Conflicting Counsels
to Confuse the Age

A Documentary Study of Political Economy
in Qing China, 1644–1840

Helen Dunstan

CENTER FOR CHINESE STUDIES
THE UNIVERSITY OF MICHIGAN
ANN ARBOR

*Open access edition funded by the National Endowment for the Humanities/
Andrew W. Mellon Foundation Humanities Open Book Program.*

MICHIGAN MONOGRAPHS IN CHINESE STUDIES
ISSN 1081-9053
SERIES ESTABLISHED 1968
VOLUME 73

Published by Center for Chinese Studies
The University of Michigan
Ann Arbor, Michigan 48109-1290

First Edition 1996

Printed and bound by CPI Group (UK) Ltd, Croydon, CR0 4YY

∞ The paper used in this publication meets the minimum requirements
of the American National Standard for Information Sciences—
Permanence of Paper for Publications and Documents
in Libraries and Archives ANSI/NISO/Z39.48—1992.

Library of Congress Cataloging-in-Publication Data

Dunstan, Helen.

Conflicting counsels to confuse the age :
a documentary study of political economy in Qing China, 1644–1840 /
by Helen Dunstan.
p.   cm.
(Michigan monographs in Chinese studies, ISSN 1081-9053 ; v. 73)
Includes bibliographical references and index.
ISBN 978-0-89264-115-4 (hardcover)
1. China—Economic policy—1644–1912.
2. China—Politics and government—1644–1912.
3. China—History—Ch'ing dynasty, 1644–1912.
I. Title. II. Series.
HC427.7.D86   1996
338.951—dc20   95-46073
CIP

ISBN 978-0-89264-115-4 (hardcover)
ISBN 978-0-472-03807-7 (paper)
ISBN 978-0-472-12751-1 (ebook)
ISBN 978-0-472-90146-3 (open access)

Contents

Preface

This documentary study of late imperial Chinese political economy is a by-product partly of my research for a forthcoming monograph on state policy towards the grain trade and the problem of popular subsistence in mid-eighteenth century China; and partly of my preliminary reading for a broader project on the evolution of economic thought in China, from the eleventh century till the early nineteenth. The present book is a contribution to the study of Sino-Manchu political economy in the heyday of the Qing (Ch'ing) dynasty (1644–1911). It has two purposes.

The first purpose is to share close readings of important sources with the scholarly community. By the rules of contemporary academic life, analysis is almost all. Sources become invisible, relegated to footnotes which consist increasingly of numbers. Sources are passive; they exist, it would appear, to have their richer parts gouged out, or else to serve as silent witness to the justice of an argument. We remember those whose interesting fragments have been drafted into someone's book; the others lose their individuality. "Sourcebooks" are for undergraduates, to give them insight into the historian's craft. For professionals, it is enough to be told where one could check the accuracy of what the analyst has claimed, in the statistically improbable event that any given reader had the motivation, opportunity, and linguistic competence to do so. The result is that, outside most scholars' narrow area of expertise, all "knowledge" becomes abstract and uncertain. One reads the monograph, understands its argument, but has no lively comprehension of the subject.

In intending the present collection partly for my fellow specialists in Chinese studies, including Qing historians, I wish neither to impugn their linguistic competence nor to deny the interest and importance of analytical monographs. The book is offered partly to people who could well have read the material in the original, had they not been reading something else. More broadly, it is for anyone who likes to pick a book up and learn something from it. Here are its "selling points." First, it offers an opportunity to watch Qing officials and others thinking through problems of political economy within the constraints of certain *genres*. Second, it shows them proposing a range of interesting approaches to the problems of their day. Third, it makes accessible some writings in political economy which are difficult because of their literary form or style. Fourth, it presents the full text of several edicts by (or at least, in the name of) the great high priest of Qing political economy, the Qianlong emperor (r. 1735–96); these have the same sort of importance, as historical documents, as public addresses by the more influential presidents of the United States.

Fifth, the book invites the reader to observe how Qing officials developed arguments on matters of political economy, with the objective of persuading colleagues or superiors. This aspect is important and merits a few words of comment. Many of the documents from which historians of Qing China routinely draw "evidence" are rhetorical (that is, their aim is to persuade). This means that the "information" they present is suspect. It is improper to use it without due attention to its author's purpose in including it, and without grasping the rhetorical structure of the text as a whole. Besides, when written communications are politically charged, there can be a substantial gap between the surface meaning of the words and what the author really had in mind. Presenting, uncut (or with a minimum of cutting), some pieces of Qing rhetoric may help to induce greater sensitivity to the nature of Qing bureaucratic documents.

Finally, of course, it is impossible to translate without interpreting, at least to some extent. For better or for worse, this book presents my interpretations of the documents I have translated.

The second purpose of this book is to make a novel contribution to the study of that topic of perennial interest for scholars, the role of the Chinese (or Sino-"barbarian") imperial state in the economy.[1] Apart from approaching this subject through the

---

[1] The most recent Western manifestations of the scholarly community's undying fascination with this topic include Jane Kate Leonard and John R. Watt, eds., *To*

translation of important texts, the present work focusses on areas of tension and controversy in (mainly) eighteenth-century approaches to that central project of Confucian paternalist administration, "nourishing the people" (*yangmin*). More exactly, it seeks to establish that there was an antithesis between belief in the activist approach those words imply, and the opinion that, in certain vital matters, it was better for the state to stand aside, and leave society's own economic institutions, trade in particular, to handle things. The case for non-intervention was sometimes based on argument that, in the matter in hand, what we should call a price or market mechanism would spontaneously function to attain the desired outcome. Although the present work attempts to represent both sides of the antithesis fairly, the materials which should be of greatest interest to Qing specialists are those which build some kind of market mechanism argument, however fragmentary.

The idea that belief in market mechanisms played a role in Qing public policy determination is less new now than it would have been ten or fifteen years ago.[2] However, at least in the West, progress in understanding the economic consciousness of Qing officials has, I think, been hampered by superficial conceptualization and an excessive preoccupation with establishing the general picture. This is unfortunate. Failure to draw distinctions between the conventional and commonplace on one hand, and the controversial on the other, can only result in unnecessarily blunt analysis.[3] There is also a need to distinguish between different

---

Achieve Security and Wealth: The Qing Imperial State and the Economy, 1644–1911 (Ithaca: Cornell University Press, 1992); and the papers by Paul J. Smith, Richard von Glahn, and Robert P. Hymes, in Hymes and Schirokauer, eds., *Ordering the World: Approaches to State and Society in Sung Dynasty China* (Berkeley: University of California Press, 1993). Of the many Chinese studies, particularly relevant to the themes of the present book is Wu Hui and Ge Xianhui, "Qing qianqi de liangshi tiaoji" [The Adjustment of Grain Supply in the First Half of the Qing Period], *Lishi yanjiu* [Historical Studies] 194 (1988): 122-35.

[2] For a recent strong statement, see William T. Rowe, "State and Market in Mid-Qing Economic Thought: The Case of Chen Hongmou (1696–1771)," *Études chinoises* 12, no. 1 (1993): 7-40.

[3] Thus the major weakness of Rowe's recent study (ibid.) is that background factors (i.e., normal Qing administrative procedures and standard Qing

levels of market awareness: on one hand, mere consciousness that (as we should say) the Chinese economy was commercialized (more or less, according to region), and that commerce played a varying but vital role; on the other hand, specific insights into how the market worked, and an opinion, resting on these insights, that its operation could be trusted.

Finally, it is necessary to distinguish between different kinds of market-oriented policy approaches. To attempt to influence grain prices by selling state reserves of grain was interventionist, although less crudely so than the conventionally repudiated policy of imposing price ceilings. Belief in the redistributive functions of private commerce, meanwhile, could inspire either interventionist or liberal policies. The concept of "economic liberalism" can be fruitfully applied to analysis of late traditional Chinese political economy. However, its applicability will not be securely established until scholars restrict its use to cases in which advocacy of non-intervention demonstrably rested on at least a rudimentary argument of the sufficiently beneficial working of a market mechanism.

Lin Man-houng has argued that economically liberal ideas and policies emerged in China in the early nineteenth century in response to the monetary crisis engendered by the well-known haemorrhage of silver.[4] The present work, applying the concept of economic liberalism in the restrictive way outlined above, demonstrates that it is possible to push this emergence back into the eighteenth century, with particularly clear expressions in debates on monetary and (more especially) grain trade policy in the late 1730s and the 1740s. Concomitantly, the book offers a

---

assumptions about sound administrative practice) are put on the same level as putative expressions of advanced faith in market mechanisms. My own impression is that Chen Hongmou, the subject of Rowe's article, did not, by eighteenth-century standards, have a particularly deep belief in market forces, and that his writings are not the best place to look for radical expressions of market consciousness.

[4] Man-houng Lin, "'A Time in Which Grandsons Beat their Grandfathers': The Rise of Liberal Political-Economic Ideas During the Monetary Crisis of Early Nineteenth-Century China," *The American Asian Review* 9, no. 4 (1991): 1-28. Also of interest in this connection is her "Two Social Theories Revealed: Statecraft Controversies Over China's Monetary Crisis, 1808–1854," *Late Imperial China* 12, no. 2 (1991): 1-35.

preliminary exploration of what can legitimately be meant by a claim that some Qing administrators had an understanding of market mechanisms and believed in them.

The findings presented here are not dramatic, but they are significant. No argument is made that the late 1730s and 1740s consciousness of market mechanisms transformed Qing economic policy thereafter; I refrain from speculation as to the balance of interventionist and non-interventionist approaches in the second half of the eighteenth century. Nor do I discuss the mixture of types of approach in the year-by-year practice of the average administrator, caught between directives from above, the pressures of specific situations, and his own, presumably changeable, opinion as to the best thing to do. For much of the time, I suspect, Qing administration muddled through, with no conception that one might attempt consistently to follow either a liberal or an interventionist approach. However, to suggest that policy was typically eclectic is not to deny the possibility that polar opposites existed and were recognized in policy debates. The objective of the present work is to inform future scholarship by clarifying the issues that were debated, the terms of the debates, and the most sophisticated positions on the liberal side.

The book has seven chapters. The first shows officials and emperors taking the activist approach to government, while the second shows such people having doubts about it. The third explores conceptions of how economic inequality within society should be regarded; the fourth addresses fiscal doctrine. The fifth presents one high official's market-conscious protests at a move to prevent "waste" of grain by banning liquor distillation. The sixth is about policy towards the grain trade, while the seventh further illustrates commercial policy and the development of market-consciousness. In the translations, and the introductory essays setting them in context, we see different Qing officials behaving as if they had no conception whatsoever of market mechanisms; intervening in the economy in various ways, some of them influenced by consciousness of the commercial world; or arguing, precisely, that a price or market mechanism can be trusted to accomplish a specific goal. Only an approach to Qing political economy that takes account of such diversity can yield genuine illumination of the subject.

*   *   *

We come to the vexed question of translation style. Everyone who has translated from classical Chinese is familiar with the dilemmas. In the first place, does one propose to render what the author said or what he (rarely she) meant? If one tries to represent, as exactly as possible, the terms in which the author formulated his understanding of a problem (which, after all, is what is wanted from the viewpoint of intellectual history), one risks unnatural or long-winded English. If, on the other hand, one recognizes that an author is referring to a concept for which a technical term exists in modern English ("indirect taxation," for example), and *uses* that term in one's translation, then one risks misleading the reader. Second, if a literary language is routinely used for bureaucratic communication, should the translation style be elegant or business-like? While it is evident that contemporary colloquial English can never be the appropriate medium for rendering classical Chinese, it is not obvious that any particular earlier form of written English (the style of Adam Smith, for instance) matches exactly either. Finally, when faithful rendering of the original would result in obscurity, one can salve one's conscience with square brackets and footnotes. Unfortunately, a text studded with square brackets alienates the less committed reader, while the more professional and therefore busier one's readership, the lower the probability that one's footnotes will be read.

It is easier to avoid obvious solecisms than to devise a satisfactory general formula for resolving these dilemmas. It is probably best not to make too great a virtue of consistency, but to trust one's discretion and the guidance furnished by the texts themselves (some have a more markedly literary flavour than others, for example). In general, my preference is for faithful rendering and old-fashioned diction, but I have not hesitated to take such liberties as replacing Chinese idioms with English ones, reformulating obscure wording enough to make the sense apparent, and breaking truly long and complex sentences into more manageable units. I have not used square brackets; footnotes explaining the sense of a passage are used only as a last resort. In short, while the translations may, like the originals, make some demands on the reader, I have made the necessary compromises to produce readable English.

A few words must also be said about the texts translated. I originally located many of them in that useful treasury, the *Huangchao jingshi wenbian* [A Statecraft Anthology of Our August Dynasty], compiled by Wei Yuan and He Changling, and first published in 1827.[5] Experience suggests, however, that reliance on a *Huangchao jingshi wenbian* (HCJSWB) version of a document is unwise. Many HCJSWB texts are abridged; in extreme cases, they may not be much more than abstracts. Useful editorial emendations are offset by unfortunate infidelities, not to mention errors. For all but two of the HCJSWB texts translated here, I have succeeded in finding at least one more trustworthy version, whether an archival document (in the case of some memorials), the version from which the HCJSWB editors were copying (often in the author's collected works), or some other version. I have, of course, always used the most reliable version as the basis of my translation, while consulting the others. However, references to the inferior versions are provided for the convenience of readers who do not have easy access to major research libraries, still less the archives in Beijing. Several of the texts translated come from sources other than HCJSWB.

In general, my policy has been integral, or almost integral, translation. The few major exceptions include cases in which texts include material that is not relevant to the section in which I have included them, and cases in which I am wholly or substantially dependent on an unpublished archival text. Here I have made cuts in order to avoid any possible infringement of archive regulations. The title given for each text is that provided by the source from which I have translated it; for the imperial edicts, however, I have had to supply a title from the alternative version in one case, and to make a title up in the three others.

Although this book has not been designed for classroom instruction, I hope that it will be found useful in advanced undergraduate and graduate courses in Chinese history and comparative political economy. For the convenience of students

---

[5] The edition used is the eight-volume reprint of the 1873 edition published by Shijie shuju, Taibei, in 1964.

and scholars from other fields, I have included rather more background explanation (usually in footnotes) than would be required by specialists in pre-modern Chinese history.

*   *   *

It remains only to make some acknowledgments. Reference works to which I have had constant recourse include Charles O. Hucker's *A Dictionary of Official Titles in Imperial China* (whose translations I have usually followed); Qian Shifu's invaluable tables of high office-holders in the Qing dynasty; the collection of short biographies of Qing personages edited by Arthur Hummel; and the Qing volume of the historical atlas sponsored by the Chinese Academy of Social Sciences.[6] My initial exploration of the *Huangchao jingshi wenbian*, and the preparation of some preliminary translations from it, were financed by a generous Fellowship in Chinese Studies from the Leverhulme Trust (Britain), under the auspices of the European Association for Chinese Studies and the European Science Foundation. Much of the research and thinking that have gone into the present book were done during my tenure of research fellowships at Newnham College in the University of Cambridge, and (more especially) the Department of Far Eastern History, Research School of Pacific Studies, Australian National University. The archival material was collected during two visits to the First Historical Archives in Beijing. The first, in 1984, was made possible by an exchange programme between the Australian National University and Peking University; the second, in 1993, was financed by a Special Opportunity for Archival Research grant from the National Endowment for the Humanities (United States), an independent federal agency. The final crystallization of my thinking for this volume was done in my

---

[6]Charles O. Hucker, *A Dictionary of Official Titles in Imperial China* (Stanford: Stanford University Press, 1985); Qian Shifu, comp., *Qingdai zhiguan nianbiao* [Chronological Tables of High Office-holders in the Qing Dynasty], 4 vols. (Beijing: Zhonghua shuju, 1980); Arthur W. Hummel, ed., *Eminent Chinese of the Ch'ing Period (1644–1912)*, 2 vols. (Washington: United States Government Printing Office, 1943–44); and Tan Qixiang, ed., *Zhongguo lishi ditu ji* [Historical Atlas of China], 8 vols. (Shanghai: Ditu chubanshe, 1982–87).

present position in the Department of History, Indiana State University, as was some of the translation.

I thank all the above funds and institutions. To turn to personal acknowledgments, I am indebted for assistance with word-processing to Oanh Collins, John Councill, and Marion Weeks. Others to whom I am grateful for comments, suggestions, encouragement, and so forth include William Atwell, Marianne Bastid, James Cotton, the late Jennifer Cushman, Christian Daniels, Mark Elvin, Herbert Franke, Philip Kuhn, Susan Naquin, Peter Perdue, Stuart Schram, Alice Stroup, Maura Shaw Tantillo, Robert Tannenbaum, Wang Gungwu, and Pierre-Étienne Will. I thank Walter Michener, Debra E. Soled, and David Rolston of the Publications Office of the Center for Chinese Studies, University of Michigan, and the anonymous readers who reviewed the manuscript; and Norman Cooprider of the Department of Geography, Geology, and Anthropology, Indiana State University, who drew the map on p. 16. Finally, I owe to those who taught me classical Chinese at Oxford University, especially Piet van der Loon, a debt which can only be repaid by doing likewise for the next generation.

Basic Information
for Non-specialists

1. Weights and measures
Weights and measures in late imperial China were imperfectly standardized; that is to say, there existed considerable regional and local variation from the published official standards. The equivalents given below should therefore be taken only as roughly indicating the official's likely understanding of the meaning of the given units, at least when used in official transactions.

Capacity. The basic unit of capacity was the *shi*, translated here as "bushel" (i.e., "Chinese bushel"). Its main decimal subdivisions were the *dou*, "peck," 0.1 bushel, and *sheng*, "pint," 0.01 bushel. The standard bushel used in the administration of the official granaries was approximately equivalent to 103.6 litres.

Weight, and the word "tael." The standard Chinese ounce, or *liang*, was approximately equivalent to 37.3 grammes, and constituted one sixteenth of the Chinese pound, or *jin*, conventionally rendered "catty." However, in the monetary system, an ounce of silver (of specified purity) was a unit of value. In monetary contexts, *liang* is conventionally rendered "tael" (abbreviated as "tl."). I observe this convention here. The subdivisions of the *liang* followed the decimal system.

Area. The basic unit of area for measuring farmland was the *mu*, a unit that was especially subject to local variation. A standard *mu* was approximately equivalent to 0.0615 hectare; 100 *mu* comprised a *qing*. The subdivisions of the *mu* followed the decimal system.

Length and distance. The three most commonly encountered linear measures are the Chinese foot, or *chi* (approximately equivalent to 31.3 centimetres); the ten-*chi* unit called a *zhang* (approximately 3.13 metres); and the *li*, which may be thought of as slightly exceeding half a kilometre.

2. Monetary system

See above for an explanation of the word "tael." Theoretically, one "string" of a thousand "copper" (actually brass) coins was supposed to exchange for one tael of silver. These brass coins are generally called "cash" in English-language writings. However, this convention can create unnecessary ambiguities. In many eighteenth-century contexts, the word "coin" is quite sufficient.

Silver was not minted in eighteenth-century China. The only silver coins were imports.

3. Governmental system

The governmental system of the Qing dynasty was fairly complex, and many excellent books and articles have been devoted to it. What follows is the bare minimum of information necessary for the reader of this book.

The central government was, of course, dominated by the court, that is, the emperor and his closest advisers and assistants, such as the Grand Secretaries and (beginning in the early Qianlong period) the Council of State, or Grand Council. Outside the court, the most important central government agencies were the traditional Six Boards, which coordinated most aspects of the administration of the empire. Especially important for the student of state economic policy is the so-called Board of Revenue (literally, Board of Households, or Board of Population). While the chief concern of the Board of Revenue was with fiscal matters, it also had jurisdiction over monetary policy, and a great many aspects of the economic life of the Chinese population were potentially within its purview. The complex business of assuring popular subsistence was, in large part, a Board of Revenue responsibility.

For the purposes of territorial administration, China Proper was divided into eighteen large units called provinces. Moving, roughly, from east to west, these were: in North China, Zhili,

The Provinces of China Proper during the Qing Dynasty

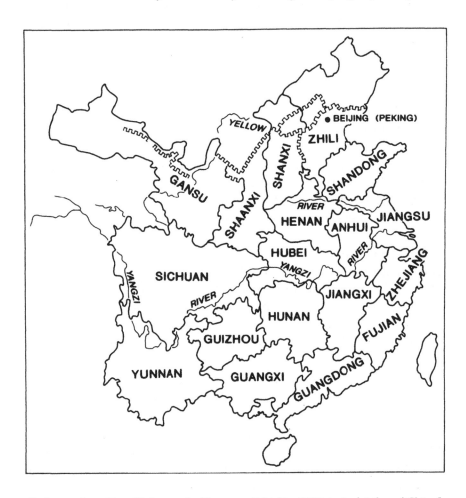

Redrawn from Tan Qixiang, ed., *Zhongguo lishi ditu ji* [Historical Atlas of China]
(Shanghai: Ditu chubanshe, 1982–87), vol. 8, pp. 3-4.

Shandong, Henan, Shanxi, Shaanxi, and Gansu; in Central China, Jiangsu, Zhejiang, Anhui, Jiangxi, Hubei, Hunan, and Sichuan; and in South China, Fujian, Guangdong, Guangxi, Guizhou, and Yunnan. In general, each provincial administration was headed by a provincial governor, whose most important subordinate was called the provincial administration commissioner; above the governor was usually a governor-general, who was responsible for overseeing the affairs of two or (less commonly) three adjacent provinces. Zhili, however, being the province wherein Beijing lay, was an exception: after 1724, it had a governor-general all to itself, but had no governor.

The most important subdivisions of the province were called prefectures; directly subordinate to the provincial government there might also be smaller units called independent departments or subprefectures. Prefectures in turn were subdivided into *xian*, "counties" (or, as some authors have it, "districts"); these were the lowest units of formal territorial administration. Since, however, there were some departments whose position in the territorial hierarchy was identical to that of counties, the phrase "county-level units" may be used to capture all the basic building-blocks of territorial administration. Departments and subprefectures could also be intermediary units between prefectures and counties.

The head official of a county is known in English as the county magistrate. This is a misnomer: the so-called magistrate was a general administrator, not a specialist in dispensing justice. It is conventional to say that tax collection, maintenance of law and order, and the settlement of legal cases were his central tasks; however, he was ideally considered responsible for all matters pertaining to the welfare of the people of his jurisdiction.

Finally, the Chinese word *yamen* is routinely used, without explanation, in English-language writings on traditional Chinese government and society. It means the headquarters of a senior official at any level of the hierarchy. Thus the county *yamen* was the complex of buildings from which the county magistrate (assisted by his staff) administered his county.

4. Reign Titles and Dates of the Three Great Emperors of the Heyday of the Qing Dynasty

Kangxi	1661–1722
Yongzheng	1722–1735
Qianlong	1735–1796

1. Activism

The texts included in this chapter reflect the assumption that the state and its agents should take an activist approach in working for the people's economic well-being. Text 1.A inventories one county magistrate's dedicated efforts to restore a complex river system, and thus make the local countryside safe for agriculture. Texts 1.B to 1.D reflect the ingenuity that officials and even emperors could show when addressing the problems of transporting large amounts of grain in order to assure the subsistence of dearth-threatened populations. Finally, in Text 1.E we see a governor-general proposing a refinement to the time-honoured tradition of state intervention in the market to stabilize grain prices in the interests of poor consumers.

As in *ancien régime* France, the reasons for state activism to assure popular subsistence were twofold.[1] On one hand, since history was believed to show a correlation between mass hunger and popular unrest, it was in the interests of the state and ruling class to take positive measures to alleviate the consequences of harvest failures, and to counteract perceived anti-social profiteering by merchants and others who controlled substantial stocks of grain. Far more in evidence in the documentary record, however, are invocations of the ideological underpinning of such activism: the emperor's assigned role in the cosmic scheme of things, and the assumptions of Confucian paternalism—or, to be more literal, parentalism. Heaven (male) and Earth (female) love life, which they themselves have generated; the emperor, as "Son of Heaven," must act as a transmitter of this cosmic love, embodying it in effective manifestations of benevolence towards his

---

[1] Cf. Steven L. Kaplan, *Bread, Politics and Political Economy in the Reign of Louis XV* (The Hague: Martinus Nijhoff, 1976), Vol. 1, pp. 1-8, for an exploration of the mixture of prudential and paternalist considerations underlying the pre-revolutionary French tradition of "policing" the grain trade to keep bread affordable for the poor.

"babes," the people. As if in tacit recognition of the complementary nature of paternal and maternal roles, however, the emperor and, still more, his local representatives, the county magistrates, should act as "father *and* mother" to the people in their charge. Concern to see the children adequately nourished is fundamental to the parent's heart.[2]

Of course, the formal position in Confucianism was that nourishing the people's bodies was important chiefly as a prerequisite for nourishing their moral natures. A central concern of Mencius ("Master Meng"), one of the founders of Confucianism, was that human beings should distinguish themselves from animals, which was to be done by respecting Confucian-defined norms for the proper conduct of a set of fundamental human relationships. The good ruler not only maintained the economic conditions in which his people could give proper treatment to their aged and their dead, but also saw that they received the instruction without which popular morality, or so the Confucians thought, was not to be expected. Expressions of these and related views are found throughout the *Mencius*. Besides the oft-quoted passage about the common people needing constant means of livelihood before they can have constant hearts, a less famous passage, to which allusions are occasionally found in late imperial statecraft rhetoric, reads as follows: "The Sage, in his governance of the Empire, will bring it about that pulse and grain are as freely available as fire and water. If pulse and grain are as fire and water, how should there be any who are inhumane among the folk?"[3] To the extent that this was read as a substantive prescription for good rulership, it set a lofty standard of economic achievement for emperors and statesmen who took the Confucian mission seriously.

---

[2] Cf. ibid., p. 5.

[3] See *Mengzi* [The Book of Mencius], 7A/23. Versions of the "constant livelihoods/constant hearts" passage are found in both 1A/7 and 3A/3; in the former case, the passage is closely followed by the statement that a ruler should ensure that his people have sufficient means of livelihood before "impelling them to goodness." For a forceful statement of the necessity of moral instruction for the people, see 3A/4, and for perception of a link between fiscal/economic maladministration and popular inability to live according to Confucian norms, 3A/3. The same point is made more positively in, for example, 1A/3.

The subject of Text 1.A, a biography, appears to have been such a statesman, albeit at a humble level. Yang Tingwang, a county magistrate and later prefect, has his life-story told here by Yang Chun, a younger kinsman;[4] it goes without saying that a flattering representation is to be expected, and that acceptance of the narrative as a complete record would be methodologically naive. At the very least, however, the text is useful in illustrating the terms in which a model local administrator would be portrayed.

Yang Tingwang's career in official service (1674–1709, although his first regular civil service appointment was not until 1686) took place during a period when there was particularly broad scope for the creative or restorative talents of Confucian-trained administrators. From the late 1620s till the late 1640s, widespread harvest failures, rebellions, droughts, famines, locust infestations, epidemics, bondservant uprisings, and, to cap it all, conquest by the alien Manchus had devastated life and property in much of North and Central China. The last two decades of the seventeenth century were years of recovery under the finally consolidated control of the Manchu (Qing) dynasty, who turned out to be infinitely better rulers than had at first been feared. As magistrate of Shangcai County in southern Henan (1686–95), Yang Tingwang devoted himself to restoring first the local agricultural economy, and subsequently the Confucian educational and ritual order. In this, he gave practical expression to his own maxim of "enriching before one instructs," an allusion to a dialogue in *The Analects of Confucius* in which Confucius is supposed to have said that given a population which was already dense, one's first care should be enrichment of the people, after which one should instruct them.[5]

The biography depicts Yang as a properly rounded local administrator, yet the topic which receives most space is his

---

[4] For a biography of Yang Chun (c. 1675–1754), see Li Huan, comp., *Guochao qixian leizheng* [Classified Biographies of Venerable and Distinguished Personages under the Present Dynasty] (1890; hereafter GCQXLZ), 124:44a-46a.

[5] See *Lunyu* [The Analects of Confucius] XIII/9. Realistically, an administrator who set out to "enrich" a local population was aspiring only to lead the people to economic security, plus a small surplus for the requisites of civilized existence.

initial rehabilitation of the river drainage system of Shangcai. It is reasonable to infer that this system (part of which was man-made to begin with) needed a certain amount of human effort (e.g., dredging) to maintain it. Such work had presumably been neglected over a long period in the previous (Ming) dynasty, and (as Yang Chun tells the story) here and there changes had been made which violated the hydraulic logic of the system. Whatever shocks the system had received during the "military conflagrations at the close of the Ming dynasty" must have been the *coups de grâce*. Yang Chun's account is written as if Yang Tingwang had accomplished the rehabilitation single-handed. This is, of course, impossible, and yet a certain literary effect is thereby realized. Yang's "guiding" of the wild rivers of Shangcai recalls the legendary efforts of the ancient Chinese culture-hero, the Great Yu, credited with eight years of dedicated labours to drain the inundated central plain and thus make civilization possible.[6] Yang Tingwang, who went on to restore the means of civilization as Confucians understood it, becomes a culture sub-hero, recognized after his death in the seasonal sacrifices of "the folk of Shangcai."[7]

More can be learned about Yang's activities as a local administrator from the two gazetteers he edited: one of 1690 for Shangcai, and one of 1711 for Quzhou Prefecture, where he was in charge from 1706 till 1709.[8] The Shangcai gazetteer is especially rich, and provides corroborative evidence that Yang possessed the technical man's eye for detail on the ground. Not only does the work include beautiful drawings of the ritual implements lovingly enumerated in Yang Chun's biography, but there are also thirty-four separate maps, one for each administrative subdivision of the county, to show the detail of the river system.

---

[6] *Mengzi* 3A/3, and also 3B/9 (which suggests that Yu's efforts, like Yang Tingwang's, were perhaps restorative rather than creative).

[7] A similar point has recently been made by Pierre-Étienne Will, who characterizes a sample mid-Ming model magistrate as *une sorte de héros civilisateur*. See Will, "Développement quantitatif et développement qualitatif en Chine à la fin de l'époque impériale," *Annales: Histoire, Sciences Sociales* 1994, no. 4, p. 888.

[8] See also the account of Yang's "virtuous administration" of Shangcai in 1690 *Shangcai xianzhi* [Gazetteer of Shangcai County], 15:126a-128b.

Such cartographic precision is unusual in seventeenth-century local gazetteers.

* * * * *

Texts 1.B to 1.D are concerned with assuring popular subsistence in two densely populated but drought-prone regions of North China: the Wei Valley region of south-central Shaanxi, and the adjacent Fen Valley region in south-western Shanxi. The Rivers Fen and Wei are both tributaries of the Yellow River; it came naturally to emperors or officials who were aware of the advantages of water transport to try to use this river network to move supplementary grain stocks rapidly to areas which needed them. Text 1.B (1704) is a Shaanxi governor's response to an instruction by the Kangxi emperor (r. 1661–1722) ordering feasibility studies of the idea of shipping grain westwards or northwards into Shaanxi or Shanxi from storage depots in Henan. The journeys would have been against the current all the way. Texts 1.C (1743) and 1.D (1748), by contrast, present proposals for bringing grain southwards with the Yellow River's current from Inner Mongolia or the northern jurisdictions of Shaanxi. Here the authors draw on observation of north Chinese merchant shipping techniques to suggest ways of using the often violent flow of the Yellow River down the Shanxi-Shaanxi border for grain transport. While the proposals may not all have been workable in practice, these three documents are remarkable for their boldness, and for the authors' positive and open-minded interest in physical realities. In Text 1.C, which is the most adventurous of the three, we also see an especially marked concern to check the viability of the proposed solution through experiment, as well as close attention both to technical detail and to the "bottom line" of transport costs and selling price.

The tone for all this adventurousness had been well set in the spring of 1704, when the chief regional administrators of Henan, Shanxi, and Shaanxi began responding to Kangxi's notion of keeping special grain reserves in Henan for emergency transport to the latter two provinces. This idea had been communicated in an edict of January 1704, which is briefly summarized in the opening paragraph of Text 1.B. The emperor envisaged that the grain from three years' special grain tax ("tribute") payments from the province of Henan might be held back in Henan Prefecture, whence it could be conveniently shipped to Shanxi or Shaanxi in the event of famine, using the Yellow River and then the Fen or Wei. He also expressed the hope that state initiative in reopening the interprovincial river route would stimulate commercial traffic.

According to the January edict, the emperor had sent a party under a prince of the blood to make a preliminary inspection of the difficult stretch of the Yellow River at the Sanmen ("Three Gates") Gorge, and this group reported the existence of some ancient man-made "eyes" up on the cliff for holding hauling-ropes. They did not, however, actually try them out with boats, and thus their survey remained inconclusive.[9] In late February, the emperor commanded the governor-general of Sichuan and Shaanxi together with the governors of Shaanxi, Henan, and Shanxi to carry out a full joint survey of the Sanmen Gorge and its perilous sequel, the Dizhu Rock. At the end of April, these dignitaries reported that their men had succeeded in hauling a boat laden with thirty bushels up through the least dangerous of the "Three Gates," but so difficult had this been that it seemed that using an overland bypass route would actually be cheaper. Their suggestion therefore was that tribute grain stocked at the seat of Henan Prefecture (i.e., the city of Luoyang) be embarked at the Taiyang Crossing in Shanzhou, some 300 *li* west.[10]

The Shanxi and Shaanxi governors' reports on the feasibility of shipping grain upstream on the Rivers Fen and Wei arrived a little later. The Manchu Ehai, for Shaanxi, replied with Text 1.B, which claims, on the basis of personal inspection, that the Wei is in principle navigable as far west as Meixian, a good way beyond the provincial capital Xi'an, but that, given the present undeveloped state of boat-building technology in Shaanxi, it is not worth

---

[9] *Da Qing Shengzu Ren Huangdi shilu* [Veritable Records of the Kangxi Period] (hereafter QSL/KX), 214:19a-20b. On the configuration of natural hazards at the Sanmen Gorge, and the ancient "trackers' galleries" there, see Joseph Needham, *Science and Civilisation in China*, Vol. 4:III (Cambridge: Cambridge University Press, 1971), pp. 274-78.

[10] QSL/KX, 215:6a and 21b-22a.

the merchants' while to go further up than Xianyang (in the provincial capital's vicinity). The strategy of choice would therefore be to import superior technology from the southern provinces, do everything possible to have the local folk adopt it, and then rely on hiring the new-style private merchant shipping when it becomes necessary for the state to rush relief supplies from Henan into Shaanxi. The Shanxi provincial governor, meanwhile, reported that the Fen was readily navigable as far north as Hongdong, about a third of the way along the river's course; from there north to Taiyuan, the provincial capital, however, there were too many rocks and shallow rapids, and it was difficult to advance without constructing small boats for the journey. For serious grain transport such as that envisaged by the emperor, the only possibility would be to build boats in the style of "Mayang river-junks"—another case of drawing on the boat-building techniques of southern China.[11]

The two reports, together with one more from the Henan provincial governor and the report of the joint survey of the Sanmen Gorge and Dizhu Rock, were considered all together by a conference of the so-called Nine Chief Ministers (actually a considerably larger high-level advisory body). According to Ehai's biography, the outcome was that he and the Shanxi governor were ordered to devise means of having the Wei and Fen dredged.[12] The next year, special granaries for storing Henan tribute grain were built in ten Henan locations near the south bank of the Yellow River, from Kaifeng in the east to Wenxiang near the Shaanxi border. The largest quantity (235,682 Chinese bushels, unhusked) was to be kept at Luoyang, while each of the remaining granaries was to stock 20,000 to 30,000 bushels. The total, 465,682 bushels unhusked (for durability in storage), would

---

[11] Ibid., 216:4b–5a, and 7a. Mayang as written is the name of a county in west-central Hunan. The reference is probably, however, to the *mayangzi* (different *yang*), the Upper Yangzi river-junks described in Needham, *Science and Civilisation in China*, Vol. 4:III, pp. 397-99, and Plate CCCXCI.

[12] QSL/KX, 216:7a; GCQXLZ, 166:1b. A conference of the "Nine Chief Ministers" brought together all the senior officials of the nine major "outer court" departments of the central government (that is, the six administrative boards, the Censorate, the Office of Transmission, and the Court of Judicial Review). It could number up to about fifty people.

seem to represent the product of only one year's tribute payment from Henan, not the three years' payments that the emperor had originally had in mind. Once the reserves had been established, routine stock rotation was to be accomplished by annually lending one third of the stock to the local peasantry in the lean ("*soudure*") period before the ripening of the new year's grain.[13] These loans would be repayable in new grain after harvest.[14] This no doubt largely explains the distribution of the stocks over so wide an area: there will have been concern, on one hand, to spread the capacity to render this "social security" assistance and, on the other, to see that the capacity of the Luoyang region's peasantry to absorb loans of old grain was not too much exceeded.

We may infer that measures were taken to replace stocks used to combat actual famine, as the granaries were still in operation sixty years later. According to the research of Pierre-Étienne Will, in 1748 they had an aggregate target stocking-level in excess of 775,000 bushels, and in 1766 actual reserves of 641,090 bushels. Will also finds that in the decades after 1705 their number was increased, in particular by the construction of new granaries north of the Yellow River.[15] These, presumably, were built with the needs of Zhili and the east side of Shanxi in view.

*   *   *

Whereas the author of Text 1.B saw a need for the state to introduce southern boat-building technology to the mercantile users of the River Wei, the authors of Texts 1.C and 1.D showed

---

[13] The term *soudure* is borrowed from French history, and refers to the period when the grain-stocks from the previous year's harvest are running out, and before the grain from the current year's harvest has become available. See, e.g., Kaplan, *Bread, Politics and Political Economy*, p. xvii.

[14] *Qingchao wenxian tongkao* [Comprehensive Scrutiny of Documents: Qing Dynasty] (1786; 1965 reprint of the 1936 *Shitong* edition; hereafter QCWXTK), 34:5174.

[15] Pierre-Étienne Will, *Bureaucratie et famine en Chine au 18e siècle* (Paris: Mouton Éditeur, 1980), pp. 175 and 239. This important work is available in English translation as *Bureaucracy and Famine in Eighteenth-Century China* (Stanford: Stanford University Press, 1990).

their respect for the commercial transport technology already in use along the Yellow River by proposing that state grain-shipping ventures imitate it. Text 1.C is an impressive document by the early 1740s Shanxi governor Liu Yuyi suggesting means of overcoming the technical difficulties involved in transporting grain down the Yellow River from the Guihua Cheng-Tuoketuo region of that part of southern Inner Mongolia that in Qing times was administratively incorporated into Shanxi Province.[16] He wished to do this because the market price of grain was high in the Fen Valley jurisdictions, and in fact throughout the south-western quarter of Shanxi. It was desirable to have extra grain on hand to sell to the population at below market rates during the *soudure* period of peak grain prices the following spring. As Liu racked his brains for cost-effective means of realizing this goal, he remembered seeing ox-hide floats used for transporting grain on the Yellow River in the Lanzhou region, in Gansu Province in the far north-west of China. He promptly embarked on the conscientious investigations detailed in Text 1.C. The positive preliminary results led him to submit the tentative proposal (to be made firm on successful completion of a full trial run) that use of ox-hide floats for shipping Inner Mongolian grain to southern Shanxi, or indeed its neighbours, be not only carried out on this occasion, but also added to the repertoire of anti-hunger measures for North China.

His ingenuity was ill-rewarded by the outcome. Two full-scale experiments were carried out in 1744 under his successor as Shanxi provincial governor, the Manchu Aligun. Aligun first had two hundred bushels of husked grain brought down by float to southern Shanxi (except for fifty bushels diverted overland to

---

[16] Guihua Cheng (modern Guisui) and Tuoketuo lie approximately 100 kilometres and 50 kilometres respectively north of the Great Wall where it meets the Yellow River on the Shanxi side. They mark two corners of a relatively low-lying area north-east of the Yellow River on the east side of the Ordos bend. Referring to the same region, Liu Yuyi's successor wrote in 1744, "At the present time, more land beyond the frontier is opened up each day, and successive years have seen abundant harvests." First Historical Archives (Beijing), *Zhupi zouzhe, Caizheng, Cangchu* [Rescripted Palace Memorials, Fiscal Matters, Granary Reserves] (hereafter First Historical Archives, CC), Aligun, Qianlong (QL) 9/9/14.

Taiyuan in accordance with Liu's plan). This expedition set out from Tuoketuo in the third moon, as Liu had envisaged. Since the results were disappointing, Aligun had the experiment repeated with a somewhat smaller quantity of grain in the fifth moon, which may have been too close to the known mid-year period of danger mentioned in Text 1.C.[17] The results were even worse. The reports of the two expeditions, duly quoted in Aligun's memorial to the throne, mention grain needing to be dried *en route*, fierce currents, "frightening waves and alarming billows," unnerved boatmen, and, in the case of the second expedition, the loss of four floats on sandbanks. Not only was the unit cost no lower than the Shanxi market price, but at the end of the second expedition, the travellers were left with grain swollen with moisture and permeated by the smell of ox-hides. "The people are not glad to buy it, nor will it keep for long in storage."

Aligun interviewed the Lanzhou boatmen whom his predecessor had originally engaged, and they confirmed that negotiating the dangerous waters and vast distances between Tuoketuo and southern Shanxi was an entirely different proposition from shipping grain along the Yellow River upstream in Gansu. Assuming that the Aligun memorial is to be taken at face value, and that the timing of the experiments was not to blame, Liu Yuyi's idea was a heroic failure.[18]

*   *   *

Liu Yuyi, based in northerly Taiyuan, had taken cognizance only of the limited amount of merchant shipping down the Yellow River that originated in Inner Mongolia. The author of Text 1.D, by contrast, being in charge of the east-central Shaanxi prefecture called Tongzhou, had had occasion to observe that merchants from the southern stretches of the Shanxi-Shaanxi

---

[17] Aligun initiated the second experiment on the eighth day of the fifth moon according to the lunar calendar. In 1744, this was equivalent to 18 June. This was neither particularly early nor particularly late: in 1740, lunar 5/8 would have been equivalent to 1 June, in 1743 to 29 June. Clearly, the lunar calendar was a poor safety guide for navigators.

[18] First Historical Archives, CC, Aligun, QL 9/9/14.

border had found their own means of travelling north against the Yellow River's current and returning south with grain. When high prices in the Tongzhou region and the south-west tip of Shanxi offered an incentive, resourceful local traders were perfectly capable of surmounting the obstacles which, according to Liu Yuyi's report, discouraged northern merchants. The secret was to use linked barges in both directions on the most problematic southern stretch, and otherwise, for travel downstream from the north, to cut down trees and make one's own round-bottomed boats. Nor was it always necessary to go as far north as Tuoketuo: at least in the late 1740s, when Text 1.D was written, stocks could be bought within the northern jurisdictions of Shaanxi, especially Fugu County on the west bank of the Yellow River immediately south of the Great Wall.

Our Tongzhou prefect, Qiao Guanglie, had taken up that post in 1746 after some seven years' experience of local administration in the Wei Valley region.[19] The 1748 drought and emerging food shortage which occasioned Text 1.D were not confined to Tongzhou, but extended throughout the eastern half of the Wei Valley, that is, the most populous and productive part of Shaanxi Province. Text 1.D is a letter to the provincial governor, the famous Chen Hongmou (1696–1771), pointing out that the level of the reserves in Tongzhou's precautionary ("evernormal") granaries was insufficient to sustain the cut-price grain sales and preliminary relief operations that were likely to be needed. Qiao therefore proposed that regional officialdom imitate the merchants' shipping techniques to bring northern grain down the Yellow River to Tongzhou. The grain would, he hints, for preference be allocated from the well-stocked ever-normal granaries of Shaanxi jurisdictions further north along the Yellow River. Failing that, it could be bought beyond the frontier.

Governor Chen appears to have taken the hint. In a directive addressing the problem of inadequate granary reserves in various Wei Valley jurisdictions, he mentions that he has already responded to what was presumably Qiao Guanglie's proposal by commanding that 100,000 bushels of grain be allocated from the granaries of Yan'an, Yulin, and Suide (all in northern Shaanxi),

---

[19] GCQXLZ, 178:35a.

and that the grain be husked and sent to Tongzhou. The remainder of the directive is devoted to instructions about planning local redistribution of surplus granary reserves within the rest of the Wei Valley region; no indication is given as to how Chen viewed Qiao's idea for transporting the grain. A clue may perhaps be found, however, in a later directive which gives details of the final allocations for Tongzhou. The supplementary stocks were to come from a total of seven ever-normal granaries located in Yan'an Prefecture and Fuzhou Department (that is, on and beyond the southern fringe of the supplying area originally envisaged). Only three of the granaries belonged to a jurisdiction directly adjacent to the Yellow River; three of the others, however, will have been close to the River Luo, which flowed directly south-east into Tongzhou. From the amounts to be provided by each granary, one may estimate that at most 62 per cent of the total is likely to have been transported on the Yellow River, and then for only a relatively short distance.[20]

*   *   *   *   *

In Texts 1.C and 1.D, we see the state preparing for intervention to protect the people's food supply not (or not only) by free grain distributions, but also by cut-price sales intended to bring down the market price of grain. Such sales, known as *pingtiao*, "[price-]stabilizing sales," were part of the Chinese state's traditional repertoire of anti-hunger operations. They embodied recognition of the fact that there were large numbers of people, beginning with city-dwellers, who were at least partially dependent on the market for their grain supply, and therefore vulnerable to seasonal price fluctuations as well as major increases induced by harvest failures. Since, moreover, city-dwellers were in principle ineligible for free grain distributions, stabilizing sales were the major state activity intended for their

---

[20] Chen Hongmou, *Peiyuan Tang oucun gao: wenxi* [Chance Survivals from the Peiyuan Hall: Directives] (n.d.; hereafter PYTOCG), 27:11a-b and 22a-24a.

welfare.[21] The concept of the stabilizing sale inspired the name "ever-normal granary" (*changping cang*), more exactly translated as "granary [for maintaining] constant [price] stability." Although the Qing ever-normal granaries doubled as reserves for free grain distributions to the peasantry, the old name was retained. There was (to simplify somewhat) one ever-normal granary per county-level jurisdiction.

The theory of the stabilizing sale can be traced back to the ancient period of Chinese history.[22] Qing dynasty practice was based on the assumption that when the state sold grain at submarket prices, the market price would be forced down partly by the simple increase in supply, but perhaps more importantly because the local, overcharging retailers now had competition. The writer of Text 1.E, the Manchu Emida, later co-authored an interesting policy discussion document which reflects his understanding of how the process ought to operate. The purpose of the document is to argue that, instead of starting with a dramatic price reduction, the state should initially offer grain at a price 10 per cent below the current market rate. Another small cut should be made once the market price had fallen correspondingly, and there should be a series of such limited reductions from each successive price level until the normal price had been achieved. Major initial price cuts would be counterproductive, went the argument, because the only rational response for the private grain dealers would be to hoard their grain until the underselling ended. The people, meanwhile, would buy only from the stabilizing sales outlets, whose limited supplies would soon run out. The merchants would then resume their profiteer-

---

[21] Cf. Will, *Bureaucratie et famine*, p. 123; and, for a rich background discussion, pp. 161-65. As Will makes clear (p. 167), it was not only urban residents who were the intended beneficiaries of stabilizing sales, especially in dearth years.

[22] See the long exposition (which assumes not a benevolent but a self-interested ruler) in the "Qingzhong" chapter of the *Guanzi*: Ma Feibai, *Guanzi Qingzhong Pian xinquan* [New Exegeses of the "Light and Heavy" Chapter of the *Guanzi*] (Beijing: Zhonghua shuju, 1979), Vol. 1, pp. 225-41. The classic ancient embodiment of the concept of price-stabilizing granaries (likewise serving the ruler's interests) was that attributed to Li Kui, fl. 400 B.C. See Ban Gu et al., *Hanshu* [A History of the Han Dynasty] (Beijing: Zhonghua shuju, 1975), Vol. 4, 24A:1125.

ing. If, however, the shopkeepers became aware *both* that there was the official competition *and* that the official price reduction was a limited one, they would be bound to bring their prices down a little "in the hope of circulation." The law, as we would say, that "where goods mass together, prices fall" (*huo ji, jia luo*) would then apply; in other words, with plenty of grain being available on the retail market, the pressure on the price level would be downward.[23]

The existence and anti-social influence of market manipulating grain dealers are the premise underlying Text 1.E, written in 1733, and addressing the popular subsistence problems of Guangzhou (the Guangdong provincial capital, loosely known as Canton in the West). Emida, as chief provincial administrator of Guangdong, was stationed in Guangzhou. Earlier in the year, he had obtained imperial assent for a plan to set up a large supplementary grain reserve for stabilizing sales in Guangzhou, in order to protect the city's population from price manipulations by the merchants who fed its markets with grain from adjacent Guangxi Province.[24] Now it was time to combat price manipulation by the city's retailers. Here too, Emida looked for a weapon in the stabilizing sales system; but this time, he sought not crude expansion, but the correction of one defect and intensified responsiveness to market price increases.

Text 1.E calmly suggests a rather devastating criticism of the stabilizing sales system as it operated in Guangzhou: the grain (in this case rice), stored, as was normal, in unhusked form to make it keep better, was being offered to the public in the same form. This, as Emida explains, made purchase impractical for the city's labouring poor. His proposed solution was to open special "husked-grain bureaux," borrowing the name (*miju*) from institutions which the current emperor (Yongzheng, r. 1722–35)

---

[23] See the 1738 document by Emida and Wang Mo summarized in QCWXTK, 36:5189-90, and *Da Qing Gaozong Chun Huangdi shilu* [Veritable Records of the Qianlong Period] (hereafter QSL/QL), 69:33a-35a.

[24] GCQXLZ, 20:59b-60a. The reserve was to be built by official buying of Guangxi grain *en route* to Guangzhou. On the structure of the Guangxi-Guangdong grain trade and the consumption needs of Guangzhou, see Robert B. Marks, "Rice Prices, Food Supply, and Market Structure in Eighteenth-Century South China," *Late Imperial China* 12, no. 2 (1991), esp. pp. 79-86.

had set up in the imperial capital five years before.[25] The basic point about the Guangzhou bureaux was that they would husk grain from the city's ever-normal granaries before putting it on sale. They would also operate on a year-round basis, being activated every time the market price exceeded the recognized norm. Thus whereas ordinary stabilizing sales were understood as a response to a deteriorating situation or actual crisis, sales from the husked-rice bureaux would prevent the situation from deteriorating in the first place. Such, at least, was the major virtue that the Yongzheng emperor perceived in Emida's proposal. He appended the following comment to the edited version of Text 1.E that appears in his anthology of leading bureaucrats' memorials and his own responses to them: "Stabilizing sales do no more than save the situation for the short term at a given point in time. If the proposed bureaux are established, it will be possible to have them operating permanently. This memorial is very highly laudable."[26]

*   *   *   *   *

In this section, we see Chinese and Manchu bureaucrats devising schemes for popular well-being with a vigour and concern for detail that would not have disgraced a Fabian socialist in modern Britain. This point is in itself of some significance, since stereotypes of the effete Confucian scholar-official die hard in non-specialist quarters. I will, however, conclude this introduc-

---

[25] The metropolitan *miju* were institutionally more complicated than the bureaux envisaged by Emida. Formally known as the "husked-grain bureaux of the Eight Banners," they had originally been created to provide the Bannermen (a kind of quasi-military caste) with a non-exploitative, and indeed paternalistic, buyer for that portion of their grain stipend that they wished to alienate. By 1731, however, the reserves of grain thus constituted were being used on a year-round basis to counteract price increases on the metropolitan grain market. In the early 1730s, the technique was credited with considerable success. For further detail, see my forthcoming *State or Merchant? Political Economy and Political Process in 1740s China*, chs. 1 and 7.

[26] *Yongzheng zhupi yuzhi* [Edicts of the Yongzheng Emperor Issued in the Form of Rescripts] (1732, 1738), Emida, 2:11a.

tion by drawing attention to a passage in Text 1.A which foreshadows the chief theme of the present book.

Yang Tingwang, as prefect of Quzhou, encountered a subsistence crisis. Despite the failure of the autumn harvest, grain merchants reportedly continued to buy up the remaining grain-stocks to supply markets elsewhere. At popular request, Yang took the obvious step of banning the export of grain, and found himself under impeachment for the offence of "blocking the purchase of grain supplies [by or for other jurisdictions]." In the view of his superiors, we may infer, he had preferred the sectional interests of the people of his jurisdiction to the proper functioning of the redistributive mechanism of commerce. Meanwhile, there were those in eighteenth-century China who would have found the whole story implausible: whoever heard of merchants "assembling" to buy the presumably expensive stocks of a region where the year's main harvest has just failed? Thus controversy was latent even when an official was simply seeking to "succour the folk" in his quasi-parental care. It will be suggested in what follows that, in opposition to the activist tradition, there was a certain body of opinion in eighteenth-century China which preferred to trust the people's economic well-being as far as possible to market forces.

*   *   *   *   *

Text 1.A

Life of His Honour Mr. Yang, Prefect of Quzhou
Date: After 1711
Author: Yang Chun, as a junior kinsman of the subject.
Source: GCQXLZ, 223:10a-14a; HCJSWB, 115:2b-4a.

His Honour's personal taboo name was Tingwang; his style was Jingru, and he was originally called Tingchang. He was a younger cousin of my grandfather, His Honour the Senior Compiler.[1] At the age of sixteen he was enrolled as a government student of Kunshan County, but he was expelled because of the tax-clearance affair and thereupon turned his attention to statecraft studies.[2] He once said: "In official service, there is nothing better than being close to the population. Closeness to the population must precede enriching and instructing them. The vice-magistrates and county registrars and downwards do not dare be close; the assistant prefects and upwards are not able to be close. It must then be the county magistrates alone who exercise this closeness. The essential point in closeness to the population surely consists in enriching before one instructs."

In 1674, he responded to an invitation from the Sichuan governor, Zhang Kunzai, to join his entourage, and in the sixth moon he arrived at Guangyuan.[3] The Great Troops were just then besieging the rebel general Wang Pingfan in Baoning. His Honour said to Zhang Kunzai: "Chengdu is the rebels' lair. The troops defending it are weak, and many of the scholars and common people are restive. If we send out surprise troops to advance down the Sword Pass and make a direct assault, Chengdu is bound to fall. If Chengdu falls, the rebels in Baoning will flee of themselves, without a battle. Otherwise, we are bound to be put into difficulties by the rebels." Kunzai did not follow this advice, and in the seventh moon the rebels attacked Guangyuan. In the ensuing battle, Kunzai was defeated, but he escaped with his life. Thereon Guangyuan was lost. His Honour wandered sojourning in Kuizhou, Xing'an, and Hanzhong.[4]

At length, in 1679, my senior uncle, His Honour the Surveillance Commissioner, was vice-commissioner for Qihuang Circuit in Huguang, and His Honour went and became his dependent.[5] When His Honour the Surveillance Commissioner was transporting military rations to Hunan, and when he was promoted to administration vice-commissioner in Guizhou, His Honour was on most occasions present in the tent assisting with the planning.[6] In 1686, as a student of the Imperial Academy, he was selected for appointment as the magistrate of Shangcai County in Henan.[7] Since the military conflagrations at the close of the Ming dynasty, the rivers in Shangcai had been overflowing, and the countryside was gone to waste. The population dwelt in wretched straits, with no recourse for their complaints. Within three days of his arrival, His Honour personally walked the paths between the fields, comprehensively surveying the rivers, and such of the old creeks as could be found. It came in all to twenty-three rivers, one stream, one brook, one pool, two channels, three reservoirs, five lakes, and 109 creeks. His Honour assessed their size and relative importance, and governed them in sequence.

The River Hong flows through the county for above 100 *li*. Its banks are low, and the water readily overflows. He guided it from north-west of the county seat south-eastwards out into Ruyang, dividing it to form the Wangsi Creek on the left side and the Branch River on the right. The River Ru is broad but shallowed by silt; the River Sha runs swiftly and will easily burst its banks. He guided the River Ru eastwards past Zhuli, where it becomes the Zhuli River, eastwards again past Caibu, where it becomes the Caibu River, and eastwards once again past Hanging-bow Bend, where it joins the River Sha to flow east-wards again into Ruyang. The River Cai has its source in the ravine springs south-west of the county seat; the waters are at first mere streams, but as they pass east of the city they gather to become a river, whose summer and autumn flooding was particularly bad. The River Hei is shallow and narrow in its upper reaches, and in the lower reaches it builds up much silt; the River Bao is topographically like a lake, and half the waters of the entire county gather in it. He guided the River Cai, diverting a first portion of its eastward flow to be the River Zhuma West, a second as the River Zhuma East, and a third to be the River Mao; he led it east again through Leian Li to meet the River Hei; then south through Gaosheng Li to meet the River Bao; and so out east into Xiangcheng.

The Boundary Creek River has its source at the town of Futai, which lies within the county. The bed had long been on a level with the surrounding land. He guided it north into Chenzhou. The Green Dragon Creek ran overflowing for almost thirty *li*. The land was desolate, the population sparse. The White Horse Creek lay at the meeting-point of the three counties of Xihua, Shangcai, and Shangshui, and at times when it was full the tomb of the Bygone Luminary Qidiao was constantly submerged by it.[8] He guided the Green Dragon Creek north-east to flow into the Longtan River of Shangshui County, and the White Horse Creek north into the River Fen of that same county. The River Shu is an offshoot of the River Ru from Xiping County. He guided it to flow into the Zhuli River. The Liuyan River had formerly flowed into the River Sha in Suiping County, but had subsequently been blocked off by the magistrate of that county, so that it had nowhere to empty itself. The Lesser Sha River was an overspill from the River Sha at Langjia Kou in Suiping County. Circumstances in Suiping were such that it was inappropriate to block it. He guided both into the Caibu River. The River-source Creek is one source of the Machang River in Ruyang,[9] the Northern Machang River being another. He guided both to flow into Ruyang. The River Cao was an offshoot of the Zhuma River. He guided it too into Ruyang. There were the five Du Creeks, all silted up completely and crossed by the River Cai.[10] A great road also had been made across them, so that they could not be reopened. He guided that part of each creek which lay north of the River Cai to flow into this river, and that part which lay south of it to flow into the Machang River in Ruyang. The Five Dragon River is a left fork from the Third Du Creek. He guided this so that the Du Creek waters, and those waters which could not flow south, would pass through it into the Zhuma River, and so into the River Hong.[11]

As for the remaining little rivers, minor creeks, streams, lakes, reservoirs, pools, brooks, and channels, here he guided them to pour into the great creeks, there he guided them to pour into the major rivers; here he dredged them, so as to let their vital energy flow freely; there he divided them, in order to abate their force; and there again he gathered them, that they might rest from their ungoverned flowings. It may be said in summary that those conducted into Chenzhou or Shangshui were two in ten; those conducted into Xiangcheng were three in ten; and those conducted into Ruyang were five out of ten. He further built eight dikes: the Hong River Dike, the Wangsi Creek Dike, the Bao River Dike, the Shu River Dike, the Sha River Dike, the Lesser Sha River Dike, the Liuyan River New Dike, and the Liuyan River Wu Family Hill Dike. In length these varied from above a hundred *li*, or sixty to seventy *li*, or forty to fifty *li*, to twenty or thirty *li*; even the short ones were above ten *li*, or five to six *li*. In width all were some thirty feet and more, and their height was eight feet. On this the waters ran contained; an arable champaign was opened up, and travellers could travel.

At the time when work was just beginning, the adjacent counties were not pleased at His Honour's undertaking dredging. Some said that he was opening rivers upon level ground; others, that he was using the neighbouring states as gullies.[12] It so happened that the provincial governor sent out a directive ordering surveys of water conservancy. His Honour wrote in his submission: "The nature of water is to tend downward. It is essential that defences upstream should be firm before one can be free of worry lest the rivers overflow; and that the dredging downstream should be deep before one is immune from fear lest they silt up. From Shangcai, 'upstream' means Xihua, Yancheng, Xiping, and Suiping, and 'downstream' Xiangcheng, Shangshui, Chenzhou, and Ruyang. If it is not firm upstream, the overflowings will continue as before; if it is not deep downstream, the blockings will be as of old. I request that the neighbouring jurisdictions, upstream and downstream, be ordered to clear their river-beds and build up their banks throughout." The provincial governor agreed with this, and His Honour furthermore uncovered seven stone bridges on the River Mao.[13] Only then did the calumnies cease.

On this, he devoted himself the more to works of dredging. He encouraged diligence in farming and sericulture; he found out and remitted above 500 *qing*'s worth of wrongfully assessed land tax paid by the people. He carried out a survey of the arable, numbering the plots and making a fish-scale cadastre.[14] The data as to owner's name, dimensions, defining boundaries, and topographical characteristics—that is to say, whether flat, low-lying, sloping, steeply sloping, hilly, or riparian—were all complete. The county was freed of concealed land-tax liabilities, and also of indemnity taxation.[15]

The county seat of learning had long been in a state of great dilapidation; His Honour made a contribution from his salary and gathered labour to restore it. He requested the promulgation of diagrams explaining ritual and music from the Board of Rites; he sent silk offerings to invite teachers of wind instruments and feather-dancing from Qufu;[16] and he asked for a printing of the scriptures and histories, together with works on philosophy and statecraft, at the Imperial Academy.[17] As to the Temple to Former Instructors, the Hall for the Illuminating of Relationships, and the shrines to the Illustrious Officials and Native Luminaries, the studies and the balconies, offices and living quarters, granary and storehouses, and gates and walls, there was not one whose renovation he omitted. Of the wine jugs, the vessels, round and square, for holding sacrificial rice or millet, the serving dishes for the salted vegetables and meat, and for the pure meat broth, the bamboo offertory baskets and the low offertory tables for fresh meat, there was not one which was not pure; of the bells and chiming stones, the flutes and pan-pipes, the *yu* and *sheng* mouth-organs, the zitherns *qin* and *se*, the ocarinas and the bamboo fifes, the sounding boxes and the crouching-tiger combs, the drums *tao* and *gu*, and the pennons and the pheasant feathers, there was not one which was not perfectly arrayed.

After a period of in all four years, the work upon the seat of learning was completed. He further set up the Shangcai Academy on the west side of the city, inviting celebrated teachers to its gates.[18] The county's finest talents were all made by it. He purchased educational trust lands for its support. The buildings comprised 63 *jian*; the land amounted to 15.78 *qing* or so.[19] He further built a temple to commemorate the Most High Sage's difficulties at Caigou; a shrine to Qidiao Kai at Huapi; and a temple to Cai Zhong, a shrine to Master Xie, a shrine to His Honour Mr. Huo the Restrained and Compassionate, and a shrine to the Three Luminaries, one at each gate of the city.[20] He purchased land in every case in order to provide for the observances. He also built a Temple of Fuxi at Shitai and recovered 25 *qing* of sacrificial land which Buddhist monks had taken over. In all cases where there were observances that should be held and yet there had of old been no directions for them, he devised an order; in cases where they ought not to be held, he put an end to them.

In 1692 and 1693 there was a great drought in Shaanxi, and the folk who came to Shangcai were numbered by the tens of thousand. Hunger found food with His Honour; cold found clothing with His Honour. Sickness found treatment and medicines with His Honour; death found gathering up and burial with His Honour; return home found funds and hatchets with His Honour.[21]

In sum, it may be said that His Honour was in Shangcai for nine years, and in that time the hundred matters were all put in hand, and men and spirits dwelt in harmony. Because His Honour had been able to enrich and to instruct his people, the provincial governor was just about to make a special recommendation of His Honour to the Court, but His Honour had already come to the expiry of his term of office and departed from the post.

In 1695 he was promoted to be vice-prefect of Dengzhou Prefecture in Shandong Province. Dengzhou lies by the sea, and, in any case, a vice-prefect has nothing to do. Over the years he merely travelled on the provincial governor's orders back and forth between the capital, Shaanxi, Ji'nan, Jining, Taian, and Wuding, and that was all. In 1706 he was promoted to be prefect of Quzhou, in Zhejiang Province. Quzhou has common borders with Jiangnan, Jiangxi, and Fujian. Its customs are diverse, its people poor. As to the terrain, the hills are high, the waters swift. His Honour considered how he might bring all to order. First he rebuilt the prefectural Confucian college, the plan and lay-out being as at Shangcai. He issued a directive that the colleges of all Quzhou's five counties should thereon be renovated. The stone dikes of Xi'an County were the most massive at the base and also the most ancient.[22] His Honour issued a directive ordering their urgent restoration. For the rest, the old prefectural gazetteer and the gazetteers of the subordinate counties may be consulted. In all his undertakings, he sent out directives of inquiry covering each several point, and instructing that what was still extant should be restored, what had been abandoned should be reinstated, and what was lacking should be introduced. In every case, he ordered matters through the method he had used to order creeks and channels in Shangcai.

There had of old been a river in the city, but for a long time it had not been dredged, and in places the folk had built houses over it. His Honour established its course and had it dredged. It was the custom to ruin one's resources in marrying off daughters; even the wealthy lineages did not raise their female offspring, but in many cases drowned them. His Honour prohibited it strictly, granting not the slightest pardon. He likewise prohibited the adulteration of silver with copper or zinc upon the markets, and the deceitful pre-absorption of water into rice. He banned gambling, drinking parties, derring-do, and fisticuffs among the populace; he forbade pettifoggers from initiating lawsuits with slanderous words and going in and out of the official buildings making mischief. Whenever His Honour had cause to prohibit something, he would be sure to spell the prohibition out in detail, going up to twice, nay thrice. If there were still those who did not follow his commandment, only then would he chastise them with the law; and his approach towards chastisement was: by chastising one, to warn a hundred. There was none of the common folk who did not bow in cowed and tremulous submission, reforming himself of his faults and making himself new.

In 1709 there was a drought. His Honour rode out with a reduced following, to go in person to the four cantons and admonish the rich folk to open up their granaries and make stabilizing sales. He further exhorted them to lend to the neighbouring poor. The poor got food to eat, but the rich became resentful. In the autumn there was no harvest. The grain-exporting merchant boats assembled like the clouds, and the price of rice rose three times in a single day.[23] Old and young were thrown into a panic, and asked His Honour to prohibit them from passing from the borders. His Honour complied, and the merchants who had lost the chance of profit were all discontented. On this they stirred each other up with groundless sayings, and His Honour was impeached for sealing granaries and blocking the purchase of grain.

In the beginning, when His Honour was in Shangcai, the people there were prudent and straightforward, and His Honour's care was to promote such things as were of profit to them. The people of Quzhou were motley and confused, and among them His Honour also worked at eliminating wickedness. There was this slight difference in his governance, and yet the populations were as one in their appreciation of him. After he had been dismissed, he was not able to go home, nor did the people of Quzhou want him to go. He therefore stayed in Quzhou three more years, and in the ninth moon of 1711 he died there. The scholars and the common folk of Qu wept in the streets; all sacrificed with tears before His Honour's bier. When the folk of

Shangcai heard of it, they set up a shrine to His Honour in the Academy, where they sacrificed according to the rites at each of the four seasons.

Notes

1. This was Yang Tingjian, who, according to Yang Chun's biography, had held the Hanlin Academy post of senior compiler under the Ming dynasty.
2. On the tax-clearance affair (1661–62), see Lawrence D. Kessler, *K'ang-hsi and the Consolidation of Ch'ing Rule, 1661–1684* (Chicago: University of Chicago Press, 1976), pp. 33-39. Yang Tingwang will not have been unusual among his peers in suffering this check to his career; on the contrary, in some parts of Jiangnan this was more or less the common experience of most "government students" (*shengyuan*, i.e., persons theoretically preparing for the provincial civil service examinations).
3. Guangyuan is a northern border county of Sichuan, and in Qing times was part of Baoning Prefecture.
4. These are, broadly speaking, neighbouring areas. Kuizhou is in easternmost Sichuan, Xing'an is to the north of it, across the Shaanxi border, and Hanzhong is north-west of Xing'an.
5. "Huguang" is the name of the old Ming province which had been divided into Hunan and Hubei in 1664. Here it refers to Hubei.
6. "Tent" is not necessarily to be taken literally. The "tent friends" of an official were the secretaries employed by himself to give advice and assistance in the more technical aspects of government.
7. This sentence indicates that Yang entered officialdom by purchase. This was the "irregular" route to bureaucratic office, and it is interesting to find it being used by someone who was apparently to be an exemplary official. In Yang's case, use of the "irregular" route was presumably an indirect consequence of the tax-clearance affair.
8. "The Bygone Luminary Qidiao" was probably Qidiao Kai, although there were three other persons of the Qidiao surname celebrated in Shangcai. All four were disciples of Confucius. See 1690 *Shangcai xianzhi*, 2:44a-b and 10:9a-b.
9. The text (both versions) has an extra *he*, yielding the translation "is one source of the Ruyang River and the Machang River." I have corrected this by reference to ibid., 3:24b.
10. The Du Creeks were named after Du Shi, who had served as chief commandant of Runan during the Eastern Han and was credited with having them dug. Ibid., 2:12b, 7:6a and 9:10a-12b.

11. This re-channelling was a later modification. The main work on the Du Creeks was done in 1686–87, but it left a problem: the creeks ran on across the Ruyang border and thus outside Yang's jurisdiction. As long as the Ruyang sections had not been dredged, the creeks could still not function as efficient conduits to the Machang River. Yang found the mouth of the old Five Dragon River in the spring of 1690 when official business chanced to take him to the area. This enabled him to divert water from the eastern three Du Creeks north into the Zhuma River, as well as providing drainage for other waters which were obstructed to the south. Ibid., 3:6b-7a and 12a-14a.

12. This is an allusion to the accusation Mencius made against a certain Bo Gui, in rejecting the latter's claims to genius in water control (*Mengzi* 6B/11). For Yang's refutation of the allegations against him, see 1690 *Shangcai xianzhi*, 3:9b-10b. His argument was that because failure to dredge downstream, across the Ruyang border, meant that Shangcai suffered flooding, it was Ruyang that was making a gully of Shangcai, and not *vice versa*. For the Shangcai gazetteer's version of the submission quoted here, see ibid., 3:32b-33a.

13. That is to say, the ruins of these bridges were discovered during dredging, thus proving beyond doubt that it was a question of clearing an old river bed, and not opening up a new one as the critics claimed. See ibid., 3:9a and 10a.

14. Fish-scale cadastres were so called because of their appearance. See Wei Qingyuan, *Mingdai huangce zhidu* [The Ming Population Registration System] (Beijing: Zhonghua shuju, 1961), Plate V.

15. The term "indemnity taxation" refers to the practice of claiming uncollectible tax payments from the community at large. An example of Yang's approach to this problem will be found on 1690 *Shangcai xianzhi*, 2:30a-b and 37a-b ff.; it involved buying land, some of it derelict, and having it reclaimed and farmed by tenants, out of whose rents the tax in question could be paid—leaving a surplus for the new Shangcai Academy.

16. Qufu was the birthplace of Confucius.

17. This probably means that the Imperial Academy kept the printing blocks for its own edition of the works in question, and that it was open to local administrators such as Yang to apply to have copies run off for the library of the Confucian College in their jurisdiction. Cf. PYTOCG, 15:15a-16a and 16:10a-12a.

18. On the Shangcai Academy, see 1690 *Shangcai xianzhi*, 2:27b-40a.

19. The *jian* is an architectural unit, effectively of area. The endowment lands had been considerably swollen by private donations, which our biographer omits to mention.

20. The first of these temples was to commemorate an incident in which Confucius "was in difficulties in the Chen-Cai area" (*Mengzi* VIIB/18; 1690 *Shangcai xianzhi*, 2:42b-43a). For Qidiao Kai, see n. 8 above; Cai Zhong was a grandson of King Wen of Zhou, and the second holder of the fief of Cai; and Master Xie was the Song philosopher Xie Liangzuo, a native of Shangcai and disciple of the famous Cheng brothers. His Honour Mr. Huo was Huo En (1470–1511), a magistrate of Shangcai who was killed and dismembered by rebels after he had led a brave but unsuccessful defence of the city against them (ibid., 9:68a-70a). "The Three Luminaries" may have been the other three disciples of Confucius named Qidiao. Yang did not found these shrines and temples; it was at most a question of his having them rebuilt.

21. "Hatchets" (for cutting down briers) was a conventional expression for travel funds. Yang was complying with the standard procedure by which famine refugees arriving in a jurisdiction were supposed to be supported over the winter, and then sent home with monetary help in time to plant the new year's crops. See below, ch. 2, introduction.

22. Xi'an was the county in which the prefectural seat was situated.

23. It is odd that both versions of the text have *tiao*, "sell grain," where we should expect the visually quite similar character *di*, "buy grain." The alternative interpretation is that these were boats importing grain to the dearth-stricken region, but selling at too high a price. However, this interpretation fits ill with what follows, and I have not adopted it.

*   *   *   *   *

Text 1.B

Memorial concerning an investigation of the River Wei, and the recruitment of boat-builders and boatmen from Jiangnan
Date: 1704
Author: Ehai, as Shaanxi governor.
Source: 1735 *Shaanxi tongzhi* [Gazetteer of Shaanxi Province], 86:60a-61b; HCJSWB, 114:8a-b.

Prostrate, I offer my opinion that Your Majesty's exhaustive cogitations on the people's needs, Your planning for the regions, are the acme of thoroughness and regard for detail. Your

Majesty's Sage breast was ever troubled by the fact that since Shanxi and Shaanxi lack riverine communications, to transport grain is difficult in the dearths and famines which sometimes befall. . . . Last year Your Majesty graced Xi'an with a visitation, and Your route passed through both Shanxi and Henan. In the time left over from inspections in the four directions and enquiries about local customs, Your Majesty surveyed the forms and configurations of mountains and streams, and reasoned to the following effect. Inasmuch as the two rivers, Fen and Wei, connect directly with the Yellow River, while Henan Prefecture lies in a central position within these three provinces, and its water routes extend in all directions: if one held back a portion of the tribute grain, and stored it up against future requirement, then should there be a need for grain in Shanxi or Shaanxi, one could forthwith build boats, and transport supplies via the Yellow River. If, having reached Sanmen, the boats could go no further, then one could still build other boats for lighterage, and so pass up the Fen or Wei to penetrate into the stricken province.

Your Majesty's Sage intelligence illuminates the most profound recesses; searching and deep are the Imperial plans! Of all things that can benefit the people's livelihood, or contribute towards plans for storing grain, there is not one for which Your Majesty does not arrange with perfect satisfactoriness, with a regard for detail that nothing escapes. Such are the means by which Your Majesty initiates a model that will prove perdurable over ten thousand years, and does not engage in calculations that pursue short-term expediency. Apart from an examination of the situation at Sanmen, made in obedience to Your Majesty's rescript, and on which I have already reported in a joint memorial, I learn from various records that the whole course of the River Wei extends over 1,900 *li*. It has its source upon the Niaoshutongxue Mountain in Weiyuan County, Lintao Prefecture, but at this point it is no more than the thin trickle of a valley stream. Only when it gains the Daodi area of Baoji County, Fengxiang Prefecture, does it become a level-flowing river. From Daodi it flows east to reach Three Rivers Mouth in Huayin County, where it debouches into the Yellow River. It was this stretch that was referred to by the ancient phrase "the 800 *li* of the Qin river."[1] In the past it was navigable, the benefits whereof were felt both far and wide, but now it is largely blocked, and fallen into disuse. I found, however, that from Xianyang east there are now trading vessels going back and forth, dealing in coal and grain; while from Xianyang west there is extremely little navigation. It seemed a reasonable fear that there was silt-congestion.

Looking upward to take to myself Your Majesty's supreme intent of opening river-courses and benefitting the merchants and the people,[2] immediately on returning to my office from the joint examination of the Sanmen Gorge, I proceeded to Baoji, lightly equipped, and with a reduced following. I went overland, but took shipping here and there on the return journey to the provincial capital. I examined the river all the way. I found that for a stretch of 140 *li* or so from Baoji to Meixian, although the river is very wide, and the current is not particularly rapid, in times of low water heavy-laden boats progress with difficulty. From Meixian east, however, the river is deep and its water smooth-flowing, and there is nothing to hinder the passage of heavy-laden vessels.

I find: to the west the River Wei reaches as far as Fengxiang; to the east it reaches the Tong Pass. Since the Wei gives access to the Yellow River and the Yellow River to the River Fen, this means that it is possible to gain Pingyang in Shanxi Province. Although the water at Sanmen may be swift-running, so that the merchants do not dare defy the danger, the navigable distance represented by the Fen and Wei comes almost to two thousand *li*. The reason for which, nonetheless, the travellers and merchants going back and forth tend to reject the water-route in favour of the land, is in all cases that the boats of Shaanxi are square-prowed and flat-bottomed, and equipped with neither sails nor rudders; nor are the boatmen skilled at handling boats. As long as they are going with the current, they can cover fifty to sixty *li* a day; but when they are travelling against the current, they go up by hauling, and can move only twenty or thirty *li* a day. The progress of the boats is sluggish, and much time is wasted; it is less handy and convenient than the land route. That is why those who use shipping are very few.

It occurs to me that, for river transport, it is essential that the boats be swift, the boatmen well-versed in their *métier*, and that plying back and forth be therefore made convenient for the merchant folk, before it will be possible to reopen the river route. Together with the governor-general Boji, I propose to contribute an appropriate sum of money;[3] hire some skilled boat-builders and practised boatmen from Jiangnan or other southern provinces; and have them make their own assessment of the water's tendencies in order to build boats, which they would fit with sails and rudders. We would have the local craftsmen, scholars, and common people study the construction method, and practise handling the craft. If the design indeed proved convenient and workable, we would direct that the folk's shipping be built on the same model. If there befell a time when Shaanxi had a poor harvest and needed the supplies of grain stored in Henan, one could immediately hire private commercial boats in order to transport the grain, and dispense entirely with the need for any other boat construction. Besides this, with the clearing of the Fen and Wei, it may by gradual degrees be possible to bring these water routes into communication with the Yellow River, causing merchants, travellers, and ordinary folk alike to enjoy benefit and favour; in order, gazing up, to set at ease the Sagely Son of Heaven's supreme intent of cherishing the populace.

Notes

1. Qin, the name of the ancient Wei Valley state which grew, by force of arms, into the infamous Qin dynasty, was a conventional name for Shaanxi.
2. This is perhaps an echo of the statement in the January 1704 edict that "If the river routes are opened, this will be of major benefit to the merchants and the people." QSL/KX, 214:20a.
3. The actual provenance of these funds is open to question, though we may give Ehai and Boji the benefit of the doubt. The use of a claim that one was oneself funding a public project was that one did not then have to account for and justify the expenditure in terms of public revenue.

*　　*　　*　　*　　*

Text 1.C

Memorial presenting plans to transport grain from beyond the
frontier into the interior using ox-hide floats
Date: 1743
Author: Liu Yuyi, as Shanxi governor.
Source: Grand Council copy of palace memorial. Held by the
            First Historical Archives, Beijing; text published in Ye
            Zhiru, comp., "Qianlong chao miliang maimai shiliao"
            [Materials on the Grain Trade in the Qianlong Period],
            Part 1, *Lishi dang'an* [Historical Archives] 39 (1990, no.
            3), pp. 29-30.

I call to mind that "the people are the basis of the state," while
"food is as the people's Heaven."[1] From time immemorial,
governance that proposes to show kindness to the people has
naturally always had as its prime task contriving the provision of
food on the folk's behalf. This is so in all the provinces, and
nowhere more than in Shanxi. The roads of Shanxi are mountainous and steep, and do not allow the passage of commercial traffic.
The price of grain is higher than in other provinces even in good
years, while whenever a poor harvest strikes, the price of millet
rises to five or six taels per granary bushel.[2] This is something of
which I became deeply aware during my former term of service
as commissioner for education in Shanxi.[3]

  This year, after assuming my present position as provincial
governor, I heard that the whole region around Guihua Cheng
and Tuoketuo has for successive years enjoyed abundant
harvests, and the price of grain is very low. The price of buckwheat is not high enough to cover the wage costs of harvesting,
and there are actually people who are leaving their buckwheat
unharvested. With such wantonness, it is not merely a question of
"when grain is cheap, this injures the farmers"; it is also a case of
"abusing and destroying Heaven-sent things."[4] One ought
naturally to take urgent measures to effect circulation. In the
interior, meanwhile, grain prices in Taiyuan, Fenzhou, Pingyang,
and Puzhou Prefectures, and Xiezhou, Jiangzhou, Xizhou, and
Jizhou Departments all range from 1.7 tl. to over two taels per
bushel.[5] Last year saw a good harvest, yet the prices are as high as

this! If we can ship grain from outside the frontier into the interior, it should be possible to stabilize these prices.

I find, however, that Guihua Cheng and Tuoketuo are over a thousand *li* from Taiyuan. It is still further to Fenzhou, Pingyang, Puzhou, Xiezhou, and the rest. If one had the grain go overland, the unit costs of hiring carts and mules would be so great as to be not much different from the current market price by the time the grain had been transported into the interior. Merchants are thus forced to take advantage of the timber rafts from the Daqing Mountains to ship grain.[6] However, the number of timber rafts per year is limited, and so not much grain is transported by this means. There are also merchants who build boats to transport grain. Because the water of the Yellow River comes cascading down as if from an inverted pitcher, and there are many sandbanks and rapids, the grain boats can only go down with the current and cannot return against it. For this reason, once the merchant-built boats have reached Cangtou Zhen in Hejin County, it is necessary to demolish them and sell the planks.[7] Each boat costs seventy or eighty taels to build, but the builder can realize only ten or so taels when he sells the timber. The impossibility of transporting goods in both directions causes constant chagrin.

Earlier, during my previous term of office as commissioner for education, the former emperor,[8] being deeply aware that Shanxi's need for grain supplies was very great, and wishing to have grain from beyond the frontier transported into the interior, gave the commander-in-chief at Guihua Cheng, Danjin, the special assignment of surveying the relevant portion of the Yellow River. At that time Danjin also advocated using timber rafts, but he proposed having the grain transported only as far as Hebao Ying.[9] It was realized that Hebao Ying lies amid myriad mountains, so that to move the grain onward would have been impossible, and the effort would have brought no benefit to Shanxi Province. Since Danjin also advocated cutting timber from the closed forests of the Muna Mountains to construct the rafts, the Board advised that the idea be dropped.

After taking up my present post, I thought the matter over more than once. I thus came to recall how, when in 1736, by Your Majesty's celestial grace, I, in my capacity as governor-general of

Shaanxi, was sent as acting governor to Lanzhou, I saw the people of Lanzhou transporting grain upon the Yellow River using ox-hide floats. The floats were thoroughly quick and convenient, and never capsized even amidst angry waves. Upon remembering this, I sent someone on a special mission to Lanzhou to hire two boatmen who were skilled in handling these floats and to buy twenty of the floats themselves. The party arrived in the Shanxi provincial capital on the twenty-fifth day of the ninth moon, and I questioned each of the two boatmen face to face.[10] According to their report, each ox-hide float costs 0.7 tl. and can carry two granary bushels. Thirty or more floats are joined together to make a raft, and each raft takes four boatmen to operate. If there are many extra floats, the number of boatmen is always computed according to this ratio. The floats can be left in the water for only six or seven days; after that, it is necessary to transfer their cargo onto dry floats and proceed downstream with these. The wet floats can be taken back by donkey to the place where grain is purchased; they are then reloaded, and brought downstream as before. Each float can be used six or seven times. Transport by these means is possible during only six months of the year, from the third moon till the fifth moon, and the seventh till the ninth. In the sixth moon, the wind and waves are too high, while from the tenth moon on, cold weather makes such transport difficult.

I find: it is 480 *li* by water down the Yellow River from He-kou Cun near Tuoketuo to Tianqiao in Baode Department, and the same distance again from Tianqiao through Xing and Lin Counties to Qikou in Yongning Department. From Qikou it is 280 *li* overland to Fenzhou, and 480 *li* to Taiyuan; thus from Qikou it should be possible to succour Fenzhou and Taiyuan. Then continuing down the Yellow River south from Qikou through Shilou, Yonghe, and Daning, it is 610 *li* to Saoshang in Jizhou, that is, the Hukou mentioned in "The Tribute of Yu."[11] At this point, it is necessary to leave the water and go overland for ten *li*, re-embarking at Qilang Wo (still in Jizhou). From there, it is another 125 *li* to Cangtou Zhen in Hejin County. From Cangtou Zhen south, there is a great abundance of boats, so that it will be possible to succour Jiangzhou, Pingyang, Puzhou, and Xiezhou.[12] It will be possible for the grain to penetrate throughout these jurisdictions, while since the Yellow River provides access to the River Wei, Shaanxi could be succoured also.

Realizing that, because it was already late in the ninth moon when the Lanzhou boatmen arrived in Taiyuan, it would not be possible to transport grain over the whole distance, I had thirty-eight granary bushels of grain bought in Baode Department and loaded onto floats for a trial shipment. It took only four days for them to reach Qikou in Yongning Department. Speeding arrow-like amidst the angry waves, they amazed all who saw them. After onward transportation overland to Fenzhou and Taiyuan, the price per bushel was some 0.4 tl. lower than the market price at Fenzhou, and 0.2 tl. lower at Taiyuan. It would seem that this is beneficial to the common people. I am now having a large number of ox-hide floats made at Guihua Cheng, with the intention of having grain bought at Tuoketuo in the third moon of next year for a further trial in which the grain will be shipped straight down to Cangtou Zhen in Hejin County. When, and only when, I have this confirmation, I will submit a memorial asking Your Majesty's permission to expend surplus monies from the meltage surcharge to buy grain for transportation to relieve the population's food needs.[13] This year the harvest in Pingyang, Puzhou, Xiezhou, and Jiangzhou has been scanty, and the price of grain is bound to rise during the time of the *soudure* next year. If it is possible to ship grain from beyond the frontier into the interior on ox-hide floats, the price of grain will naturally stabilize. This measure will become an eternal source of benefit to Shanxi, while when Shaanxi and Henan are short of grain, it will also be possible to divert a portion for the succour of these neighbour jurisdictions. As in duty bound, I submit this memorial.

Notes

1. These well-known clichés of Confucian statecraft are, respectively, a quotation from the ancient *Book of Documents*, and an allusion to a passage in a now lost section of the *Guanzi*.
2. The granary bushel was the standard bushel for administrative purposes. See Pierre-Étienne Will and R. Bin Wong, *Nourish the People: The State Civilian Granary System in China, 1650–1850* (Ann

Arbor: University of Michigan, Center for Chinese Studies, 1991), p. 236.
3. Liu Yuyi had been the Shanxi provincial commissioner for education during 1723–26.
4. Liu is using two stock phrases. The first can be traced back to some words attributed to the "Legalist" minister Li Kui (fl. c. 400 B.C.), quoted in *Hanshu*, Vol. 4, 24A:1124. The second is from *The Book of Documents* (ch. 23).
5. The jurisdictions listed cover the whole south-western corner of Shanxi.
6. The Daqing Mountains lie to the north of the region whence Liu Yuyi was planning to ship grain into south-western Shanxi.
7. Cangtou Zhen lies in southern Shanxi, somewhat more than 100 kilometres upstream from the point where the Yellow River begins to flow east instead of south.
8. This refers to the Yongzheng emperor.
9. Hebao Ying is the site of the modern Hequ county city in northern Shanxi. For further information on this episode of 1725–26 (which Liu does not seem to have remembered with complete accuracy), see First Historical Archives, comp., *Yongzheng chao Hanwen zhupi zouzhe huibian* [Collected Chinese-Language Imperially Endorsed Palace Memorials of the Yongzheng Period] (Nanjing: Jiangsu guji chubanshe, 1986; hereafter YZZZHB), Vol. 13, p. 884 (memorial of 1728). This shows that the Yongzheng emperor did not fully relinquish the idea when it appeared infeasible, but instructed a slightly later Shanxi governor to make further investigations.
10. I have emended the date of the boatmen's arrival from 9/15 by the lunar calendar to 9/25. This is on the basis of the statement later in the text that they arrived "late in the ninth moon" (literally, in the last ten-day period of the ninth moon).
11. "The Tribute of Yu" is a chapter in *The Book of Documents*.
12. I have emended "Chenzhou" to "Puzhou."
13. The meltage fee was a surcharge on the land tax nominally intended to compensate the government for the metal lost when the odd weights of silver collected from the taxpayers were melted down and recast into standard ingots. An unauthorized expedient in early Qing times, the fee was legalized during the Yongzheng period to provide funds for supplementing the hitherto inadequate official salaries, and for meeting the expenses of local and provincial administration. See Madeleine Zelin, *The Magistrate's Tael: Rationalizing Fiscal Reform in Eighteenth-Century Ch'ing China* (Berkeley: University of California Press, 1984), passim, esp. pp. 180-83.

* * * * *

Text 1.D

Letter to Governor Chen discussing transport of grain for famine relief via the Yellow River
Date: 1748
Author: Qiao Guanglie, as prefect of Tongzhou, Shaanxi.
Source: Qiao Guanglie, *Zuile Tang wenji* [Collected Writings from the Zuile Hall] (1756), 1:14a-17a; HCJSWB, 44:6b-7b.

I have heard that there is no extraordinary strategy for the relief of famine. The approach of the men of old was that if calamity arrived they had the wherewithal to withstand it, and that if the year was one of hunger they had the wherewithal to satisfy it. As they withstood it, even though there was calamity, it could inflict no harm; as they satisfied it, even though there was hunger, it could bring no hardship. And what in fact was their technique? I say again: it was nothing more than that their precautions were complete. If the granaries are amply stocked, one may rely on them for making distributions; if the stores have surplus, one may rely on them for drawing of supplies. As for when the granaries and stores are not in a fit state to be depended on, and, even while one points or turns one's head to look, the famine is upon one, then even lightning plans, it may be feared, will come too late. For coping with a famine is like putting out a fire: one really may not pause an instant in one's planning.

When spring gave way to summer, Tongzhou suffered a long spell of unrelenting drought. Although some rain has fallen by degrees since the beginning of autumn, the soil has not been adequately moistened. In two of the subordinate jurisdictions, Huazhou and Huayin, throughout the southern hills of Tong-guan, and in the vicinity of Tongguan city, here there are springs or channels, and there the land has *yin* at its back, and so is rich in moisture; thus, fortunately, the autumn grain remains unscathed. As for the north-facing acreage, much of it is already parched. North of the River Wei, of all the territory of Dali, Chaoyi and the other five counties,[1] only an area some twenty *li* or so in circumference in the Zhichuan area in Hancheng has channels in which water runs; for the rest, high and low fields alike are already badly drought-stricken. All the early millet crops, together with the cotton and beans, are dried out, scorched, and withered. Even if more rain came now, it would effectively impart no succour. As far as Dali, Chaoyi, and the other counties are concerned, not only is there not much well or spring irrigation, but the moistening that comes from seasonal precipitation has long been cut off completely. There are scant prospects for the ripening in the west; it is a year of dearth already.[2] Although the folk are ploughing even now, and looking up to Heaven to pray for rain so as to sow the wheat, the fiery dryness of the red sun and the searing wind grows only more intense. If the planting cannot be accomplished, it will truly be a great embarrassment for next year's springtime budgets.

Prostrate, I call to mind that the territory of this prefecture is narrow, and the population dense. Even in years of abundant harvests, the local grain has ever been inadequate to feed the population. At present, grain is scarce and prices high. The folk's resources are already stretched, on top of which the autumn harvest, in the nature of the case, can only be a sorry garnering. The needy people's difficulty in acquiring enough to eat will be still harder to describe with words. When autumn finishes and winter starts, to make some stabilizing sales in order to force down the market price will be the first priority. If there is a soothing distribution, it will be necessary to give the aid in silver as well as grain, in the hope that this will help the needy.[3] In order to ensure the proper mix, supplementary grain supplies will be required everywhere. Calculation reveals that in the ever-normal granaries of the ten counties there remain no more than 227,000 odd metropolitan-measure bushels of unhusked grain, which basically is far from ample and will not suffice to save the situation.[4] Your Honour's predecessor was greatly exercised by this, and made enquiries of the provinces of Henan and Hubei. While the riverine counties and departments of Henan had no granary-held grain to make available, the rice of Hubei would have had to be transported over a long and rugged route, which would not have been easy. And so despite this situation justifying the most desperate concern, this reality of human throats anxious and restless waiting to be fed, he yet remained devoid of any means to deal with the one or to contrive the calming of the other.

Now with taking thought for a calamity before it starts, putting the plan in readiness beforehand to assure material assistance, I take the liberty of stating that to fix designs on distant parts is not as good as taking what one needs from near at hand; devoting effort to the difficult is not as good as putting it into the easy. Of late, I have made enquiries, and learned that the Yellow River is a route of direct access from the territories of Yulin and Yan'an to Tongzhou Prefecture. The upper reaches are essentially pacific; only for the stretch of seventy *li* leading to Yumen in Hancheng do sheer precipices starkly face each other, the current in between them running swiftly, with many whirlpools at the sides. Boats advance with considerable danger. Because in recent years the two prefectures of Puzhou in Shanxi and Tongzhou in Shaanxi have had poor harvests and the price of grain has risen, the folk from all along the river take ten or so barges at a time, and range them side by side at the Yumen Zhen river station, hooks pulling them together so as to form a wall of stone. When these go up against the current, the whirlpools cannot do them any harm.[5] Those who engage in trade betake themselves to Guihua Cheng and Fugu County, where there is much grain assembled, and buy supplies of grain. They cut down trees to make round-bottomed boats, which they float down with the current from the Fugu and Jiazhou river stations as far as Saokou, and on again to Great Fall Lookout in Yichuan County. The land is high, and the current rushes swiftly, falling suddenly in a sharp drop, so that it is impossible for boats to pass; hence the name Fall Lookout. When the round-bottomed boats arrive at this point, the boatmen get onto the bank and unload the grain for haulage overland. At the same time, they also bring the boats onto the bank, and draw them onward. After altogether thirty *li*, they make their way from the flank of the hills back to the water's edge, and put the round-bottomed boats onto the river to resume transport by water. Once they reach Da Chuanwo, the round-bottomed boats cannot be used, and they unload the grain onto the barges.[6] The barges are larger and more stable than the round-bottomed boats, and each can carry some hundreds of bushels of grain. Starting from Da Chuanwo, the barges proceed as far as

Longmen, a distance of no more than sixty *li*. From there, the grain is transported to Hancheng, Heyang, or Chaoyi; or to Ronghe or Yongji in Shanxi. The grain is put on sale in the markets.

The region is already gaining much assistance through the grain transported by this route. On a rough estimate, the transport costs, overland and water, per market bushel are no more than 0.4 tl. or thereabouts. The mercantile folk derive considerable profit. I have written secretly to the magistrate of Hancheng County, Zheng Zi, who reports that there are at present upwards of 100 boats moored at Saokou. Their load of grain is upwards of 10,000 bushels. Prostrate, I reckon that the territories of Yulin and Yan'an have year after year enjoyed abundant harvests, and the stocks in their granaries are piled high. That I did not earlier propose exploiting them was because the land route is rugged and steep, and pack transport over hills and valleys would be difficult. It now transpires, however, that to come down with the river's current is as easy and convenient as has been described; nor are the transport costs excessive. Either one might allocate and ship stocks from the granaries of those county-level jurisdictions of the said regions which lie directly on the Yellow River; or grain might be procured beyond the frontier. If over 100,000 bushels of millet—no matter of which kind—can be acquired, shipped, and stored in Heyang, Chaoyi, and the rest in order to provide for relief grants and sales during the three winter months, there will be grounds to hope that the administration of relief can proceed calmly, avoiding panic at the time of crisis.

I have, however, heard that after Falling Dew the river freezes over, so that navigation cannot well proceed.[7] This present juncture is critical. If the thing is only managed expeditiously, all can yet be done in time. As to distances and stages, the size and number of the boats to be employed, and the amount of grain per boat; the official personnel to take charge of the operation, and the distribution of responsibility among them; together with the requisite funds for transportation, and all other expenses and equipment, I have considered these with care and thoroughness. I have set out my conclusions in twelve articles, which I respectfully present.[8]

Notes

1. Dali was the name of the county which housed the Tongzhou prefectural seat. The other five counties of Tongzhou north of the Wei were Baishui, Chengcheng, Hancheng, Heyang, and Pucheng.
2. The expression "ripening in the west" comes from the opening chapter of *The Book of Documents*. The west represents the autumn.
3. On "soothing" relief distributions (also known as "preliminary" or "urgent" distributions), see Will, *Bureaucratie et famine*, p. 119. Issuing a portion of the famine relief doles in the form of silver could be a means of coping with shortages of grain in the state granaries, but in the 1740s there were those who advocated this practice on more positive grounds. See below, ch. 7, introduction, and Will, ibid., pp. 121-23.
4. The official assumption was that 50 per cent of the volume of unhusked grain would be lost during husking (Will, ibid., pp. 120-21). Taken literally, this would imply that the actual quantity of cereal food available in the Tongzhou ever-normal granaries was only 113,500 bushels.
5. HCJSWB's emendation of *yi* (a river name, etc.) to *su* ("go up against the current") is to be accepted here.
6. Da Chuanwo may also have been in Yichuan County, since 1753 *Yichuan xianzhi* [Gazetteer of Yichuan County], Maps:1b, shows a Xiao Chuanwo. Yichuan, on the Shaanxi side of the river, is roughly opposite Shanxi's Jizhou (cf. Text 1.C), and is the next county north from Hancheng in Tongzhou, Shaanxi. However, there was also a Chuanwo Zhen on the Shanxi side, some way south of Jizhou.
7. "Falling Dew" was one of the twenty-four solar periods into which the year was traditionally divided. It corresponded roughly to the fifteen days from 23 October till 6 November.
8. These articles are omitted both in Qiao's collected works and in HCJSWB.

*   *   *   *   *

Text 1.E

Memorial respectfully setting out a plan to help the poor buy food

Date: 1733
Author: Emida, as Guangdong governor-general.
Source: YZZZHB, Vol. 24, pp. 520-21; *Yongzheng zhupi yuzhi*,
           Emida, 2:9a-11a; HCJSWB, 40:5a-b.

I take the liberty of finding that upward surges in the price of rice all arise from speculation by hoarders. In keeping rice shops, they are interested in nothing but profit, and frequently put about false rumours so as to push up the price of rice. If at some time it happens to be windy, they say the wind surely presages drought; if there is rain for two days in succession, they say that it must be an augury of flood; and in a single day they put the price up several times. When one establishment puts up its prices, all the others follow suit. It is known as "solidarity within the trade," and no one dares dissent.[1] The rich with their domestic grain stocks do not care when prices are thus made to soar, for it does them no harm; but the artisan poor are frequently unable to afford their food, despite working their fingers to the bone the livelong day.

Even if the authorities make stabilizing sales of the unhusked rice kept in the granaries, it is in the last analysis of no great service to the real poor.[2] For the daily earnings of the real poor— whether they carry wares by shoulder-pole or on their backs, or work as hired labourers—are almost negligible. They cannot buy much of the unhusked rice—only a matter of a pint or half a pint, which will be eaten on the day that it was bought. Thus even though there is the unhusked rice available for stabilizing sales, when the poor purchase it they do not instantly have husked rice suitable for eating. Supposing that, wishing to acquire one pint of husked rice, they buy two pints of unhusked:[3] not only is it impossible for every household of the poor to own the implements for husking; they also have no time at all left over from their daylong bustle.[4] How are they to obtain the husked rice ready for the pot? If they would therefore rather buy rice at high prices from the husked-rice shops, it is not that they are unaware that the official unhusked rice is cheaper, but that they have no option. If one wishes to confer a boon on these poor people, the best thing would be to open official husked-rice bureaux.

I was born and grew up in the capital, and have seen with my own eyes how, in the Eight Banners, since Your Majesty sent down a rescript commanding the establishment of husked-grain bureaux, over some years grain prices have not been high.[5] This has been all because, the bureau prices being at the normal level, would-be speculators cannot shoot at profit. The method is sound and the intention excellent, and it should in fact be adopted everywhere.

Prostrate, I bear in mind the facts that in Guangdong's provincial capital there are particularly great numbers of poor people needing to be fed; that the wicked, seizing every opportunity to shoot at profit, often plague the people with high prices; and that my close enquiries show that, even if there are frequent stabilizing sales, these are of no very great service to the extremely poor. In view of these considerations, I propose to set up three husked-rice bureaux in the said provincial city. (There are not many people living in the vicinity of the north gate of the city, and so there is no need to put a bureau there.) I would put one bureau at the south gate, using the grain of the Guangzhou prefectural granary, and under the management of the keeper of that granary; one at the east gate, using the grain of the Panyu county granary, and under the management of that county's gaol warden; and one at the west gate, using the grain of the Nanhai county granary, and under the management of that county's transferred vice-magistrate.[6] Each bureau would submit a daily account of sales for the inspection of the appropriate magistrate or prefect, and once in every ten days these latter would each forward a report to the provincial and circuit offices for filing. The grain and post intendant would additionally be instructed to perform occasional inspections. As to the quality of the rice, some extra pounding would be done after decortication, so that the result would be equivalent to the medium-grade rice available on the market. As for the price, a set level of one tael per bushel by granary measure would be established as an everlasting rule, to be neither diminished nor increased. As long as the market price remained below one tael, the population would be left to buy rice from the ordinary shops; but as soon as the market price had risen slightly higher, sales would be made from the official bureaux at the set price of one tael.[7] Those going to the bureaux to make their fragmentary purchases would be allowed to pay in coin or silver as best suited their convenience.[8] When they buy a pint or half a pint, there must be no resentment of the bother of repeatedly assisting them; nor should they be allowed to buy more than one peck, since that would create the risk that the rice would be used for trade.[9] The cost of staffing the bureaux would be met by selling the bran and broken grains left after husking. Instructions would be given that the silver realized by the husked-rice sales should be taken, as convenient, to places where grain is cheap and used to make restocking purchases, so that there is continuous replenishment.

Now if there is an established level for the price, there will be no room for the self-seeking of the clerks; as the bureaux would always be there, the speculators would be unable to derive monopolistic profit. All those who seek their living bearing wares on shoulder-poles or on their backs, or else as hired labourers, with their few coppers in their hand, would stand to benefit. . . . I further find that the general-in-chief, provincial governor, and provincial commissioners and intendants are all based in the provincial capital. Since there are many eyes and ears, when the prefect and magistrates established the bureaux, they would definitely not be able to commit abuses. The policy would truly be one of benefit uncompromised by harm.

As for the prefectural capitals, rice from their prefectural granaries would be husked and used to open bureaux, for making fragmentary sales to the local poor. Each bureau would be managed by the keeper of the prefectural granary or, in places where there is no keeper, by the prefectural registrar. The prefect would duly inspect the accounts. All such matters as the rice's quality and selling price would accord with practice at the bureaux in the provincial capital, and the responsible circuit intendant would be charged to carry out inspections. It would seem that this is indeed fit for general and uniform adoption. . . .

Notes

1. "Solidarity within the trade" is a somewhat free translation of *qihang*. William Rowe, in *Hankow: Commerce and Society in a Chinese City, 1796–1889* (Stanford: Stanford University Press, 1984), pp. 254 and 297, translates this term "trade combine," but my experience of seventeenth- and eighteenth-century usage suggests that *qihang* is the action of combining, not the combination formed. *Qihang* action is described in a 1738 imperial prohibition directed at shopkeepers. This forbids "collecting subscriptions and combining" (*lianfen qihang*) and "combining [to] raise prices" (*qihang zhangjia*)—practices whose content, according to this text, is that in the name of "jointly deliberated rules of the trade" (*gongyi hanggui*), the shopkeepers in a given line of business set prices (and a standard quality for silver), and fine anyone who sells for less. The fine includes the obligation to provide a feast for the remaining members of the combination. See 1899 *Qinding Da Qing huidian shili* [Imperially Authorized Collected Statutes of the Great Qing Dynasty: Precedents and Regulations] (hereafter 1899 DQHDSL) 765:13b-14a.
2. As opposed, presumably, to better-off households which took advantage of concessionary sales which they did not really need, not to mention commercial interests which (according to quite frequent allegations) fraudulently bought the cut-price grain for trading purposes, including speculation. Cf. Will, *Bureaucratie et famine*, pp. 167-68.
3. For explanation, see n. 4 to Text 1.D above.
4. Such consciousness was not necessarily unique to Emida. In a 1742 questionnaire to the county magistrates of Jiangxi—a questionnaire whose purpose was both to gain an overall view of conditions in the province and to find out whether the magistrates were doing their job properly—Chen Hongmou asked whether in the annual stock-rotation sales from the ever-normal granaries the rice was sold off husked or unhusked (PYTOCG, 14:7b). His wording would bear the interpretation that rice sold in urban settings was expected to be husked. Notice also, in QSL/QL, 50:7a (1737), a censor's statement that "if rice is not husked it cannot be eaten, which means that if it is not husked it cannot well be sold."
5. The expression "the Eight Banners" normally refers to the socio-military structure into which the Manchu population was organized. Sometimes included is the corresponding structure (eight banners each) for the descendants of those Chinese and Mongol people who

had joined the Manchu side before the conquest. Here, Emida refers to that part of the capital in which the Bannermen resided.

6. Panyu and Nanhai were the two county jurisdictions between which Guangzhou City was divided. On the relocation of the Nanhai vice-magistrate's headquarters, see GCQXLZ, 20:58a.

7. On the status of "one tael per bushel" as the "canonical" grain-price, see Will, *Bureaucratie et famine*, p. 122, n. 13. Table D-9 (pp. 154-60) of Han-sheng Chuan and Richard A. Kraus, *Mid-Ch'ing Rice Markets and Trade: An Essay in Price History* (Cambridge, Mass.: Harvard University, East Asian Research Center, 1975) suggests that, while the concept of a "normal" rice price for Guangzhou was perhaps questionable, to assume this price to be one tael per bushel would not have seemed unrealistic in the early 1730s.

8. For a brief explanation of the Qing monetary system, see below, ch. 2, introduction.

9. Cf. n. 2 above.

2. Doubts

The purpose of this chapter is to suggest, in a preliminary way, that some Confucian-educated officials in eighteenth-century China had their reservations about state activism, and about public and private "do-gooding" generally. Text 2.A, a pleasant frontispiece, shows a county magistrate celebrating the principle of the simple solution to a thorny local problem (in this case, an inter-community dispute over water control). Text 2.B, a commemorative inscription on the foundation of a philanthropic ferry service, unexpectedly suggests that self-interest and the profit motive have their virtues after all. In Text 2.C, we see a censorial official with the audacity to insinuate that the state, with its ever-normal granaries, is nothing but the biggest anti-social hoarder of them all. Texts 2.D and 2.E are edicts of the Qianlong emperor (r. 1735–96) which, in decidedly rhetorical fashion, raise the issues of welfare dependence and abuses of public welfare provision. Finally, Text 2.F, an attack on a series of highly interventionist measures to ameliorate the exchange rate between brass coin and unminted silver, enunciates a theory of what we would call a self-regulating market mechanism that makes state action unnecessary.

Text 2.A, a commemorative inscription, shows a county magistrate congratulating himself on a job well done. Han Xizuo had become the magistrate of Yucheng County in north-west Shandong in 1749. As Yucheng magistrate, he had participated in a drive to improve the river drainage systems of Shandong, and thus reduce the risk of flooding. He had taken advantage of his work in clearing the course of a certain River Yin to resolve a dispute between two neighbouring villages. One village had wanted to dig a channel to drain its easily waterlogged land; the village on whose land the channel would have ended very reasonably objected. The quarrel had come to blows. Once the River Yin was cleared, however, it had become possible to resolve the dispute by redesigning the proposed channel to flow into it. Once the channel had been dug, not only was the agricultural economy of the first community restored; so also was (in Han's account) rustic good humour between the simple-minded yokels of both villages.

While Yang Tingwang (Text 1.A) might have seen in this a perfect small-scale example of "enriching" the people before attempting to improve their morals, the point on which Han focusses in his inscription is the simplicity of the solution. No matter, for our purposes, that the solution's precondition was an episode of classic state hydraulic activism, or, that by some standards, Han might himself have been regarded as an activist local official.[1] It is sufficient, as an introduction to this section, to have one eighteenth-century official asserting the principle that "things of profit to the population need not necessarily be multifarious and complex."

*   *   *   *   *

Text 2.B, also a commemorative inscription, was written *circa* 1785 by Qian Feng (1740–95), a Yunnanese whose main claim to fame was fearlessness in speaking out against the improper dominance of the imperial favourite Heshen at the late Qianlong court.[2] When Qian wrote Text 2.B, however, he was serving as the Hunan provincial commissioner for education. His duties as examiner took him to the prefectural city of Yuezhou (also known as Baling), which was situated at the southern end of a short neck of water connecting the great Dongting Lake with the River Yangzi. While he was there, his examinees (that is to say, the government students, *shengyuan*, theoretically enrolled in the local Confucian college) asked him to write the text for an inscription to immortalize the recent philanthropic gesture of a

[1] For Han's work in improving the drainage of Yucheng County generally, and his efforts in promoting higher education there, see 1839 *Ji'nan fuzhi* [Gazetteer of Ji'nan Prefecture], 38:32b. On Han as a poet, stylist, and calligrapher, see Dou Zhen, *Guochao shuhua jia bilu* [Jottings on the Calligraphers and Painters of the Present Dynasty] (1911), 2:34a-b.

[2] On Qian Feng's censorial career, see biography by Knight Biggerstaff in Hummel, ed., *Eminent Chinese of the Ch'ing Period*, Vol. 1, pp. 150-51.

local man called Zhao Dengmo.[3] Zhao had made an impressive contribution of both silver and agricultural real estate in order to endow a philanthropic ferry service, with supported ferrymen, for the many hundreds of ordinary, impecunious people who daily crossed the Yangzi into Hubei at a place called Chengling Beach. Establishing a philanthropic ferry meant displacing a number of fare-charging operators.

The case for the philanthropic ferry, in terms of the public interest, was twofold. In the first place, the existing operators were accused of overcharging. Secondly, the inevitable hazards of the crossing were said to be magnified by the greed that led the ferrymen to overload their boats. According to Qian's account, there was quite some local feeling against them. What is surprising is that in his closing reflections, where one would have expected to find nothing but praise for Zhao's public spirit, Qian takes up the cause of ordinary, gain-motivated private enterprise and hints that Zhao's initiative, besides being limited from a moral point of view, may also be not fully wise. True, Qian suggests, the displaced ferrymen may have been overloading, but if so, self-interest must have made them attach great importance to keeping their boats in good condition. There was no guarantee that hired ferrymen, whose own the boats were not, would be as conscientious. Great was the tragedy that might ensue.

The idea that private selfishness might lead to public benefit was not new in China when Qian Feng expressed it. The famous scholar Gu Yanwu (1613–82), for one, had made a similar point over a hundred years before, although as a matter of political theory rather than of political economy, and although the "invisible hand" posited by Gu was that of the sage who

---

[3] Once enrolled, through highly competitive examination, in a state Confucian college, the *shengyuan* remained subject to examination by the provincial commissioner for education twice every three years: once in order to reclass them, and once in order to establish eligibility to proceed to the next rung on the ladder to the civil service. See Chang Chung-li, *The Chinese Gentry: Studies on Their Role in Nineteenth-Century Chinese Society* (Seattle: University of Washington Press, 1955), p. 17. Since the upper-level examinations were also highly competitive, it was possible to remain a *shengyuan* for the rest of one's life. Thus Qian's examinees may well have included mature men with well-established interests in community affairs.

consciously built recognition of self-interest into his designs for governmental structure.[4] There is no difficulty, either, in suggesting motivations for Qian's writing as he did: exploitation of a hook on which to hang a moralistic discourse, desire to avert disaster through a warning permanently inscribed and publicly displayed. Nonetheless, his text is very striking. This is almost the last place in the world in which one would have expected to find greed and the profit motive vindicated on pragmatic grounds.

*   *   *   *   *

Yang Eryou, the author of Text 2.C (1742), was a supervising censor at the Office of Scrutiny for Works. This means that, along with the investigating censors represented by the author of Text 2.F, he belonged to a group of professional administrative watchdogs and policy critics—men whose policy discussions, although not always well-informed and sometimes carrying the marks of prejudice, could be the most radical, daring, and innovative of any generated by the Qing bureaucracy, at least during the 1740s.[5] Text 2.C, an attack on the operation of the ever-normal granaries, is a magnificent example.

The late 1730s and early 1740s were a time when fierce criticism of the ever-normal system was being provoked by a naive and generally unsuccessful effort to expand the granary reserves

---

[4] The passage occurs in Gu's famous argument for adjusting the system of centralized bureaucracy by giving county magistrates a personal stake in their jurisdictions (e.g., by permitting them to appoint their successors, the presumption being that they would appoint their sons or younger brothers). It reads: "Each member of humanity cherishes his own family and is partial to his own offspring, and this is normal. His disposition to act on behalf of the Son of Heaven or for the people's good will assuredly be less strong than his mind for acting for himself; it was thus already in the time of the Three Dynasties and earlier. The Sage will take advantage of this, and will use the selfishness of the whole world's population to realize his individual public-mindedness, and all the world will be well governed." The county magistrate will become a model administrator once his self-interest has been appropriately recognized in institutional arrangements. Gu Yanwu, *Gu Tinglin shi wen ji* [Collected Poetry and Prose of Gu Yanwu] (Beijing: Zhonghua shuju, 1976), p. 15.

[5] This judgement, admittedly impressionistic, is based on my research on the 1740s public policy debates. See my forthcoming *State or Merchant?*, chs. 4 and 5 for further examples.

dramatically in order to provide improved insurance against famine. Maintaining the same kind of policy direction that had characterized the reign of his father, Yongzheng, the young Qianlong emperor, abetted by the regional bureaucracy, had set a goal of approximately doubling reserves by requiring payments for titular studentships in the Imperial Academy (i.e., *jiansheng* titles) to be made in the form of grain.[6] The adverse commentary that promptly started did not typically take the form of a direct attack on the new policy, perhaps because that would have been too confrontational. Rather, it challenged the basic assumption underlying the emperor's initiative, viz., that the influence of the ever-normal system on the working of the grain market and the welfare of the people was self-evidently beneficial.[7]

Text 2.C, like many of the other documents generated by what was in the event a fifteen-year controversy, focusses on the alleged negative aspects of the perennial process of buying grain in order to restock the granaries. The need for restocking arose in two ways. First, of course, when grain was issued to the public to relieve a food shortage, it had to be replaced. Second, the problem of the perishability of grain was met by annually rotating a prescribed proportion of the stock (in principle 30 per cent, although the proportion varied according to regional climatic conditions). The oldest grain was put on sale in the springtime *soudure* period, when it was most likely to meet a real need among the poor; it was replaced by purchase after the autumn harvest when grain prices were low. Such was at least the theory; the difficulties of making such a system work in practice have been ably analyzed by Pierre-Étienne Will.[8] The topic here, however, is not the actual performance of the restocking arrangements, but rather how they were perceived by critics in

---

[6] See, e.g., First Historical Archives, CC, Board of Revenue, QL 6/5/2 (1741); QSL/QL, 61:1b-3a; Dunstan, *State or Merchant?*, ch. 5; and Will and Wong, *Nourish the People*, p. 49. For further material on the sale of studentships, see below, ch. 7.

[7] For a full analysis of the documents on which this statement is based, see Dunstan, *State or Merchant?*, chs. 5 and 6. A detailed study of the early Qianlong period debate on the ever-normal granaries will be found in that work.

[8] See Will and Wong, *Nourish the People*, pp. 142-78.

the early 1740s. Yang Eryou, in Text 2.C, makes two complaints, which lead up to a forcefully expressed objection to the entire ever-normal institution as it operated in his day.

Part of the argument of Text 2.C is hard to follow because Yang does not spell out all the implications and connections. In summary, however, Yang's first complaint is that county magistrates typically receive inadequate funds from the provincial treasury to buy the requisite amounts of grain at current market prices. This happens because of systematic underreporting of the level of local grain prices, coupled with deductions at source to cover an administrative fee. The magistrates then pass the buck. Either they call in the local power-holders, who are presumably able to do what magistrates would feel awkward doing, viz. cajole or force local suppliers to sell at a sub-market price; or else they parcel out the purchase quota among the granary staff and the state's liaison persons in the villages. Each of these hapless individuals absorbs a portion of the unmet cost. Yang's concern is simply that this burden on subalterns is both heavy and improper.[9]

The point of departure for Yang's second complaint is the belief, widely held among the 1740s opponents of the ever-normal system, that official buying for the granaries harms consumers by driving up grain prices. While there was a variety of views as to the mechanism by which this happened, Yang's account portrays the process as distinctly sinister. He represents local officialdom as continuing to bleed the market of grain until well into the *soudure* period, apparently irrational behaviour whose motivation is revealed in the dénouement. In the stabilizing sales, inaugurated only when the scarcity of grain is acute to the point of crisis, the price charged for official grain is only slightly below the current market rate. Officialdom thus reaps substantial profit. Small as the official price reduction is, however, it suffices to frighten away the merchants who would otherwise have been attracted by the soaring market prices to bring grain into the area.

---

[9] Yang's account was probably unusual in stressing the financial burden that, he claimed, underfunding of the restocking process imposed on lowly servants of the local government. Other critics focussed rather on the suffering of landowners and others allegedly forced to part with their grain at a sub-market price. Cf. Will and Wong, *Nourish the People*, pp. 168-78.

The state, in short, has abused its power to become engrosser, market-manipulator, and monopolist extraordinary.

It would not have been hard for knowledgeable contemporaries to fault Yang's memorial on grounds of both factual inaccuracy (or at least incompleteness) and implausibility. Only funds for replacing grain distributed in relief operations were issued to the magistrates from the provincial treasury; the annual routine buying was performed with the proceeds of the springtime sales, which, even if they did not remain under the magistrates' control, were as likely to be deposited in prefectural or circuit treasuries as in provincial ones.[10] There was, as we have seen (chapter 1, introduction), a rationale for the small price reductions in the stabilizing sales. And it is highly dubious whether any sensible market manipulator would continue to buy grain on a scarcity-afflicted market right up till the time when he began to sell. Yet all this, while important, is beside the point. Text 2.C shows that the same ever-normal granaries whose level of reserves occasioned such anxiety to conscientious prefects such as Qiao Guanglie (Text 1.D) could be denounced as sources of popular hunger in themselves.

*　　*　　*　　*　　*

By the second third of the 1740s, the Qianlong emperor was willing to allow his edict writers to commit him to positions whose implications were potentially anti-activist.[11] In Texts 2.D and 2.E, he questions the appropriateness of the state devoting vast resources to the economic well-being of people represented as too indolent and feckless to contrive their own subsistence. If the people merely abuse welfare provision, the state should limit its commitment rather than encourage them.

---

[10] Will, *Bureaucratie et famine*, pp. 168-69; Will and Wong, *Nourish the People*, pp. 44-46, 148-49, and 161-68.

[11] The processes by which the court's social welfare policy orientation shifted in the 1740s are charted in Dunstan, *State or Merchant?*, passim. Suffice it to note here, first, that documents such as Text 2.C were not entirely without effect; and second, that the policy of massively expanding the ever-normal granary reserves was abandoned in 1743 (QSL/QL, 189:1b-4b).

Text 2.D (1744) is an imperial protest against what it represents as the excessive tendency of high officials to request that *ad hoc* appropriations from the tribute grain be made for famine relief or granary restocking in the provinces. The grain tribute was an additional land tax levied on eight provinces.[12] Paid mostly in rice, the grain tribute was destined, in principle, for the support of the civil and military officials, Bannermen, and other members of the state establishment residing in Beijing. In fact, however, as the Yongzheng and Qianlong emperors were well aware, it also made a substantial contribution to the provisioning of the general population of the capital, including visitors and sojourners. Tribute grain might either "trickle down" to ordinary people through the market, when officials and Bannermen sold the surplus portion of their grain stipends, or it could be released to them by deliberate governmental measures such as stabilizing sales and winter "gruel kitchens."[13] Thus the tribute grain was indeed of considerable significance for the security of the court and central government; the Qianlong emperor was not exaggerating where, in Text 2.D, he insisted upon its strategic role.

As Will has pointed out, however, the amount collected annually from the taxpayers was high enough to leave a certain margin.[14] Given the belief in state paternalism, it came naturally to emperors and their policy advisers to consider that a portion of the surplus should be used to feed the hungry elsewhere in the empire. The reserves in county ever-normal granaries were only expected to suffice for feeding local peasant populations during minor crises, or enabling them to hold out until supplementary stocks arrived from elsewhere in more serious disasters. While such supplementary stocks could be obtained by purchase, or by transfers from the surplus stocks of other granaries, it was highly convenient that there should be surplus tribute grain available for the same purpose. The 1705 establishment of special precautionary reserves for Shanxi and Shaanxi (chapter 1/introduction) was a matter of using diverted tribute grain to found permanent anti-

---

[12] The tribute-paying provinces were Henan, Shandong, Jiangsu, Anhui, Zhejiang, Jiangxi, Hubei, and Hunan.

[13] See e.g. QSL/QL, 51:6a-b, 76:16b, and 566:4a; and QCWXTK, 37:5197.

[14] Will, *Bureaucratie et famine*, p. 241.

famine institutions. The usual procedure, however, was to let grain be allocated on an occasional and *ad hoc* basis for the relief of famine either in the province of collection, or in another, preferably nearby, one where supplementary grain was needed. By 1744, a *de facto* precedent had also been created for letting tribute grain be used to restock ever-normal granaries.[15]

In Text 2.D, the emperor details some recent substantial allocations for relief and restocking, and indicates that such munificence is not to be taken for granted in the future. Whether motivated by intensified concern about the food security of the capital, by a changing attitude towards welfare provision and its beneficiaries, or by unease about the state of the work ethic among peasants, he orders that local officialdom explore the alternative approach of admonishing the people to take more responsibility for their own subsistence. The burden of the edict is that the state cannot and should not support the entire population; that officials' habitual activation of state famine relief procedures risks giving the opposite impression to the people; that the correct approach would be to devote full ingenuity to guiding all the folk into productive occupations, so that they could keep their own precautionary reserves; but that as things stand, there is real danger of the folk beginning to rely *entirely* on state provision for their every need.

From the point of view of the paternalist tradition, this is a most subversive document. Interesting if only because of its anticipation of the creed of economic individualism (third paragraph),[16] the edict succeeds in imposing on the reader because of its kernel of validity. Since the state's capacity to give relief was ultimately limited, it was indeed advisable that society be in a position to postpone and minimize its calls on state

---

[15] The above account owes much to ibid., part 3, ch. 1, esp. pp. 237 and 240-45. See also QSL/QL, 150:3a-4b; Will and Wong, *Nourish the People*, pp. 46-49; and Wu Hui and Ge Xianhui, "Qing qianqi de liangshi tiaoji," pp. 124-25.

[16] I refer to the assertion of the primacy of "own particular designs" (or "individual objectives"? Cf. Phyllis Deane, *The Evolution of Economic Ideas* [Cambridge: Cambridge University Press, 1978], p. 17, quotation from F. H. Knight). The claim appears to be that an economically well-functioning polity is to be expected only if all parties pursue their own (institutional or private) objectives, as opposed to looking after others.

assistance even in subsistence crises. In the edict, however, this prudent proposition is surrounded by much forceful language suggesting that the people, on the contrary, are greatly given to fecklessness, improvidence, and the mentality of welfare dependence. While the idea that peasants need superiors to organize and monitor their labours was an ancient and fundamental concept of Chinese political economy, seldom can a statesmen have gone so far to insinuate that the ordinary folk of his own day are prone to neglect their livelihoods as soon as they perceive the prospect of state welfare. That there was a strong element of hyperbole in the emperor's rhetoric would have been obvious at the time. The question was: what did the hyperbole signify?

*   *   *

Text 2.E, which actually denigrates welfare recipients, suggests an answer to this question. The court would not hesitate to do away with elements of the paternalist tradition if people who were capable of standing on their own two feet did nothing but take advantage of the state's goodwill. The more strident the court's accusations of abuse, the easier to curtail the provision while still appearing socially responsible.

Text 2.E (1748) was the second of two edicts effectively abolishing the system whereby, if famine refugees arrived in a jurisdiction beyond the stricken region, the host authorities were supposed to care for them over the winter, and then automatically send them home, with funds for the journey, in time to plant the new year's crops.[17] It is reasonable to assume that the concern expressed in this edict about abuses of this system was based, at least in part, on actual reports. In particular, it is likely that the most vituperative part of the document, that which accuses the disorderly and cunning beneficiaries of making a permanent livelihood out of the travel grants, was extrapolated from experience in Zhili, where the practice of paying rather generous

---

[17] For detailed discussion of this policy, see Will, *Bureaucratie et famine*, pp. 195-205; and for further exploration of the implications of the abolition, Dunstan, *State or Merchant?*, ch. 7.

grants to clear famine refugees out of the capital does seem to have created understandable temptations.[18] It was sensible for officials to worry that the prospect of free food over the winter, followed by a dole of cash, might attract both fraudulent claimants, and dearth victims who were not yet desperate, and to whom, on social order grounds, the state would rather have supplied relief in their home districts.[19] One should, however, also note Will's point that certain restrictions in the rules for issuing relief were probably themselves responsible for many peasants taking to the roads as famine refugees. To the emperor, it was an abuse if half the family claimed famine refugee assistance, while the other half stayed at home and drew regular famine relief. However, such occurrences were more or less inevitable, since no relief was to be issued for the able-bodied adult male members of families classified as only "moderately poor."[20]

The first of the abolition edicts argued that in the case of severe, protracted famines resulting from repeated harvest failures, there was no point in sending people home since there would be nothing for them to eat when they arrived, and they would inevitably take to the roads again. When such famines occurred in future, therefore, there should be appropriate provision for "those who most extremely lack support," but the able-bodied should be left to seek the help of friends or relatives, or to support themselves by hiring out their labour.[21] It was only the second edict (Text 2.E) which based the case for abolition on the alleged abuses of the system. Although this edict allowed regional administrators the discretion to continue to assist the genuinely helpless, it was considered to have finally ended the state's long-standing commitment to re-establishing famine refugees on their home fields.[22]

---

[18] Will, *Bureaucratie et famine*, pp. 198-99 and 204.

[19] Ibid., loc. cit., and pp. 195-97.

[20] Ibid., pp. 203-4.

[21] 1899 DQHDSL, 288:22b-23b.

[22] Ibid., 288:23b-24b. The travel grant system went back at least to late Ming times. Will, *Bureaucratie et famine*, p. 198.

It is beyond the scope of the present book to unravel the complex of motivations underlying the decision to abolish. Suffice it to say that Text 2.E illustrates doubt about a practical expression of paternalism taking the form not of suspicion that it did not appropriately help the people, but rather of professed concern that it was turning criminally inclined and feckless individuals into permanent state pensioners.

*   *   *   *   *

Text 2.F was influential in ending an episode of extreme state interventionism in the Beijing money market during 1744–45. In eighteenth-century China, there were two forms of metallic currency: silver, which circulated generally by weight, and whose quantity was essentially independent of government planning; and brass coin (the so-called copper cash), which was minted by the government according to fixed quotas. It was assumed that coin would normally be used for small transactions and was therefore, above all, the currency of the poor. Silver was thought likely to be used for large transactions, such as those in the wholesale sector and in the retail of luxury commodities. In the first half of the eighteenth century, these assumptions corresponded to reality to a considerable extent, although there was significant regional variation.[23] Theoretically, one thousand brass coins were supposed to be worth one tael (Chinese ounce) of silver.

The conventional position among eighteenth-century administrators was that when (as was generally the case) one thousand cash did not exchange for exactly one tael in the market-place, this was in principle an aberration which should be corrected. In the Yongzheng and early Qianlong periods, concern focussed particularly on *low* cash to silver ratios (e.g., one tael buys 800 cash), since such ratios were perceived as reflecting a shortage of coin. It is important to note that where we would speak in terms of the "exchange rate," Qing officials spoke routinely of the "price

---

[23] For further exploration of this issue, see my "'Orders Go Forth in the Morning and Are Changed by Nightfall': A Monetary Policy Cycle in Qing China, November 1744–June 1745," *T'oung Pao*, forthcoming.

of coin." In certain contexts, coin was conceived as a *de facto* commodity, which people went to buy at "coin shops" (while in Beijing there were literal "coin markets" for wholesale transactions). A high price of coin was perceived not only as signalling inadequate government performance in keeping society appropriately supplied with currency, but also, more concretely, as being a source of hardship for the poor.

The state response to high coin prices was sometimes analogous to that routinely triggered by high grain prices. In 1731, for instance, a mechanism was set up by which the coin collected from the Beijing population during stabilizing sales of grain would be channelled back onto the market through the Banner husked-grain bureaux, at a cash to silver exchange rate a few percentage points above that offered by the private money-changers. The goal was to edge the market rate up towards the official norm (1,000 cash/tael) through an operation which the reigning emperor (Yongzheng) explicitly conceived as parallel to stabilizing sales of grain, and which he deemed necessary, like stabilizing sales, because of private sector profiteering.[24]

With coin, unlike grain, the obvious measure of first resort for counteracting perceived shortage was simply to increase supply. When, however—as in the mid-1740s—the output of the mints had been increased very significantly over a period, yet the "price" of coin in Beijing remained high, an alternative prescription seemed to be required.[25] In the autumn of 1744 (by which time Qianlong was on the throne), the imperial grand secretaries pronounced the key to the problem to be "wasteful dissipation" of the capital's existing stock of money, and introduced eight

---

[24] *Shangyu qiwu yifu* [Edicts Concerning Endorsed Proposals on Banner Affairs], Yongzheng 9:4b-8a; and E'ertai et al., comps., *Baqi tongzhi chuji* [Gazetteer of the Eight Banners: First Edition] (1739), 69:19b-23a. On the Banner husked-grain bureaux, see above, ch. 1, introduction, n. 25.

[25] For the empire-wide rise in minting output since the second decade of the eighteenth century, see Hans Ulrich Vogel, "Chinese Central Monetary Policy, 1644–1800," *Late Imperial China* 8, no. 2 (1987), Graph 6 (p. 48). See also Vogel's Table 3 (pp. 17-26), and Graph 1 (p. 43) for the movements of the cash to silver exchange rate in Beijing and Zhili during 1567–1857. His data suggest that, while low cash to silver ratios were characteristic for much of the eighteenth century, the late 1730s and the 1740s did indeed represent a trough.

extraordinarily interventionist measures to end such "dissipation." The forms of "dissipation" that they had in mind were the perennial bugbear of illicit melting, together with practices which, whether innocent or not, had the effect of temporarily removing coin from circulation or draining it out of the capital entirely.

The eight measures ranged from a reassertion of the existing ban on hoarding coin to a complex scheme by which the coin received by Beijing's pawnbrokers was to be compulsorily recycled to the market through two new "official coin bureaux." Also noteworthy was the provision by which brassware manufacturers (prime suspects as regards illicit melting) were to be moved into official premises, where official personnel would monitor the amounts of metal daily entering each workshop in the form of raw material, or leaving it as finished products.[26] The measures were implemented in the capital, and so optimistic must the court have been that many provincial governors-general and governors were ordered to report on whether, and if so how, six of the measures could be applied in their own jurisdictions. However, by the time the provincial reports arrived (beginning in the late spring of 1745), the emperor had changed his tune, and started to repeat the adage that "methods are only as good as the individuals who administer them." His enthusiasm was gone.

The seeds of doubt as to the advisability of the eight measures had been sown partly by two memorials by the investigating censor Yang Kaiding. More directly influential, however, was Text 2.F, by his sexagenarian colleague, Li Shenxiu. Yang's memorials devoted most space to arguing that certain of the measures were in fact dysfunctional if not counterproductive, but he also showed signs of dissatisfaction with the whole principle of close state efforts to control the coin/silver exchange rate.[27] The interest of Text 2.F, by contrast, lies in the fact that, while the eight measures are condemned in passing as "harsh and

---

[26] QSL/QL, 226:8b-14a. A full account of the eight measures, and of the subsequent discussions and their resolution, will be found in Dunstan, "Orders Go Forth in the Morning and Are Changed by Nightfall."

[27] First Historical Archives, *Zhupi zouzhe, Caizheng, Huobi jinrong* [Rescripted Palace Memorials, Fiscal Matters, Currency and Finance] (hereafter First Historical Archives, HBJR), Yang Kaiding, QL 9/11/11 and 10/2/4.

vexatious," the case against them is argued entirely on principle. The key to Li's approach, moreover, is the claim that close state regulation is *unnecessary*.

Text 2.F, written in April 1745, was provoked by a redirection of the regulation policy. As Li indicates in his preamble (omitted here), the emperor had authorized the additional measure of searching all returning grain tribute boats and sea-going vessels that might conceivably be carrying coin exported from the capital. Concerned, however, that action of this kind did not touch the root of the problem, the emperor had also issued an edict "commanding that inasmuch as silver is properly the standard when goods are bought and sold, the folk should likewise value silver for their everyday transactions." In other words, demand for coin was to be reduced by encouraging society to make more use of silver. To this end, decreed the emperor, the grand secretaries and other responsible authorities should prepare proposals for a further set of regulations, and for means of publicizing them effectively.[28]

For Li Shenxiu, this was the last straw. In Text 2.F, he comes as close as any sensible official would have dared to sarcasm at the emperor's expense, pointing out that ordinary people hardly need officialdom to teach them the value of silver. More substantially, he constructs an argument purporting to show that low coin/silver exchange rates are not detrimental to consumers, because the retail price level automatically adjusts. Since commercial accounts are kept in terms of silver, merchants defend their profit margins by routinely revising prices set in terms of coin as the exchange rate fluctuates. This effect operates in the event of both upward and downward fluctuations; it operates in exact proportional manner; and it is the expression of unchanging principles, or "patterned forces." If coin is cheap, prices must rise, or else the merchants will make losses; if coin is dear, prices must fall, or else the merchants' goods will go unsold. There is, therefore, no need for action to restrain the market price of coin.

---

[28] The edict is quoted in First Historical Archives, HBJR, Grand Secretaries and Nine Chief Ministers, QL 10/5/7.

The significance of Li's memorial for the history of Chinese economic thought is twofold. First, it shows that at least one Confucian-educated eighteenth-century Chinese bureaucrat could conceive of economic laws more sophisticated than the mere "where goods mass together, prices fall."[29] Second, in the final paragraph, our bureaucrat, with his advice that the market be left alone to adjust itself, and the merchants to "do what they find convenient," was applying, in effect, the basic injunction of *laissez-faire* liberalism (a doctrine of which he had never heard), on the basis of the law that he had posited. For the Beijing population at the time, the memorial was influential in leading to the abandonment of the whole interventionist approach to the exchange rate issue. A full conference of the grand secretaries and "Nine Chief Ministers," reporting in early June, did not declare itself persuaded by Li's argument. It did, however, recommend rescinding the original eight measures, except for two which had already been rescinded, two which had been merely reassertions of existing prohibitions, and one which fell within the scope of the sole positive measure the conference supported. The emperor's idea about reducing the demand for coin should be translated into a simple enactment requiring the use of silver in wholesale transactions—a practice which was basically normal. The emperor assented to these recommendations. This marked the transition to a policy of "governing [the exchange rate] by non-governance," as he was later to call it.[30]

*   *   *   *   *

---

[29] See ch. 1, introduction.

[30] First Historical Archives, HBJR, Grand Secretaries and Nine Chief Ministers, QL 10/5/7; QSL/QL, 314:7a.

Text 2.A

Inscription for the Lesser Simple River channel at Han Family Stockade in the Western Canton of Yucheng County
Date: c. 1750
Author: Han Xizuo, as Yucheng magistrate.
Source: Han Xizuo, *Huayi ji* [The Huayi Collection] (1874), 5:21a-22b; 1839 *Ji'nan fuzhi*, 67:83b-84b; HCJSWB, 115:11b-12a.[1]

With affairs, there are cases where one wants to see to something but is unable so to do; but where, when one moves on and sees to something else, then on the contrary it becomes possible to see to the first matter. The channel at Han Family Stockade is an example of this.

Han Family Stockade is situated fifteen *li* into the West Canton of Yucheng. The territory is low-lying, and the water from protracted rains accumulates readily. Not only this, but the waters from some tens of *li* south from Xing Family Village all flow into it. When summer yields to autumn, clouds form and the rain bestows itself, the eddies gathering to form a standing pool, so that where it is deep the water wets one's clothes, and where it is shallow one still lifts one's robe.[2] Walls collapse, houses fall down. If it dries out speedily, the people can plant wheat; if not, then even wheat is held from them. If one takes the kindness shown by Heaven above in sending rain and dew, and blames it for disaster and calamity, this is indeed occasion for affliction of the heart. Previously, the folk of Han Family Stockade had asked permission to dig out a channel, wishing to conduct the flow into Liupu. The Liupu people rose up and fought to obstruct this. The legal plaints were followed by affrays, on which the matter was laid down and not proceeded with further.

In the winter of 1749 I became magistrate of Yucheng, and the people came once more complaining of Liupu's obstruction of their digging out the channel. I said: "They are quite right to obstruct it. You want benefit; would they be wanting harm?" It happened that the provincial governor, His Honour Mr. Zhun, having received an Imperial Edict, was minded to eliminate the fear of flood from the Three Qi for ever.[3] He sent directives to the intendants and prefects, requiring them to undertake broad consultation and far-ranging enquiries, treading out and measuring the paths between the fields, in order to establish the design for creeks and channels. Under His Honour Mr. Liu, the prefect, I personally oversaw the business; and thus I was enabled in the process to give my attention to the River Yin, south of the official highway in Yucheng. I scoured away the blockages and drained the stagnating waters, so that with the swiftness of a horse's gallop or an arrow's flight, they took their way into the Tuhai River. The Yin is the river that runs through Liupu. On this, I summoned the folk of Liupu and spoke to them as follows. "Will you still obstruct the channel from Han Family Stockade? If you had not obstructed it before the River Yin was cleared, this would have been to call down flooding on yourselves, to your own ruination. To bring down ruin on oneself is contrary to nature. If, now that the River Yin is cleared, you still obstruct it, this will be to block the water off, to the ruin of others. To bring down ruin upon others spells ill luck." They all assented.

On this, I asked permission, through the prefect, of the provincial surveillance commission, and commanded the folk of Han Family Stockade to begin work on the seventh day of the fourth moon of 1750. Starting to the south of Han Family Stockade, they dug out a channel twelve feet wide at the top and half that at the bottom, and five feet deep. To the north it flowed into the River Yin, and its total length was 14,700 feet or so. In fewer than ten days, the project was completed. The young grain plants stood thick and plentiful; the farmers were congratulating themselves upon the prospect of a harvest. As to the folk of the two neighbourhoods, they who had previously nursed enmity like that between opposing states, now talked and laughed and entertained a social intercourse, each admonishing the other not to speak about the former business of the obstructing of the channel. There was no end of sweat upon the blushing faces.

All requested that a name for the new river be determined and inscribed on stone. The thought came to me that things of profit to the population need not necessarily be multifarious and complex. The length of the River Yin is only thirty *li* or so; that of the Han Family Stockade channel, only seven *li* or so. The employment of the people's strength was only for three or four days. Is this not indeed simple? Whereas formerly, with the requests for digging out a channel to drain off the maleficent waters, a hundred plans expressed the wish to see to it and yet all failed, now in a single morning it was put in hand. The population of the Western Canton of Yucheng is all but ten thousand households. Security from the encroachments of the flooding waters, and enjoyment of sufficiency in granaries and grain-bins; release from the recriminations of the suits at law, and clearance for the pleasures of convivial wine: it was not only the folk's initial expectations that did not extend to this. Even in my own case, who as the responsible official desired to rescue the people from their drowning, my initial expectations too did not extend to this. Then, if one is afraid of blockage, one should dredge and deepen it; if one desires greater width, one should make the sides perpendicular, and thereby expand it. Do not let earth build up in it, intending thus to speed your crossings; do not plant crops in it, appropriating to your single selves the fatness of the millet grains. Every year lay out the strength of seven or eight men to scythe it and to clear the weeds. This is a flawless and far-reaching plan to last a hundred years. So will the work of upkeep be more simple still. Of old, the name of one of the Nine Rivers was the Simple River.[4] Because it lies hard by the Tuhai River, I name this the Lesser Simple River, and have written its whole story for inscription.

Notes

1. The *Ji'nan fuzhi* version (which is presumably closest to the inscription actually carved in Yucheng) is markedly different from the other two. One supposes that Han later reworked the text, and that it was this revised version that was included in his collected writings.
2. This is an allusion to Ode 34 in the ancient *Book of Odes* (also translated as *The Book of Poetry*), one of the Confucian scriptures.
3. "His Honour Mr. Zhun" was in fact the Manchu Zhuntai. "The Three Qi" refers to Shandong.
4. The Nine Rivers were the nine important tributaries of the Yellow River in the time of the Great Yu (the ancient hydrological culture-

hero). They included the Tuhai; and Tuhai, in Han Xizuo's time, remained the name of the major river that bisected Yucheng before flowing northeast across the Shandong Plain into the sea.

*   *   *   *   *

Text 2.B

An account of how Mr. Zhao of Baling gave land and money to set up a philanthropic ferry

Date: c. 1785
Author: Qian Feng, as Hunan provincial commissioner for education.
Source: Qian Feng, *Qian Nanyuan Xiansheng yiji* [The Collected Works Bequeathed by Master Qian Feng] (1872), 5:8a-9b, or *Nanyuan wencun* [Surviving Writings of Qian Feng] (1881), *Ji*:46a-47b; GCQXLZ, 457:29a-30a; HCJSWB, 95:5a-b.

If in the sentiments of all a thing is of advantage, it will in every case be right to press ahead with it as a matter of urgency. But once such urgency has been imparted, one must allow plenty of time before it can come slowly to fruition. This shows the difficulty that besets initiators.

Lake Dongting is the greatest pool in all the world. From the south it gathers many waters; to the north it lets them out into the Yangzi. Only when one reaches the two beaches downstream from the city of Baling does one espy the bank. The southern beach, within the jurisdiction of Baling, is known as Chengling Beach; the northern one, within the jurisdiction of Jianli, as the Jing River Head.[1] Each day more than a thousand persons hail boats to make the crossing. Because this crossing does not lie upon a major route, arrangements are not made by the authorities. Persons on either side used to equip themselves with boats and oars; their passengers duly paid them a fare, but when the crossing was completed they invariably wanted something more. The authorities issued repeated prohibitions, which would go unheeded. Farming folk and petty traders, and paupers with no means of livelihood who seek their food with empty hands, were bitterly distressed by this as they went back and forth. Not only this, but the ferrymen never considered what their boats would bear, but were solely concerned to take the maximum on board. In summer and autumn the water's force is at its height, and the Yangzi will sometimes regorge into the Dongting Lake. As the great waves rage and swell, a heavy boat that falls foul of the current has but to be shaken once or twice, and it will all go to the bottom. Even in winter and spring, when there is little water in the lake, a squall can arise at any time, and the disaster for an overloaded boat will be no different.

Mr. Zhao of Baling made an unstinting contribution of his substance, amounting to some 3,000 taels and more, with the proposal to set up a philanthropic ferry. Those who had hitherto been profiting joined in association and took desperate measures to obstruct the plan, going so far as to bring actions before the governor-general, governor, and both surveillance commissioners.[2] In response to the Imperial selection, I had come as educational inspector: it was not as if I had a territorial charge. Even so, if there was one who brought a document of suit to me, there were a number. Each party had its own view of the rights and wrongs, but in the end the profit-makers failed to win the day. What they were scheming for was nothing but the private interest of a single individual or single family, besides which they had become the focus of general anger. This winter, I have been presiding over the examinations in Yuezhou.[3] The project having meanwhile been completed, the student body of the entire jurisdiction has asked me to prepare a composition to inscribe on stone for a commemoration.

Mr. Zhao's given name is Dengmo, and he has served as an official in Zhejiang.[4] The original value of the paddy fields that he contributed was 1,800 taels. Once the land tax has been paid, the annual rents will go entirely to keep the ferrymen. He also gave 400 taels in silver with which in all five boats were made. A further 800 taels financed the laying of foundations and the putting-up of buildings by the ferry wharfs on either bank; and a last 100 is to earn interest to provide for annual repairs.

I was delighted that the matter was successfully concluded, and said to the students: "This move of Mr. Zhao's is altogether righteous, and will, moreover, be found advantageous in the sentiments of all. However, those who sought to obstruct him were never numerous; if it took until now for the flames to be extinguished, the point is that their benefit depended on themselves; their hearts were dedicated, their will as fellows joined together, one. Those who will be succoured by the founding of the philanthropic ferry are many, but that by which they are to benefit depends on others. The achievements of a wise man ultimately rest upon the physical exertions of the foolish. From now on, will every man who accepts pay and plies a boat be capable of taking as his heart the heart of him who made a contribution of his substance and set up the ferry? With the common run of men, there is not one who does not love ease and hate toil. In my experience, there is not one or two in ten who will exert himself the livelong day for others without tiring. Not only this, but the fellows who were profiting before, in their preoccupation with taking the maximum on board, were bound unfailingly to take the precaution of making their boats both tight and sound. Their masts, poles, sweeps and such-like were also bound to be in perfect condition. Only thus could they expect prospective passengers not to withhold their custom out of doubt and fear. Although there is not the slightest suspicion of an imperfection in the boats which now have been provided, those who ply them will consider that they are not their own, which means that their sparing and cherishing the boats will perhaps not be entirely assured. The boats may easily wear out; and when this has happened, the boatmen will fear censure and fail to report the matter urgently. How should the calamity that would result be trifling?

It is difficult to undertake a project at its first beginning, harder yet to sustain it in the ensuing period. It may be felt that to make over to posterity one's entire surplus of the moment still leaves something unfulfilled, when measured against the wisdom of the princely man in undertakings. Now if the heart that seeks the good of others is devoted, it is further imperative that those who are our fellows and associates should also, every one of them, be of a single purpose. This is the eternal and imperishable way. Yet even so, how can we be too gentle with those who shall come after us? Where the beautiful intention of a forerunner survives, they should look to see what strength of theirs can bring about, and there will be nothing that they will not bring about. Let them put their strength into becoming princely men!

Notes

1. Chengling Beach is just south of the junction of the lake "neck" with the Yangzi, while the county of Jianli is north of the Yangzi in Hubei. The lake's hydrology was more complicated than Qian's remarks suggest. For a good account, see Peter C. Perdue, *Exhausting the Earth: State and Peasant in Hunan, 1500-1850* (Cambridge, Mass.: Harvard University, Council on East Asian Studies, 1987), pp. 198-200.
2. This presumably means the provincial surveillance commissioners for both Hunan and Hubei.
3. In other words, Qian Feng was back in Baling.
4. One word has been changed in the GCQXLZ text, so that it suggests that Zhao served not as an official, but as a private secretary in the entourage of an official. It is conceivable that this is a deliberate, and accurate, correction by the GCQXLZ compiler, who was presumably interested in biographical exactitude.

* * * * *

Text 2.C

Memorial requesting, first, that the practice of forcing subalterns to make good shortfalls in grain purchase funds should be prohibited; and second, that stabilizing sales be at cost price, with the addition of an element for wastage

Date: 1742

Author: Yang Eryou, as a supervising censor at the Office of Scrutiny for Works.

Source: Grand Council copy of palace memorial. Held by the First Historical Archives; text published in Ye Zhiru, comp., "Qianlong chao miliang maimai shiliao," Part 1, p. 25.[1]

My previous memorial explaining that official buying for the granaries harms the people by pushing up the price of grain has been considered by the Nine Chief Ministers, whose response was to the following effect. There being no perfect technique for precaution against famine, it would not be proper to halt purchasing outright; as for the problem of price rises, and their injurious effect upon the people, there is almost nothing to be done in mitigation. However, I have heard that rampant abuses in the practice of official buying in both Zhili and the provinces are occasioning what would appear to be still worse problems.

Except when their jurisdictions are visited with actual calamities which they do not dare conceal, it has long been the practice of county-level magistrates to report 50 to 60 per cent successful harvests as 70 to 80 per cent successful ones, and 70 to 80 per cent successful harvests as 90 to 100 per cent successful ones. In their grain-price reports, they represent a price of 0.8 to 0.9 tl./bushel as only 0.6 to 0.7 tl./bushel.[2] The purpose is to suggest that all has gone well with the jurisdiction's crops, and there is no need to disturb the peace of mind of their superiors. This is an entrenched habit. The governor-general and governor are responsible for the affairs of the whole province, and since their mental energies cannot reach everywhere, they in turn draw up their memorials solely on the basis of their subordinates' reports, expecting thus to soothe the sovereign's Sage breast. When the time comes to issue funds for the official buying to the county-level magistrates, because the provincial administration commission clerks levy their so-called fund-collection fee, it is not possible to give the magistrates the full amount.[3] Unable either to cover the shortfall by diverting funds, or to carry out the buying personally,[4] they will inevitably either engage the powerful degree-holders of the locality, or else divide the task among the grain-measurers, village officers, and so forth. They may even go so far as to issue the funds in silver of inferior purity, so that the true amount is short. With the fleecing that takes place at level after level, the burden of indemnity borne by the actual purchasers becomes unspeakable. Then when official deputies go to neighbouring provinces to buy for the granaries, the governors-general and governors of those provinces are likewise bound to parcel the task of procurement out among their county-level magistrates, and the abuses are like those described above. This means that even before we reach the problem of official buying promptly pushing up the price of grain, the abuse by which subalterns make good official shortfalls is already in evidence. This practice should be urgently eliminated.

Subsequently, the official buying starts, and the price of grain immediately rises. By the time that spring is giving way to summer, grain is scarcer still, and its price even higher. A price which had been 0.8 to 0.9 tl. per bushel has actually reached 1.6 to 1.7 tl. per bushel. The masses wail aloud, for it is naturally hard for them to survive from one day to the next. Only when things have reached this pass do the responsible county-level magistrates propose a temporary halt to buying and request permission to proceed with stabilizing sales. Now, everybody knows that stabilizing sales represent the admirable virtue and beauteous intentions of our Dynasty. However, if we look into the price at which the stabilizing sales grain is sold, we find that the regulations prescribe a reduction of but 0.05 to 0.1 tl. per bushel from the current price. The official selling price is some few times the price at which the grain was bought. Because there is grain being made available through the stabilizing sales, the merchants bind their feet and fail to come forward, with the result that grain is even dearer, the folk plagued even more. Officialdom, with its buying, has hitherto been burdening the people's food supply with price increases, and is now, through its stabilizing sales, successfully competing for sources of profit which should be the people's. The virtuous intention of the Court has, in the last analysis, become no different from the speculative hoarding of the wealthy. How can we wonder that the people fail to perceive the virtue but regard it as a grievance?

I request that henceforward the price of stabilizing sales grain in Zhili and the provinces should cease to be determined on the basis of reduction from the current price. Only an appropriate amount per bushel to cover wastage and transport costs should be added to the price at which the grain was bought, so that the selling price will not be very much above the latter. There should also be a strict prohibition of improper purchases by rich merchants and wicked clerks, so that the petty folk may all be blessed with solid bounty.[5]

If I have made so bold as to importune Your Majesty with the above, it was in recognition of a hidden source of grief among the people which could not, of itself, have come to Your Majesty's attention. Prostrate, I beseech Your Majesty, in Your Sage perspicacity, to adopt my suggestions.

Notes

1. For the original palace memorial, see First Historical Archives, CC, Yang Eryou, QL 7/4/18. I have corrected one apparent error in the published version on the basis of Yang's original.
2. Especially after the beginning of the Qianlong period, reporting grain prices was a routine activity of the Qing bureaucracy. Provincial chief administrators were required to send the court detailed monthly price statistics for each prefecture within their jurisdiction. These upper-level price reports, available in the central government archives in Beijing and Taibei, now form the basis of important studies such as those presented in part 1 of Thomas G. Rawski and Lillian M. Li, eds., *Chinese History in Economic Perspective* (Berkeley: University of California Press, 1992). One hears less about the process of reporting prices at the lower levels of the territorial hierarchy.
3. The provincial administration commission managed the provincial treasury. The fee in question was probably payable when personnel sent from each county-level jurisdiction collected the grain purchase funds. Yang presumably intends the reader to understand that the allocations for each county are in any case too low, because they correspond to the underreported local prices mentioned in the first half of the paragraph.
4. Yang must mean that the magistrates cannot be seen buying grain in person at sub-market prices.
5. Reading *di* ("buy grain") for *tiao* ("sell grain"). Cf. n. 2 to Text 1.E above.

*   *   *   *   *

Text 2.D

Instructions to local administrators to exhort the people and assign them tasks, to make the population's food supply sufficient
Date: 1744
Author: Issued in the name of the Qianlong emperor.
Source: *Shangyu dang* [Archive of Imperial Edicts] (microfilm), QL 9/3/23; QSL/QL, 213:10a-12b.

The lord of men takes nourishing the people as his urgent business. The true way of nourishing the people lies in causing them to follow Heaven's times above and be observant of Earth's opportunities below, going to the limit of their industry and toil in order to support their families. It is not a matter of their basking in the willingness of those above to make good what they lack, and save and succour them, so that they depend upon it permanently as their strategy for the support of life. In ancient times, those who were skilled at planning the state's course used to say that where the folk are nourished by the lord there will not be enough, but where the folk are caused to nourish themselves there will be ample and to spare. This is truly an unalterable precept.

The state annually transports tribute grain in order to solidify the capital. It is a matter of provision for the income and outgoings of the Heavenly Garner; it is of the most weighty significance. It may happen that, because dearth or disaster chances to befall and there is absolutely no alternative, one adopts the plan of having tribute grain diverted or held back. This may be done only on the odd occasion: how should one proceed to look upon it as a constant rule? Nowadays, the ministers and officers within and without are ever asking that the tribute grain should be held back; and We, in Our acute concern over the folk's support, have likewise repeatedly concurred. It flows in each case from one time's exigency. In fact, although the Metropolitan Granaries' stocks are said to be enough for five years if not ten, and to be required, in principle, only for official salaries and military rations, if one reckons with the capital's whole population, it is to be feared that they will not suffice for so much as a year or two. How much the less if one desires to portion them out further for relief grants and loans for Zhili and the provinces! Why have they not considered this? In the reigns of Emperors Wen and Jing of Han, the grain of the Great Granary had new stocks heaped on old unendingly, to the point where it went red and rotten and became inedible.[1] How should it be that at that time there were no regional disasters? Yet We have yet to hear of portionings or reductions being lightly advocated. This is truly because the great calculations for managing the state require imperatively that one plan with the long term in view.

Within officialdom and among the folk, in the capital and in the provinces, there is none but has his own particular designs. If one forsakes one's own designs and goes contriving aid as well to others, there will, in the event, be many inconveniences, besides which, in the nature of the case, it will not be within one's power. As soon as there is some deficiency, both parties suffer harm. Since ancient times, this has not been adopted.

Last year the granaries of different provinces urgently needed grain. This being so, in proper adaptation to this accidental circumstance, We had 100,000 bushels each out of the tribute grain of Jiangsu, Anhui, Zhejiang, Jiangxi, Hubei, and Hunan retained within each several province, besides which We instructed Jiangsu and Zhejiang to transport 100,000 bushels each to Fujian, and Jiangxi to transport 100,000 bushels to Guangdong. Further, because Tianjin and Hejian in Zhili Province were suffering from natural disaster, We had altogether 800,000 bushels allocated from the Tongzhou granaries as provision for relief.[2] This year, once again, We had Shandong retain 200,000 bushels, and have it stored in different places for use in relief. These were all cases in which, the people's lives being at stake, We could not but show some flexibility in managing the situation. Suppose the little folk have not knowledge enough each to devote his efforts to his livelihood, but are dependent solely on official grain. Setting aside the absolute impossibility of giving to all the needy masses as well as the soldiers and officials, one may point out that, although for places which are near the tribute-paying network it is possible to advocate retention or diversion of the grain, the distant, border provinces are without tribute grain to keep or have diverted in their favour. From whence will they supply themselves?

We bear in mind that a given region's endowment of Earth's opportunities will properly be capable of nourishing that region's population. A given family's endowment of human strength will properly be capable of nourishing that family's whole membership. In ancient times, nine offices employed the myriad people. The first was that of the three kinds of farmer, who raised the nine grain-crops. The second was that of the gardener, who grew herbs and trees. The third was that of the forester, who brought up the useful products of the hills and marshes. The fourth was that of the wetlands keeper, who reared and propagated birds and beasts.[3] Which one of these was not an art for the support and nourishing of life? If one is father and mother to the folk, the folk's affairs are one's own family affairs, and one should be exhorting them and setting them on tasks wholeheartedly, apportioning and reapportioning the work from time to time, in order that none of Earth's opportunities may be left unexploited, none of the people's forces left unspent. This being done, each family will have its own reserves, and will naturally be able to "draw on them to nourish and draw on them to soothe," so that whether caring for their children or their parents, they will not lack.[4] If the governors-general and governors have not the ability to give direction to the local authorities, and if the local authorities, for their part, do not concern themselves with fields and farmsteads, domestic animals and trees; if, in years of bad harvests, they only ask permission to release stocks from the granaries and to hold back the tribute grain; if this is assumed to be sound anti-famine strategy for governors-general, governors, and local magistrates, so that the folk are caused to say that there is no need for precaution against flood or drought, and make no plans for living on the fruits of their own toil; and if the point is reached where vagabondage turns into a vogue, and the vital matters of the food and clothes of self and family are all entrusted to the state authorities—this is not to love the people, it is actually the way to harm them.

Set against the vastness of the Empire, the great number of the billion trillion people, the regular prestations total but a certain small amount; how would it be possible to succour everyone?[5] We therefore specially send down this Edict, commanding the governors-general and governors of Zhili and the provinces each to consider, and to instruct the local guardian officials each to consider, of what affairs is it that they are governors-general? Of what affairs is it that they are governors? Inasmuch as they are designated as "having cognizance of prefectural affairs," or "having cognizance of departmental, or of county, affairs," of what affairs is it in fact that they ought to have cognizance?[6] Whatever they do on the folk's account is also what they do upon their own account. If, acting on the folk's account, they do not cause the folk to understand that each must act upon his own account, then how far are they capable of acting on the folk's account? From now on, let each of the governors-general and governors take to himself Our heart. Let them not neglect the folk's affairs, but let them earnestly instruct and guide; and let them exhort the good local authorities to be particular to see to it that all the common people know that they must contrive for themselves, in order to enrich the source of nourishing and sustenance. They should not vainly look for grace or hope for favour; but in these conditions grace and favour, when applied, will truly be enough to be of use, which being so, in the abundant years they will rejoice in the felicity sent down, while in the years of dearth they will be able to depend on being without fear. We wish to share Our servants' efforts in this cause.

Notes

1. Cf. Sima Qian et al., *Shiji* [The Records of the Historian] (Beijing: Zhonghua shuju, 1972), Vol. 4, 30:1420, which cites this state of affairs as evidence of the prosperity of the times. The reigns referred to occupied the period 179–141 B.C. It does not seem to trouble the Qianlong emperor that the surplus grain could, arguably, have been better diverted to famine relief than left to rot.
2. For the 1743 tribute grain reallocations in favour of the granaries of central and southern China, see QSL/QL, 196:18a-b. On the diversion of tribute and other grain held in the Tongzhou granaries (near Beijing) for famine relief in Zhili during 1743–44, see Will, *Bureaucratie et famine*, pp. 138-55.

3. The list of "nine offices" is borrowed from a Confucian scripture, the *Zhouli* [The Rites of Zhou] or *Zhouguan* [The Officers of Zhou], which purports to describe the governmental structure of the hallowed Zhou dynasty (traditional dates 1122–256 B.C.) in its idealized early heyday. For the reference, see Sun Yirang, ed., *Zhouli zhengyi* [The Rites of Zhou, with Correct Exegesis] (first published 1905; *Guoxue jiben congshu* edition) 2:54. That the emperor did not go to the end of the list is readily explained: while offices nos. 5-8 are, in order, "the hundred kinds of craftsman," "the merchant," "the waiting-woman," and "the male or female servant," no. 9 is "the unengaged [*xianmin*— conventionally understood as idle people], who have no constant office, but shift from one employment to another."

4. The words for "draw on them to nourish and draw on them to soothe" (*yin yang yin tian*) are borrowed from a context (in ch. 31 of *The Book of Documents*) in which they mean something else. Here again the emperor alludes to a scriptural passage which is hardly in accord with the spirit of his edict. The burden of the passage is that a good ruler's instructions to regional authorities (in this case, feudal vassals) stress caring government, which should extend even to pregnant women. In giving orders to his vassals and administrative officers, the ruler "leads them on to nourish and to soothe [*yin yang yin tian*] the people." See Bernhard Karlgren, *The Book of Documents* (Stockholm: Museum of Far Eastern Antiquities, 1950), p. 46.

5. The phrase "regular prestations," whose archaic sound is explained by its origin in *The Book of Documents*, refers essentially to the land tax, including the grain tribute.

6. The emperor is alluding to the literal meaning of the words "prefect" (*zhifu*, "know-the-prefecture"), "magistrate" (*zhixian*, "know-the-county"), etc.

* * * * *

Text 2.E

Second of two edicts abolishing the system of automatically providing for famine refugees over the winter, and then sending them home with monetary assistance[1]
Date: 1748
Author: Issued in the name of the Qianlong emperor.
Source: QSL/QL, 314:15a-17a.[2]

Because, in Zhili and the provinces, the system of returning wandering people to their homes with monetary assistance not only occasions great expense to neighbouring provinces, but in fact is also of no benefit to the disaster-stricken, We earlier sent down a special edict proclaiming Our instructions. We have recently noted, from an implementation report by Anning, the acting governor of Jiangsu, that he still fails to understand Our meaning.

It may be pointed out that since the rule of winter feeding and an assisted return home came into force, there have been those among the cunning folk of every province who have left their grain and tools with relatives after the autumn harvest and set off with their families, falsely claiming to be famine victims. There have also been poor people in disaster-stricken areas who, having obtained relief tickets, have sold them for money and set out to rove.[3] There have been cases of half the family staying at home to draw relief, while the other half takes to the roads as famine refugees.

When the famine refugees of any province leave its borders, their home jurisdiction has no way of keeping watch on them, while the neighbouring provinces have still less means of telling whether or not they are real famine victims. They have no option but to take in anyone they see, in order to conform with the set regulations. Besides, they are afraid that if the multitude is great and they do not oblige it with accommodation, there may arise some further trouble. Even when the visitors should not be taken in, they will still stretch a point and carry out the rule. Such are the problems of the winter feeding system.

When the term specified in the host province's report draws to its close, and it is just the time for starting on the springtime toils,[4] the host province may indeed wish to speed the visitors on their homeward way, and duly send them off in batches. However, with the delays *en route* caused by foul weather, it invariably happens that several batches become merged. Massed together in their hundreds and thousands, the returnees demand at will, even going so far as to ransack shops, revile the *yamen* personnel escorting them, and defy senior officials, finding a hundred pretexts for disputes. As soon as they have entered their home jurisdiction, their one fear being investigation on the part of the authorities, they raise a final clamour and disperse. The two or three escorting runners cannot stop them. After they have scattered, they again depart the jurisdiction and claim to be famine refugees. They travel back and forth and are each time sent back with monetary help, so that it is an endless cycle; they finally rely upon this as a lasting strategy for the support of life. Those who genuinely settle and resume their occupation are not one or two out of a hundred. Such are the problems with the assisted return home.

Besides, the rations provided to famine refugees are actually larger than the relief doles that they could draw if they remained at home. There is therefore a saying that to be a famine victim in one's home is not as good as to become a refugee upon the roads. With gradual habituation, taking to the roads becomes a custom and grows daily commoner. The point of view of the authorities is that, since it is a question of famine victims, they would rather err on the side of generosity. They do not realize that this is to entice the people to be refugees.

The cost to neighbouring provinces is incalculable, and those who are assisted home are in the last analysis not real members of the poor and needy. It is a detraction from munificence, and the service of an empty name; it is in no way consonant with proper government. One might cite the example of this year's famine victims from Shandong. Those who crossed the northern frontier numbered almost in the tens of thousands. Beyond the frontier there is no question of assisted returns home, and yet one never saw them drifting and becoming destitute.[5] Besides, if one attempted to provide assisted returns home to everyone, there would, in the nature of the case, be ways in which it would be hard to do this. It would be better to let these people seek food and contrive a livelihood themselves, while issuing clear and incisive proclamations so that the folk understand that there is nothing to be gained by drifting and by taking to the roads, and will not lightly leave their neighbourhood or forsake their old source of livelihood. Such alone is the way to correct the root and purify the source.

You should convey to the governors-general and governors that they are to manage matters satisfactorily according to the circumstances, and should not feel obliged to cleave to the established rules.[6] If an area is actually severely stricken, and the poor have no means of keeping themselves alive, or if it is a question of the old, the very young, the crippled, or infirm who have no one to lean on as they flee from famine, and who would be unable to survive and go back to their neighbourhood without the winter feeding and assisted return home, then it should be permitted for the governors-general and governors to make appropriate *ad hoc* provision. Let them take Our intent to heart, and understand that it is imperative that, in dealing with such matters, they act with a view to real assistance to the disaster-stricken masses. They are not to let mere captivation with the fine repute attendant upon winter feeding and assisted return home perversely lead them into fostering mean habits in the populace.

Notes

1. This title has been supplied by the translator.
2. The entries for the fifth moon of 1748, when this edict was issued, seem to be missing from the microfilm of the *Shangyu dang*. I have therefore had to rely on the *Veritable Records* text alone.
3. As part of the preparation for official famine relief operations, relief tickets, i.e., relief eligibility certificates, were issued to those peasant households which an *ad hoc* survey classified as "poor" or "moderately poor" (the great majority of households in any given rural community). The tickets, which specified the head of household's name, the village, and the household composition, were obviously not intended to be transferable. However, poor organization at the relief distribution centre (which served many villages), or connivance by the village officers, could conceivably have resulted in transfer of tickets going undetected. See Will, *Bureaucratie et famine*, pp. 107 and (for the contemporary notion of a *well*-organized distribution centre) 131-33.
4. That is, it is just the time to plough the fields in preparation for planting spring-sown crops.
5. During the first half of the Qing dynasty, immigration into Fengtian (southern Manchuria) and the Mongolian border areas of Xuanhua and Chengde served as a significant channel of escape from economic hardship for the peasantry of Zhili and Shandong. After 1740, such immigration was in principle forbidden, but already in 1743, at the time of a severe drought in Zhili, the emperor had ordered that

famine refugees arriving at the major passes in the Great Wall should be quietly let through (Will, *Bureaucratie et famine*, pp. 52-53 and 196). This evidently set a precedent for similar tolerance in 1748.

The present edict was promulgated at the beginning of June. The emperor had hardly allowed much time for resettlement problems among the Shandong famine refugees to show themselves!

6. The edict was addressed to the grand councillors, who would now have the task of forwarding the emperor's text to the governors-general and governors in the shape of a "court letter."

* * * * *

Text 2.F

Memorial explaining that high coin prices are not detrimental to the people, and requesting that the bans be dropped in order to avoid harassment
Date: 1745
Author: Li Shenxiu, as an investigating censor.
Source: First Historical Archives, HBJR, Li Shenxiu, QL 10.

[In his preamble, Li refers both to the original eight interventionist measures introduced the previous autumn, and to the emperor's more recent orders that new measures be devised to guide the people into "valu[ing] silver for their everyday transactions," and thereby to reduce demand for coin.]

One cannot say that this is not the ultimate in taking thought for the coinage. However, on the basis of a close examination, and having regard for the great constancies in the working out of patterned forces, I take the liberty of saying that all need not be as Your Majesty envisages. I beg leave to expound this for Your Majesty in detail.

I was born in 1685, and remember how in 1699 and 1700 one tael of silver would exchange for 1,200 or so small coins. In terms of today's large standard coins, this was only 600 or so.[1] Coin may be said to have been extremely dear, yet commodities on the contrary seemed cheap, and the people never found the situation inconvenient. By 1703–4, the price of silver had shot up to the point where one tael would exchange for 2,200 small coins. In terms of today's large standard coins, this was as much as 1,100 cash. Coin may be said to have been extremely cheap, yet the prices of commodities were at least twice their former level, and so this time the people failed to benefit.

I submit that, in the case of trade in the metropolis, profit and loss accounting is done entirely in silver.[2] If coin is cheap, the prices of commodities must rise; otherwise, there will be losses of capital. If coin is dear, the prices of commodities must fall; otherwise, the goods will pile up unsold.[3] To push on from these principles, even if the price of coin rose to the point where one tael of silver exchanged for no more than 500 cash, one cash would naturally and necessarily perform the service of two-thousandths of a tael. If the price of coin fell daily to the point where one tael of silver exchanged for 2,000 cash, then 2,000 cash would necessarily be demanded for goods which had previously cost 1,000. This is all the inevitable working out of patterned forces, once-fixed and unchanging.

Given the above, what good or harm do changes in the price of coin do to the people, that there should be so much anxiety? The eight measures devised by the high ministers and now in force are harsh and vexatious, and the merchants are already greatly burdened by them. Prostrate, I peruse Your Majesty's edict. While comprehensively and penetratingly well-versed on the primacy of silver over coin, and on the usage of each of these forms of currency, Your Majesty, fearing that the folk do not appreciate the superiority of silver, has ordered the high ministers to determine new provisions and proclaim them in compelling fashion.

Having turned the matter over in my mind, I would definitely not venture to concur immediately. Even severe laws are unable to ban practices which are convenient; even sages are unable to change customs which are well-established. It is true that "in the lower Yangzi provinces there are places where silver is used for hundredths and thousandths of a tael."[4] However, this is a practice of long standing that has gradually become habitual; it was not created by the force of law. As for the children and uneducated fellows of the north, who know nothing of scales and fine weights and would be hard put to determine purity:

measures such as Your Majesty envisages will necessarily involve setting a line of demarcation above which silver must be used, below which, coin. If there are situations in which the rules prescribe the use of silver, but the needy folk only have coin and are devoid of silver, what is to be done? In these circumstances, even if one had the wisdom of Xiao He, one would certainly be unable to propose any sound scheme that would accommodate the people.[5] As to the superiority of silver, even foolish fellows and their wives are well aware of it without the benefit of proclamations. The reason for their use of coin is simply that they opt for its convenience; it is not because they fail to realize the value of silver.

According to my unenlightened view, it would be best to leave these matters entirely as they were before. The harsh and vexatious measures devised by the high ministers should all be completely done away with. Let the price of coin be left alone to rise or fall, and let the people be left to use either coin or silver. Let the Boards continue to pay silver for those items for which they have hitherto paid silver, and coin for those for which they have hitherto paid coin.[6] There is no need either to devise new regulations or to post notices and proclamations. If one merely lets the merchant folk do what they find convenient, and refrains from binding them with the laws of officialdom, not only will one avert confusion and inconstancy in governmental ordinances, but one will also spare the folk disturbance and harassment. This would seem to be extremely simple and extremely easy; it is easy both to understand and follow. Prostrate, I beg Your Majesty to discern whether my rustic, boorish views are apposite, and put them into practice.

Notes

1. There was apparently a time during the Kangxi period when coins of sub-standard size were minted. Two of these small coins were deemed equivalent to one standard coin. See Frank H. H. King, *Money and Monetary Policy in China, 1845–1895* (Cambridge, Mass.: Harvard University Press, 1965), pp. 60, and 257, n. 30.
2. Literally, "capital and profit are reckoned entirely in silver."
3. By "prices," Li means "prices expressed in terms of coin."

4. This is a not quite word-for-word quotation from the edict. For reference, see n. 28 to the introduction to this chapter.

5. Xiao He, right-hand man of the founder of the Han dynasty (202 B.C.–A.D. 220), gained his reputation for wisdom by providing the intelligence and logistical support which enabled the Han founder to defeat his rival for imperial power. In particular, when the Han founder's army occupied the Qin capital in 206 B.C., Xiao He made a point of seizing the maps and other administrative records of the Qin government while the Han military leaders were all vying to claim the wealth locked in its storehouses. See *Shiji*, Vol. 6, 53:2013-16, and *Hanshu*, Vol. 7, 39:2005-9.

6. Li is referring to a passage in the edict in which the emperor complains about what he perceives as the irrational propensity of officials to convert appropriations from the silver in which they were issued into coin before expending them. He prohibits this practice, making an exception only for the Board of Works, which is to be permitted to continue to pay coin for "those items for which coin ought to be issued."

3. Inequality

As long as the world has both rich and poor, a fundamental question in political economy will be the proper attitude and role of government (that is, state power) towards the fact of inequality. In the twentieth century, the issue has presented itself quite starkly as the choice between pursuit of the communist vision of a classless society (and, ultimately, a withered-away state) and defence of the inegalitarian capitalist alternative on pragmatic or libertarian grounds. From the viewpoint of the 1990s, maintenance of structures based on inequality appears as the path of normality and common sense, while the efforts to realize communism seem aberrant. Confirmed Western preference, at least, is now for a rather low level of state activity to soften the contrast between rich and poor, instead of the ultimate state activism of communism as the world has actually known it.

In the Chinese élite tradition also, from Song times on if not before, the upholders of egalitarian ideals, or at least of strong-arm action by the state to limit inequality, were a minority, and on the losing side. That the ancient egalitarian "well-field" system of land distribution could not be restored was a *cliché*, and symbolized a general (and understandable) lack of interest on the part of the élite in attacking the *de facto* principle of private, including corporate, property.[1]

This much is common knowledge. Less well studied, at least in the West, has been the traditional discourse upholding the social function of the rich, associating wealth with virtue, and

---

[1] The partly mythical "well-field" system was so called because each of the units in its rectilinear grid-plan looks like the Chinese character for "well" encased within a square. According to the major source for the traditional belief about this system, each well-field unit was a square containing 900 *mu* of arable. This area was divided into nine equal holdings, eight of which were allotted to individual families, while the ninth was cultivated by all eight families to yield tax grain for the state. *Mengzi 3A/3.*

pointing out the ways in which the state can harness private wealth so as to realize social welfare goals.[2] Such discourse, while serving the purposes of social conservatism, was ideologically nonconformist, since the convention in Confucian political culture (and, no doubt, much popular thinking also) was to associate virtue with relative poverty, and wealth with wrong-doing, avarice, and general ethical vulgarity.[3]

The selection of texts for the present chapter reflects both the minority status of egalitarianism in traditional Chinese élite thought, and the need for closer attention to the counter-cultural defence of private wealth. Text 3.A is the one plea for egalitarianism; it can also be read as a somewhat mystical prescription for enlightened autocracy, the role of the judicious and, presumably, abstemious ruler being to keep society homogeneous. In Text 3.B the tables are turned: it is the state itself which sucks wealth from society, thereby vitiating the natural process whereby wealth is constantly generated and flows from its possessors to the needy. Text 3.C, taken from a famine relief manual, both makes and quotes forceful assertions about the moral worth and social value of the rich, while arguing that officialdom should cherish wealthy families as insurance against future need to draw on their resources and goodwill (to supplement official relief efforts). Text 3.D, whose purpose is to urge county magistrates to promote conditions in which private grain-lending will flourish, reiterates some rhetoric about the value of the rich, and defends a certain interest-charging practice which at first sight seems unconscion-

---

[2] See, however, for Song dynasty (960–1279) arguments supporting private wealth, Peter K. Bol, *"This Culture of Ours": Intellectual Transitions in T'ang and Sung China* (Stanford: Stanford University Press, 1992), pp. 251-52; and Winston Wan Lo, *The Life and Thought of Yeh Shih* (Hong Kong: University Presses of Florida and the Chinese University of Hong Kong, 1974), pp. 118-20. For Qing government use of wealthy landowners in famine relief operations, see the work of Will cited in n. 17 below.

[3] As we saw in ch. 1, introduction, virtue was not thought to be associated with hunger and destitution (except, perhaps, in the case of real paragons such as Confucius's disciple, Yan Hui). Just how relative poverty could be is illustrated where we read in one of Ho Ping-ti's social mobility case studies of a family "so poor that [it] could not afford a wet-nurse" for three infant sons spaced close together. See Ho, *The Ladder of Success in Imperial China: Aspects of Social Mobility, 1368–1911* (New York: Columbia University Press, 1962), p. 286.

able. The theme of the alternative, amoral view of economic exploitation emerges with more clarity in Text 3.E, a largely poetic dialogue in which we learn that "murder shops" paying hungry and emaciated cottagers low prices for their cloth are doing nothing but responding normally to market fluctuations.

As if to symbolize the fundamental nature of the issue which they all address, these texts, with one exception (3.D), are all private writings, not documents generated by the day-to-day business of bureaucratic service.

* * * * *

The starting point of Texts 3.A and 3.B is similar: both authors hold the ruler's personal example ultimately responsible for the economic morality of society at large, while conveying a strong hint that the example set by contemporary rulers is deficient. As already indicated, however, Text 3.A is, so to speak, a "statist" document, while Text 3.B evinces strong suspicion of the whole state apparatus. Text 3.A is a literary composition of considerable power and artistic richness; it is, I think, best understood as a rare Chinese example of the *genre* known in the Judaic and Christian tradition as prophecy.[4] Its author, Gong Zizhen (1792–1841), appears to have been given to radical thinking; at least, as an advocate of social and political reform, he made various proposals which have been hailed as "revolutionary" for their day.[5] Text 3.A, "On Equality," is, on the face of it, hardly a revolutionary document, since it calls only for careful corrective action by an astrologically guided monarch to

---

[4] Prophecy is not, of course, a recognized *genre* of Chinese literary writing. I do not wish to speculate about the possibility that our present author had been influenced by reading the prophetic books of the Old Testament in translation. Creativity within the Chinese cultural tradition would have been sufficient to produce Text 3.A.

[5] Fang Chao-ying in Hummel, ed., *Eminent Chinese of the Ch'ing Period,* Vol. 1, p. 433. Gong's concerns included the civil service examination system, opium addiction, foot-binding, and the general level of political morality. For a brief view of his thought, see Judith Whitbeck, "Kung Tzu-chen and the Redirection of Literati Commitment in Early Nineteenth Century China," *Ch'ing-shih wen-t'i* 4, no. 10 (1983): 1-32.

even out society's imbalances. Insofar as it has revolutionary implications, these lie in the earnestness of Gong's warning that extreme inequality leads to social cataclysm and dynastic downfall. The assumed institutional framework is not revolutionary; the dramatized treatment of the theme of inequality may be.

In the opening of Text 3.A, Gong uses the metaphor of a community's demands on an exhaustible body of drinking water to explain the causal relationship between monarchical avarice and economic competition in society, and to warn of the dangers inherent in the latter, assuming finite resources. The sumptuary hierarchy of the hallowed "Three Dynasties,"[6] in which the allocation of graduated shares (bowlfuls for lords, ladlefuls for ministers, and wine-cupfuls for ordinary subjects) provided the means, presumably, to "bring peace to" society, already represented a decline from an earlier stage in which "lord and population drank together" and there was perfect "equability."[7] Once sumptuary inequality was thereby instituted, the way was open for struggle between those with great and those with small entitlements, with the lord's assistants trying to snatch resources from the populace, and *vice versa*. After a period of neglecting the greed-driven strife within society, the rulers started to join in, with demands commensurate with their status and in keeping with their by now predatory natures. Once again, where the sovereign had led, society followed, and soon everyone, both sovereign and subjects, was scooping water by the "bushelful." The consequence was that the supply sometimes ran out, leaving all the drinkers incapacitated ("prostrated") by thirst.[8]

---

[6] The Three Dynasties were the ancient dynasties of Xia, Shang, and Zhou, and their early institutions (especially those of the Zhou dynasty) were considered to provide a model of ideal government.

[7] Gong Zizhen agrees with the ancient Confucian philosopher Xunzi in perceiving competition over limited resources as the fundamental problem of human society, and in associating (implicitly and with incomplete approval in Gong's case) the hierarchical allocation of shares with the pacification of society. Cf. A. C. Graham, *Disputers of the Tao: Philosophical Argument in Ancient China* (La Salle, Ill.: Open Court, 1989), pp. 255-57; and *Xunzi* 9, lines 15-18 in the Harvard-Yenching Institute Sinological Index Series concordance text.

[8] My interpretation differs from that of Wolfgang Bauer, in *China and the Search for Happiness: Recurring Themes in Four Thousand Years of Chinese Cultural*

This image introduces a prose poem in which Gong implicitly admonishes the ruler to redistribute resources, in the interests of his dynasty's survival. Gong's analysis of the ill-effects of inequality within contemporary society is not very explicit. We are probably meant to infer that the progressive development of inequality is far advanced and that the poor are indeed "dwelling on the brink." Otherwise, we gather only that the proximate cause of the impending civil war and dynastic collapse will be the deterioration of "prevailing customs" that has been induced by inequality; also, that the unprincipled commercial instinct has been one important factor leading to both inequality and moral degradation. To illustrate the link between commercialism and moral decadence, Gong cites the prostitution of both female beauty and (referring to the civil service examinations) Confucian scriptural study. However, the most pressing threat to dynastic survival and, indeed, the survival of mankind itself, is the "festering ether" generated by all the hatreds and the acts of greed and callousness produced by inegalitarian society.

The interest of Gong's programme for corrective action lies in the fact that, just as the rulers of old relied on the divinations of the Grand Astrologer to tell them about the imbalances within society and their own hearts, so the redistributions carried out by the ruler who heeds Gong's advice are to be cosmological as well as social. Exactly what is meant by, for example, "ladling out [the superfluity] from Heaven and pouring [it] into Earth" is not made clear. We can infer, however, from elsewhere in the text, that Gong's concern is with the adequacy of resources born from Earth, and that he means to suggest that a ruler who can hold his heart in balance with a balanced cosmos will be able to ensure "abundance of production." Once it is a question of cosmological

---

History, trans. Michael Shaw (New York: Seabury Press, 1976), p. 256. Bauer has lord, ministers, and populace competing for the soup in a tureen, and it is the tureen which is overturned (my "prostrated") in the chaos. There is, however, nothing in the original except the reference to spoons (my "ladles") to suggest that the liquid in question (*shui*, "water") may be soup, while no container of any kind is mentioned. It seems to me that, given Gong's high seriousness and the vagaries of China's climate, the image of greedy competitors prostrated by thirst is not only more dramatic than the farcical scene conjured up by Bauer, but also the more plausible interpretation.

rulership, the stakes are raised, because the potentially totalitarian project of evening out accumulations of private wealth within society gains supernatural endorsement.

It is, perhaps, beside the point to discuss how far this text is "revolutionary" (in the conventional sense of contributing to the ideological foundation for egalitarian social revolution). In practical terms, the text was presumably as ineffectual as its author, by reason of its eccentricity.[9] It remains, however, a forceful literary statement of the hazards of social inequality. As such, it is worth preserving less for its historical than for its universal human value.

*   *   *

Text 3.B, an essay called "On Enriching the People," is less abstruse than "On Equality," but also a fine piece of literary writing. Its author, Tang Zhen of Suzhou (1630–1704), was quite an outspoken critic of "big government," and opposed his ideal of personal solidarity between sovereign and subjects to the reality, as he perceived it, of a predatory state apparatus staffed by voracious officials. For Tang, nothing the state apparatus of his day could do was right. Its centralized appointment system, which deprived the administrator of any natural personal stake in the good order of his jurisdiction, was dysfunctional; its reliance on the written word put barriers between the officials and those whom they governed; founded on the butchery of the conquest period in the 1640s, the *régime* remained a government of brigands; and it tolerated the exclusive use of silver as a medium of exchange in all but very small transactions. Not only did the bullion-based monetary system cause depression at a time when silver was in short supply; silver, being light and compact, and thus "the easiest of things to concentrate," was admirably suited for the avaricious schemes of corrupt and high-placed functionaries.[10]

---

[9] On Gong's failures and frustrations as a public man, see Fang Chao-ying in Hummel, ed., *Eminent Chinese of the Ch'ing Period*, Vol. 1, p. 432.

[10] See Tang's essays "On Authority," "On Changing the Currency," and "A Domestic Conversation," in Tang Zhen, *Qianshu fu shi wen lu* ["A Book to Be

As is well known, many of these themes were common to a number of late seventeenth-century "statecraft" thinkers, that is, political economists who were mostly outsiders to the Qing bureaucracy, their normal expectation of a life of government service having been frustrated by the change of dynasty in 1644.[11] Although Tang Zhen did serve as magistrate of Changzi County in south-east Shanxi for several months, probably during 1671, in his writings he is very much the disaffected private intellectual.[12] In another of his essays, he expresses something of the "physiocratic" view—which is at least implicit in much other seventeenth-century statecraft writing—that wealth is to be identified not with precious metals but with the produce of the soil.[13] In Text 3.B, he seems mostly to use "wealth" in the more

---

Hidden," with Poems and Prose Texts Appended] (Beijing: Zhonghua shuju, 1963), pp. 115-18, 140-42, and 196-97; Jacques Gernet, "L'homme ou la paperasse: aperçu sur les conceptions politiques de T'ang Chen (1630-1704)" [Human Beings or Red Tape? An Outline of the Political Ideas of Tang Zhen], in *State and Law in East Asia (Festschrift Karl Bünger)*, ed. D. Eikemeier and H. Franke (Wiesbaden: Harrassowitz, 1981), pp. 117-24; and Nakayama Mio, "Shindai zenki Kōnan no beika dōkō" [The Secular Trend of Rice Prices in Jiangnan in the First Half of the Qing Period], *Shigaku zasshi* [Journal of History] 87, no. 9 (1978), p. 22.

[11] The more relevant works on the late seventeenth-century "statecraft" thinkers and their political background include Étienne Balazs, *Political Theory and Administrative Reality in Traditional China* (London: School of Oriental and African Studies, 1965), Parts 1 and 2; Hu Jizhuang, *Zhongguo jingji sixiang shi* [A History of Chinese Economic Thought] (Shanghai: Shanghai Renmin chubanshe, 1983), Vol. 3, chs. 12-14; Wm. Theodore de Bary, *Waiting for the Dawn: A Plan for the Prince. Huang Tsung-hsi's* Ming-i-tai-fang lu (New York: Columbia University Press, 1993); and Ono Kazuko, "Shinsho no kōkeikai ni tsuite" [On the Scripture Study Circle of the Early Qing Period], *Tōhō gakuhō* [Journal of Oriental Studies] (Kyōto) 36 (1964): 633-61. The most sophisticated introduction to the economic thought of the period is Kishimoto Mio, "Kōki nenkan no kokusen ni tsuite—Shinsho keizai shisō no ichi sokumen" [On the Kangxi Depression: Some Aspects of Early Qing Economic Thought], *Tōyō Bunka Kenkyūjo kiyō* [Annals of the Research Institute for Oriental Culture] 89 (1982): 251-306; abridged in English as "The Kangxi Depression and Early Qing Local Markets," *Modern China* 10, no. 2 (1984): 227-56.

[12] On Tang's short-lived career as an official, see *Qianshu fu shi wen lu*, pp. 269-75.

[13] Ibid., p. 140; cf. Kishimoto, "The Kangxi Depression and Early Qing Local Markets," p. 243.

everyday sense of a given household's resources, especially monetary ones; yet the physiocratic understanding may have contributed to his depiction of the process of wealth-generation as a natural and spontaneous one, which begins with the soil, domestic animals, natural materials, and quotidian human labour. Here, too, he was not alone: his use of the growth of the willow tree as a metaphor for the enrichment of society finds an analogue in an essay by his contemporary, Yi Xueshi. Yi implicitly likened the proper growth of wealth to the shooting up of young grain plants, or the multiplication of domestic animals.[14] What is striking about Tang's discussion is that he views the generation of wealth, sometimes from minuscule amounts of capital, as a constant process involving all members of society, and normally providing more than amply for society's requirements.

In Tang's view, the natural way in which poor people gain such external support as they may need is through dependence on the rich. The rich support the poor by acting as employers, customers, and lenders; and, in the aggregate, they do this on a substantial scale. The best service that the state can render is simply to leave the economy alone, so that the natural principles of mutual dependence may continue to function normally. Unfortunately, however, to the contrary, the state permits its ruthless "avaricious functionaries" (meaning the degree-holding members of the regular bureaucracy) to ransack society, and thus feed their unbounded private coffers. Thus is society impoverished. Not only does Tang argue that the remedy for this state of affairs lies with the sovereign, who must set a good example; he drops a muted hint that the emperors of his day are guilty of complicity in the despoliation. Their conspicuous consumption sets the pattern for the mandarinate, and can be sustained only by imprudent spending and immoderate exaction from the population.

---

[14] Yi Xueshi, "On the Management of Wealth," in HCJSWB, 26:1b. Yi's position in this essay is very similar to Tang's in Text 3.B. The only help that the process of wealth-generation needs is removal of sources of harm; the biggest source of harm is the despoliation wrought by the state apparatus, and this is fundamentally the work of the harsh, avaricious functionaries.

*   *   *   *   *

Text 3.C comes from a manual of famine relief administration by one Yang Jingren, originally published in 1826. Its advice represents only a small part of the author's relief strategy. It purports to be inspired by concern that the stocks of grain available in a famine-stricken county's ever-normal and community granaries may not suffice to feed all the hungry people in the event of successive harvest failures.[15] This concern would have been sensible at any time; it was probably especially realistic in the early nineteenth century, when the state and state-sponsored famine relief institutions were long past their prime.[16]

If the state and state-sponsored granaries lacked adequate resources to prevent local starvation, an obvious supplementary measure was to appeal for assistance to the county's rich. As Will has shown, even in the mid-eighteenth-century heyday of Qing state famine relief, officialdom relied on local wealthy people to fill the gaps in its own programmes; as the state's power and effectiveness declined, dependence upon private wealth was likely to increase.[17] However, if appeals to the rich were to succeed, the local officials needed to maintain good relations with them. There was the rub. Not only, as Yang says, were the rich the natural targets when there was some local "public undertaking" that needed contributions; they could also, as he fails to mention, be positive enemies both of state paternalist endeavours over popular subsistence and (especially when wealth was combined with formal élite status) of good order generally. Many

---

[15] Community granaries (*shecang*) were theoretically supplementary reserves of grain built with private contributions; administered by relatively well-to-do members of local society under official supervision; and, commonly, intended to provide loans of grain rather than outright grants. Recent research suggests that, as intense imperial and official efforts to promote the *shecang* system were made from the 1720s to the 1770s, these principles were not treated as sacred. See Will, *Bureaucratie et famine*, pp. 176-80; and Will and Wong, *Nourish the People*, pp. 37-40, 63-69, and 86-89.

[16] On the decline of the Qing granary system, see Will and Wong, *Nourish the People*, ch. 4, and for a searching analysis of the problems that made decline probable, chs. 5-8, which are by Will.

[17] Will, *Bureaucratie et famine*, pp. 125-28.

a local official wrung his hands at the perceived immorality of wealthy landowners and others who hoarded grain during subsistence crises, while official impulses towards social justice in such matters as taxation were repeatedly frustrated by the manoeuvres of local magnates with illegal or improper vested interests to defend.[18] In practice, prudent administrators reached an accommodation with the local power-holders, to make government possible and prevent damage to their own careers; in principle, officials and the anti-social wealthy should have been at daggers drawn.[19]

Yang's approach to dealing with this problem, as an author, was to simplify it. Acknowledgment of the dual nature of the local rich, as both potential saboteurs and needed allies, would have detracted from the persuasiveness of a call to cherish and support them (and thus, presumably, court their goodwill). Instead, in Text 3.C, he constructs an image of the rich as virtuous but vulnerable. On one hand, the rich, who represent the nation's "fundamental soundness," are the only persons with the wherewithal to practise moral conduct (in the sense of materially helping others). Meanwhile, they are also liable to gradual impoverishment through the demands of local officials. Not only do officials look preferentially to the rich when public contributions for some project are required, and take advantage of these occasions to feather their own nests; their despoliations are also sometimes actuated by a prejudice against the rich which is entirely at variance with the latter's real character. To make this

---

[18] See, e.g., ibid., pp. 59-66, for a thoughtful exploration of the problem posed officialdom by the social antagonisms between famine victims and the "immoral" rich who profited by their distress, whether through speculation or through usury. For a brief survey of the ways in which holders of state academic titles (the so-called Chinese gentry) exploited their position at society's expense, see Ch'ü T'ung-tsu, *Local Government in China under the Ch'ing* (Cambridge, Mass.: Harvard University Press, 1962), pp. 185-90. On official policy on speculative hoarding, see below, ch. 6, introduction, and Dunstan, *State or Merchant?*, chs. 1 and 3.

[19] This is not to say that local officials never risked confrontation with powerful local interests. For an interesting late Ming example, which led to the forced resignation of the courageous magistrate, see Hamashima Atsutoshi, "The Organization of Water Control in the Kiangnan Delta in the Ming Period," *Acta Asiatica* (Tokyo) 38 (1980), p. 91.

last point, Yang quotes Li Gou, an eleventh-century writer, as having claimed that rural wealth is the result of diligence, thrift, superior mental characteristics, and a generally respectful attitude towards the natural order and official authority. To jeopardize the continued existence of such a valuable group within society because of prejudice would go against the real interests of the state.

Yang's own argument runs parallel to this. Private wealth, belonging to the nation's only truly solid citizens, must be protected so that it may serve as a resource in times of famine. Officialdom, therefore, must cease to milk the rich. Yang buttresses the pragmatic appeal of this point of view by establishing it as part of a long tradition with roots in scriptural authority. The phrase "leaving the rich in peace," which he takes as his text, is from the canonical *Zhouli* [The Rites of Zhou].[20] While he also alludes to two stories from the "legalist" *Guanzi* book, and to a substantial late Ming exposition of the social function of the rich, he quotes from two pieces of commentary on the *Zhouli* phrase. The Li Gou quotation comes from such commentary, and near the beginning of Yang's essay there is a very interesting remark by, probably, the Qianlong emperor, linking the concept of "protecting the rich" with the idea that the state cannot alone "provide for everyone."[21] Text 3.C supplies a concrete illustration of what Qianlong might have meant.

Although Yang would thus have been the last to claim that his approach was novel, his rhetoric is striking. One is no more accustomed to seeing actual *wealth* explicitly proclaimed as a prerequisite for goodness in Confucian discourse than in Christian. The lesson drawn from the two *Guanzi* tales is also unconventional. Where others used these stories to promote the view that a wise ruler encourages his people to attach more importance to prudently accumulated grain reserves than to mere monetary wealth, for Yang the propaganda purpose was to exalt

---

[20] On the nature of the *Zhouli*, see above, n. 3 to Text 2.D.

[21] For references, see notes to Text 3.C.

the principle of private wealth, and urge that to protect one's own wealth was a duty.[22]

*   *   *

Text 3.D is a directive about rural credit by the Jiangxi governor Qin Cheng'en. It too was written in the early nineteenth century (1804), and its framework of concerns is similar to that of Text 3.C. The reserves of the ever-normal granaries, limited to begin with, have been eroded by diversion of some grain to other purposes; the only hope is to rely on supplementation by the local rich. For Qin as well as Yang, the wealthy are the nation's "fundamental soundness"; they are "the mothers of the poor," and have to be "preserved" so that the poor may benefit. At this point, however, the differences become as salient as the similarities. Qin is interested in the rural rich specifically as sources of subsistence or seed-grain loans to peasants in the *soudure* period; and the threat from which the rich must be preserved comes not from the bureaucracy but from their own clients.

Text 3.D consists largely of a set of contrasts between urban pawnbroking and rural grain-lending. It is a little hard to read, because what at first appears to be a descriptive analysis is gradually revealed as being partially prescriptive. Qin seems to be simultaneously stating what is the customary pattern in the countryside and giving aspects of the customary pattern his official sanction. At the end of the analysis, there is a shorter discussion of the role of wealthy grain-controllers in anti-famine strategy, and in community welfare generally. Here, Qin goes so

---

[22] Cf. the essay "On Enriching the People" by Yu Tingcan (*jinshi* of 1761, d. 1798), in HCJSWB, 39:2b-3a. This essay, like Yang's, focusses on the need for the state and state-sponsored granary reserves to be supplemented by private grain stocks in the hands of "wealthy commoners." In Yu's text, the potential social functions of the *prudent* rich are pointed out through evocation of an unspecified past in which the wealthy *did* save grain, and thus were able to assist officialdom in times of crisis. More recently, however, a tendency towards extravagance has led to a situation in which "the wealthy commoners began to lead each other on to lay stress upon coin and precious metal, and not to find grainstuffs to their advantage and convenience." It is while decrying this state of affairs that Yu tells the two *Guanzi* stories. He advocates that "wealthy commoners" be required to keep substantial grain reserves, on pain of unspecified penalties.

far as to suggest that the ideal anti-famine policy would be to encourage wealthy households to build, through purchase, grain reserves which, in the aggregate, would soon become "one hundredfold the size of those of the authorities." Smoothing their present path as grain-lenders would be one practical first step towards persuading the wealthy to embark on such an undertaking.

The two parts of the directive hint at two different ways in which the poor threaten the interests of the rich. In the closing discussion, the concern is that the resentment of the poor may find expression in menacing or violent collective actions. Indeed, the inference is clear that such expressions have already taken place; from reading between Qin's lines, it looks as though two years earlier there had been incidents arising out of popular anger at speculative hoarding on the part of wealthy grain-holders. Qin's prescription here is nothing out of the ordinary: the poor must be brought to an appreciation of their own best interests and made to "feel some regard" for those who save them from starvation. More interesting are the suggestions in the technical analysis of the two forms of credit that the needy clients, in their very role as borrowers, undermine the economic interests of the rich.

The general theme of Qin's ten-point comparison of urban pawnbroking and rural grain-lending is that the latter is by far the less rewarding, and the more hazardous and burdensome. Whereas urban pawnbrokers can turn their capital over continuously throughout the year, lending to all comers, the lending pattern of the rural rich is determined by the agricultural cycle and by community relationships. Rural lending takes place at the time of hunger in the spring, with repayment due after the autumn harvest; the borrowers are those whose who borrow from a given wealthy household every year.[23] The enterprise is vulnerable, because each lender's stocks are limited (as well as being perishable), and repayment depends on the vagaries of harvest conditions. This vulnerability, combined with the vital

---

[23] Are the borrowers typically the tenants of their creditors? It is reasonable to suspect this, for Jiangxi, but Qin says nothing on the subject. Does his silence suggest that there was no consistent pattern, or is it symptomatic of a lack of interest in critical social analysis?

nature of the rural credit system, imposes a discipline unknown in urban pawnbroking. The only guarantee the lender has that loans will be repaid is the desperation of the borrower to avoid being excluded from the system the following spring. The pledges deposited are of insufficient value to permit the lender to recoup his capital in the event of default. Worst of all, when the principles of the broader, monetized economy are factored in, it becomes apparent that the borrower is weakening the lender (or, to borrow Qin's startlingly precise formulation, "occasion[ing] an invisible loss" to the lender's capital).[24] The grain borrowed in the spring was a high-priced commodity; the grain used, after harvest, to repay the loan is cheap. Specious as this last point may be (because the repaid grain will appreciate), Qin cites it as justification for the practice of charging every borrower the legal maximum interest for a year-long loan (30 per cent), even though the standard duration was considerably shorter.

The ancient text putting the case for state operations in the grain market had expressed strong opposition, partly on political grounds, to the idea of monopolistic traders "taking advantage of the people's want to realize hundredfold returns upon their capital."[25] The ruler was to buy, stock, and resell grain himself in order to prevent such profiteering and the undesirable concentrations of financial power that would have resulted from it. It is striking how Qin's document reverses such a formula. For Qin, by far the greatest part of the task of creating reserves out of the marketed grain surplus would ideally be entrusted to rich households. These households were already authorized to set their interest charges in a way which, however it might be justified, must certainly have tended to perpetuate the borrowers' dependency, and thus the lenders' power. There was, of course, also a reversal from the rhetoric of the state expansionism of the 1730s, when the ideal had briefly been that in years of good

---

[24] The original reads *qiongmin yijing an kui fuhu zhi ben* ("the poor have already occasioned an invisible loss to the rich households' stock").

[25] Ma, *Guanzi Qingzhong Pian xinquan*, p. 225.

harvests, "half the grain will be in the hands of the authorities, and half among the people."[26]

The reversal prompts reflection on the processes summed up by the term "dynastic cycle," and may, perhaps, additionally be taken to illustrate, from the angle of official consciousness, what William Rowe has called "a long-term trend toward the privatization of many sectors of the Chinese economy."[27] The point that I would like to stress, however, is that the cold abstraction of Qin's argument that poor agrarian borrowers invisibly erode their creditors' capital hints at the possibility of a very different style of discourse from that upholding the rich for their quasi-parental patronage of needy neighbours. One is accustomed to thinking of the "cold" style as "modern," and of the moralistic style as "traditional," and to assuming that the former threatens to subvert both the latter, and the world view on which it rests. Within the framework of Qin's document, at least the idea of subversion seems applicable: the closing rhetoric about the rich being the "mothers" of the poor is belied by the recognition that considerations of capitalistic gain and loss do enter into the relationship.

* * *

It would, of course, be wrong so lightly to dismiss the question whether a modern-style, amorally economistic way of thinking arose in China in the eighteenth and early nineteenth centuries, and began gradually to undermine earlier traditions based on the assumption that economic behaviour is to be discussed in moral terms. The question is important; the problem is that this is not the place to grapple with it systematically. Text 3.E, however, provides exceptionally strong *prima facie* evidence at least for the first part of the proposition. This excerpt from a long poetic dialogue, probably written in the early nineteenth

---

[26] *Yongzheng zhupi yuzhi*, Wang Rou, 85b-87a; reference from Abe Takeo, *Shindaishi no kenkyū* [Studies in Qing History] (Tokyo: Sōbunsha, 1971), p. 496.

[27] Rowe, *Hankow: Commerce and Society*, p. 341. For some especially pertinent remarks on the articulation of cycles in the locus of responsibility for famine relief with the dynastic cycle, see Will, *Bureaucratie et famine*, p. 267.

century, shows "a certain Mr. Wise-in-Practical-Affairs" rebutting four concerns of a "Hermit of Correct Meditations," with whom the poet's sympathies appear to lie. Two of these concerns have to do with the basic human needs of local people, threatened by the heartlessness of those who channel local products (cloth and grain) into the interregional market economy. A third concern addresses the related issue of local food security *versus* production for the market, while the fourth has to do with fears of environmental degradation bringing reduced rice yields. Mr. Wise-in-Practical-Affairs, who pooh-poohs the environmentalist concern, speaks for business principles, market forces, and the monetized economy. He also points out that the high rice prices deplored by the Hermit benefit the local farmers. The dialogue is set in Songjiang, the major cotton-growing region in which Shanghai is located, and of which the poet, Qin Shan, was a native.

The portion of the excerpt in which the theme of inequality most strongly features is that in which the merchant princes of North China, customers for Songjiang cloth, appear in close juxtaposition with the peasant families in which the cloth is woven. Two views are presented of the latter. First, the reader is invited to contemplate the peasant women of Songjiang, whose skills are apparent in the wonderful variety of weaves made in the area, but who are also at risk of overwork. Later, we meet their menfolk, wretchedly hungry in the last days of the *soudure* period, marketing the cloth in exchange for subsistence rations. The villains of the piece are not the merchant princes, but the "crafty brokers," low down in the hierarchy of middlemen, who underpay the peasants for their cloth.[28] They do this in establishments graphically known as "murder shops," *shazhuang*.

That is the picture painted by the Hermit. Mr. Wise-in-Practical-Affairs dismisses his objection to such exploitation by pointing out that economic expectations must respond to market

---

[28] On the structure of the Lower Yangzi cotton industry, including the tortuous route travelled by each piece of cloth from peasant weaver to capitalistic wholesaler, see Mark Elvin, *The Pattern of the Chinese Past* (London: Eyre Methuen, 1973), pp. 278-82; and James C. Shih, *Chinese Rural Society in Transition: A Case Study of the Lake Tai Area, 1368–1800* (Berkeley: University of California, Berkeley, Institute of East Asian Studies, 1992), pp. 120-23.

conditions; that the middlemen are only looking to their profit margin, which is the normal thing for anyone in trade to do; and that, whatever the experience of individual peasant weavers, the profits generated by the trade as a whole are great. Qin Shan, presumably, created the dialogue because he was dismayed that such justifications for indifference to grass-roots suffering had become current in commercial Songjiang.

*   *   *   *   *

Text 3.A

On Equality
Date: Early nineteenth century
Author: Gong Zizhen, in a private capacity.
Source: Gong Zizhen, *Gong Ding'an quanji leibian* [The Complete Works of Gong Zizhen, Classified by Category] (Shanghai: Shijie shuju, 1937), pp. 62-64, or *Gong Zizhen quanji* [The Complete Works of Gong Zizhen] (Shanghai: Shanghai Renmin chubanshe, 1975), pp. 77-80; HCJSWB, 7:7a-8a.[1]

Master Gong says: For one who possesses All-under-Heaven, there is nothing higher than the exaltation of making it equable.[2] So was it in the earliest beginnings. Coming down from this, they merely brought peace to All-under-Heaven; coming down from this again, they merely dwelt in peace with All-under-Heaven; coming down from this again, they merely fed off All-under-Heaven.

In the highest antiquity, lord and population drank together.[3] At the highest point of the Three Dynasties, to speak as if it had been water, the lord would take by bowlfuls, the ministers would take by ladlefuls, and the populace would take by wine-cupfuls.[4] Coming down from this, those with the ladlefuls encroached on those below them, while those with the wine-cupfuls encroached on those above them. Coming down from this again, the lord would take a bushelful, and the populace would also want a bushelful. There were therefore times when it dried up, and they were left prostrated. When they took bushels full to overflowing, there was extreme unequability; when it dried up and they were left prostrated, there was again extreme unequability. He who has All-under-Heaven will say: "I wish to have it as it was during the earliest beginnings; then shall I take that which is full to overflowing and ladle out from it? Or that which has too little, and pour into it?" Then, flocking, all will put their mouths to it and drink. As a rough guide to calculation, the further apart the levels of the full to overflowing and the underfilled, the swifter the impending fall. If they are rather close together, then, contrariwise, so much the swifter the establishment of governance. Over a thousand times ten thousand years, fate as to governance or chaos, rise or fall, has tallied directly with this.

The condition of men's hearts is the basis of the prevailing customs; the prevailing customs are the basis of the monarch's destiny. If men's hearts go to perdition, the prevailing customs will become depraved; if the prevailing customs are depraved, the monarch's destiny will alter in mid-course. If he who reigns as monarch would take thought for his own self, wherefore does he not take thought for human hearts and the prevailing customs? If it is the case that the poor grind each other down, while the rich dazzle each other; that the poor dwell on the brink, while the rich enjoy security; that the poor fall daily into ever worse collapse, while the rich grow daily ever more entrenched; then, whether they manifest themselves in envy or resentment, arrogance or meanness, strange, ungenerous customs come forth in their hundreds and cannot be stopped, until at length the ultimate in inauspicious ethers starts to fester, shut in betwixt Heaven and Earth. Having festered for a while, it must inevitably break forth as the flames of war or in the form of pestilence; and of the living populace, the chewing kind, there will remain no solitary survivor. Man and beast will sorely grieve; the ghosts and spirits will be thinking of replacement on the throne.[5] To go back to the origin, it is no more than the effect of inequality between rich and poor. Small inequality grew gradually into great inequality; great inequality led straight to the loss of All-under-Heaven. Alas! This shows that what is of account is that the monarch grasp the fundamental, and adjust and blend according to the times.

Above, there are the five ethers; below, there are the five powers. With the population, there are the five abominations;

with things, there are the five materials.[6] What brings about their dissolution or their growth, containment or release, is nothing but the monarch's heart. On this account, in ancient times, the Son of Heaven's ritual was that at the year's end, the Master of the Music took the pitch-pipe and announced the sound, while at the end of every month, the Grand Astrologer looked out and announced the ether. In the east there was no accumulation of water, to the west there was no accumulation of wealth, to the south there was no accumulation of grain, and to the north there was no accumulation of soil. To the south there was no accumulation of the population; to the north there was no accumulation of the winds. The monarch's heart was equable: he listened to equable music, and the hundred officers knew blessedness. As the *Ode* expresses it: "He kept his heart sincere and deep, and the tall steeds and mares were three thousand in number."[7] For if the monarch's heart is deep and equable, the very livestock will shoot up in number; how much the more with men? Elsewhere we find: "At the Sovereign's pool, the horses snort forth sand, and the Sovereign's kinsfolk are stern and proper in demeanour"; and in the following stanza, "At the Sovereign's marsh, the horses snort forth jade, and the Sovereign's kinsfolk receive grain."[8] This speaks of the abundance of production, such that men were able to show sternness and correctness of demeanour, and to feed the multitude belonging to the inner precincts; and all because goodness enjoyed a goodly reputation.

Suppose the Grand Astrologer's announcement were: "In the east there is accumulation of water; in the west there is accumulation of wealth; in the south there is accumulation of grain; in the north there is accumulation of soil. In the south there is accumulation of the population; in the north there is accumulation of the winds. The monarch's heart is unequable: he listens to declivous music; he rides a slanting chariot and grasps a loaded balance-beam, and the hundred officers suffer reproof." On this the monarch would search out All-under-Heaven's imbalances and alter them. As the *Ode* expresses it: "He examined the north-facing and south-facing slopes; he surveyed the flowing springs." Again, it says that he "measured the western slopes." This was speaking of the survey of the site for a new city.[9]

Thus the ether of accumulated wealth or grain is stagnancy; stagnancy means much fog, and the population's sound is bitter. Bitterness injures loving-kindness. The ether of accumulated population is licentiousness. Licentiousness means much rain, and the population's sound is clamorous. Clamorousness injures decorum and righteousness. The ether of accumulated soil is wastefulness. Wastefulness means many days, and the population's sound is turbid. Turbidity injures wisdom. Accumulated water and accumulated wind both arise because the State is suffering from mental darkness, and are the concern of the officials.

Besides, he who succeeds to loss will be a ruler of prosperity; but he who succeeds to prosperity will be a ruler of impending crisis. He will say to the common people: "Do you fear the flames of war? Then I shall raise my great-great grandsire and great grandsire from the tomb and consult them. Do you fear dearth and famine? Then see the farmers here." For a sovereign who succeeds to prosperity to be glorious is hard indeed. Master Gong says: "It should arouse concern! It should arouse concern; it should be changed, but not with suddenness." Besides, the lords of Tang and Yu detailed a separate official to take charge of every matter, such was their care.[10] Although the population did not yet know trade, and was not yet able to match want and possession, these lords already feared, and said: "In after generations there will be those who show my folk the way to opulence, who show my folk the way to poverty; it would be best if I myself enriched or made them poor, for thus at least it will be possible to hold it!" The *Ode* says: "Unknowing, uncognizing, following the Sovereign's laws."[11] Now Yao indeed was greatly apprehensive of the people's having knowledge and cognizance, and considered that it would be best to prevent them from knowing or cognizing, so that they would be obedient to him.[12] Water and soil were equable, and men and women reproduced, with never an ending for three thousand years. A thing which to the rich and honourable is of the very smallest urgency, the mean and poor will notwithstanding put their sinews' strength into the making of it, and take months and years in the perfecting of it; if this were put aside, the mean and poor would have nothing to which they might entrust their lives.

However, a walled hamlet of five families must have its shop; a village of ten families must have its trader; a town of thirty families must have its merchant. As for shops which deal in freakish clothing; shops which deal in freakish food; shops which deal in freakish baubles; shops at which young men croon the sacred texts in quest of rank and salary; shops where sageliness and worth are wrongfully appropriated, and trade is done in human-heartedness and righteousness; and shops in which young women sell their faces: there are ringleaders among the shops, champions among the traders, and outstanding talents among merchants. Their hearts are all desirous of taking the whole wealth of those five or ten families and making it their own; although their cunning is not up to it, such is their slogan. However, if he who possesses All-under-Heaven is to change it, it will not be by slogans and orders. There are five ladlings-out and five pourings-into: he should ladle out from Heaven and ladle out from Earth; pour into the populace and ladle from the populace; pour into Heaven and pour into Earth; ladle out from Heaven and pour into Earth; and ladle out from Earth and pour into Heaven. The *Ode* says: "We ladle the water from there and pour it here, and with it we may steam our food; the gladsome, mild lord is father and mother to the people."[13] There are three things to be feared: he should fear weeks; he should fear months; he should fear years. There are four things which he should not fear: bragging words are not to be feared; whispered words are not to be feared; groundless words are not to be feared; insinuating words are not to be feared. If, on the other hand, he tries it out with a supremely testing law; makes it even with supremely assured punishments;[14] and draws it all together with a supremely impassive heart; then, says Master Gong, within the decade he who has All-under-Heaven may almost achieve equability.

Notes

1. Both editions of Gong's complete works note variant characters throughout this difficult, and sparely worded, text. Here, I draw attention only to the more important variants.

2. One variant reading is "there is nothing higher than the exaltation of equality." Another replaces "exaltation" with a word meaning "emblem" or "manifestation."

3. Following Bauer, *China and the Search for Happiness*, p. 256, one could also read this as "lord and subjects were as people who have clubbed together for a feast."

4. One variant substitutes the word "some" (*scil.* people) for each of the words "lord," "ministers," and "populace." It is presumably the same version that eliminates the words "lord" and "populace" in the next sentence but one.

5. This is an allusion to *Mengzi* 7B/14, a famous paragraph beginning: "The population has the highest value, the gods of soil and grain come next, while the lord is of the least importance." The relevant (concluding) part reads: "Should the feudal lords imperil the gods of soil and grain, one will replace them. Should the sacrificial animals be sleek, the offerings of grain be pure, the sacrifices be observed at the due season, and yet there happen flood or drought, in that case, one will replace the gods of soil and grain." The implications for the overlord are clear.

6. The "five powers" (or "five phases") are water, fire, wood, metal, and soil, but there certainty ends. The set intended by "the five ethers" may be cold, heat, dryness, wetness, and wind, and that by "the five materials" metal, wood, leather, jade, and earth, but other dictionary enumerations seem almost to identify both of these "fives" with the five powers.

7. See *Shijing*, Ode 50; translation after Bernhard Karlgren, *The Book of Odes* (Stockholm: Museum of Far Eastern Antiquities, 1974), p. 33.

8. These lines are from *Mu Tianzi zhuan* [The Legend of the Emperor Mu] (c. A.D. 300; *Sibu congkan* edition), 5:26b. In the original, it is a different character *huang* which stands at the beginning of each stanza, so that the translation would not be "At *the Sovereign's* pool/marsh." The second "Sovereign" in each stanza stands, however.

9. See Ode 250; translation after Karlgren, *The Book of Odes*, p. 208. This ode tells how a certain Prince Liu founded his capital at Bin.

10. The "lords of Tang and Yu" are the mythical ancient sage rulers, Yao and Shun.

11. See Ode 241; cf. Karlgren, *The Book of Odes*, p. 196.

12. A variant reading has, more simply, "was greatly apprehensive of the people's having knowledge and cognizance wherewith to break his laws."

13. See Ode 251; translation after Karlgren, *The Book of Odes*, p. 208.

14. Variants for "testing law" and "assured punishments" include "reasonable law" and "undifferentiating ordinance" respectively.

* * * * *

Text 3.B

On Enriching the People

Date: Between c. 1670 and 1704
Author: Tang Zhen, as a private writer.
Source: Tang Zhen, *Qianshu fu shi wen lu*, pp. 105-7, or *Qianshu zhu* ["A Book to Be Hidden," with Annotations] (Chengdu: Sichuan Renmin chubanshe, 1984), pp. 309-15; HCJSWB, 7:4b-5b.

Wealth is the treasure of the nation and life of the population. The treasure ought not to be thieved; the life ought not to be stolen. The Sages had the common people as their children and grandchildren, and all within the Four Seas as their storehouses and treasuries; there was not one of them who thieved the treasure or purloined the life. For this reason, households and families dwelt in plenty, women and the young were all at peace. Those who went against these principles delivered the stolen wealth into the homes of favoured ministers, or stored it in the vaults of the great houses. If the pests are many, then the tree will wither; if the tumour has grown fat, the body will decay. This is the source of poverty or wealth, the difference between governance and chaos.

He who is harsh in taking will, in taking one tael from a man, lose him a hundred taels; and, in taking from one house, he will bring loss upon a hundred houses. Outside the East Gate of Yan there was a seller of cooked-mutton dishes. His family had been at the trade for two generations, and what with his wife and sons and errand-boys and so forth, those who got their food by it were ten or more. Someone falsely accused him of stealing sheep, and he was fined three bushels of grain. When those above hunt one part, those below steal ten: he sold all his cooking-pots and vessels, and this still was not enough. Thereon he lost his source of livelihood and begged along the wayside. This is what is meant by taking one tael from a man but losing him a hundred taels. In the Western Hills of Lu, there was a certain Mr. Miao, whose family was rich through iron-smelting.[1] They had been at the business for some generations and attracted many merchants from the four directions. Those who depended for their food upon the hammering and boring, or the blowing up of fires and the draining off of water, or the carrying or carting, were forever upwards of a hundred men. Someone falsely accused him of harbouring thieves. When those above hunt one part, those below steal ten: his smelting was thereon abandoned. Those who had hitherto depended on it for their food had now no means of gaining sustenance, and all dispersed and took their flight upon the Yellow River and the Zhang. This is what is meant by taking from one house but bringing loss upon a hundred houses. If one takes with harshness such as this, then not to take at all would actually be the proper course.

To the right of Long, they pasture sheep; north of the Yellow River, they rear swine. South of the Huai, they fatten ducks; beside the Lake, they reel silk. The people of the countryside of Wu weave mats and raincoats made of straw.[2] These are all the most minute of livelihoods, and yet the daily increase and the annual turnover are beyond calculation. All these are cases in which, by wielding one tael of capital, one can realize a hundred taels of profit. If in a community there is a household worth a thousand taels, when it disposes of a daughter or takes in a bride, when it mourns a death or celebrates a birth, with the healing and the praying for its sick, and with its drinking and its feasts, its gifts and presentations, its requirements in point of fish, meat, vegetables, fruit, cinnamon, and pepper, those who do trade with it will not be few. The string of cash or drachm of silver, these the petty traders borrow;[3] the bushel of wheat or half of rice, these the tenant farmers borrow; the length of cotton cloth or foot of silk, these the neighbours, friends, and kinsmen borrow: the times of their reliance on it are not few. This means that by depending on one house's opulence one may secure one hundred houses' nourishment.

Now with the wealth of the sea-girt world, there is no soil that does not bring it forth, no man who does not produce it. As months pass into years, without the need for calculation, it remains sufficient of itself; while poor and rich, without the need for contrivance, depend upon each other. The Sages, for this reason, had no art of wealth production: they gave rein to the spontaneous springs of profit, doing nothing to their interference, and the wealth was more than could be fully used. Now take the willow, which of all things under Heaven is the easiest to grow. If one breaks off a twig, some inches or a foot in length, and plants it, in no more than three years it will become a tree. Each year one may snip off its branches, and so make baskets square and round, and fascine bundles to defend against the River.[4] It will be more than can be fully used. Its endless service is all born of a twig some inches or a foot in length. If, at the time of its first planting, some lad had pulled it out and thrown it on the ground, then how could one have hoped to snip its branches every year and make good use of them? Its endless service would all have been cut off together with that twig some inches or a foot in length. He who does not vex the people is the planter of that twig, with its endless potential for production. He who takes with harshness from the people is the uprooter of that twig, who cuts off its potential for production. But who is it that takes with harshness?

Of the great banes of the Empire, there is nothing worse than avarice. It would be fair to say that it is ten or a hundred times as bad as heavy taxes. For those who enter by breaking holes in walls will fail to uncover other people's secret hoards. Those who advance with serried blades will not be able to deprive them of their homes and land. Those who hold up travellers upon the roads will not be able to destroy their houses. Those whose marauding does not stop at slaughtering and arson will not be able to exhaust the hills and valleys, and to cover all the sea-girt world. But as for those who fill the role of functionary, they are distributed like stars across the Empire. Day and night they hunt men's wealth. Once their takings have become substantial, there will be someone who breaks in on them and makes off with the caskets on his back. Loss being sustained above, they take again from those beneath.[5] Now again they lose and now again they take, like filling in a valley, past all satisfying. In short, thievery does not finish a man, nor brigandage a generation; but as for the injury inflicted on the folk by avaricious functionaries, there is nowhere between Heaven and Earth that they can flee it. For this reason, over the past few decades, the rich houses have been empty, those which had middling property have been destroyed, and the poor have nothing to rely on. Wives desert their husbands; sons go from their fathers. They ever sigh, lamenting that their lives are not as those of dogs and horses.

With those who fill the role of functionary nowadays, one suit of furs will cost two or three hundred taels; their brocade and embroidery will be comparable. The decorative costume of their players will invariably cost thousands of taels; their other baubles will be comparable. The gold cups, silver pitchers, pearls, jades, corals, and strange and cunning implements will be innumerable. One who is like this is called an able functionary. The people of the market-place admire him; the villagers revere him. Those who have sons or younger brothers to instruct use him as an example. If there is anyone who fills the role of functionary and possesses probity, who has no palanquins for his excursions, no meat at his table, no furs in his wardrobe, he is said to be without ability. The people of the market-place contemn him; the villagers make sport of him. Those who have sons or younger brothers to instruct will use him as a warning. For the hardening of men's hearts by avarice is great indeed.

In treating textiles silk or cotton, if one bleaches them they will be white, and if one dyes them with black dye they will be black. If, starting from the customs of the present day, one wishes to transform the present avarice, this is to seek for whiteness from black dye. The proper way of treating avarice is to induce without exhorting and destroy without affrighting: one must achieve it gradually, through example. *The Book of Rites* enjoins that one must "know whence the example comes."[6] In former times, the underclothes and jackets of the founder of the Ming were all of simple shuttle-cloth.[7] Now clothes can be of common cloth; why insist on brocade and embroidery? Vessels can be earthenware; why insist on gold and jade? One can eat one's fill on fine grain and good meat; why insist on bear's paw and jade-field rice? I have heard that in the heyday of the Ming, the folk of Wu did not eat fine grain and good meat. Among the common throng there was no finery; the womenfolk did not wear ornaments until they put their hair up. In the markets no one stocked strange goods, and those with guests to feast did not offer a range of viands. The houses were without high walls, but thatched cots stood in neighbourly proximity. The ways of Wu are to esteem extravagance: how should there have been plainness such as this? It must have been the example of the simple cotton clothes. If the lord of men can exercise restraint, the hundred mandarins will be transformed by it; the common folk will be transformed by it. On this, the mandarins will not harass the populace; the populace will not injure the wealth. If the lord of men can exercise restraint, his taking he will regulate by the production, and his spending he will regulate by what he takes. For each ten parts that are produced, he will take one; for each three parts he takes, he will leave one unspent. On this, the population will not feel the taking, nor the state the spending. It will be possible to make pulse and grain become as fire and water, coin and precious metal common as the soil; and a great governance will be established in the Empire. Of all the joys of being lord, is any greater than this?

Notes

1. Mr. Miao must have lived in either Changzi or Tunliu County, Lu'an Prefecture, Shanxi. Tang Zhen had, of course, served as the Changzi magistrate.
2. The expression "to the right of Long" refers to a large region of central Gansu. "The Lake" is Lake Tai, in southern Jiangsu and northern Zhejiang; the area to Lake Tai's south-east was indeed famous for sericulture. "Wu" can refer generally to Jiangsu, specifically to the Suzhou area, or, more loosely, to the whole area to the east and south-east of Lake Tai.
3. A string of cash was, theoretically, one thousand brass coins strung together through their square central holes. The "drachm" (*zi*) was an archaic weight equivalent to a quarter of a tael. As has been mentioned, silver circulated generally by weight in late traditional China.
4. A fascine bundle was a bale of *gaoliang* stalks used to reinforce dikes or close breaches in them. See Needham, *Science and Civilisation in China*, Vol. 4:III, pp. 341-43, and Plate CCCLXXXIII.
5. There seems to be a hint here that those who rob the functionaries are not common burglars, but their administrative superiors.
6. The quotation is from the *Zhongyong* [Doctrine of the Mean] chapter.

7. On this interesting subject, note Nishijima Sadao, *Chūgoku keizai-shi kenkyū* [Studies in Chinese Economic History] (Tokyo: Tokyo University Press, 1966), pp. 840-41. Material quoted here suggests the existence of a belief, going back at least to the late fifteenth century, that the imperial underwear of Ming times was all made of Songjiang cotton "triple shuttle cloth."

*   *   *   *   *

Text 3.C

On the importance of leaving the rich in peace for the salvation of the poor
Date: 1826
Author: Yang Jingren, as author of a famine relief manual.
Source: Yang Jingren, *Chouji bian* [A Manual of Famine Relief Planning] (1883 edition), 10:24a-26a; HCJSWB, 41:21b-22a.[1]

I note that the six kinds of "protecting to let multiply" conclude with "leaving the rich in peace."[2] The commentary has it that if one "keeps their liability to *corvée* fair and does not make a point of taking from them," the principle of "leaving the rich in peace" will certainly be there. I take the liberty of saying that the good are the moral essence of the polity, while the rich constitute its fundamental soundness. If one is not rich, one lacks the wherewithal to perform acts of goodness.

In ancient times, if subjects of King Wu of Zhou had a full hundred *gu*-measures of grain, when it came to guard duty, they escaped the "draft for laying weight on coin." As for the subjects of Duke Huan of Qi, two families which had completed granaries were visited with gifts of *bi*.[3] These, the subtle manipulations of rulers of men for spurring on the age and training the dull-witted, were actually supreme plans for storing wealth within the population. For if one fails to save grain, one will not be equipped to relieve famine; thus those able to keep reserves of grain were excused from service or rewarded. This caused the folk to understand that private wealth was valued by the sovereign, and that each person should protect his riches.

Respectfully perusing the *Imperial Annotations to the "Exegesis of the Officers of Zhou*," I find the words: "Leaving the rich in peace is the most important of the kinds of 'protecting to let multiply.' For if the rich do not have peace, the folk will not pursue accumulation, and there will be many who lose their source of nourishment. How can the sovereign provide for everyone?"[4] With Sagely instruction as incisive and profound as this, how is it that officialdom does not take pains to leave the rich in peace, but on occasion vexes and harasses them?

Until the end of the Three Dynasties, land was allotted through the marking out of well-figures, and the power of enrichment was wielded by the sovereign.[5] At that time there were no very poor people, nor yet any very rich ones. Once the well-fields had been abolished, the people's livelihood was left entirely to their own contrivance, and what was known as wealth came half from trade. It did not all come forth from farmers' fields. Hence the distinction found in *The Records of the Historian* between wealth basic and derivative.[6] Now, only if a person is already rich will he be good. In all the world's affairs, there has never been anyone who, having no surplus himself, was able to supply another man's deficiency. This being the case, if one "draws on excess to supplement paucity," not only will the basic wealth be found dependable, but one will be able to make use of the derivative wealth too.[7]

In recent generations, the population has been growing daily more abundant, the throng of idle vagrants daily swelling, customs becoming daily more neglectful. If the petty folk have any surplus, they generally squander it. When there is some public undertaking in a locality, it is only the rich households that are called upon, and the officials sometimes take the opportunity to despoil and affront them. With the daily flaying and the monthly fleecing, before long the wealthy become poor. *The Book of Odes* says:

The rich are fine;
Pity these solitary and supportless people![8]

The solitary and supportless are indeed worthy of pity, but how can all the rich be fine?

Li Gou of the Song said of the rich:

All arable can be cultivated, and all mulberry trees can be used for sericulture. That they alone have become rich through these is because their minds were knowledgeable and their efforts diligent; because they rose early and retired after nightfall; and because they tackled hardship and ate tasteless food—all this in order to keep pace with Heaven's seasons, and to observe the commands of those above them. If one is so perverse as to detest such people, making their assignments heavy, multiplying one's demands on them, and ensuring that expense and toil invariably fall upon their shoulders, then it will not be long before the rich turn into paupers. If all the empire's wealthy people are turned into paupers, will the ruler find this beneficial or the contrary?[9]

During the Ming dynasty, there was a request that the rich households of the Jiangnan region should be rounded up and directed to report to the authorities and surrender their possessions. The Grand Secretary Qian Shisheng responded with a memorial in which he said: "That there are wealthy families in the prefectures and counties certainly means provision of food and clothing for the poor. It has never been other than beneficial for the state. If this proposal is once advocated, ne'er-do-wells and outlaws will conspire to make trouble for the wealthy families."[10]

The words of these wise men of former times show eminently far-reaching understanding. Suppose the rich have not been left in peace, but are daily sliding towards ruination, and that there are recurrent famines. Given that one does not dare take it upon oneself to touch the funds belonging to the local treasury and, further, that the issuing of grain out of the ever-normal and community granaries will not suffice, whence will one draw the wherewithal to save the lives of all the needy masses, standing in a circle waiting to be fed?

My point is that only if one nurtures the rich households during normal times will one be able to rely upon their strength in times of crisis. If in normal times one keeps the *corvée* light and taxes low, and pays attention to protecting and upholding the rich households, then when the time arrives such works as stabilizing sales, free gruel distributions, assistance and relief, and loans of seed may all be furnished by them. And yet this cannot be elicited coercively. If there are ways for leading and supporting them, and means for urging and inducing them, then very miserly though the Old Men Grainenough may be, when they perceive the local officer's easy instruction of them, and how he treats them with the fullest courtesy, they will all feel it to be an act of glory, and leap up obedient to the call.

In 1724 there was an Edict to the following effect: "The establishment of community granaries is properly for meeting the emergency needs created by famine and dearth. It is Our opinion that, in exhortation of the common people, one must let the people make their contributions of their own accord, according to their own convenience; one ought not to bind them with the laws of officialdom. Respect this."[11] Now the grain of a community granary means no more than some few pecks or half-bushels by way of assistance to the little people; and yet the Sage heart of the Sovereign felt such concern as this! It was because of deep misgivings lest local officials implement the system badly, resulting in harassment. And so, whenever one exhorts the wealthy to share their resources, how can it be right to bind them with the laws of officialdom, so that it borders on an imposition? I will say nothing of cases in which public business is used to further private interests, reflecting a mentality that is unworthy of discussion. Even if, through ardour for the public cause and love towards the populace, one issued cogent proclamations and imposed strong prohibitions, forcibly insisting on compliance, one would either be pressing the rich too hard, without first having won their confidence, or making over-extravagant demands of them, without having considered their resources. I take the liberty of fearing that, although one's will would be on the salvation of the poor, one would inevitably first disturb the rich.[12] Now the urgency of succouring the poor is not to be permitted to induce one to disturb the rich; it is with the surplus wealth left with the rich that the poor are to be saved. If he who is a pastor to the people will apply those concepts of *The Officers of Zhou*, "protecting to let multiply," and "leaving the rich in peace";[13] if he will nurture the fundamental soundness on behalf of our polity, so that it may be relied on in emergencies, while rich and poor protect each other, then this will not be far off.

Notes

1. The HCJSWB text is greatly abridged. It is especially noticeable that the HCJSWB editors have eliminated Yang's assertions that personal wealth is a prerequisite for goodness.
2. Yang's reference is to *The Rites of Zhou*: see Sun, ed., *Zhouli zhengyi*, 5:19, p. 97. The first five kinds are "showing affection to the young," "nourishing the old," "succouring those who are without recourse," "showing compassion on the poor," and "showing lenience to the infirm." The commentary from which Yang quotes is the original one by Zheng Xuan of the Eastern Han.
3. A *bi* was a circular jade disc with a central hole conferred by ancient Chinese rulers as a mark of honour. Yang is referring to two stories from the *Guanzi* (see *Guanzi* 77:85 and 83:113 in the *Guoxue jiben congshu* edition). In the first, King Wu, founder of the Zhou dynasty, seeking to deter his people from preferring monetary wealth to grain, set up a special "frontier guard draft for laying weight on coin" and exempted those who had 100 *gu* of grain. In the second story, Guan Zhong, the famous prime minister of Duke Huan of Qi, noticed that two families had just finished building capacious granaries and suggested that the duke reward them. Duke Huan thereon conferred the gifts of *bi*.
4. The *Exegesis of the Officers of Zhou* (*Zhouguan yishu*) was an official commentary to *The Rites of Zhou*, commissioned by the Qianlong emperor and published in 1748. The *Imperial Annotations* quoted by Yang were evidently by one of the Qing emperors, probably Qianlong.
5. Yang is referring to the egalitarian "well-field system," which was attributed to the Three Dynasties. See n. 1 to the introduction to this chapter.
6. *The Records of the Historian* is China's first great comprehensive history, the *Shiji* of Sima Qian (c. 145–c. 86 B.C.) For the present reference, see *Shiji*, Vol. 10, 129:3272. Sima Qian in fact names three kinds of wealth: the third, and most inferior, is "wealth ill-gotten." "Basic wealth" (*benfu*) would have been understood as referring to wealth from agricultural sources, and "derivative wealth" (*mofu*) as wealth from trade.
7. The phrase "draws on excess to supplement paucity" is borrowed from *The Book of Changes*, and refers to balancing or redistributive activity. Yang's logic is a little difficult to follow here, but what he seems to be doing in this rambling paragraph is (a) using the discourse of historical progression to remind his reader that, although he seems mainly to be discussing agrarian wealth, commercial

wealth exists as well; (b) reiterating the point that surplus wealth has to exist before it can be socially useful; and (c) suggesting that, provided that this principle is borne in mind, rich merchants can also be induced to contribute to famine relief efforts.

8. See Ode 192; translation after Karlgren, *The Book of Odes*, p. 137.
9. Li Gou (1009–59) was a Northern Song intellectual who wrote extensively on matters of government and political economy. The present passage is quoted (with some omissions and interpolations) from Li's commentary on the *Zhouli* concept of "leaving the rich in peace," which is in the "State Resources" section of his *Discourse Concerning How* The Rites of Zhou *Brought about Grand Tranquillity*. See *Li Gou ji* [Collected Works of Li Gou] (Beijing: Zhonghua shuju, 1981), p. 90.
10. Yang refers to a 1636 incident in which a military state student called Li Jin submitted a memorial denouncing Jiangnan's influential families and rich merchants, and asking that they be required to submit truthful statements of their taxable assets, on pain of expropriation. Qian Shisheng, a member of a rich and élite Jiangnan lineage, responded with a long exposition of the social functions of the wealthy; Yang's "quotation" actually consists of phrases from different parts of the memorial, cobbled together with much editing. Qian's defence of the rich rests on the following claims: that agricultural estate owners provide a livelihood for tenants; that merchant capital helps the poor survive the *soudure* period through pawnshops; that rich landlords shoulder certain economic burdens for their tenants, as well as paying the taxes; and that the rich are called upon in times of crisis to provide famine relief (through stabilizing sales) or organize tenant militias. See Donald L. Potter in *Dictionary of Ming Biography, 1368–1644*, ed. L. Carrington Goodrich and Fang Chao-ying (New York: Columbia University Press, 1976), Vol. 1, p. 238; and (for partial transcription of Qian's memorial) Kawakatsu Mamoru, "Sekkō Kakō-fu no kanden mondai—Minmatsu kyōshin shihai no seiritsu ni kansuru ichi kōsatsu" [The Problem of Cross-Boundary Landholdings in Jiaxing Prefecture, Zhejiang: An Inquiry Concerning the Establishment of Gentry Dominance in the Late Ming Period], in *Shigaku zasshi*, 82, no. 4 (1973), p. 43.
11. For the edict from which these sentences are quoted (with incomplete fidelity), see QCWXTK, 35:5177.
12. Reading *bi*, "inevitably" for *bi*, "abuse."
13. *The Officers of Zhou* is an alternative title for *The Rites of Zhou*.

*   *   *   *   *

Text 3.D

Instructions re. encouraging pledged loans of grain among the population
Date: 1804
Author: Qin Cheng'en, as Jiangxi governor.
Source: HCJSWB, 40:17b-19a.

I find that what the poor of every province can rely on for the mediation of want and possession and supplying of their daily food is nothing other than the pawnshop. The pawnshop, however, deals only in silver and coin and makes no difference to the level of grain prices. Among the grain-possessing families of Jiangxi, there are some which, at the commencement of the labours of the East, suffer the farming folk to borrow on security the grain which they have spare, and so supply their toil.[1] After the autumn harvest, the account is cleared with interest. Compared with the pawnshop, it is even more convenient. However, if one wishes that the poor shall benefit, one must first ensure the preservation of the rich households.

It may be observed that lending grain upon security is different from lending coin or silver upon pawn. Pawnbrokers are found mainly in towns and cities, places where human life is concentrated, and have coin and silver as the stock for their advances. With but a mat-sized plot of land, the coin and silver can be stored deep underground. The rich households are in rural villages and isolated areas, and to accumulate their grain they must build granaries, as only then can it be gathered in and stored. They must also hire someone to keep watch on it. This is the first point of difference. The pawnbrokers' capital is invariably in excess of some few tens of thousands, and the pledges are redeemed at any time. Mother and child come into balance; profit again gives rise to profit, operations supplying further operations in an unbroken flow, the turnover unfailing.[2] The rich households have grain as their stock. Where this is small, it will be a hundred or so bushels to some few hundred bushels; at the most, it will not exceed some few thousand bushels. The loans being made in spring and paid back in the autumn, they can lend but once a year. This is the second point of difference.

In lending coin or silver upon pawn, while pledges are indeed redeemed in times of cheapness, they will also be redeemed in times of dearness. The stock, therefore, need not run out. With lending grain upon security, if prices are low the pledges are redeemed; if they go high, redemption stops. If the pledges taken in Year One are not redeemed, there is no stock for Year Two's lending. This is the third point of difference. In lending coin or silver upon pawn, a pawn-ticket is used as evidence. No matter whether the customer is known to him or not, the pawnbroker will let him borrow coin in quantities from some few hundred cash, or silver up to some few hundred taels. The more the customers, the greater the profit. With lending grain upon security, there is nothing of the nature of a pawn-ticket. The customers, without exception, are the farming folk of the vicinity, who bear their loans across their shoulders as they go away on foot, in order to supply their daily needs. Each loan can be no more than a few bushels to some ten bushels or so. If the borrowers are many, the stock for the advances will be readily exhausted. This is the fourth point of difference.

With lending coin or silver upon pawn, if the stock is large the profit will be great. Not only does one not select the customer; one also does not fix the sum. If in Year One a customer does not redeem his pledge, he will still be permitted to pledge further in Year Two. With lending grain upon security, the grain-stock is not large, and there is fixity regarding the recipients. One cannot cut out A, who borrows every year, and give instead to B, who has not borrowed previously. In other words, those who repay during Year One are those who will be pledging in Year Two. If, moreover, they have borrowed five bushels in Year One, in Year Two this cannot be increased to six, nor yet reduced to four. If A, having repaid his grain, does not wish to pledge again the second year, it is appropriate to let the rich household make the loan instead to B. Again, if in Year One a loan of five bushels has been made, the repayment plus the interest come to 6.5 bushels. If, however, after the autumn harvest A repays no more than four bushels, not only has he paid no interest, but it falls short of the principal. This means that, as he has been guilty of a breach of faith, it is appropriate to let the rich household allocate the grain he has repaid to someone else the second year. A is not allowed to enter on a further, and concurrent, loan by pleading some excuse. This is the fifth point of difference.

With lending coin or silver upon pawn, the established regulation is that a value of ten secures a loan of five.[3] If by the expiry of the term the pledge is not redeemed, it is permitted for the pawnbroker to sell it, so as to recoup his capital. There will not be any very great discrepancy. With lending grain upon security, the pledges tend to be items of clothing made of coarse material, which when sold do not fetch enough to cover the principal. The reason for which, nonetheless, the poor cannot do other than redeem them, is in order that the grain which they restore in one year they may borrow and consume the next, so that they do not jeopardize the springtime ploughing. This is the sixth point of difference.

With lending coin or silver upon pawn, there is no such thing as wastage, besides which disbursements and receipts follow cyclically upon each other, profit giving rise to profit. For this reason, the 3 per cent interest is calculated on the basis of the actual months and days of the duration of the loan.[4] With lending grain upon security, not only is there fear of wastage during measuring and handling whenever grain is lent out or collected in, but there are also risks of spoilage at the top and bottom of the granary, of rat damage and mildewing.[5] In name the interest is 30 per cent, but in reality the gain is almost negligible. How much the more when one can lend but once a year! If a loan of one bushel of grain is made on the first day of a given year, and repaid on the last day of that year, it is not permitted to take more than three-tenths of a bushel by way of interest. If the same loan is made on the first day of the fifth moon and repaid on the first day of the sixth, the interest is still three-tenths of a bushel. For what reason? The point is that pledged borrowing of grain occurs during the *soudure* period, when the price of grain is very high. Repayment does not happen until after the autumn ripening, by which time the price has fallen. It may therefore be that at the time of borrowing, the value was above two taels, while at the time of paying back, it is not even one. Even with this 30 per cent interest, imposed according to the regulations, the poor have already occasioned an invisible loss to the rich households' stock. If, on top of this, one forced the latter to reduce the interest *pro rata* on the basis of the actual duration of each loan, thereby preventing them from "cutting from the long in order to make up the short," then how could one expect them to comply with pleasure? It is, moreover, to be feared that this would open the way for seekers after profit to begin to borrow grain on pledge for trading purposes. This is the seventh point of difference.

In lending coin or silver upon pawn, one recognizes the pawn-ticket but not the customer. Kinsmen and neighbours may equally well pledge on his behalf. With pledged borrowing of grain, however, even the closest kinsman or the dearest friend may not make the transaction for him. If A pays back five bushels in Year One, in Year Two it will again be necessary for him to deposit his security in person. Otherwise, an uncle or a brother might lay a pledge falsely in his name. He himself would come only to find the grain already gone, and this would very easily give rise to strife. This is the eighth point of difference. A pawnbroker applies for a licence and pays tax, the amount not exceeding some few taels a year. This keeps the artful from making insinuations. The grain stocks of families which lend grain on pledge are not substantial, and ... the interest which they earn is very slight. The artful, taking advantage of the fact that they have not applied for licences, often accuse them of running illegal pawnshops, and snatch away their ledgers and intimidate them. They will even go so far as to collude with *yamen* clerks and servicemen to blackmail them, with the consequence that the rich households become afraid, and will only sell their grain, not lend it. This is the ninth point of difference. With lending coin or silver upon pawn, there is no demarcation of territories. Irrespective of the distance of his habitation, anyone may pledge. With lending grain upon security, however, the artful fellows often take control of operations and do not allow the folk of distant villages to carry grain away. This is the tenth point of difference.

The above ten counts will still be tolerable in a year of plenty; but as soon as there is a scant harvest, they will most easily give rise to trouble. It is necessary to give clear advance instruction during ordinary, quiet times, so that every family and household understands, and when the time arrives will naturally have the sense to keep within its station. From ancient times there has been no sound strategy for the relief of famine: what all amount to is that one must take precautions during years of plenty, and yet the ever-normal granary reserves are mostly short of their quotas, since drawings have been made on them for public purposes. Besides, if as many as the populace of a whole county are to look to the authorities for as long as a whole year, it will naturally be difficult for the relief to extend everywhere. It is what the men of old summed up in the expression "for the folk to get a peck or pint, the authorities must spend a hill or mountain"; it is truly no different from tossing a cup of water at a cart of blazing firewood.[6] Suppose that one is able to spur on the rich households to buy grain supplies. They would not be required to take out a licence and would be left to operate the stocks themselves. Whether they began with some few tens of bushels, some few hundred bushels, or some few thousand bushels, they could in each case build up gradually, and go from less to more. If one household acts like this, so also will the next one; if one village acts like this, so also will the next one. Once the policy has been in operation for some time, throughout the county there will not be anywhere that does not act like this; the whole province will indeed be acting like it. Within a few years, the population's grain holdings can be one hundredfold the size of the authorities'. Should the occasional famine year befall, the population's food will be provided from its own grain holdings. It is, at bottom, the ancient conception of "surplus for one year from three years' cultivation; surplus for three years from nine years' cultivation."[7]

Now if one wishes to ensure the preservation of the rich households, one must first make the poor see their own interest in the matter, for only then can one apply reproof and exhortation. It may reasonably be asserted that the rich are the mothers of the poor and constitute the nation's fundamental soundness. If the rich households fall into decline and ruin, not only will the indigent lose their support, but the fundamental soundness too will suffer injury. In 1802, a drought gave rise to dearth, and for a long time the price of grain did not come down. As governor, I was tormented with anxiety day and night, truly fearing that the families with stocks of grain would wait for a good price before they sold. I issued notices exhorting them, which was but an *ad hoc* expedient for the short-term adjustment of the people's food supply, and had the purpose of suppressing moves by artful people to find pretexts to harass and vex. This year, rain and shine come at their proper seasons; the early rice is harvested and has come onto the market, and the price of grain has already fallen greatly. I look to you, in conjunction with the provincial administration commissioner and the circuit intendants,[8] immediately to command all subordinate authorities to issue telling and incisive proclamations in conformance with the above points, ensuring without fail that they are universally understood by rich and poor in the remotest rural areas and most isolated districts, so that each remains within his station in adherence to the law. There must be no more treading in their former tracks.

It may be said in sum of the relations between rich and poor that the strong are bound to be oppressive, and the weak covetous.[9] Now, inasmuch as the rich households rescue the needy out of their extremity, it is incumbent on the latter to feel some regard for them. Since in normal times the one relieves the other through all ups and downs, when trouble comes there should be mutual assistance in the watch.[10] Let thoughts alike of covetousness and oppression be forgotten, and the spirit of harmony and concord will of itself become robust. The achievement of this outcome depends on careful guidance and instruction by capable local officials, causing customs daily to revert to plainness and simplicity. As governor, I place great hopes in them.

If within individual county-level jurisdictions there are, by reason of the population's temperament or local custom, slight differences from what I have indicated, once these are verified it is permitted for the local authorities to make changes as appropriate, the accommodation of the people being always the prime consideration. They are further ordered to establish pledging-tickets on the model of those used by pawnshops. These are to be issued to the client households when they pay back their grain, for them to keep as proof of their entitlement to pledge the following year. This too should eliminate a cause of strife.

Notes

1. East represents the spring, and thus this phrase (from *The Book of Documents*) refers to ploughing, sowing, etc.

2. "Mother and child" refer, respectively, to capital and profit.

3. High as this ratio may seem, the author appears to accept it as no higher than appropriate for securing the pawnbroker against significant loss in the event of a default. The explanation is presumably the need to compensate him for any loss of interest plus the opportunity cost of having capital tied up over the full pledge period. Cf. T. S. Whelan, *The Pawnshop in China, Based on Yang Chao-yü*, Chung-kuo tien-tang yeh [*The Chinese Pawnbroking Industry*], *with a Historical Introduction and Critical Annotations* (Ann Arbor: University of Michigan, Center for Chinese Studies, 1979), p. 36.

4. Three per cent per month was the legal maximum interest rate on private loans and pawn transactions in Qing China. See, in the Qing Code, the statute on "Interest-charging such as contravenes prohibitions," classified under *Revenue, Money loans*.

5. On "spoilage at the top and bottom of the granary," see Will and Wong, *Nourish the People*, p. 118.

6. This is an allusion to *Mengzi* VIA/18.

7. Allusion to the idea of "surplus for one year from three years' cultivation" will recur in other texts translated here. The *locus classicus*, in the "Kingly institutions" chapter of the *Liji* [The Book of Rites], reads: "If a state does not command nine years' reserves, it is said to suffer insufficiency; if it does not command six years' reserves, it is said to be in crisis; if it does not command three years' reserves, it is said to be no longer worthy of the name of state. From three years' cultivation there must necessarily remain food for one year; from nine years' cultivation there must necessarily remain food for three years. To take the full sweep of a period of thirty years, although there may be bale-bringing drought and flooding of the waters, the folk will be without a famished look; and then and only then the Son of Heaven will take his food daily accompanied by music."

8. It is reasonable to infer from this that Text 3.D was addressed to the provincial surveillance commissioner.

9. Cf. the closing lines of *Ode* 33, and also *Lunyu* IX/27.

10. This is an allusion to a passage describing community friendliness and solidarity in *Mengzi* 3A/3 (the same discussion as that containing the canonical account of the well-field system).

*   *   *   *   *

Text 3.E

Excerpt from *Questions Relating to Songjiang*
Date: Early nineteenth century?
Author: Qin Shan
Source: Qin Shan, *Jitang wengao* [The Prose Compositions of Qin Shan] (1820), 1:1a-4a; HCJSWB, 28:7b-8b.

A certain Mr. Wise-in-Practical-Affairs was wise regarding the affairs of the present age and frequented the gates of major personages. His path never crossed that of the Hermit of Correct Meditations. One day, he called upon the Hermit in his alleyway, entering his study with a foolish air, at odds with himself, and speechless. At length he said: "I have long known of your reputation. You live in Songjiang, and must be well informed concerning its affairs. Tell me, wherein do the splendid riches of Songjiang actually lie?"[1]

The Hermit raised himself hastily, and replied: "Heaven bestows and Earth produces, thereby nourishing the people. If Songjiang had none of their riches, how would the people be preserved? But whereas in the past Songjiang was bravely decked out by its riches, now it is exhausted by them, and it will eventually be left with no riches at all. I have lived upon its soil like my ancestors before me, and its pains and pleasures have been mine. In my leisure moments, my heart is ever thumping in alarm at this, so that I cannot sleep.[2] But why would you have this teaching?"

The visitor breathed a sigh, and knelt down on the mat.

"I have travelled much within the Empire," he said, "and paid close attention to the riches of Songjiang. I have seen the brave decking out, but I have not seen the exhaustion. What is the cause of your anxiety? I pray that you will make it plain for me, item by item."

The Hermit spoke as follows:

"Songjiang has the riches of dry cultivation:

Along the east edge of the prefecture,
Straddling rivers, overstepping creeks;
Twisting and turning for a hundred *li*,

Rank and wild, darkly winding on unendingly:
A bamboo-covered ridge, a sandy spine,
A high plain, soil dry and friable,
A convex bank, as hung with tiles.
The level ground is open to the sky;
The clods are hard, the feel dry,
And what grows well is cotton.

The cotton-growing folk,
In winter they are drenched in sleet,
In spring they are stuck for the cash for cakes.[3]
They hoard up dung like gold,
In covered trenches mixing it with water.
Holes dug one foot apart:
The liquid goodness is plopped in.
They go out shouldering their hoes,
Man and wife and wife and man,
Their sweat to shed upon the sunken patches,
Each one with two *mu* to tread.

Green the shoots;
Yellow the sprouts.
Rank on rank and line on line:
Rows perpendicular and rows aslant.
Young blades and tender heads;
Strong leaves and rampant flowers.
With seven sweeps they take the weeds to task,
Striking to their hearts, and deadening their thrust.
Heaven's breezes gently blow;
Nectarines effortlessly redden.
The swans outstretch their wings
And fly off in a swirl of down.
Grasping the fore, the whiteness all behind,
They wield blades of Wei to gather in the floss.
    And, as the final total from the labours of one hoe
    That worked throughout the livelong year,
    Ten thousand cash per *mu*: riches indeed!

And yet,

As the stalks are bundled, the straw baled,
They clothe themselves from close at hand, but seek their
food afar.
Their funds may easily be dissipated in the east,
But grain is not so readily imported from the west.
And when the demon of the drought wreaks his calamity,
This stone-like soil is the first to redden;
When the moisture-bringing rains miss their due season,
The soft bells are bereft of strength.

At times like these,
In a tumultuous confusion,
They drift off roving westwards,
Girls and boys in tow
To have the marker straws put in their hair
And be cried out for sale.[4]

The experience of some few years ago has not become remote.
Latterly,

The plough-fellows, fatigued
And foolish, gawping at generous profits,
Upon the arable beside the river banks
Have taken to the planting of
Cotton along with paddy.
Deep stagnant pools are left undredged;
The soil's proper suitability is disregarded.
To get an extra hundred catties' cotton
They will forgo two bushels of rice.

Is this not bad farming practice?"

"Why your lack of wisdom about practical affairs?" returned
the visitor. "The true way of preserving human life gives equal
weight to grain and money. If one can get money, one need not
fear not having grain. Indeed, granted the mutability of needs
and circumstances, to place the greater emphasis on money is in
fact still more convenient. Discarding paddy in favour of cotton is
no bad strategy."

"Songjiang has the riches of labour at weaving," went on the
Hermit:

> This is true of all seven counties.
> Bundled and loaded, their handiwork will go ten
> > thousand *li*,
> The merit of which is the womenfolk's.
> Cotton, I say, cotton!
> The cotton has spilled out in seeds:
> Short the iron rollers.
> The cotton has been turned out all in clumps:
> Slow the wooden bow.
> The cotton has come floating up all fleecy:
> The needles draw it into rovings.
> The cotton has been twisted into yarn:
> The reeling-frame must pull the threads together.
> Compressed within the hand, it feels like curd cheese;
> Spread out, it makes one think of tailor's chalk.
> Held up, it forms a single cylinder;
> Laid flat, it is suggestive of a waterfall.
> To sweep it up takes all the effort of lifting a tripod;
> To get it properly assembled means
> Eyes down, as if for study.

> And, once the loom-reels have been swept with warp,
> Before the bobbin-shuttles are in motion with their woof,
> The stars of daybreak twinkle in the distant void,
> The night-time lamps burn with refulgent gleam;
> And men are in the land of dreams.
> Not merchants, not officials—
> Ten thousand looms go into action all together.[5]
> Humming, they make as if to speak;
> Creaking and whining come their plaints.
> If these are sounds of sorrow, hearts are free of care:
> For on the morrow, they will sell the cloth.

> Purple Flowers and Iris Watersmeet;
> Flying Flowers and Mao Bay;
> Bird-in-the-Mud and Eye-of-Elephant;

Dragon Flower and Herbal Mixture.
Nine-inch and Double-thread;
Seven-times-precious and Jinshan;
Southern Reservoir and Northern Reservoir;
Broad Width and Narrow Width.
Tight weave to surpass the cloud-like silk;
Loose weave reminiscent of the misty crêpe.
The left hand rests upon the piled-up whiteness;
The right hand makes the breadth-wise tear.

Ten feet of weave
Bring in a hundred cash.
Accumulate the industry of one loom;
Wear out the strength of one woman,
And in a month you can get thirty *zhang* of cloth.
The great merchants of the north
Come with their capital of millions:
From Dai and Long, from east and west,[6]
From within and without the passes of the seas,
They contract for donkeys and they purchase horses,
And they gallop southwards night and day.
They drive their chariots across the frozen Yellow River;
They sail their great ships down the mighty Yangzi;
They take their meals in the wind and lodge upon the
                                                    water,
And so they come to Su and Chang.[7]

Signs help them tell the shops apart:[8]
Unless it is the produce of Songjiang they will not buy.
A monopolizer's mound set down upon an even road:
The neighbouring commanderies feel cause to harbour
                                                    grudge.
I have it from a Suzhou merchant
That, as a commandery, Songjiang
In its autumn sales of cloth
Disposes of 150,000 lengths a day: riches indeed!

Alas!

Farmers in autumn are parched—blackened and emaciated—
by the time the autumn paddy-crop is ripe. It is too green for
cooking, and so their lives depend upon the shining threads.

> Going hungry two days out of three,
> Clutching their cloth, they go into the market.
> The price is low as that of mud,
> And there are what are known as murder-shops

run by the crafty brokers of these recent times. Whereas, before, a
zhang of cloth would fetch five pints of rice and more, now it
fetches only two or so. Is this not a bane to distaff labours?"
      "Why your lack of wisdom about practical affairs?" returned
the other. "Weavers and trading masters are alike in that they
raise or lower their sights according to the times. To part with
things at a high price and acquire them at a low is but the natural
demand of the technique. What question can there be of murder?
Besides, the gains of a hundred shops, when put together, are
substantial, the losses of the single loom but slight. The effect is
not unbountiful."
      "Songjiang has the riches of wet plantation," said the Hermit:

> To the prefecture's east, west, and north,
> The polder-lands, both great and small,
> Are interhooked and closely laid
> Like logs that form a raft,
> And cover fifty thousand *qing*.
> The springs are sweet, the soil rich,

And, if we exclude the thirty per cent which is taken up by
hillside, lakes, roads, or marshy areas, and is therefore unculti-
vable, thirty per cent yields one harvest a year, and forty per cent
is double-cropping.

> Mountains for immortals by the sea;
> Northern pavilion by new river;
> White sands and tall bamboos;
> Grand persons high and prosperous.
> Pine-tree for pillow, snooze the day away;

The hamlets stand each in each other's sight.
Herein are many tenant farmers,
Their heads plastered with mud.
In the first moon they burn off the stubble;
In the second they must plough their squares.
In the third they turn the grasses over;
In the fourth they sow the thronging seedlings.
They pick the seedlings out for rice-plants:
Like streaming tears the farmer's sweat;
They cherish the rice-plants for paddy-rice:
Repletion is in prospect for the farmer's belly.
Pluck it, lay it down in bundles,
Spread it, scoop it up;
Pour it in libations, dedicate it.

As they look into the water
The warm liquid washes round their feet;
As they pull away the weeds
The fineness of the stalks pierces their gaze.
Lively and lithe,
Thrusting upwards, sprouting,
Surging, billowing,
Ripening to a serried sea of heads.
Slope-grown and grown between the levees,
The glutinous and the plain,
The red kind and the white,
The yellow and the rush-like,
The non-glutinous and the rustling,
The purple-bearded and the adlai,
The lotus-like, the forked-head, and the arrow-like,
The crow-beak dwarf:
Fifty old-established kinds,
New varieties more numerous than they.
Cold grains within ponderous ears
Fill all the space between the criss-cross paths.
Harvest it, winnow it, hull it,
Pound it in the house,
Carry it to the dealer's shop;
Cover it up in storage bins,

> Load it onto boats and carts.
> The tenants know nothing of tax,
> But raise rent-payments from their fields;
> The landlords do not till the soil,
> But render tax to the authorities.
> Drachms and quarts depend upon each other,[9]
> And there is a secret profit in it.

And, moreover, according to the words of the old farmers eighty years of age and more,

> In the old days when you opened up the blades
> Each *mu* yielded three bushels of grain;
> But these days when you open up the blades
> Each *mu* yields but three halves.
> The terrain is as it was before,
> And yet the former richness has been turned to poverty;
> The breaths of Earth are what brings this about,
> And the farmers' fat is being daily pared away thereby.

Now if we take the average appetite, the annual individual rice consumption is something under four bushels. Songjiang's acreage is four million, its population two million. Provided there arise no bale of the soil,

> With husks a-plenty, generous supplies of chaff,
> By dint of making good the short by chopping off the
> > long,

The people should still be preserved from suffering extremes of hurt, or dying drought-stricken; but, that is, for the fact that

> Before the whale-troubled depths have settled,
> Evil-hearted persons in receipt of stolen grain
> Put it in hostelries by night, in warehouses at morn,
> And on large barges and swift skiffs
> Thievingly load it, and make good their flight.
> The market knows no constant price,
> For every three days sees a rise,

And what once bought a peck
Now buys a mere five pints.

This is the hard situation that has faced the needy masses in their cooking watery gruel and eating all coarse fare over the past ten years."

"Why your lack of wisdom about practical affairs?" returned the visitor. "That from the same acreage the yield is now half is but the talk of rustics. Why must you believe it? That for the same amount of rice the price has doubled is unquestionably greatly to the profit of the farmers."

Notes

1. The character translated in this text as "riches" is *li*, "profit," "advantage." While *li* often means "profit" in the technical economic sense, the meaning can be broader. In Qin's poem, it means the entire economic and topographical potential given by Heaven and Earth to Songjiang, and realized in that prefecture by human activity. It thus embraces the agricultural, manufacturing, and commercial profits generated in Songjiang, but it is not confined to these. I have duly varied my translation of *li* according to the context.
2. Reading *chang*, "always," for the *chang* indicating "it has been known to happen."
3. These will have been "cakes" made out of oil wastes and used for fertilizer.
4. My interpretation here is based on a late Ming reference to the use of straws stuck in the hair to indicate that a person is for sale. See Lü Kun, *Lü Gong Shizheng lu* [Mr. Lü's Notes on Practical Administration] (1593; 1797 edition), 2:25a.
5. Despite appearances, this line does not refer to factory production, since the last line of the stanza makes it clear that the weavers are independent producers who market their own cloth. The suggestion of synchrony is poetic licence. In the previous line, I have emended *gong*, "palace," to *guan*, "official," following HCJSWB.
6. That is, from Shandong in the east to Gansu in the west.
7. That is, Suzhou and Changzhou, two prefectural capitals on the Grand Canal south of the Yangzi which served as major marketing centres for the cotton cloth of the Yangzi Delta.
8. These "shops" are evidently wholesaling establishments.

9. In other words, the "small" tenants and their "large" patrons, the landlords, are dependent on each other. There is, alas, a mixed metaphor here: *zi*, "drachm," was a small unit of weight, while *fu*, which I have loosely rendered "quart," was a quite large unit of capacity, albeit smaller than a bushel.

4. Fiscal Doctrine

The essays by Tang Zhen and Yang Jingren in the previous chapter allude to two concepts which are fundamental to conventional Confucian notions of good government. One is the idea that wealth should, for preference, be "stored within the population," rather than being siphoned off by the government. The other is that the ideal agrarian taxation rate is "one in ten," loosely understood to mean 10 per cent of annual production. These notions are of venerable antiquity, and were generally taken to imply modest consumption by the court and a benevolent approach to rulership.[1]

Associated with these beliefs was the Chinese version of the doctrine that a government should live within its means. This was usually formulated as an injunction to determine expenditure, that is to say commitments, in the light of income (*liang ru wei chu*). If the state's legitimate income was limited to one tenth of what the farmers could produce, plus miscellaneous revenues from commercial taxes and the state's formal entitlement to "the profits of mountains and marshes," it followed that state aspirations must be limited.[2] Government should be small, and so should the state apparatus. As one late seventeenth-century writer bluntly put it, "The hallmark of good ruling is to keep the number of officials low; the hallmark of good government is to

---

[1] The *locus classicus* for the 10 per cent taxation rate is in *Liji* 47/par. 4, with mentions also in *Mengzi* 3A/3 and 6B/10. The expression "storage of wealth among the population" appears in the commentary to the *Liji* passage expounding the necessity for a state to set aside reserves for one year from the fruits of every three years' cultivation (see n. 7 to Text 3.D).

[2] The state's traditional claim to the fruits of exploiting the empire's wastelands and wildlands provided the ideological underpinning for the state monopolies. The monopolies, especially that on salt, made significant contributions to the state's income at least during the major imperial dynasties.

keep the burden of taxation light."[3] In reality, the late imperial state apparatus was large, and its activities multifarious. However, to the exponent of conventional fiscal morality, state gigantism must be kept in bounds.

The seeds of challenge to this conservative position were logically contained within it. If the state was entitled to take 10 per cent of agricultural production, it could enrich itself without oppressing the farmers by taking measures to enlarge the agricultural economy. Other components of the tax base could surely be expanded too. The most radical practitioner of this counter-approach was the eleventh-century reformer Wang Anshi, who had gone so far as to increase the size of the bureaucracy in the belief that deeper government involvement could help society to "create wealth" (*shengcai*).[4] Wang was a heretic within Confucianism; his policies, controversial at the time, were repudiated by conventional Confucian political economists thereafter. But rejection of the extremist challenge did not bring uniform compliance with the conventional ideals. Later dynasties also had their episodes of state expansionism, while diverse opinions on matters of fiscal principle and policy were expressed in most periods.

The great episode of state expansionism in Qing history was the reign of the Yongzheng emperor. It is true that the aim of Yongzheng's fiscal reforms was partly to reduce the overall burden of the state apparatus on society, by regularizing, and thus bringing under control, that portion of the territorial bureaucracy's irregular exactions which was actually necessary for running the underfunded local and regional administrations. Unambiguously illegitimate private predation would be easier to check once necessary expenditures were properly provided for.[5] However, Madeleine Zelin has argued that a by-product of the

---

[3] See the preface by Li Yesi (1622–80) to Wan Sida's *Zhouguan bianfei* [A Demonstration That *The Rites of Zhou* Is Spurious]; quoted in Ono, "Shinsho no kōkeikai ni tsuite," p. 659, n. 14.

[4] Paul J. Smith, *Taxing Heaven's Storehouse: Horses, Bureaucrats, and the Destruction of the Sichuan Tea Industry, 1074–1224* (Cambridge, Mass.: Harvard University, Council on East Asian Studies, 1991), pp. 111-18.

[5] Zelin, *The Magistrate's Tael*, pp. 88-97 and passim.

reforms was the creation of discretionary funds and, sometimes, regular budgetary appropriations for state activities tending to enhance public welfare.[6] Another of the Yongzheng emperor's schemes, introduced briefly below, provides a clear case of actual fiscal growth being linked to an increase in state economic and welfare activities. The Yongzheng emperor's overall proclivity for interventionism is well known; Pierre-Étienne Will has recently written of Yongzheng-period economic policies and their continuation in the early years of Qianlong's reign in terms likely to evoke thoughts of the Great Leap Forward.[7]

The aim of the present section is not to focus on the differences between the Yongzheng-period approach to government finance, and the less demanding fiscal styles commonly associated with those conventionally admired emperors, Kangxi and Qianlong. It is rather to illustrate (a) the expression of fiscally positivist views by persons other than Yongzheng and his assistants; and (b) the process by which Yongzheng's positivism gradually gave way to *laissez-aller* and conventional fiscal morality under his son, Qianlong. Thus Text 4.A, an extraordinary disquisition of c. 1680 by a famous high official of the Kangxi period, criticizes contemporary governance for not forcing society to be more productive, and thereby generate more revenue for the state coffers. Text 4.B is an edict by the Qianlong emperor, in the third year of his reign, defending the practice, developed in the Yongzheng period, of state financial capitalism as a fund-raising technique. Text 4.C, by that luminary of mid-eighteenth-century provincial administration Chen Hongmou, asserts the necessity for deliberate official spending in order to achieve worthwhile goals. Turning to the case against fiscal positivism, Text 4.D, from the very beginning of the Yongzheng period, introduces some stock rhetoric against perceived state monopolization of economic

---

[6] Ibid., pp. 169-83, esp. 180-83.

[7] Will, "Attempts at Reviving the Zhengbai Irrigation System in the Wei River Valley of Shaanxi in the Late Imperial Period: A Preliminary Investigation" (paper presented at the Conference on the History of the Environment in China, Hong Kong, 13-18 December, 1993), pp. 22-32, esp. pp. 22-23 and n. 54. For a general account of Yongzheng's style of government, see Pei Huang, *Autocracy at Work: A Study of the Yung-cheng Period, 1723–1735* (Bloomington: Indiana University Press, 1974).

opportunities, while Text 4.E is an attack, from early in the Qianlong reign, on a central aspect of the state's investment operations. Finally, Text 4.F, submitted within five months of the Qianlong emperor's accession, is a fairly conventional *exposé* of vexatious state demands on the incomes of merchants, fishermen, and duck-rearers. What makes it interesting is its attention to the link between state taxes and consumer prices, and its suggestion that a way for the state to do effective economic good would be to limit its exactions.

* * * * *

Text 4.A (c. 1680) is strange, fascinating, and extremely long. The first of three memorials responding to an imperial command to frame proposals on the state's financial problems, it is partially concerned with a pet reclamation project of the author's.[8] Explanation of this project, based on what the author calls the "creeked fields" irrigation system, occupies approximately the last quarter of the text and is omitted here. The author is Jin Fu (1633–92), a celebrated expert in river control who served as director-general of the Grand Canal and Yellow River from 1677 until he was dismissed in 1688. The resentments caused by Jin's "creeked fields" project seem to have been one factor leading to his fall from grace, although policy and factional disputes were more important.[9]

In the main part of the memorial, Jin argues as follows. Calculation shows that the empire's capacity to generate agrarian tax revenues is more than ample to meet the state's military expenditures, sustain the government establishment, and provide adequately for the state's ritual responsibilities. The present fiscal

---

[8] The financial problems were presumably chiefly those engendered by the campaign to suppress the Revolt of the Three Feudatories (1673–81). The text of the Board of Revenue's plea for counsel is excerpted in the memorial of another respondent, Mu Tianyan (see HCJSWB, 26:13b-14a). The Board's immediate concern appears to be the fiscal implications of current natural disasters.

[9] See J. C. Yang, in Hummel, ed., *Eminent Chinese of the Ch'ing Period*, Vol. 1, pp. 161-62; Zhang Aisheng, *Hefang shuyan* [Record of a Dialogue on River Control] (late seventeenth century; *Siku quanshu zhenben sanji*, no. 169), pp. 57a-59a; and GCQXLZ, 155:20a.

difficulties are to be attributed to the state's failure even to aim to collect the full potential revenue. To the contrary, it annually sets out to collect less than a third of what could be available. In order to solve its fiscal problems on a long-term basis, the state must cause society to bring forth an annual volume of grain more nearly commensurate with the empire's cultivable acreage. It will then be able to fill its coffers properly with a tax of one in ten.

Mobilizing society for expanded production is a matter of battling with "three great mischiefs" entrenched in Chinese political economy for "long ages" past. These mischiefs are failure to undertake major water conservancy projects; failure to tax at a sufficiently high rate to force the rural population to be diligent; and toleration of an excessively high ratio of consumers to producers. In the portion of the memorial translated here, Jin gives most attention to the second and, more especially, third points. In particular, indignation about the extent of parasitism in the empire leads Jin into a diatribe against Buddhism and Daoism, and into some extremely interesting allegations about the ways of beggars in his day.

Calls for restoration of the 10 per cent taxation rate in late imperial discussions are usually signals that their authors think present exaction rates to be too high. Jin Fu is exceptional in calling for an *increase* in agrarian taxation rates to 10 per cent. That there could be difference of opinion on the matter is easily explained. The basic agrarian tax was in fact a land tax, and the rate was expressed as a fixed sum per *mu* of land within each grade. While the rates per *mu* were intended to reflect differences in productivity, the rationality of the system was severely compromised by the fact that it was the product of a long and complex evolution in which the principle of quotas had been approximately as influential as that of rates. At least an element within each county's tax rates was likely to be attributable to division of one or more pre-existing quotas among the county's registered taxable acreage.[10] Calculation of the percentage of

---

[10] Such division was especially likely to have occurred as part of the late Ming tax rationalization process known as the "Single Whip Reform." See Ray Huang, *Taxation and Governmental Finance in Sixteenth-Century Ming China* (Cambridge: Cambridge University Press, 1974), pp. 109-33. For a useful survey of the principles and practice of tax assessment under the Qing, see Wang Yeh-

annual yields that a given county's tax rates represented thus required local agronomic knowledge. Calculation for the empire at large was fraught with the hazards of generalization.[11]

The one piece of eye-witness evidence Jin gives to back his claim that subnormal tax rates are inducing idleness comes from the region straddling the northern part of the Jiangsu-Anhui border. This region has always been ecologically problematic, from the human point of view, and had further suffered in the popular rebellions of the end of the Ming dynasty.[12] What Jin perceived was that tax rates of 0.01 to 0.02 tl./*mu*, which do indeed seem on the low side, were encouraging the local people to live by mowing wild grass, for which there was a market in the cities, instead of expending the labour necessary for proper farming (i.e., the systematic cultivation of cereal, pulse, and fibre crops). In Jin's eyes, the waste of territory involved in this one case would seem to have been sufficiently substantial to justify regarding undertaxation as a national problem, without enquiry as to whether similar conditions existed elsewhere. He hints, however, that they do. His implicit message to the central government is that the key to eliciting popular cooperation with the calls for reclamation which are being "frequently sent down," is to impose on landowners tax rates corresponding to 10 per cent of the *potential* yield of their land if properly exploited.

---

chien, *Land Taxation in Imperial China, 1750–1911* (Cambridge, Mass.: Harvard University Press, 1973), pp. 20-39, esp. 21-31 on the importance and stability of quotas.

[11] Ray Huang has hazarded an empire-wide estimate for the sixteenth century, and his finding tends to support Jin Fu. He concludes from a survey of a wide range of evidence that, before the beginning of the seventeenth century, statutory taxation "was in general . . . less than 10 per cent of the estimated farm output at the normal local grain prices." Elsewhere, he claims that the real burden of the ill-famed tax increases of the early seventeenth century has been greatly exaggerated. Huang, *Taxation and Governmental Finance*, pp. 174 and 308. If Jin was mistaken about the burden of the land tax in his own day, this was presumably mainly because he was overlooking the effects of deflation.

[12] For a rich study of the ecology of the Huai'an-Xuzhou-Fengyang region, and its impact on local society, see Elizabeth J. Perry, *Rebels and Revolutionaries in North China, 1845–1945* (Stanford: Stanford University Press, 1980), ch. 2. Perry refers to depopulation and destruction of water control installations as a result of the late Ming rebellions on p. 13.

Jin devotes the most space to his third "mischief," the excessively high ratio of consumers to producers. He opens this section of his text with a quantitative discussion purporting to show that society can be adequately fed, with reserves kept in case of famines, only if 70 per cent of the population works full time at agriculture. The remaining 30 per cent will be fully accounted for by the other functionally necessary orders of society: scholars, artisans, merchants, and petty servants of the government bureaucracy. Unfortunately, the toleration of "Buddhist and Daoist monks and priests plus vagabonds and beggars" has increased the dependency ratio from 30 per cent to 50 per cent. This means inadequate food supplies in good years, widespread starvation during famines, and unnecessary social order problems. Jin does not trouble to spell out the effect on tax revenues.

It is difficult to account for the contumely which Jin visits upon Buddhism and Daoism in terms of the real influence of those doctrines in his day. A different kind of explanation is suggested below. While Jin's estimate that vagabonds, beggars, and full-time religious devotees account for 20 per cent of the population was surely quite arbitrary, his description of the excesses to which beggars go probably reflects the continuing influence of the socio-economic disasters earlier in the century, not to mention the more recent disruptions wrought by civil war. Infants are not maimed to enhance the appeal of begging operations in well-functioning economies. Jin's allegation on this score is valuable, since details of this sort tend to drop out of historical accounts of "glorious" reigns.

Striking features of Text 4.A are the pretensions of its style, its systematic (not to say laborious) theoretical expositions, and the way it is shot through with allusions to the Confucian scriptures. These points are interrelated: part of the exposition is directly borrowed from the scriptures. The arithmetical ratiocination in the opening paragraph is modelled almost exactly on a passage in the "Kingly institutions" chapter of *The Book of Rites*. The premise, at the beginning of Jin's discussion of the dependency ratio, that the individual farmer may, according to his skill, feed five, six, seven, eight, or nine people, comes from the same source.[13] In both these quantitative sections of his essay, Jin explicitly stresses that principles established in antiquity provide a model still applicable in his own day. The 10 per cent taxation rate is, itself, such a principle. Jin begins his account of each of the three "mischiefs" with at least one scriptural allusion, or reference to the sages of the hallowed past.[14] The principle of the four-class society, standard among Confucians and central to Jin's prescriptive sociology, can arguably be traced back to *The Book of Documents*.[15] Finally, his "creeked fields" plan was consciously adapted from a model in *The Rites of Zhou*.[16]

Scattered allusions to the Confucian canon are commonplace in Qing regional administrators' addresses to the throne, but not the general permeation that we find in Text 4.A. The concomitant rigidity of outlook in Text 4.A is also quite unusual. Jin is against diversity: he wants a uniform pattern to prevail throughout society, with universal diligence. Most administrators had their hands full grappling with the real world. That Jin makes an excursion into grand theory suggests that he is casting himself in a role, perhaps that of the statesman who provides sound counsel to a monarch creating the institutional foundations for a dynasty still young. A hint about Jin's self-image is perhaps to be found in his quotation, in the dependency ratio discussion, from Han Yu's essay, "Essentials of the Moral Way."[17] Han Yu (768–824) has traditionally been acclaimed as the founder of the Confucian revival after the dark ages of Buddhist ascendancy; the essay is his most famous reassertion of Confucian values. The whole last section of Text 4.A, with its anti-Buddhist diatribe, was arguably

---

[13] *Liji*, 5/pars. 2 and 55.

[14] Besides the obvious allusions, there is one which might pass unnoticed. This is the expression "the management of rural areas," used in the account of the third "mischief." This comes from the opening sentence of the *Zhouli*.

[15] For the phrase *simin*, "four [orders of the] people," see *Shangshu* [The Book of Documents], ch. 40. The orders are enumerated in *Guanzi*, 20:100-102. For the fifth occupational group accepted in Jin's scheme of things, the "commoners in the official service," see *Liji*, 5/par. 2.

[16] GCQXLZ, 155:20a-b and 26a-b.

[17] I have borrowed Charles Hartman's translation of the title. See the valuable discussion of this essay in his *Han Yü and the T'ang Search for Unity* (Princeton: Princeton University Press, 1986), pp. 145-62.

inspired by Han Yu. Jin Fu is posturing, but he is also participating in the late seventeenth-century élite reassertion of Confucianism's "eternal truths" about the cosmos and the social order. This reassertion was a reaction to the alleged excesses of late Ming intuitionism, which had been receptive to Buddhist influence, and which was accused, by some, of having greatly contributed to the late Ming breakdown of the social order.[18]

Robert Hartwell has characterized Wang Anshi's approach to government as "classicist," meaning that Wang sought to revive the institutions described in the Confucian "classics" (scriptures) without attention to historical experience.[19] Jin Fu may have aspired to take on the mantle of Han Yu; but he was perhaps closer than he knew to Wang Anshi.

*   *   *   *   *

Some institutional background is necessary for understanding Texts 4.B and 4.E. It concerns the development of state investment operations under the Yongzheng emperor and in the early part of Qianlong's reign. The basic principles of this system of state finance were that substantial sums were lent, at interest, to private businesses, or even used directly by state agencies to create their own money-spinning ventures. Such operations had a distant precedent in the Tang dynasty. In Qing times, funds were already being placed with private managers quite early in the Kangxi period, in order to raise interest payments for the Shengjing Board of Revenue and branch treasury of the Imperial Household Department.[20] There were also some state loans of

---

[18] See, e.g., Wm. Theodore de Bary, "Individualism and Humanitarianism in Late Ming Thought," in *Self and Society in Ming Thought*, ed. de Bary and the Conference on Ming Thought (New York: Columbia University Press, 1970), pp. 171-78; and Okuzaki Hiroshi, *Chūgoku kyōshin jinushi no kenkyū* [Studies on the Gentry Landlords of China] (Tokyo: Kyūko shoin, 1978), esp. parts 2, 3, and 5:4.

[19] Robert M. Hartwell, "Historical Analogism, Public Policy, and Social Science in Eleventh- and Twelfth-Century China," *American Historical Review* 76, no. 3 (1971), pp. 691, 693, and 727.

[20] See Denis Twitchett, "Merchant, Trade and Government in Late T'ang," *Asia Major* 14 (1968), pp. 73-74; and Wei Qingyuan, "Kangxi shiqi dui 'shengxi

capital to individuals in the Kangxi period, as well as special credit funds for Bannermen, but the primary purpose of these kinds of lending was probably accommodation of the borrowers, not profit for state treasuries.[21] The closest precedent for the new institutions of the Yongzheng period was the loan of 60,000 taels made by the Board of Revenue to the Imperial Clan Court in 1702, to set up an investment fund. The profits from this fund would provide grants for the wedding and funeral expenses of the imperial clansmen, and the collateral relatives of the imperial house.[22]

The Yongzheng emperor's initial concern was to create investment funds that would provide permanently for grants to Bannermen and, later, all rank-and-file military personnel, for their life-cycle expenditures. The Bannermen, that is, the descendants of the Manchu, Mongol, and Chinese contingents who had conquered China for the Manchus in 1644, were paid stipends to remain nominal soldiers, but the lower ranks were subject to growing impoverishment by the second quarter of the eighteenth century.[23] The expenses of weddings and funerals were notorious among censorious Confucians for reducing poor people to penury; when members of the state's military establishment were involved, an emperor as politically minded as Yongzheng saw cause for government assistance.

In the first year of Yongzheng's reign, investment grants of 100,000 taels per Banner were made from the Imperial Household

---

yinliang' zhidu de chuchuang he yunyong" [The Introduction and Operation of the "Investment Funds" System in the Kangxi Period], *Zhongguo shehui jingji shi yanjiu* [Journal of Chinese Social and Economic History] 1986, no. 3, pp. 62-63. The Imperial Household Department managed the business of the Court; Shengjing (Mukden, Shenyang) was the Manchus' capital for two decades before they conquered China, and became an "auxiliary capital" thereafter. See Robert H. Lee, *The Manchurian Frontier in Ch'ing History* (Cambridge, Mass.: Harvard University Press, 1970), pp. 60-63.

[21] Wei, "Kangxi shiqi dui 'shengxi yinliang' zhidu," pp. 64-68, and references there cited; and Abe, *Shindai-shi no kenkyū*, pp. 389-90.

[22] Abe, *Shindai-shi no kenkyū*, pp. 394 and 402, n. 3.

[23] Susan Naquin and Evelyn S. Rawski, *Chinese Society in the Eighteenth Century* (New Haven: Yale University Press, 1987), pp. 4-5 and 141; and Wu Wei-ping, "The Development and Decline of the Eight Banners" (Ph.D. dissertation, University of Pennsylvania, 1969), esp. chs. 6 to 8.

Department treasury in favour of the Manchu and Mongol Bannermen in the capital. Profit at the rate of 12 per cent *per annum* was to be deposited in a special fund for helping the Bannermen with their wedding and funeral expenditures. By 1730, such a system had been extended to the Chinese and Manchu Banner forces stationed in the provinces, and to the major regular (Chinese non-Banner) provincial forces also. Further extensions were made over the next two decades, including, in 1736, grants of 25,000 taels apiece for the Chinese Banner units in the capital. Beginning in 1732, the Yongzheng emperor accepted some diversification in the uses to which income from the investment funds was put. New uses included the establishment of military granaries to supply grain to the servicemen during times of high prices; disaster relief for servicemen; burial of deceased servicemen; assistance to the families of those who had died in combat; and acquisition and maintenance of military equipment. While the funding for the original provincial grants came from provincial treasuries, a 1757 accounting statement put the total investment funds awarded out of the Household Department treasury at 1,953,000 taels (a figure which includes grants to various imperial agencies and guard detachments as well as the Banners).[24]

Such were the foundations of the system of *yingyun shengxi yinliang*—literally, "funds to be managed to generate profit." The word *xi* in fact covers not only profit but also rent and interest. Research by Abe Takeo and Wei Qingyuan suggests that the commonest ways in which the military and Banner units used their investment funds were, in roughly this order, to open

---

[24] See Abe, *Shindai-shi no kenkyū*, pp. 391-93; Wei Qingyuan, *Dangfang lunshi wenbian* [Historical Essays from the Archives] (Fuzhou: Fujian Renmin chubanshe, 1984), pp. 24-26, and "Yongzheng shiqi dui 'shengxi yinliang' zhidu de zhengdun he zhengce yanbian" [The Reorganization of, and Evolution of Policy towards, the "Investment Funds" System in the Yongzheng Period], *Zhongguo shehui jingji shi yanjiu* 1987, no. 3, pp. 35-36; Saeki Tomi, *Chūgoku shi kenkyū II* [Studies in Chinese History, Second Collection] (Kyōto: Kyōto University, Tōyōshi Kenkyūkai, 1971), pp. 307-9; Sasaki Masaya, "Shindai kanryō no kashoku ni tsuite" [On Money-Making by Qing Bureaucrats], in *Shigaku zasshi* 63, no. 2 (1954), pp. 30-31; *Shangyu qiwu yifu*, Yongzheng (YZ) 1:5b-7b; and *Da Qing Shizong Xian Huangdi shilu* [Veritable Records of the Yongzheng Period] (hereafter QSL/YZ), 6:27a-b.

pawnshops; to lend to salt merchants and private pawnbrokers; to run miscellaneous kinds of businesses; and to buy real estate for rental purposes.[25]

The early years of Qianlong's reign (until the early 1750s) saw further extensions and rationalizations of the above system, with continuing efforts to spread access to the benefits more evenly and to new recipients.[26] At the same time, a parallel system was emerging in civil provincial finance. Text 4.B, from 1738, was occasioned by an attack on Emida, governor-general of Guangdong and Guangxi, for asking leave to lend 100,000 taels from the customs revenues to salt merchants, so as to earn interest to finance dike restoration in Chaozhou Prefecture. Later, as governor-general for Hunan and Hubei in the mid-1740s, Emida was to be involved in at least three more instances of investment income being raised to finance civil engineering work—though in one case his role was to propose replacing an original investment of 30,000 taels with a more modest 5,000 taels.[27] Other scholars have cited instances, spanning the period from 1735 to 1752, of state investment funds being used to finance improvements in law and order maintenance, urban firefighting, and educational provision, as well as general purposes.[28]

---

[25] Abe, *Shindai-shi no kenkyū*, pp. 397-400; Wei, "Yongzheng shiqi dui 'shengxi yinliang' zhidu," pp. 36-44, and *Dangfang lunshi wenbian*, pp. 31-32 and 38. The lines of business undertaken by the military and Banner units included money-changing, grain, cloth, medicinal substances, coal, oil, second-hand clothes, and dyeing. Only in the last instance does the investment seem to have been in manufacturing or processing.

[26] QSL/QL, 23:27b, 51:25a-b, 68:4a, 164:34b, 205:15a-b, 225:5b, 315:16b-17a, and 324:9a.

[27] The original investment (for financing maintenance work) had been made in 1737, and subsequently discontinued. See QSL/QL, 53:13a-b, 229:8a-9a, and 253:21a-b.

[28] Abe, *Shindai-shi no kenkyū*, pp. 405 and 409 n. 4; Saeki, *Chūgoku shi kenkyū II*, p. 315; Zelin, *The Magistrate's Tael*, pp. 281-83; and Pierre-Étienne Will, "State Intervention in the Administration of a Hydraulic Infrastructure: The Example of Hubei Province in Late Imperial Times," in *The Scope of State Power in China*, ed. Stuart R. Schram (London: University of London, School of Oriental and African Studies; Hong Kong: Chinese University of Hong Kong, Chinese University Press, 1985), p. 316 n. 48.

Text 4.B is an edict, addressed to the advisers to whom the Qianlong emperor had referred the document attacking Emida. The attack was a reassertion of the conventional position that those in government ought not to "talk of profit."[29] The advisers had been split on the issue: those supporting Emida had been led by E'ertai (1680–1745), one of Yongzheng's most trusted counsellors, while the president of the Board of Personnel, Sun Jiagan (1683–1753), had spoken for those opposing Emida's initiative.[30] The emperor decided in favour of Emida. His argument was simple. Scripture shows that the disjunction between "righteousness" and "profit" is a false one, erected in Confucian discourse only because of the danger that inferior people will reject the former and pursue the latter. In fact, from an ethical point of view, all that needs to be rejected is self-interested profit-seeking; to seek to profit others (the intent behind Emida's proposal) is righteousness itself. Meanwhile, flexibility is sometimes necessary in government. In any case, the merchants benefit from the low-interest loans.

The argument itself is undistinguished. What is significant is that the Qianlong emperor was making it. By 1760, he had changed his tune.

*   *   *

Text 4.C, by Chen Hongmou, supplies a quietly eloquent coda to the part of this chapter illustrating fiscal positivism. In fact, it was not originally written as a single document. The editors of the 1827 *Huangchao jingshi wenbian* welded together material from letters to different people, representing the whole as a single letter to unspecified "responsible officials." Improper as this procedure may have been, the result is so felicitous that I have preserved their arrangement. The interests of historical accuracy are served by textual annotations.

---

[29] It was the advocates of state monopolies and other fiscalist measures in the famous "Debate on Salt and Iron" (81 B.C.) who had especially given a bad name to "ministers who talk of profit." For the scriptural *locus classicus* for "profit" as a dirty word, see note 3 to Text 4.B.

[30] QSL/QL, 70:23a (ref. from Abe, *Shindai-shi no kenkyū*, p. 409 n. 4). Sun Jiagan features prominently in ch. 5 below as a defender of the North China liquor industry, and explicator of the workings of the agrarian market economy.

Text 4.C is partly a *cri de coeur* against the fiscal timidity that, in Chen's view, plagues all levels of the bureaucracy and results in the false economy of neglecting necessary expenditures until it is too late. The problem he addresses is not one of ideology but, rather, one of the self-interest of civil servants, who have careers to protect and prefer to avoid unnecessary complications. Chen's ideal, by contrast, lies in identifying undertakings that would positively benefit the people of one's jurisdiction, and finding the means to push ahead with them, even if the cost is great. A hint is given, through his quotation from the "Great Learning" chapter of *The Book of Rites*, that Chen shares Wang Anshi's belief in state activism as a means of spurring on society to "create wealth."

The concluding paragraph presents a sustained plea for bold spending on carefully planned, worthwhile projects for the betterment of local or regional conditions. Chen warns his reader to expect difficulties, including the scepticism and rebukes of colleagues. There begins to be something a little pathetic in Chen's image of the bureaucratic innovator, sustained against all vicissitudes by the strength of his convictions. Recent research by Will suggests that an economic project which Chen himself pursued for thirteen years was not outstandingly successful.[31]

*   *   *   *   *

While it was in the Qianlong period that there was a significant reaction against Yongzheng-style fiscal positivism, reservations about state economic activism were expressed at other times as well. Text 4.D is a letter, written by a central government official, Li Fu (1675–1750), in 1723, to raise concerns about the Yunnan provincial government's copper monopsony, which had been set up in 1705. Li's central complaint was that, while compulsorily acquiring the entire output of the Yunnan copper mines, the authorities were actually paying for only about two-thirds of it. He accurately represented the official operations as a *de facto* monopoly of the mining itself. Although the miners were

---

[31] See the section entitled "La promotion des textiles" in Pierre-Étienne Will, "Développement quantitatif et développement qualitatif en Chine à la fin de l'époque impériale," pp. 891-99.

technically private entrepreneurs, most of them were receiving payment for their copper in the form of an advance to fund production costs. The mining also took place under official supervision.[32] The crux of Li's argument was that state selfishness in monopolizing the economic bounties of "the hills and seas" leads to a constriction of those bounties (as witness the current copper shortage). The policy of choice for future operations would be for the provincial government to leave mining entirely to private capital, and pay for copper at the market price.

From a historian's point of view, Text 4.D was influential but inaccurate, or at best partial. It was addressed to one "Administration Vice-Commissioner Li" in the Yunnan bureaucracy,[33] but part of its wording, and that of a companion letter on the administration of the Yunnan salt monopoly, was recycled in a mid-1723 memorial by the supervising censor Zhao Dianzui.[34] Zhao's version was not identical: the style is simpler and less vigorous, and there are differences in content. For Zhao, the central abuse in the Yunnan copper administration was that the price paid to the miners for their copper left the provincial government with an unconscionably large profit margin when it sold the copper to those buying for the central government mints, located in Beijing.

It was a propitious time for policy departures, because, as Li Fu mentions, a decision had been made to mint the copper in Yunnan in future, rather than sending it all the way to Beijing. After high-level discussion of Zhao's memorial, the Board of Revenue proposed that the Yunnan governor and governor-general be ordered to report in detail on the provincial copper industry. However, it did not wait for the report before making a recommendation which broadly met the views of Zhao and Li.

---

[32] Basic sources on Yunnan copper mining in the late Kangxi period include QCWXTK, 14:4977 and 15:4981; *Gongzhong dang Yongzheng chao zouzhe* [Secret Palace Memorials of the Yongzheng Period] (Taibei: National Palace Museum, 1977–80; hereafter GZD/YZ), Vol. 2, pp. 185-89; and 1826 *Yunnan tongzhi gao* [Draft Gazetteer of Yunnan Province], 75:3b-16b.

[33] This may have been Li Shide, who was in charge of Yunnan copper matters from 1721 until his death during the spring of 1723. See GZD/YZ, Vol. 2, pp. 188-89.

[34] GZD/YZ, Vol. 1, pp. 379-82.

The provincial government's monopoly should be dismantled, and the monopsony replaced by a pre-emption system; official buying was to be done fairly, and at market prices.[35]

The Yunnan chief administrators' report, written in January 1724 to defend the provincial government's monopoly, casts that monopoly in a quite different light from Li's and Zhao's. Li must have gathered the material for Text 4.D in 1717, when he was in Yunnan as provincial examiner. In 1717, reported copper output had been only just beginning to recover from the trough of the immediately preceding years, and the provincial authorities had indeed had the impression (as Li mentions) that they were confronted with resource depletion and diminishing returns. Between 1717 and 1723, however, reported annual output had more than recovered, and the problem was no longer failure of supply, but collapse of demand. Because of the remoteness of Yunnan, commercial demand for the province's copper remained problematic, while the administrations designated to procure copper for the Beijing mints were buying, after 1719, from their preferred source of supply, Japan. The decision taken, within a month of the Yongzheng emperor's accession, to start minting Yunnan copper in Yunnan was partly a matter of straightforward economic rationalization, of the sort for which Yongzheng is famous. However, the Yunnan governor had requested such a change as early as 1721, and saw it as a solution to the pressing problem of disposing of the growing copper stockpile for an acceptable return.[36]

The main issues addressed by the 1724 Yunnan report are the *raison d'être* of the provincial government's monopoly, and the justification for the allegedly excessive profit margin. The former is explained in terms of the uncertainty of demand for Yunnan

---

[35] 1767 *Qinding Da Qing huidian zeli* [Imperially Authorized Collected Statutes of the Great Qing Dynasty: Precedents and Regulations] (hereafter 1767 DQHDZL), 44:15a-b; QCWXTK, 15:4982; and GZD/YZ, Vol. 2, p. 189.

[36] GZD/YZ, Vol. 2, pp. 187-88, and 528-32 (I owe the latter reference to the manuscript of Hans Ulrich Vogel's major study of the Qing Yunnan copper industry, which I thank him for letting me see); QCWXTK, 15:4981 ff.; QSL/YZ, 1:23b-24a, and 2:40a-b; and Yang Duanliu, *Qingdai huobi jinrong shi gao* [A History of Currency and Finance in the Qing Dynasty] (Beijing: Sanlian shudian, 1962), pp. 49-51.

copper and the lack of interest by private capitalists in buying up the miners' output. The miners lack the capital to continue production for the two or three years it may take to sell a given stock. This is why the provincial government steps in with the capital advances, and with marketing arrangements centred on its warehouses. As for the suspected profit margin, this is more or less completely accounted for by further costs. These are listed and explained, and most of them are quantified in a financial statement for a twenty-four-month period in 1721–23. In this twenty-four-month period, according to the figures given, there was indeed at best a negligible profit margin in the official copper business. In keeping with the tenor of the early Yongzheng period approach to fiscal matters, the report's authors conclude by setting goals for profit in the future, when the new provincial mints will be the buyers. They offer nothing but a sop to Li, Zhao, and the Board of Revenue: allot any new deposits that may be discovered to the private sector, but keep the known resources to supply the mints and generate a profit for provincial government and military expenditures.[37]

It was necessary to provide the above information, so as to warn the reader against accepting Text 4.D as an accurate depiction of the Yunnan copper industry in the early 1720s.[38] The episode has some significance, in that it confirmed the pattern of state dominance that would prevail in the Yunnan copper industry throughout the eighteenth century. The rich new deposits found in 1726 were not, in the event, surrendered to the private sector. Meanwhile, the 1724 report and Text 4.D furnish a most instructive contrast. On one side is hard-headed discussion of the problems and prospects of state enterprise; on the other, sensitivity to the hardships of low-status producers and moving

---

[37] GZD/YZ, Vol. 2, pp. 185-90. The report is summarized in Zelin, *The Magistrate's Tael*, pp. 141-42, but the summary is marred by Zelin's apparent assumption that the authors accepted the idea of ending the monopoly. For the broader context of the 1723-24 debate, see ibid., passim, and pp. 136-48.

[38] This mistake was made in older studies whose authors had not seen the answering report. See Yan Zhongping, *Qingdai Yunnan tongzheng kao* [An Investigation of the Yunnan Copper Administration in the Qing Dynasty] (Shanghai: Zhonghua shuju, 1948), pp. 6-8; and Yang Duanliu, *Qingdai huobi jinrong shi gao*, pp. 24-25 (where the text is erroneously dated 1736).

rhetoric about the fiscal and economic benefits of "sharing" with the people.

*   *   *

Text 4.E is an attack on the Yongzheng emperor's investment funding system for the Bannermen and regular armed forces. It was made in the same year (1738) as the young Qianlong emperor's defence of the principle of state profit-making, but it helped to lay the ideological foundation for Qianlong's later repudiation of this method of state finance. The author was the Manchu Shuhede (1711–77), but his argument was impeccably Confucian. On one hand, profit-making was the business of merchants, and thus incompatible with the proper dignity of government; on the other, the cumulative profit-spinning that was taking place, with part of the return being turned into capital, was inevitably taking wealth away from society, and enriching the state sector at society's expense. As others would have put it, using a well-known *cliché*, the state was improperly "competing with the folk for profit."[39] It would be better at least to require the provinces to moderate their capitalistic zeal, allowing "the wealth . . . to circulate among the populace."

What is striking about Shuhede's approach is his failure to be excited by the idea that "a limited quantity of public funds" could be "used to contrive endless profit." In fact, two officially sanctioned uses of surplus profits that had emerged by 1738 were the creation of capital grants for military units that had not yet received them; and (as Shuhede's discussion suggests) the repayment of the original capital grants of the successful units. Such repayment had become expected after 1735;[40] for Shuhede, this was a development to be encouraged, since it would put a

---

[39] The idea that the state (or those empowered by the state) should not compete with society for profit seems to have become influential in the Han dynasty, although its origins may well be earlier. See, e.g., Sima Qian, *Shiji*, Vol. 10, 119:3101; Huan Kuan, comp., *Yan tie lun* [The Debate on Salt and Iron] (between 73 and 49 B.C.; Taibei: Shijie shuju, 1967), 1:1; and Ban Gu, *Hanshu*, Vol. 4, 24B:1176, and Vol. 10, 72:3077.

[40] GZD/YZ, Vol. 24, pp. 702-3 (ref. from Wei, "Yongzheng shiqi dui 'shengxi yinliang' zhidu," p. 35); cf. QSL/QL, 192:8a-b.

brake on secondary profit-spinning. His recommendations therefore centred on insisting that the provinces repay their grants and that their future operations should be modest, with all the profits dedicated to assistance to the servicemen.

Shuhede's position may reflect distrust as to the use to which fund managers would ultimately put the excess income; but we may also say that his imagination was not captured by the idea of "creating wealth," despite that concept's canonical origin.[41] By implication, he accepted the more conventional assumption that the world's wealth was ultimately fixed, so that gain for the state necessarily meant less wealth for society. His reassertion of conservative fiscal morality at this early stage of the Qianlong period is interesting, as it provides a parallel to the late 1730s ideological attacks on Yongzheng's rationalization of illegal surcharges.[42] These attacks were followed by a long period in which, although the Qianlong emperor never dismantled his father's reforms of local and provincial finance, he allowed their effectiveness to be gradually eroded, until, by the end of the century, it was as if they had never been.[43]

In the case of the investment funding system, reforms in 1742 and 1743 were followed by moves towards abolition in the 1750s.[44] Abolition took a long time to accomplish, and at no time meant the abolition of *all* capitalistic operations by the imperial establishment. The reasons for the abolition were complex and are not yet completely clear, but they certainly involved a great deal more than ideology.[45] The implications, however, reinforced the

---

[41] For the *locus classicus* of the idea of "creating wealth" in the "Great Learning" chapter of *The Book of Rites*, see n. 1 to Text 4.C below.

[42] Zelin, *The Magistrate's Tael*, pp. 266-69. The assumption that the world's wealth is fixed features in these attacks as well.

[43] Ibid., ch. 7.

[44] For the 1742-43 reforms, see QSL/QL, 164:34a-b and 192:8b. While not identical with Shuhede's recommendations, these reforms went in the same direction.

[45] The practice of using investment profits to fund life-cycle expenditures assistance grants to metropolitan Bannermen was abolished in 1750, while the emperor called for the phasing out of all investment operations in the provinces in 1759. The background to the 1750 abolition was that there had already been large-scale misapplication of the metropolitan Bannermen's investment funds, a

trend of growing fiscal weakness. Life-cycle expenditures assistance for Bannermen and servicemen became a new call on conventional revenue sources. Investment funding for miscellaneous public projects was outlawed as well, resulting in a further strain on local budgets.[46] It proved, in fact, impossible to do without investment funding, which resurfaced even as the Qianlong emperor was struggling to abolish it;[47] but recourse to this system in the late eighteenth and nineteenth centuries had an entirely different meaning from the fiscal expansionism of Yongzheng times.

*   *   *

Text 4.F, submitted in the first moon of 1736, offers the kind of advice to which a new ruler was likely to be susceptible: relieve the people's sufferings by sparing them the burden of vexatious and improper taxes (non-agrarian taxes, in this case). At first sight, it is not particularly interesting, except for the glimpse into the worlds of fishermen and duck-rearers, the author's application of the 10 per cent norm to commercial taxes, and the hints of negative side-effects from Yongzheng era fiscal-mindedness. The document's main significance, however, lies in its treatment of the principle of indirect taxation and in its influence on policy between 1737 and 1749.

The author, Gan Rulai (1684–1739), clearly understands how indirect taxation works, although he has no name for it and does not recognize it as a distinct and valid way of taxing society at large. Commercial taxes are, in principle, taxes on the income of

---

situation for which Qianlong himself bore some responsibility. It looks as though, by 1750, funds intended for the benefit of rank-and-file Bannermen were instead being lent to Bannermen who had official ranks. See Abe, *Shindai-shi no kenkyū*, pp. 406-7, 409 n. 6, and references there cited; and Wei Qingyuan, "Qianlong shiqi 'shengxi yinliang' zhidu de shuaibai he 'shouche'" [The Decline and Abolition of the "Investment Funds" System in the Qianlong Period], in *Zhongguo shehui jingji shi yanjiu* 1988, no. 3: 8-17.

[46] Assistance for the metropolitan Bannermen was to be funded out of salt revenues, and for provincial servicemen out of regular tax revenues (after 1781). QSL/QL, 367:2b-5a, 582:2b-3b, and 799:19b-20b; QCWXTK, 41:5240 (all refs. from Abe, *Shindai-shi no kenkyū*, pp. 406-7, and 409 notes 6 and 8).

[47] Abe, *Shindai-shi no kenkyū*, p. 407.

merchants. In fact, however, higher taxes on distributors are reflected in higher consumer prices. Higher consumer prices are an additional evil of oppressive commercial taxation. The effect is particularly to be lamented in the case of grain, a commodity unlike all others because lives fundamentally depend on it. Grain prices could be lowered if the transit taxes which affect them were removed.

The understanding that commercial taxes told on the price level was not new with Gan Rulai.[48] However, there is as yet no evidence that the policy of remitting the transit taxes on grain cargoes destined for dearth-stricken regions, already carried out sporadically before 1736, had been inspired by this understanding. The rationale seems, rather, to have been that the remission would give merchants an incentive to import grain to the stricken regions, where the increase in supply would bring about a fall in prices. This rationale continued to be articulated after 1736.[49] The argument that removing transit taxes would directly cause a fall in grain prices (because the merchants would no longer have a burden to pass on) began, however, to appear in policy pronouncements in 1737.[50] During 1737–38, as a result of Gan's memorial, the practice of remitting transit taxes at the internal customs stations on the routes into dearth-stricken zones was made into a regular procedure.[51]

This was a compromise, called forth by the opposition of a number of governors, governors-general, and customs station superintendents to Gan's proposal for complete suspension of transit taxes on grain. Gan had, however, laid the theoretical foundation for an experiment with just such a suspension half a

---

[48] Kōsaka Masanori, "Kenryū-dai zenki ni okeru kanzei shukoku-zei menjo-rei ni tsuite" [On the Suspension of Internal Customs Duties on Staple Foodstuffs in the Early Qianlong Period], *Bunka* [Culture] 32, no. 4 (1969), p. 42 (quoting a source of c. 1650).

[49] See Will, *Bureaucratie et famine*, p. 187; Kōsaka, "Kenryū-dai zenki ni okeru," pp. 73-75 note 9, sub-notes 14, 21, and 22.

[50] Kōsaka, "Kenryū-dai zenki ni okeru," p. 73, notes 6 and 9, sub-note 8.

[51] Ibid., pp. 49-50. Gan's requests concerning the taxation of coastal fishing-boats, duck-wharves, and fish-traps had received imperial assent in 1736. See GCQXLZ, 72:18b, and QCWXTK, 31:5136.

decade later. This experiment, begun in 1742, was declared unsuccessful and terminated in 1749. Positivism in fiscal self-denial was no infallible prescription either, it appeared.[52] Perhaps this failure too contributed to the gradual decline of active civil governance in the long Qianlong reign.

* * * * *

Text 4.A

First memorial on the creation of wealth, and the enrichment of the funds for military supplies (excerpts)
Date: c. 1680
Author: Jin Fu, as director-general of the Grand Canal and
           Yellow River.
Source: Jin Fu, *Jin Wenxiang Gong zoushu* [The Memorials of Jin
           Fu], 7:28a-48a; HCJSWB, 26:6a-9b.

I submit that, under our present Dynasty, the carriage-gauges and the forms of writing are made uniform; and that down to the sea itself, both within and without, there is none but reveres and loves the Sovereign. From the days of Tang and Yu down to the present, the breadth of territory in the Empire has never been as it is now in this our present Dynasty.[1] Now, with an area as great as this, one would expect that wealth and revenue would daily mount until the cords were rotten and the grain decayed;[2] if, nonetheless, those at the Board of Revenue are fretting with anxiety lest military funds should not suffice, this passes understanding. I find that an area of one *li* square contains 5.4 *qing* of arable. An area of 10 *li* square, being 100 times the area of one *li* square, contains 540 *qing* of arable. An area of 100 *li* square, being 100 times the area of 10 *li* square, contains 54,000 *qing* of arable.

---

[52] The 1740s suspension did not apply to the tonnage tax mentioned by Gan, a limitation that turned out to be serious. For detailed discussion of this whole episode, see Dunstan, *State or Merchant?*, ch. 2. Existing accounts are Kōsaka, "Kenryū-dai zenki ni okeru," pp. 53-54 and 59-66, and He Benfang, "Qianlong nianjian queguan de mianshui cuoshi" [Exemptions from Internal Customs Duties in the Qianlong Period], *Lishi dang'an* 28 (1987, no. 4), pp. 90-91. Also relevant is Text 7.E below.

An area of 1,000 *li* square, being 100 times the area of 100 *li* square, contains 5,400,000 *qing* of arable. If, going by what is written in the "Kingly institutions,"[3] we take away one part in three for hills and mountains, woods and forests, streams and marshes, creeks and channels, inner and outer city walls, halls and palaces, and streets and lanes, each area of 1,000 *li* square will in fact contain 3,600,000 *qing* of arable. Provisionally subtracting the fourth part of this, which is 900,000 *qing*, to take account of any cotton, vegetables, fruit, water chestnuts, lotus roots, medicaments, and the like that may be under cultivation (because these crops are not of the five kinds of grain) there still in fact remain 2,700,000 *qing* of arable.

To take from the population at the rate of one in ten was the normal institution of antiquity. Counting together summer wheat and autumn rice, each *mu* of arable, however poor the soil, will yield a bushel of grain per year. If this is taxed according to the rule of one in ten, with one tenth of a bushel levied from each *mu*, ten bushels of tax-grain will be receivable from every *qing* of arable. From 2,700,000 *qing*, 27,000,000 bushels of tax-grain will be receivable. If out of this one tenth is payable in kind, each year 2,700,000 bushels of grain may be collected. Nine tenths will be commuted, at an average rate of four tenths of a tael per bushel; nor does this allow for what accrues from cloth, silk, fish, and salt. The total area of Zhili and the fourteen provinces is not below 5,000 to 6,000 *li* square, but measured straight across by pace and bow, it comes to no more than 4,000 or so. If for the moment we calculate on the assumption that it is only 3,000, there will be nine areas of 1,000 *li* square. The annual quota-governed taxes should amount to as much as 24,300,000 bushels of grain and 87,480,000 taels of silver. Here I have shown what should be so to-day by drawing on the standards of antiquity, and based my calculations on the minimum assumptions. It is a matter of unalterable logic, of figures necessarily obtained, not uninformed and arbitrary speculation.

Now what is needed by the Board of Revenue, roughly speaking, is no more than the funds for army rations, military equipment, and the postal relay system, plus salaries and wages for official personnel and runners, and funds for works and sacrifices. For it may reasonably be observed that if the soldiers have no rations, there will be nothing to ensure that men feel full and horses prance; if the officials have no salaries, there will be nothing to nourish their integrity and virtue; and if the runners have no wages, there will be nothing for the support of their families,[4] nothing to ensure that they put heart and mind into their errands. If the above three kinds of payment are not properly provided for, the resulting mischiefs may in each case harm the common people and injure the basis of the State. Military equipment, furthermore, is the prerequisite for sweeping out banditti; the postal relays are the life-force-bearing ducts that run throughout the nation. These, together with building and maintenance of city walls and palaces, and sacrifices to Heaven and Earth and various divinities, all absolutely may not be dispensed with. I have, however, calculated roughly, and I find that a sum of 20,000,000 taels *per annum* will more than suffice to feed the armies. Even should the sum required for official salaries and wages increase several-fold, and allowing also for some increase in the staff and horses of the postal relays, these, together with all military equipment, construction works, and sacrifices would cost no more than an additional 20,000,000. This again is on the basis of extreme assumptions. Supposing that the State's annual receipts of grain and silver were indeed the sums that I have calculated, then even putting each year's spending at the maximum, it still would not reach half the income. The funds accumulated in the treasuries would unquestionably fill them up right to the ridge-poles, occupying all the courts; what grounds could there remain for fearing insufficiency? In fact, however, the quota-governed taxes now collected in Zhili and the provinces do not amount to even one third of the figure which I calculated. It is naturally no wonder that those at the Board of Revenue cast their eyes towards the ceiling.

Now since the Empire has a given actual land area, there should naturally be a corresponding assured output of grain; there being an assured output of grain, there should naturally be a corresponding amount of tax due. If we now measure the empire's dimensions in order to compute its acreage, we find the latter to be very great; but if we use the "comprehensive regis-ters" to ascertain the volume of the quota-governed taxes, we find this to be very small.[5] And for what reason? The reason is that there are three great mischiefs in the Empire which no one of this generation has discerned. They did not arise during the present time, but have come down from the defunct Ming dynasty; indeed, long ages previous to the defunct Ming partook of these same mischiefs. Because, however, with the passage of the generations, investigation is now difficult, I shall not discuss this aspect further. What are the three great mischiefs? The first is that water conservancy is not put in hand; the second is that taxes are light and the people lazy; the third is that producers are few, consumers many.

Investigating in the scriptures, we perceive that Master Kong, in praise of the Great Yu, observed that he "held palaces and mansions in but low esteem, devoting all his strength to creeks and channels." Master Meng, replying to Duke Wen of Teng, remarked "the population's business may not be deferred."[6] The sages and wise men of antiquity profoundly comprehended that the population "takes food as its Heaven," and thus whenever they discoursed upon the proper way of ordering the State and quieting the Empire, they invariably took the satisfying of the population as the chief concern, and agriculture as the prime prerequisite. Qi used the strategies of Guan Zhong to make itself the wealthiest state east of the mountains; Qin used the techniques of the state of Zheng to establish its strength within the passes. Even from Han and Tang times down, there have been openers of channels and irrigators of the fields. All were able to profit the population and to bring advantage to the State; the only pity is that they practised merely in one corner, and never planned for the whole Empire. Because of this, there was, in the end, much land left waste, and later generations were not able to reap the full benefit.

The breadth of our Dynasty's territory at the present time is rivalled by nothing in antiquity, yet land lying uncultivated and not put in order is to be found ubiquitously. Even what has been put in order is for the most part level plain, devoid of the facilities of water storage and dispersal.[7] Without awaiting great floods or extraordinary droughts, if rain and shine are even slightly out of season, the harvest on such territory promptly fails. The result is that the taxes due the State fall daily into worse arrears, while the people's lives fall daily into greater hardship. Such is the mischief of the failure to cultivate conservancy of water.

When Yao and Shun were taking from the people, they always made one part in ten their standard. When Bo Gui wished to make it one in twenty, Master Meng rejected the idea.[8] The point is that if it is more than one in ten, it will be difficult for the population's strength to furnish it, while if it falls below, the State's requirements will not be adequately met. In ancient times, the Empire's riches lay entirely in the north-west. As for the prefectures of Suzhou, Songjiang, Changzhou, and Zhenjiang in Jiangnan, and Hangzhou, Jiaxing, and Huzhou of Zhejiang, before the Han and Tang they were a land of swamp and nothing more. After Qian Liu had got the land by theft and occupied it, and the Southern Song established their partial dominion there, the people congregated and the land was opened up, becoming thereupon a reservoir of wealth and revenue.[9] In their early years, the defunct Ming perceived that the south-eastern revenues were adequate to furnish their requirements, and thought thenceforward only to exhaust the south-east's riches, giving no further thought to the north-west. The consequence was that the tax revenues from the north-west diminished daily, while the population daily grew more indigent; until, in the concluding generation, thieves and robbers burst forth like thickets, and could not be put down.

After our present Dynasty set up its tripods, it did away entirely with the defunct Ming's mischief-ridden policies. Only in the matter of the true way for creating wealth has it so far failed to restore the ancient practices of the Three Dynasties. Although commands to reclaim waste and open up new soil are frequently sent down, the responsible authorities being, every man of them, devoid of any searching exploration of the problem, these orders have as yet resulted in no concrete benefit.

I am now charged to oversee the works upon the Yellow River, and as I bend my hasty steps over the flat and empty countryside, what strikes my gaze is that wild grass predominates over cereal crops within the territory of Huai'an, Xuzhou, and Fengyang.[10] It was because of this that previously, in my "On managing the Yellow River works" memorials, I asked permission to recruit "accretion men" to reclaim and cultivate the waste beside the river, for the consolidation of the dikes.[11] When we were just about to utilize these wastes, owners emerged to claim them, many of them saying that this was their tax-paying arable. Bewildered, I enquired in detail, and learned for the first time that the people of Huai'an, Xuzhou, and Fengyang put no effort whatsoever into farming labours, but merely look to Heaven and Earth to nourish and raise up on their behalf. Their rice, hemp, pulse, and wheat are often planted higgledy-piggledy amidst the wild grass and rushes. They do not plough or weed and are ignorant of irrigation and manuring. There are even cases in which rice, hemp, pulse, and wheat have not been planted at all, and the land-owners merely mow the grass in order to supply their livelihood. This happens everywhere within this region.

Upon enquiry as to the cause, one finds that, generally speaking, the annual yield of grass per *mu* of ground will be above 1,000 catties where the grass is thick, 400 to 500 where it is but thin. When he who cuts 1,000 catties takes them to the city, their worth is five or six tenths of a tael of silver. If we subtract half for the cost of transport, he will actually gain some two tenths odd. When he who cuts 400 catties takes them to the city, their worth is two tenths of a tael. If we subtract half for the cost of transport, he will actually gain one tenth. Meanwhile, the quota-governed tax demands no more than one or two hundredths of a tael per *mu*. From the point of view of the small people, on one *mu* of land, without expenditure on seeds or oxen, without the effort of ploughing and weeding, and paying no more than a hundredth or so of a tael per year in quota tax, they can gain one or two tenths of a tael and more in payment for their grass. This is why the practice has grown up into a custom, bringing the abandonment of the Dynasty's territory to the pass which I have mentioned. Such is the mischief of the taxes being light, the people lazy.

Since antiquity, the basis for the management of rural areas has been that a superior farmer feeds nine people, a second-class farmer eight people, a third-class farmer seven people, a fourth-class farmer six people, and a fifth-class farmer five people. Now it may reasonably be observed that the land the farmers have received will vary in fertility, so that the numbers fed per farmer differ in accordance; but generally speaking, where an individual toils diligently the whole year round, the grain that will be harvested by one who has received fertile soil will feed no more than nine, while the grain that will be harvested by one who has received poor soil will still feed five. I have made enquiries of the people of Suzhou, Songjiang, Jiaxing, and Huzhou, and learned that one able-bodied individual can cultivate no more than twelve or thirteen *mu* of paddy. His annual harvest will not be more than thirty bushels or so for fertile land, and if his land is poor, he ought still to reap twenty. On the assumption that each person eats one pint of grain a day, he who harvests thirty bushels or so can feed nine people, and he who harvests twenty, five to six people. When we take the standard of antiquity and test it in the light of present-day experience, we shall find no discrepancy.

If, out of the five classes of farmer, we take the average of the capacities of the top, third, and fifth grades, each individual can feed seven people. From these we must deduct the farmer and his womenfolk, together with his aged father and his juvenile sons, who will between them eat about a half; there then remains the other half for feeding others. In antiquity there were four categories of the population and no more, and these were scholars, farmers, artisans, and merchants. Scholars were able to make clear the true way of the former kings, and to assist the lord of men in governing the Empire. Farmers were able to exert their strength in plots and fields, harvesting the grain for the nutrition of the Empire. Artisans made necessary implements to serve the Empire's uses; merchants mediated between want and possession, and assembled wealth and riches for the Empire's profit. There were also commoners in the official service, similar to the clerks and runners of the present day: being absolutely indispensable for government, these were allowed to be appended at the end of the four categories. And of the thus-divided population, those who toiled at agriculture were seven out of every ten, while scholars, artisans, and merchants, and the commoners in the official service, numbered three in ten. For this reason was it that, out of the Empire's annual harvests, apart from what was needed to supply the Empire's food requirements, there still remained reserves against the famine years.

The attainment of good order in the Empire depends on every family being provided for, every individual having sufficient for his needs. Disorder comes from cold and hunger, drifting and dispersal. If the Empire's population can really be made able to have surplus in the good years and be free of difficulty in the bad, who will not wish to rejoice peaceably in the broad sunlight of Sagely governance, but prefer to bring death on himself through brigandage and evil conduct? Thus if one desires good order in the Empire, this can be achieved only if one will first ensure that those who labour in the fields form the majority. And yet, ever since the end of the Three Dynasties, outside the four categories, there have additionally been Buddhist and Daoist monks and priests, plus vagabonds and beggars. Each one of them eats without ploughing and is clothed without weaving, rejecting duty and destroying loving-kindness, plaguing the population and infesting the State.

[At this point, Jin digresses for a long attack on Buddhist and Daoist doctrines. The main burden of his refutation is assertion of the reality of the natural order; of the privileged place of man within the natural order; and of the necessity of the political and social institutions established by the sages to prevent disorder among human beings. These institutions include the Confucian code of precepts governing human relationships, but Jin's emphasis is noticeably on the virtues proper to subordinates. When the sages' institutions are functioning properly, "the practice of loving one's superiors and dying for one's seniors bursts forth, and all the vastness of the sea-girt world relies on this for lasting peace and order." The ruler, for his part, must govern with the correct mix of "active governance" (zheng), "penal law" (xing), "virtue" (de), and "ceremony" (li) to prevent disorder and to make the people moral.

Unfortunately, Jin complains, not only do Buddhist and Daoist transcendentalism fly in the face of basic facts about the natural order and human society; they are also undermining the court's present efforts to realize the above formula for proper governance. The prevalence of Buddhist doctrines in society is causing:

... the mentality of homage to the ruler to express itself instead in homage to the Buddha, and the effort spent in serving parents to be shifted into service to the bonzes. Believing in the notion that one can avoid disaster through repentance, the folk make light of law-breaking; believing in the claim that one may seek good fortune by reciting sutras, they are reckless in donation. When it is a question of their fathers, elder brothers, kinsmen through the male line, neighbours, affinal relatives, and friends, they balk at lending so much as a pint or peck of grain or some small quantity of money; but when it comes to renovating shrines, constructing temples, carving graven images, or feeding monks, they throw around sums in the hundreds and thousands like so much soil. Only when the treatment appropriate for intimates and that appropriate for strangers have thus been thoroughly reversed do they feel gratified with their behaviour.

Buddhist and Daoist doctrines, in short, are not only undermining the state's authority but also sapping fidelity to society's most fundamental bonds.]

... [Not only are Buddhist and Daoist doctrines politically and socially pernicious, but] persons at a loss for means of livelihood, discontented and frustrated elements, together with law-breakers with no place to flee their crimes, frequently worm their way into the company of bonzes. Now discoursing on the sutras and preaching the *dharma*, now reciting mantras and inscribing charms, now striking chiming-stones and tapping bells, now wandering the four directions with begging-bowls up-raised, they mass into their hundreds and their thousands ... to delude the foolish men and foolish wives. In the last analysis, there is no form of robbery and fraud which people of this ilk do not commit; even should there be some so-called real devotees or reverent observers of their doctrine, these are still exactly like unworthy sons or younger brothers who desert their closest kin in order to take up with outlaws. Is such conduct not greatly to be lamented?

As for the path of beggary, although when spoken of it seems to be an object for compassion, the mischief of it is beyond expression. Issuing forth his government and dispensing his humanity, King Wen never failed to accord priority to widowers and widows, the childless and the orphaned, which was because they lacked the strength to fend for themselves, and in their destitution had no one to turn to.[12] When later generations set up almshouses for the reception of the poor and solitary, this was still like the idea which comes down from King Wen. Who could have anticipated that the beggars of these recent times should for the most part have been sturdy fellows? In their hands they carry foul and venomous objects to intimidate the decent people, and in overall command of them, there are the beggar heads. The rations for the poor and solitary are all collected by the beggar heads, who share the fat with vermin *yamen* menials: they do not get to fill the stomachs of the poor and solitary.[13] Not only this, but on any of the folk's occasions . . . for congratulation or condolence,[14] the hosts must be sure first to call in the beggar heads, regaling them with food and wine, presenting them with coin and silver. Otherwise, the beggar crowd throngs forthwith at their doors, shouting and behaving coarsely, and stopping at nothing. From time to time, the beggar crowd will also importune the urban shopkeepers, relying on the foul, and in every way unprepossessing, figures that they cut to make their victims dare be angry but not dare be mean. Half the coin and silver which they thus obtain they use to eat their fill and get drunk on the streets; the other half goes to the beggar heads.

Thus is it that in prosperous areas, all the beggar heads possess substantial riches, live at ease, and eat the bread of idleness. Their warm and well-fed look indeed outmatches what is seen among the families of scholars, farmers, artisans, and merchants. To get one's food in idleness becomes established as a custom, upon which there emerge people who secretly abduct the little boys and girls of decent families, breaking their limbs or removing their ears or eyes, and raising them to take over the captor's begging garb and bowl.[15] When one speaks or thinks of this, it is utterly detestable. As for the rest, such as chanters of ballads and singers of vulgar melodies, practitioners of the martial arts, conjurors, sellers of quack remedies, invokers of transcendents and writers with the planchette, cinnabar-refiners and exorcists, and chicken-stealers and cut-purses, these will not bear enumeration. What are these people? Han Yu wrote, "Those who in ancient days made up the population were of four sorts; those who make up the population now, of six. For every farming family, six consume its grain; for every family of artisans, six use its manufactures; for every trading family, six are supplied by it." Here he was speaking with reference precisely to Buddhist and Daoist monks and priests. Who would have anticipated that of recent generations, quite apart from Buddhist and Daoist monks and priests, there should yet further have been added this limitless flock of vagabonds and idlers, none of whom but looks for his support to the decent and virtuous of the local district?

Now if what is sought is that the Empire's population should have surplus in the good years and reserves against the bad, this lies entirely in there being an excess of those who toil at farming over scholars, artisans, and merchants. If, therefore, for each ten individuals one reckons farmers seven, and scholars, artisans, and merchants three, it is with the good reason that when one subtracts the half that they consume themselves from the seven portions reaped by seven farmers, there still remain three portions and a half for sale to the scholars, artisans, and merchants. It is, moreover, further necessary that the scholars, artisans, and merchants should consume no more than three portions, so that there remains half a portion in reserve. Since the theories of the Buddha and of Master Lao gained currency, one could not help but sacrifice one individual from the seven farmers to be a monk or priest. If we add the beggars, vagabonds, and idlers, all of whom seek food with empty hands, we must subtract a further half an individual, and of the seven farmers there remain a bare five and a fraction. And then in no case are the food and drink, clothing and utensils, wealth and possessions of the Buddhist and Daoist monks and priests inferior to those of scholars, artisans, and merchants, so that already they have not the frugal character of farmers; while the costs of their construction works, equalling those of kings and marquises, exceed those of the scholars, artisans, and merchants by a hundredfold. Since the Buddhists and Daoists are without techniques for gaining supernatural supplies, in logic we cannot but drive another half an individual from among the farmers off to be their artisan or merchant. This means that of ten individuals, farmers account for a mere five, while scholars, artisans, and merchants, together with the heterodox and vagabonds and idlers, plus the artisans and merchants in the service of heterodoxy, account likewise for five. The three non-farming individuals of former times—that is, the scholars, artisans, and merchants—were entirely dependent for their food on the three portions and a half of surplus from the seven individuals who toiled at farming, for which reason there was always grain left over. Now, however, of the seven farming individuals there remain but five, which means a cutting of the surplus to two portions and a half. If, with two portions and a half of grain, one had to feed the three non-farming individuals of former times, there would already be fears of inadequacy; how much the more when one adds in two more to represent the heterodox and vagabonds and idlers, plus artisans and merchants in the service of heterodoxy, who have arisen in their throngs and vie for feeding! No wonder, then, that cold and hunger are not avoided even in good years, while in the bad years corpses lie in piles. Such is the mischief of producers being few, consumers many.

Alas! These three mischiefs are of the deepest and most pressing relevance towards the population's livelihood and the budget of the State; how can we fail to design countermeasures with the utmost urgency? The proper way for such designing lies solely in developing conservancy of water. Once conservancy of water has been put in hand, in every place the soil will be rich and fertile. This achieved, if, adhering to the rule of one in ten, one levies tribute in accordance with the different types of soil, the taxes will not be light, nor yet the people lazy. One should then place a severe interdiction on all the heterodox, and on all vagabonds and idlers, forbidding authorities and public alike to show them charity, but having all of them reform themselves and become decent people. Each single one of them ought to be given land and entered in the population registers, so that they may eat the fruits of their own toil, using their surplus efforts in the service of the Sovereign. If this is done, within the decade prosperity will reign among the populace, abundance among material things; the tax receipts will multiply, and we shall evermore be free of sighs of desperation at the Board of Revenue.

Notes

1. The names Tang and Yu refer to Yao and Shun.
2. Jin's reference to cords (for stringing coins together) is a literary archaism: in Ming and Qing China, the central government reserves were kept in silver bullion.
3. The "Kingly institutions" chapter of *The Book of Rites*.
4. Reading *ba*, "eight," for *ren*, "person."
5. The "comprehensive registers" are the "comprehensive registers of land taxes and service imposts" compiled at provincial level to record the tax liabilities of each subordinate jurisdiction.

6. "Master Kong" is Confucius, and "Master Meng," Mencius. For the quotations, see *Lunyu* 8/21, and *Mengzi* 3A/3.
7. Following HCJSWB, 26:7a, I have emended *pingyang* ("level and of a *yang* nature") to *pingyuan* ("level plain").
8. See *Mengzi* 6B/10. When the politician Bo Gui expressed a wish to tax at 5 per cent, Mencius retorted that so low a rate would not sustain the governmental apparatus necessary to a civilized society, and was fit only for barbarians. The idea that 10 per cent was the taxation rate of Yao and Shun is found in this passage.
9. Qian Liu was the founder of the Kingdom of Wu-Yue, one of the independent states among which China was divided after the collapse of the Tang dynasty in A.D. 907. His capital was at Hangzhou, and the state's territory embraced much of the highly productive region to which Jin has just alluded. Jin also refers to the retreat of the Song court to Hangzhou after North China was lost to the Jürchen in 1127. In fact, the economic development of the "Wu-Yue" region had begun much earlier.
10. Emending *haocai* to *haolai*, as do the HCJSWB editors. If *haocai* is correct, the literal meaning would appear to be some kind of artemisia or daisy. A literal reading is not necessarily appropriate, however.
11. Jin's reference is probably to his "Seventh memorial respectfully expounding the management of operations" (*Jin Wenxiang Gong zoushu*, 2:26a-32a). This advocates the stationing of troops along the sites where dikes were to be built, in the first instance to supervise construction, and subsequently, once the dikes were finished, to guard them against wreckers. Some of the dikes were to be built initially to a width of sixty Chinese feet at the bottom and twenty at the top. They would then need to be built up thicker and higher year by year by the addition of more soil, a process called *jiabang*. The responsibility for doing this, Jin suggested, should fall to the soldiers. Since, however, the task was too heavy for the troops alone, each soldier was to recruit four "accretion men" (*bangding*) to live together with him on the dike, and share the work on the 450 Chinese feet of dike for which he was responsible. It was for the subsistence of this work force that Jin proposed the reclamation of the waste beside the river. He wanted to designate all land up to 1,800 Chinese feet away from the dikes as "river land," and to distribute it to the "accretion men" for cultivation. Wherever there was land within this belt which was already growing grain and paying tax, the owner was either to become an "accretion man" himself, or else to assign some members of his family to be "accretion men."

12. King Wen was the benevolent and virtuous father of King Wu, founder of the ancient Zhou dynasty. For Confucians, Kings Wen and Wu were second only to Yao and Shun as the ultimate role models for rulers.
13. "Rations for the poor and solitary" were a regular, quota-governed allocation from that portion of each county's annual tax revenue which was retained within the county for the needs of local administration. By the late seventeenth century, they were probably commonly issued in monetary form.
14. Jin is referring to family occasions such as weddings and funerals.
15. These shocking allegations (which are surely quite believable) were presumably too much for the HCJSWB editors, who replaced them with the following, less offensive, wording: "there emerge those who abduct and sell the sons and daughters of decent families, or who form gangs and break and enter, thieve and plunder, and go out on the rampage."

*   *   *   *   *

Text 4.B

Edict defending the principle of the state deriving income from lending investment capital[1]
Date: 1738
Author: Delivered orally by the Qianlong emperor.
Source: *Shangyu dang,* Qianlong 3/6/14; QSL/QL, 70:23a-25b.

The word "profit" has always been something not shunned by Sages, although the merely worthy will approach it with some circumspection. In explicating the four concepts of "origination," "development," "profit," and "soundness," the *Wenyan* appendix to *The Book of Changes* says "Profit is the harmonization of righteousness.... [The princely man] ... will profit things to such an extent that righteousness is harmonized." The *Xici* commentary has it that "to use resources profitably, make one's words correct, and forbid the people from wrong-doing, is called righteousness." *The Analects* likewise says "to profit the people through what they find profitable," which serves precisely to illuminate the meaning of *The Book of Changes.*[2] It is only selfishness and being led by profit that are improper. For there is basically no disjunction between righteousness and profit. If one uses them to profit things outside oneself, then one is public-spirited and broad; profit in this case is righteousness. If the use one makes is to profit oneself, then one is covetous and narrow; in this case, profit is harmfulness. The men of later ages only saw the harmfulness of talk of profit, on which they separated righteousness and profit, and made them into two distinct paths, as mutually incompatible as ice and burning coals, or fire and water. It was because Mencius feared that people would forsake righteousness in talk of profit, daily scurrying towards harm without being aware of it, that he pronounced those words "Why insist on saying 'profit'"?[3]

What is meant by "profiting things outside oneself" is to contrive the population's food and clothing through their own resources; those in authority above them do no more than to direct and plan on their behalf. What is meant by "profiting oneself" is to fleece and amass with heavy taxes, taking the subject people's fat to fill the treasuries of the Court, so that the people's strength is ever more exhausted while their resentment daily mounts. What harm is there greater than this? Now Emida has memorialized about the people's dikes of Haiyang and five other counties of Chaozhou Prefecture in Guangdong, asking leave to lend 100,000 taels of customs revenue to merchants, so that they may manage the funds and produce interest with which restoration may be gradually put in hand. This was discussed by the Board of Revenue, who advised approval. Opining that a governor-general should not talk of profit, the censor Chen Gaoxiang submitted a further memorial, which We turned over to you for joint deliberation. Each expressing his opinion, you in turn presented two divergent points of view. Perusing the second of these statements, We find that it holds that it is not right to lend government funds for management, in order to carry out public business. There is nothing incorrect about such a position. However, when it comes to managing the Empire's affairs, it is necessary to grasp the total situation, with an eye to feasibility. The restoration of the dikes of the six counties is a task for which the petty populace is properly responsible. It is because their resources are insufficient that they depend upon the government to do the restoration, and yet the public funds available in

Guangdong in turn do not suffice to meet the needs of public business in that province. There is no option but to take the step of entrusting funds for management.

We find that the merchants of Guangdong have not much capital. They often borrow, without flinching at the heavy interest, in order to contrive their profits. It is for this reason that government funds have always hitherto been lent to them, as a plan for showing liberality to merchants, who pay the interest and buy salt. If now customs revenues are lent to them, not only will it be possible to bring about some small alleviation of the merchants' difficulties, but there will also be benefit to the people's farmland. It would certainly be worthy of description as accommodating to both parties. If one thinks lending official funds for building dikes to be improper, so also is the merchants' borrowing of official funds in order to buy salt. If one extends this to the funds for gracious succour to the servicemen both in the capital and in the provinces, these are all derived from monies managed to yield a return. If one considers profit-making to be wrong, then should one suddenly break off the awards made up till now to servicemen in order to provide for their wedding and funeral expenses? Since the gracious succour to the servicemen cannot be broken off, and there is regularity in State expenditures, from whence are these extraordinary awards to be financed? When in the future someone adduces the precedent of the Haiyang dike-works to request the discontinuation of these last investments, do you think that you will recommend approval or rejection? It may be seen that there is a principle of flexibility according to the times, and that this should commend itself to those deliberating on the Empire's business. One's understanding cannot but be broad.

We have already thoroughly considered the distinction between taking righteousness as profit, and taking profit to be profit.[4] In present circumstances, there is truly nothing for it but to calculate on a broad basis and act according to expediency. If at a future date the State's resources are abundant, and every family and individual among the people has sufficient, however could it not be possible to make adjustments to the measures now adopted? It is commanded that this matter be dealt with in accordance with the first report. You are to circulate the texts of both reports together with Our Edict, so that the governors-general and governors of all provinces may note the following. To think profit-producing management of funds *for its own sake*—that is, when it is not a question of bringing substantial benefit to the folk's livelihood—to be a good way of performing public business, is to fail to understand the proper essence of administration.

Notes

1. This title has been supplied by the translator.
2. For the "four concepts" and the *Wenyan* exegesis on them, see under the first hexagram of *The Book of Changes*. There is an error (corrected in the *Shilu* version) in the quotation from the *Xici* commentary, 2/1. *Li*, "profit" should read *li*, "regulate," etc. The corrected version reads "to manage wealth" instead of "to use resources profitably," and the quotation loses its point. For the quotation from *The Analects*, see *Lunyu* 20/2.
3. This is an allusion to the famous opening lines of *Mencius*, in which the philosopher, asked by the King of Liang what he has brought to profit the kingdom, replies, "Why must Your Majesty insist on saying 'profit'? I have nothing more to offer than benevolence and righteousness." See *Mengzi* 1A/1.
4. Cf. the concluding paragraph of the "Great Learning" chapter of *The Book of Rites.*

*   *   *   *   *

Text 4.C

From letters to responsible officials discussing operational expenses
Date: Mid-eighteenth century
Author: Chen Hongmou, in various capacities.
Source: HCJSWB, 26:20b-21a; text compared with Chen Hongmou, *Peiyuan Tang shouzha jiecun* [Surviving Copies of Correspondence from the Peiyuan Hall] (1823; edition of 1872), 1:16b and 17b-18b; 2:7b; and 3:8b.

In managing wealth on behalf of the State, restraint and care are vital; "to determine expenditure on the basis of income" is naturally correct doctrine. In my humble opinion, however, one should ask for what purpose the expenditure is to be made. If it is something that could well be dropped, as being of no consequence or practical effect, then even if the sum involved is small, it should be grudged. If it is something that is of far-reaching consequence as regards the population's welfare, then even if it means heavy expenditure, this ought not to be grudged. In terms of the *Great Learning's* "great way for creating wealth," it is the maxims "let there be urgency in promoting it," and "let those creating it be many" that are applicable to spending which produces long-term benefit, and not "let the expenditure be slow."[1] How much the more since whether undertakings fail or succeed is influenced by timing. If something that ought to be put in hand is left undone because of the expense, even if later great expenditure is made, it will not be possible to do it at that stage. Or it may be that it can be carried out, but much damage will already have been done.

As those in charge of planning see it, to add one thing to their responsibilities is less desirable than to shed one, for in the latter case they not only gain immunity from present censure but also minimize their subsequent entanglements. From the point of view of personal considerations, this is truly most convenient. One's only worry is that were everyone to take this attitude over every matter, each district's various affairs would daily move towards abandonment. This is indeed not good strategy![2] If the project is one of far-reaching, long-term implications, one should neither be constrained by normal guidelines nor be looking for immediate results. Yet as soon as some slight hitch arises in the implementation, such a project will become the object of gossip. The onlookers will not speak of the uncertainty inherent in positive action but, rather, will invariably say that the thing cannot be carried out. This encourages a daily slide towards expedients and schemes of instant efficacy, which are assumed to be safer.[3] Those in charge of treasuries all take fiscal caution and avoidance of malfeasance for ability, and so, in the nature of the case, inevitably confine themselves to plans that do not see beyond the end of the same day. At the time when the expense would be but slight, they are unwilling to embark on necessary undertakings; they act only once the damage done is great, and the cost has become substantial. This was precisely the Sage's meaning when he included fiscal meanness as the last of the "four evils."[4]

How can a poor, straightforward man of books with no superfluous possessions in his house, and some experience of official life, be unaware of the difficulties of mobilizing funds, or unmindful of the hardship of personal liability? Nonetheless, if it is something that ought to be done, the expenditure should not be grudged. Although on some occasions not to spend will mean a saving, on others spending much will also mean a saving. One can only make a mature reckoning as to whether what one has in mind is of utility or not: one may not fear the subsequent embarrassments to oneself, and so forget the long-term interests of the State.[5] I will venture the suggestion that one who, while in office, does not expend both mental energies and material resources, and who adopts ideas as soon as they have been put forward, will certainly realize no worthwhile project. Even if what he does is worthwhile, it will not last. Any lasting, worthwhile project is bound to meet with several obstacles and to suffer several tribulations. It will cause one's colleagues within official-dom to change their expressions and admonish one, taking one to task for wasting one's time. But only if the individual is able to think his plans through, and devote himself energetically and unfalteringly, will he be able to make any contribution in the matter. Once it has been brought to fruition, the previous vicissitudes will all appear as having served as hones and whetstones. This is something that has always been so, and is not only so today.[6]

Notes

1. Chen is alluding to the following passage from the "Great Learning" chapter of *The Book of Rites.* "There is a great way for creating wealth. If those creating it be many, those consuming it but few; if there be urgency in its promotion but unhastingness in its expenditure, then wealth will ever be sufficient." See *Daxue,* par. 19. What Chen means is that in the case of capital investment on projects of long-term benefit, one should ignore the "Great Learning"'s advice to be

thrifty, and concentrate instead on increasing society's wealth and, thereby, the state's resources. He refers to the "great way for creating wealth" again in a letter to Fang Bao, in *Peiyuan Tang shouzha jiecun*, 2:23b.

2. The text down to here is Chen's 1741 letter to the Manchu Deling ("De Songru") as it appears in ibid., 1:18a-b.

3. The above is Chen's letter to one "Lei Cuiting" (ibid., 2:7b). "Lei Cuiting" was probably Lei Hong. The HCJSWB editors have omitted the last sentence, which reads "This has of late become a general malady among officialdom."

4. Cf. *Lunyu* 20/2. The above is an excerpt from Chen's letter to one Gong Erquan ("Gong Yiyun") in *Peiyuan Tang shouzha jiecun*, 1:17b-18a. Material omitted at the beginning reiterates the importance of strategic spending, while the final sentence translated above is a contraction. In the original, Chen says that at first, he was unable to understand why "the Sage" (Confucius) included "fiscal meanness" as one of the "four evils." However, his investigations over recent years have led him to the insight that Confucius was referring to the kind of false economy that he (Chen) has been discussing.

5. The above is Chen's letter to the Manchu Guzong ("Gu Yongfang"), on ibid., 1:16b.

6. The above is from Chen's letter to one "Zhu Xiaoyuan," on ibid., 3:8b. Zhu may have been one of Chen's subordinates, to judge by the omitted opening sentence. This tells the recipient that now that his temporary assignment elsewhere is completed, he should turn his attention to his jurisdiction, and "carry out one or two projects that are beneficial to the people's livelihood."

* * * * *

Text 4.D

Letter to Yunnan Administration Vice-Commissioner Li discussing copper matters

Date: 1723

Author: Li Fu, who at the time was probably acting vice-president of the Board of Personnel.

Source: Li Fu, *Mutang chugao* [The Writings of Li Fu: First Collection] (1740; edition of 1831, contained in *Li Mutang shi wen quanji*), 42:4b-6b; HCJSWB, 52:14b-15a.

On the salt administration, I have already expressed myself in full in my earlier communication;[1] but there is another matter with which I must importune you. Of all the sources of mischief in Yunnan, there is none surpassing salt; but of all the province's sources of profit, there is none superior to copper. In Yunnan heretofore, copper and coinage were two separate matters; but just recently a special new decree has been received, commanding Yunnan to mint coin. This means that Yunnan copper and the Yunnan coinage will now in fact become a single matter.

Fifty to 60 per cent of the Empire's copper is produced in Yunnan, and 30 to 40 per cent in other provinces. Before the seas were opened, most of the Empire's copper was supplied by Yunnan, yet it sufficed to meet requirements, and one never heard of shortfalls from the quotas at the Precious Spring and Precious Source Bureaux.[2] If now, when the seas are open, and copper is being bought abroad, the supply contrariwise shows shortfalls from the quotas, this is because the copper of Yunnan is not being brought forth. Why is Yunnan copper not being brought forth? Ever since the Province of Yunnan established its official copper warehouses, the copper of Yunnan has failed to be brought forth.[3]

When the mining folk enter the mountains to extract copper, the authorities must issue them a price of 4.5 tls. per 100 catties in advance. Once the copper has been smelted out, twenty catties are abstracted as tax for the State, plus an extra thirty catties through the loading of the weights, so that, in all, 150 catties are made over.[4] It is this uncapitalized metal that is the reason for the miners' hardship. If there are any miners who do not wish to take the advance price, but lay out the production costs themselves, ... then, once the copper has been smelted out, they are required, at their own expense, to transport it by pack-animal to the provincial warehouse, and receive their silver. For every 150 catties, they are paid five taels. Again, the wasted days drag on without their being able to collect the payment; on this, the miners who own capital also fall into hardship. If there are those who traffic in the copper privately among themselves, this is designated contraband; the copper is confiscated, and a penalty inflicted.

Now when the miners extract copper, they incur extremely great expenses. There are the expenses of oil and rice; there are the expenses of sledge-hammers and chisels; and there are the expenses of the furnace fires. In transporting copper to the provincial warehouse, there are the expenses of carrying charges. The sums expended are extremely great, and the official price is not enough to cover them. In consequence, the miners will invariably make the plea that the galleries are old, the mountain empty, which is simply their pretext for desertion. In fact, there is no question of the galleries being old, nor yet the mountain empty. Now with the profits of the hills and seas, if one shares them with others, they will be diffused and plenteous, but if one selfishly monopolizes them within the government, they will be concentrated and scanty. If one shares them with others, one will be able to enrich the State and bring abundance to the people; if one selfishly monopolizes them within the government, one will finish by harming the people and embarrassing the State. By the time the miners have deserted, there is a lack of copper, and the government tax revenues are also in arrears, the mischievous practice of concentrating profits will actually have brought about a total failure of profits. This is often found to be the case.

If, from now on, the Province of Yunnan runs mints and casts coin, it stands to reason that, when it needs copper, it cannot but set up official warehouses. However, although official warehouses must be set up, an official price should definitely not be issued. If it is possible, first, to put out notices proclaiming that, except on cultivated land, house-sites, and grave-sites upon which they have no claim, the people are invited to mine wherever they please; and second, to pay the miners for their copper at the market price; then, men vying to direct their steps towards the place where profit lies, the output of copper is naturally bound to rise to several times the ordinary level. Above, it will be possible to lend assistance to the Court's design of minting coin. Not only will what I propose be advantageous for the coinage, but the copper output being higher, tax receipts must necessarily increase, and it will also bring enhancement to State revenues. Below, it will be possible to have poverty-stricken folk enter the mountains and dig copper; acquiring silver by extracting copper, they will be enjoying the natural profits of Heaven and Earth. Not only will this be beneficial to the folk: much copper being produced, the personnel responsible for its procurement will be spared the penalty for shortfalls from the quotas, and it will also be found advantageous to officialdom. The copper output being great, the copper-purchase funds will stay within Yunnan, which will be beneficial to the vagabondish, violent, and perverse elements. If one assembles them on mining sites, so that they can get their food and clothing, and learn gradually to value themselves, thieves and robbers will grow few in number, lawsuits will decline and cease, and customs and governance will both be improved. For profits which conduce to common profit will be profitable everywhere they go; this indeed is the necessary drift of nature's workings, and something to which those responsible should pay urgent heed....[5]

Notes

1. Following the HCJSWB version, I read *yi*, "already," instead of *yi*, "taking," "in order to," etc.
2. The Precious Spring and Precious Source Bureaux were the two metropolitan mints, attached to the Board of Revenue and Board of Works respectively. The seas were "opened" for trade in 1684, after two decades of prohibition inspired by military concerns.
3. Li is using the establishment of the official warehouses (in 1705) as a symbol for the creation of the provincial monopsony. See QCWXTK, 14:4977, and GZD/YZ, Vol. 2, p. 185. The latter source alleges that before the 1705 reform, all Yunnan's silver and copper mines were the private, untaxed enterprises of the provincial chief administrators.
4. The tax to which Li refers was central government revenue.
5. The final paragraph, omitted here, briefly mentions three problems that may arise in Yunnan's minting programme.

* * * * *

Text 4.E

Attack on the investment funds system used by the Eight Banners and Green Standards army[1]
Date: 1738
Author: Shuhede, as a censor.
Source: Excerpts transcribed in Wei Qingyuan, *Dangfang lunshi wenbian*, p. 30.

Plans should be made to discontinue the investment funds held by the Eight Banners and each province. I find: the Eight Banners and the provinces all hold investment funds, whose purpose is to provide for the wedding and funeral expenses of the soldiers. This is truly a good policy. However, making ends meet through trade is the affair of merchants, and is inconsistent with the proper order of the Court.

Those who discuss the matter fear that, were these funds to be abolished, the soldiers would be left without recourse. In my foolishness, I consider this a superficial argument. If, in the capital and all the provinces, quite apart from the activities of merchants, officialdom is setting up businesses and making profits to finance awards, to the apparent benefit of all concerned, this is actually nothing more than collecting the population's surplus wealth, and the regular funds intended for the soldiers' pay, to create a basis for perpetual funding.[2] Besides, if the State's princes and high officials are administering the system, it is still more pertinent to ask what has become of the Court's dignity.

. . . The investment funds system has been in operation for over a decade, and although the accumulated returns already exceed the capital, that same originally granted capital is still being used to earn more profit. This means that a limited quantity of public funds is being used to contrive endless profit. Although the purpose may be to bestow awards on servicemen, after some years of operation there really cannot help but be the mischief of "enriching those above at the expense of those below." As for the provincial investment funds, I find that there are cases in which the original capital has been repaid, and the profit is now being used as capital, and there are still also cases in which the original capital has not yet been repaid in full.

I ask Your Majesty to send down a command to all the high officials concerned, ordering that those provinces which are using profit as capital refrain from deploying all these monies in officially managed operations.... Only a light rate of return should be exacted. There should be no piling capital on top of capital, profit on top of profit; every year the income gained should be distributed in awards to the servicemen. Those provinces which have not yet repaid their capital in full should be ordered to complete their payment in installments; once their accumulated profits are sufficient to replace the capital, they too should follow the guidelines above. If this is done, instead of being held by the authorities, the wealth will be able to circulate among the people, while it will still be possible to avoid shortage of funds for grants to servicemen. The State, it may be hoped, will thus escape the taint of trade.

Notes

1. This title has been supplied by the translator.
2. "The population's surplus wealth" presumably refers to the funds in provincial treasuries, from which the capital grants to provincial Banner and Green Standard units had been financed. It is not clear to what Shuhede refers where he alleges that some of the capital had come from army pay funds.

* * * * *

Text 4.F

Memorial requesting that vexatious imposts be eliminated, so as to spread August benevolence and revive the mercantile folk
Date: 1736
Author: Gan Rulai, as president of the Board of Military Affairs.
Source: First Historical Archives, *Zhupi zouzhe, Caizheng, Guanshui* [Rescripted Palace Memorials, Fiscal Matters, Customs Tariffs], Gan Rulai, QL 1/1/18; HCJSWB, 51:2b-3a.

I take the liberty of finding that merchants and traders mediate between want and possession for the convenience of the folk, while the Superintendents of the Markets offer up wealth so as to make tax revenues sufficient.[1] Thus at barriers and fords there are taxes on goods in transit, and at towns and markets there are taxes on unloading.[2] An assessment is made of the amount of profit gained, and no more than 10 per cent is taken to supply taxation revenues. Below, it does not harm the merchants; above, it can assist the State. The principle is long-established. Because, in their bad implementation, the authorities often take excessively, sums known as "surplus" have emerged. Of recent days, the quantity of surplus has been taken as the basis for recommendation for administrative honours.[3] For this reason, the internal customs station superintendents and other responsible authorities devote all their strength to harsh exaction, finding many ways of realizing the extra revenue. They even go so far as to ignore whether or not there is a quota laid down in the regulations, merely using the difficulty of producing surplus as an excuse for ceaseless exaction, leaving not a hair. Alas for these commercial voyagers! How should they bear this fleecing? How much the more when the injury of it falls not only on the merchants! For every extra portion of tax imposed upon the merchants, the price of commodities goes up one portion, and the equivalent amount of harm is suffered by the population. In other words, the so-called surplus is not the capital of wealthy merchants but the fat of needy folk.

Prostrate, I perceive how Your Majesty loves and spares the masses; Your virtue is immense, Your grace is all-pervading. In the single matter of the contract forms for real estate transactions, the boon of abolition has already been bestowed, which was profoundly to the population's benefit.[4] I take the liberty of thinking that in the matter of commercial taxes also this same sentiment should be applied, and some measure of rectification carried out. I request that Your Majesty command the governors-general and governors of Zhili and the provinces, together with the superintendents of all customs stations, to revise the regulations at all places where commercial taxes are collected. All that is collected should be reported; just as embezzlement and concealment should be forbidden, there should be instructions against realizing extra revenue by harsh exaction. If this is done, the mercantile folk will all enjoy the blessing of it. Here, I will respectfully set out for Your Majesty those things which I have ascertained through my own eyes and ears, and which I positively know to be disadvantageous for the merchants.

1. The same merchandise should not be taxed repeatedly.
I find that the original reason for setting up several customs stations within any given province was that one has to place a customs station at each strategic point of passage. The intention was not that goods already taxed should be subjected to another levy after travelling for a few hundred *li*. And yet in Jiangsu, Zhejiang, Guangdong, and Guangxi there are stations at every step. As soon as the merchant has passed through one station, and paid duty there, the next station is in turn demanding payment. This was not the original purpose of establishing the stations, but is actually the result of bad administrative practice. I request that henceforward, whenever merchandise is passing though a given province, when the first station it reaches in that province taxes it, a receipt should be issued, and the remaining stations should merely inspect the receipt and let the bearer go. They should not repeat the collection or oppress the merchant.

2. The duty on grain should removed.
I find that food is as the population's Heaven. There is no comparison between it and other commodities. Originally, the various provinces had no tax on grain, except that in Guangxi alone each station collected it; thus only Guangdong suffered increased grain prices.[5] For the rest, although the Kui and Huai stations and others do not levy a duty on grain as such, all exact a tonnage tax based on each boat's dimensions, which still means that grain cargoes will be taxed.[6] Now grain is a necessity for poor people, and regions where the land is cramped and densely populated, or which happen to have suffered flood or drought, will in all cases be dependent on the neighbouring provinces or prefectures.[7] If one station's tariff charge is added, the grain's price will be raised by that one step. Would it not be better to remit this trifling levy, and let the little people gain the boon of hunger satisfied? I request that, henceforth, whenever a grain

boat reaches a customs station, it should only be inspected to see whether it is carrying contraband salt or other forbidden articles. The collection of customs duties and tonnage should be completely stopped. Then will the little folk derive endless effective bounty.

3. The fishing boats of the sea-shore ought not to pay tax.
I find that, along the coast, all is a vast expanse of emptiness; the people living there have only fishing and shrimping with which to sustain their lives. Their boats are single-masters, unable to go out on the high seas to trade. The normal practice used to be merely to issue them with permits at their local county offices and keep a check on their departures and returns; there was no question of their paying tax. I have heard of late that the maritime customs superintendents are making even single-masters apply for customs office tokens and pay tonnage, exactly like two-masted, sea-going trading ships. This means that, irrespective of the amount of tonnage due, the very application for the customs office token will cost from four to six taels every time by way of customary fees.[8] Alas for these poor fisherfolk! How can they bear it? I request that the governors-general and governors of coastal provinces be commanded that all single-masted boats should be exempted from obtaining tokens and paying tax, once it has been established that they are indeed fishing boats, not sea-going trading vessels. It may then be hoped that, the poor people of the sea-shore being able to make a living, and not being driven into robbery by hardship, officials and commercial folk will alike enjoy the blessing of tranquillity.

4. The tax on fish-traps and duck-wharves should be entirely removed.
Among the coastal poor who have no land for their support, some catch fish with bamboo traps, while others rear ducks on the wharves. In Fujian and Guangdong, a tax is always levied by the trap or by the wharf, reducing the livelihood of these poor folk to even worse extremity. The receipts from this tax do not amount to much; it makes basically no contribution to the budget of the State, but is of enormous harm to the poor people. It behoves me to request that it be done away with altogether, to the lifting of the people's troubles.

5. The charging of "food cash" at customs stations should be forbidden. When travelling merchants arrive at a customs station, before any mention has been made of the regular duty, "food cash" is demanded. It has been known for the "food cash" paid by merchants with no great amount of merchandise actually to exceed the regular duty several times over. I request that the governors-general and governors of all provinces and the superintendents of all customs stations be commanded to give the clerks and runners severe instructions to the effect that when a merchant arrives at the station, they should collect only the regular duty, in accordance with the regulations. In no case may they exact "food cash." If there are any further creatures of illegality who fleece the merchant folk, and governors-general, governors, or superintendents turn a blind eye to such conduct, the censors should be permitted to impeach them at any time, recommending a severe administrative punishment.[9]

The above are all matters of which I know through my own eyes and ears; I know full well that they are thoroughly injurious to the merchant folk, and therefore I have dared, without shrinking from vexatious detail, to make a crude and vulgar exposition of them. As to whether or not my words should be adopted, prostrate, I beg Your Majesty's Sage discernment to direct.

Notes

1. The reference to "Superintendents of the Markets" is an archaism. The allusion is to the *Zhouli*. See Sun Yirang, ed., *Zhouli zhengyi* (*Guoxue jiben congshu* edn.), 7:27, pp. 77-91.

2. Cf. the 1736 definition of these two kinds of taxes quoted in QCWXTK, 27:5085: "There is the distinction between transit taxes [*guoshui*] and *in situ* taxes [*zuoshui*]. Transit taxes are the taxes payable in transit on goods being taken to another place to sell. *In situ* taxes are those applying in the case of goods bought in another place arriving at a shop to be put on sale, that is to say, they are taxes on unloading [*luodi shuiyin*]."

3. This was presumably a Yongzheng-period aberration from the normal practice in the late imperial period. Cf. Huang, *Taxation and*

Governmental Finance, p. 229, and Zelin, *The Magistrate's Tael*, p. 210 ff. The translation "administrative honours" is borrowed from Thomas A. Metzger, *The Internal Organization of Ch'ing Bureaucracy: Legal, Normative, and Communication Aspects* (Cambridge, Mass.: Harvard University Press, 1973), p. 457.

4. See QCWXTK, 31:5136, edict of 1735 (presumably from after Yongzheng's death, which was in early October) abolishing a system introduced by Tian Wenjing (1662–1732) under which official, pre-stamped contract forms and counterfoils were issued from the provincial administration commissions to the subordinate county-level jurisdictions. This, it was claimed, had merely furnished local government clerks with a new pretext for exaction from the public, and they had made the most of it. In future, members of the public were to be left to draw up their own contracts, and pay tax according to the rate applicable. See also ibid., 5136-37, for a subsequent refinement.

5. Gan is referring to Guangdong's dependence on rice imports from Guangxi.

6. Gan's information here is somewhat at variance with the systematic data later collected by the Board of Revenue as part of the consultation over his proposal to suspend the transit tax on grain. See Kōsaka, "Kenryū-dai zenki ni okeru," pp. 45-46, and 1899 DQHDSL, 239:16a-b.

7. My hunch is that *jun*, "prefecture," is a slip of the pen, and that the word *sheng*, "province," should have been repeated. The translation of the next sentence would then begin "For every levy imposed by a neighbouring [exporting] province. . . ."

8. Customary fees were a form of non-statutory official income whose basic function was to meet necessary administrative expenses for which tax funds were not available. Their irregular nature conduced to improprieties such as extortionate collection. For a good introduction to the subject, see Ch'ü, *Local Government in China under the Ch'ing*, pp. 25-32. The general direction of the Yongzheng-period reforms was to attempt to obviate the need for such non-statutory funding, but it proved impossible to do this in the case of the customs administration (Zelin, *The Magistrate's Tael*, pp. 211-15). Grossly oppressive collection such as that alleged by Gan was very much at variance with the spirit of the reforms.

9. For the translation "administrative punishment," see Metzger, *The Internal Organization of Ch'ing Bureaucracy*, p. 115.

5. The Early Qianlong Liquor Prohibition

Texts 5.B to 5.E present dissenting views about a piece of well-intentioned classicism (advocated in Text 5.A). The famous Neo-Confucian scholar Fang Bao (1668–1749) was moved by scriptural precept, historical precedent, and the economic problems of his day to argue for a ban on distilled liquor preparation in the greater part of northern China. His paternalist concern was that "wasting" grain by turning it into spirits aggravated the risk of famine. In 1737, the Qianlong emperor accepted his ideas and promulgated such a ban, which he later supplemented with a ban on yeast-making. The provincial governors-general and governors generally reported favourably on their endeavours in implementing these new measures, while Fang Bao pressed for their extension. The implementation reports are, of course, revealing about the political culture of the early Qianlong period, but they are somehow less interesting than the criticisms of those who were dissatisfied with Fang Bao's antiquarian common sense.[1] In particular, the protests of Sun Jiagan (Texts 5.B, 5.D, and 5.E) are remarkable for the originality with which they mix expressions of market consciousness with conventional rhetoric about the risk of petty tyranny by civil service underlings.

Prohibition of liquor distillation was not an entirely new policy when the recently acceded Qianlong emperor decided on

---

[1] For a good collection of implementation reports, spanning both the initial ban in North China and its subsequent extension into Central China, see Ye Zhiru, comp., "Qianlong nianjian Jiangbei shusheng xing jin xiqu shaojiu shiliao" [Materials on the Yeast and Liquor Prohibitions in Several Northern Provinces in the Qianlong Period], Part 1, *Lishi dang'an* 27 (1987, no. 3): 27-35, and Part 2, *Lishi dang'an* 28 (1987, no. 4): 16-21, 59; and "Qianlong nianjian Jiangnan shusheng xing jin xiqu shaojiu shiliao" [Materials on the Yeast and Liquor Prohibitions in Certain Yangzi Valley Provinces in the Qianlong Period], *Lishi dang'an* 25 (1987, no. 1): 13-20.

firm action. Already in 1641, before the conquest, the Manchus had enacted a rule against liquor sales in time of dearth. Subsequently, distillation bans, applying to the Shengjing area and/or parts or all of Zhili, were reasserted several times, especially in bad years, before and after 1700. There is some evidence that the Yongzheng emperor was interested in extending prohibition to other provinces, while text 5.A (c. 1720) mentions a "comprehensive ban on wine distilled from glutinous setaria."[2] While the position immediately before 1737 was probably that liquor distillation was theoretically illegal, even in years of good harvests, what seems to have been lacking was determination to enforce perennial prohibition rigorously.

This was what dismayed Fang Bao. Probably in c. 1720, this moralist from Central China, aged about fifty and a scholar in residence to the Kangxi emperor, wrote a letter (Text 5.A) to the Manchu Xu'yuanmeng ("Xu Dieyuan"), president of the Board of Works. Xu'yuanmeng was wont to consult Fang about the explication of the three canonical books on ritual (*Yili*, *Zhouli*, and *Liji*), which were Fang's special field as a scholar.[3] In Text 5.A, Fang gave his pupil all the scriptural grounding he could have desired for the policy initiative of totally prohibiting all private liquor manufacture. He cited *The Officers of Zhou* (i.e., the *Zhouli*, "The Rites of Zhou") three times to justify the idea that preparation of the small amount of wine required for ritual purposes should be a state monopoly, that the state itself should distribute wine to the population, and that less wine was actually needed for ritual purposes than was commonly assumed. Besides three further allusions to *The Book of Rites*, Fang also quoted the line from the *Mencius* about the sage's role of making pulse and grain "as freely available as fire and water." This was to be a motif in his later prohibitionist memorials.[4] Finally, Fang argued that the

---

[2] Kawakubō Teirō, "Shindai ni okeru shōshu no seikō ni tsuite" [On the Popularity of Alcoholic Spirits in the Qing Dynasty], *Shūkan Tōyō-gaku* [Papers in Oriental Studies] 4 (1960), pp. 24-25 and 29; and QCWXTK, 34:5169.

[3] Fang Chao-ying in Hummel, ed., *Eminent Chinese of the Ch'ing Period*, Vol. 1, pp. 235-36.

[4] See *Mengzi* 7A/23, and above, ch. 1, introduction. For the reappearance of this notion in Fang's late 1730s memorials, see Fang Bao, *Fang Bao ji* [Collected

grain saved in three years through prohibition would be equivalent to one year's food supply. This would mean realization of the canonical standard of building a reserve sufficient for one year out of the surpluses from every three years' cultivation.

The last years of the Kangxi period were not a good time for proposing mobilization of the bureaucracy in a coercive campaign against accustomed social practices. However, fifteen or so years later, in 1736, there was a new monarch with a need to show an interest in at least the rudiments of sagely rule. Fang Bao, at sixty-eight, a friend of Qianlong's recently deceased and influential tutor Cai Shiyuan (1682–1734), was well-placed to act the role of sagely counsellor.[5] In 1736 he submitted a memorial which, as Kawakubō Teirō has suggested, would seem to have inspired the deliberations leading to the 1737 liquor ban.[6] This memorial, concerned throughout with economic policy, espoused some interesting causes: prohibition of diverting good crop land to tobacco cultivation; conservation of forest and fishing resources; reversal of deforestation; prohibition of the maritime exporting of grain and cotton cloth, and so on. Whether or not one approves of Fang's economics, his concern with assuring society an adequate supply of the necessities of life was probably sincere and rested largely on personal observation.

One cannot say, however, that the whole memorial gives the impression of unmediated engagement with the real world. In particular, a strong degree of classicist flavour was imparted to the section advocating liquor prohibition by Fang's recycling some of the phraseology of Text 5.A. His recommendations, however, were more modest than the sweeping ban proposed in that document. As a beginning, only the "burnt liquor" of the northern provinces should be prohibited, since North China was especially vulnerable to famine, and "burnt liquor" preparation presumably consumed over 10 million bushels of grain per year.

Works of Fang Bao] (Shanghai: Shanghai guji chubanshe, 1983), Vol. 2, pp. 529, 532, 547, and 553.

[5] For Fang's friendship with Cai Shiyuan, see Harold L. Kahn, *Monarchy in the Emperor's Eyes: Image and Reality in the Ch'ien-lung Reign* (Cambridge, Mass.: Harvard University Press, 1971), p. 159.

[6] Kawakubō, "Shindai ni okeru," p. 25.

In order to assist enforcement, the making of yeast should be forbidden, and the liquor tax should be repealed. Stills should be destroyed, existing yeast stocks registered with the authorities, and a deadline set within which all existing liquor must be sold.[7]

Such was the background to the issuing of Qianlong's first prohibition edict, in the summer of 1737 (which was in fact a year of drought and high grain prices in Zhili). The edict argued that burnt liquor was indeed responsible for much waste of grain in "the five provinces north of the Yellow River" (Zhili, Shandong, Henan, Shanxi, and Shaanxi). The waste was complete, and also socially undesirable: burnt liquor was of no use for ritual and other proper purposes, but was consumed in "wanton drinking" only, and conduced to brawling. Being cheap but potent, it was very popular. If it were effectively banned, over 10 million bushels a year would be saved for the private grain reserves of individual households. Such a result would realize a most important principle of good disaster planning. "Although those families possessing grain will not all be capable of sharing what they have to aid the needy, the grain that has been saved will naturally be among the people, and it will be possible to make shifts and adjustments to ensure relief." The need for perpetual prohibition in the five provinces being therefore beyond doubt, the "Nine Chief Ministers" were to advise the emperor on punishments and sanctions.[8]

* * *

Text 5.B was an immediate response to the 1737 edict by one of the "Nine Chief Ministers," Sun Jiagan. Sun, then president of the Board of Justice, also had his pretensions to Neo-Confucian scholarship, but, unlike Fang, he was a native of North China. He came from an at least relatively poor family.[9] The gist of Text 5.B is that the newly declared prohibition will not only fail to promote domestic grain reserves; it will, on the contrary, be

---

[7] *Fang Bao ji*, Vol. 2, pp. 529-36.

[8] QSL/QL, 42:12a-13b; reference from Kawakubō, "Shindai ni okeru," p. 25.

[9] Li Man-kuei in Hummel, ed., *Eminent Chinese of the Ch'ing Period*, Vol. 2, pp. 672-73.

positively harmful both to the reserves and to the livelihoods of farming families. Part of Sun's argument addresses the administrative problems of enforcing prohibition of a form of manufacture that can, he says, be carried out by any household, using everyday equipment; the suppression policy will be an open invitation to local administrators to indulge their worst proclivities, whether towards corruption or excessive zeal. More interesting, however, is his economic argument.

The argument for prohibition, Sun suggests, has failed to distinguish between different kinds of liquor, made with different kinds of grain. The high-quality "yellow liquor" does require the sacrifice of fine food grains; the commoner and cheaper "burnt" or "white" liquor is made basically from *gaoliang* (sorghum), eked out with chaff and bean pods.[10] Sun's case rests on the claim that while *gaoliang* stalks are essential to the rural economy, the real value of the seeds is not as food, but rather as a saleable commodity to bring needed monetary income into farming households. Suppression of the liquor industry will destroy the market for *gaoliang*. Deprived of their accustomed source of monetary income, the farmers will be forced instead to sell basic food grains (wheat or millet), thus weakening their domestic grain reserves. The demand for the unbanned yellow liquor will meanwhile soar, occasioning increased "waste" of its high-quality ingredients. The hapless farmers, when in need of wine, will deplete their wheat and millet stocks still more to raise the money for the high-priced yellow liquor.

The most fundamental way in which Sun challenges the rationale for liquor prohibition is by suggesting that policy for rural areas must address the problems of glut as well as those of scarcity. By the 1730s and 1740s, although problems of glut were not unknown,[11] the idea that basic food security was the empire's central economic problem was pretty much taken for granted in official circles. Thus although concern with farmers' monetary

---

[10] Even this classification was a little crude. According to the Henan governor, the *gaoliang*-based spirits included both true burnt liquor and a commoner and weaker variety known as *mingliu*. See Ye, comp., "Qianlong nianjian Jiangbei shusheng," Part 1, p. 27.

[11] See, e.g., QCWXTK, 35:5183-84; QSL/QL, 223:32a.

income was nothing new or shocking in Chinese political economy, Sun's suggestion that there could be any question of grain being "piled up unused" was bound to strike his readers as eccentric.[12] In the event, Text 5.B generated keen debate. The emperor ordered the special privy council convened for the duration of his statutory mourning period to join the "Nine Chief Ministers" for careful reconsideration of the distillation ban. Unable to reach unanimity, the deliberators submitted two reports. Although these broadly favoured prohibition, the emperor rejected both, on the grounds that their recommendations were too indecisive. While the deliberators were revising their proposals, at the emperor's command, the views of the governors and governors-general for the five provinces were canvassed.

Preparing their revised report during the autumn of 1737, the deliberators were faced with a range of opinions from the provinces. Provincial proposals included: no ban at all; a severe ban in perpetuity; loose enforcement of the ban in good years, and severe in bad; and a severe ban on "wanton yeast-making" and commerce in liquor and yeast. The proposal for a ban on yeast production had been made by four respondents and was adopted in the deliberators' revised report. In general, they opined, the question of direct liquor suppression should be left to the discretion of the provincial chief administrators; but yeast (the *sine qua non* for fermentation) was the source of all the trouble, and the advisability of banning it was clear. The emperor was persuaded, and thus the issue was resolved for the time being. Fang Bao was not content, however; even before the deliberators had submitted their report, he drew up a new memorial systematically and vigorously disputing the expressed objections to determined, direct liquor prohibition.[13]

---

[12] On the long history of Chinese concern with farmers' monetary incomes, see Robert M. Hartwell, "Classical Chinese Monetary Analysis and Economic Policy in T'ang-Northern Sung China," *Transactions of the International Conference of Orientalists in Japan* 13 (1968), esp. pp. 72, 74 and 77-80.

[13] Sun Jiagan, *Sun Wending Gong zoushu* [The Memorials of Sun Jiagan], 8:21b-22a; QSL/QL, 44:9b-11b and 52:13b-14b; QCWXTK, 30:5125; and *Fang Bao ji*, Vol. 2, pp. 546-50.

* * *

In the course of the above deliberations, one of the privy councillors received some informal advice in the shape of a letter (Text 5.C) from a promising junior metropolitan official. The privy councillor was E'ertai, who had served as a grand secretary since 1732 and was extremely influential.[14] His correspondent was Chen Zhaolun (1701–71), an accomplished younger scholar from Hangzhou with a post in the Hanlin Academy (imperial literary chancellery), who had served as a secretary in the Grand Secretariat for a time in 1735. Chen writes as if he had been personally present at the initial top-level discussions. This is conceivable, since he had also been appointed as a secretary to the important Office of Military Strategy before the end of 1735. As the Office of Military Strategy was shortly afterwards merged into the mourning-period special privy council, and this was a transitional period in court institutions, it may be that Chen was in attendance on the joint meeting of the privy council and the "Nine Chief Ministers," despite his more recent appointment to the Hanlin Academy.[15]

Text 5.C makes very interesting reading. In this letter, Chen conjures up the image of a world of abject poverty in which people unable to afford full sets of clothing rely on the subjective warmth of alcohol to make the winter tolerable. In this world, it is only the possession of the tiny quantity of grain required to supply a wayside drinking booth that keeps many a poor person from utter destitution. All the poor have stills, if only they have a roof over their heads; most are presumably making liquor at least

---

[14] For the leading political role of E'ertai in the late Yongzheng and early Qianlong periods, see Beatrice S. Bartlett, *Monarchs and Ministers: The Grand Council in Mid-Ch'ing China, 1723–1820* (Berkeley: University of California Press, 1991), pp. 90, 139-48, 175-76, etc.

[15] Zhao Erxun et al., *Qingshi gao* [Draft Standard History of the Qing Dynasty] (Beijing: Zhonghua shuju, 1976–77), Vol. 35, 305:10,517; and, for Chen's brilliant early career (which included success in the 1736 special examination for outstanding scholars), Tu Lien-che in Hummel, ed., *Eminent Chinese of the Ch'ing Period*, Vol. 1, p. 81. On the institutional changes of the Yongzheng-Qianlong transition, see Bartlett, *Monarchs and Ministers*, pp. 128-43.

partly for their own consumption. This picture is intended to apply at least to all of Zhili and Shandong; if it is veracious, it provides a valuable new perspective on the so-called golden age of eighteenth-century Qing China. For Chen, however, the significance is different. He hints at the possibility of a social upheaval if the whole people of North China are suddenly deprived of so vital a part of their economy and culture. Sun's argument, he suggests, is over-ingenious, and misses the real point. Only when the people see a collapse of food availability staring them in the face will it be feasible to suppress burnt liquor preparation.

The fears raised by Chen may have lain behind the privy councillors' and "Nine Chief Ministers'" preference for the compromise policy of banning yeast. Meanwhile, specific parts of Chen's argument brought him into direct conflict with Fang Bao. Chen claimed, on the basis of personal observation, that many poor people distilled for profit, whereas Fang had argued that only families of at least middling means could engage in such enterprise. The emperor, presumably under Fang's tutelage, had gone so far as to insinuate that the distillers were all "wealthy commoners" with funds enough to bribe the *yamen* underlings. In his autumn memorial defending the idea of liquor prohibition, Fang conceded the existence of the wayside booths, but claimed that they accounted for only one per cent of the liquor business. In general, only those whose capital was large could run distilleries and accumulate the stockpiles of grain required to feed them. There was, he claimed, no reason why the wayside booths should not sell yellow wine instead.[16]

The argument that spirits were needed as a defence against the cruel North China winter was not made by Chen alone, but also (at this time or later) by the governors of Shanxi and Gansu. The irrepressible Fang Bao eventually responded to this point as well. It was nonsense to suggest that a mere cup of liquor could counteract the combined effects of nakedness and hunger; if indeed the poor had cash enough to spare for buying liquor, they could save their liquor money for two months and buy winter

---

[16] *Fang Bao ji*, Vol. 2, pp. 531 and 547; QSL/QL, 42:13a.

clothes instead.[17] Here too, Fang was implicitly assuming that the distillation was being done commercially, and not by the consumers.

* * *

The rationale for the yeast prohibition, as expounded by the Henan governor Yin Huiyi, was as follows. Weak *gaoliang* spirits could indeed be made by every household and were ubiquitous, which would make enforcement difficult. The problem with *gaoliang* grain, meanwhile, was its perishability; most distillation simply involved ordinary farmers sensibly using grain which they could not store to earn cash income. Wheat and barley, however, the raw materials for yeast, were staple food grains which should not be squandered; and yeast preparation was big business. "The yeast required for wine-making in the provinces of Zhili, Shanxi, and Shaanxi is all alike supplied from Henan; and therefore every year, after the wheat and barley have risen to harvest, rich merchants and great traders take up their stations at the ports along the land and water routes, and at the famous towns and markets. They buy up grain from miles around, and open workshops for yeast preparation. How should the quantity of wasted grain be merely between some few thousand and ten thousand bushels?" Elimination of capitalistic yeast production would directly rescue all this wheat and barley, as well as being a more feasible way of stifling the liquor industry.[18]

The yeast suppression policy decreed in the autumn of 1737 strictly forbade large purchases of wheat or barley by "rich merchants and great traders" for yeast preparation and large-scale distillation. By way of criminal sanction for offenders, two months in the cangue were added to the hundred strokes with the heavy bamboo that heretofore had been the punishment for

---

[17] Ye, comp., "Qianlong nianjian Jiangbei shusheng," Part 1, p. 33 (1738); Part 2, p. 19 (1743, but hints that this argument had been used with reference to Shanxi in 1737); *Fang Bao ji*, Vol. 2, p. 552 (1738).

[18] Ye, comp., "Qianlong nianjian Jiangbei shusheng," Part 1, pp. 27-28; HCJSWB, 51:8a-b; or Yin Huiyi, *Yin Shaozai zouyi* [The Memorials of Yin Huiyi] (*Congshu jicheng* edition), 2:16-18.

illicit distillation. A new supplementary article to this effect was added to the penal code.[19] In the spring of 1738, however, the policy was revised in order to avoid any possible impediment to the normal functioning of the grain trade. As the emperor put it, "if the merchant folk trade wheat and barley, food grains will circulate, and it will be of succour to the population. It is not appropriate to exercise surveillance, to the impeding [of this commerce]."[20] Watching the grain merchants for signs that they were diverting wheat or barley into yeast production would, it seems, have hindered the commercial redistribution of grain surpluses. The emperor does not seem to have been worried by the fact that peasant households could release grain for commercial distribution only at the expense of those domestic grain reserves whose growth was the ostensible objective of the anti-liquor policy.

To resolve the problem that it did perceive, the court proceeded on the assumption that there was a distinction between the yeast makers and the dealers who supplied them. On one hand were the "wicked" merchants "who [went] with substantial funds to the large market-towns and nodal places on the water-routes, and [bought] new grain, to sell it solely to the yeast makers"; on the other were the yeast makers, who "[built] great barns and [bought] in grain on a large scale, fearing only that the quantity [they bought might] not be great." Only the latter were to receive the state's attentions: they were to be located, and prohibited from engaging further in yeast manufacture, on pain of heavy punishment. The court was choosing to ignore the indications, in more than one report, that the grain buyers themselves ran yeast production workshops.[21] At about the same

---

[19] QCWXTK, 30:5125; QSL/QL, 52:13b-14b; and 1899 DQHDSL, 755:15a-b.

[20] QSL/QL, 65:2a.

[21] Ibid., 65:1b-2a. The most detailed account of the structure of the yeast industry is in a 1738 memorial by the Anhui governor. This describes rich merchants coming in person to "places where there is much wheat," buying large stocks of it (in some cases through futures transactions), and opening yeast workshops. These operate for up to a month, after which the yeast is all transported out of the district. The merchants employ local people to make the yeast using their own equipment. The local rich may also accumulate large stocks of wheat and convert them into yeast, which they hold until it fetches a good price. See Ye,

time, it extended the ban on making yeast to Anhui and Jiangsu, in which there were a number of well-known yeast-production centres.[22]

Such is the background to Text 5.D, Sun Jiagan's protest against the yeast-suppression policy. This was occasioned by yet another edict, criticizing the inappropriate enforcement measures taken by Yang Yongbin, till recently the Jiangsu governor. Yang's offence had been, in part, to contravene the policy of protecting the grain trade. He had informed the emperor that, besides having all yeast-making equipment impounded and destroyed, he had ordered his subordinates, if not actually to ban all trade of wheat and barley in the province, at least to impose close surveillance on it. The emperor had rapped Yang on the knuckles and transferred him to a less demanding metropolitan position;[23] but at the end of his edict he took provincial chief administrators generally to task for insufficient diligence in implementing yeast suppression. This was presumably in order to prevent them from reading the wrong message in Yang's transfer.[24]

In Text 5.D, besides declaiming against over-zealous implementation (which, he assures the emperor, is not confined to Yang Yongbin), Sun basically rewrites his earlier economic

---

comp., "Qianlong nianjian Jiangnan shusheng," p. 14. The situation in Shaanxi was somewhat different: the yeast workshops of Xianyang and Chaoyi were under local ownership, but production was capitalized by merchants from Shanxi and Henan who came each year and placed their orders with the workshops. See Ye, comp., "Qianlong nianjian Jiangbei shusheng," Part 1, p. 34. See also Yin Huiyi, *Jianyu Xiansheng fu Yu tiaojiao* [Yin Huiyi's Directives as Henan Governor] (1750; *Congshu jicheng* edn.), 3:21.

[22] Ye, comp., "Qianlong nianjian Jiangnan shusheng," p. 16; also QSL/QL, 68:6a-b for a reassertion of the anti-yeast ban two months later. The following centres of yeast production outside Henan and Shaanxi are mentioned in imperial edicts or the memorials transcribed by Ye: in Shandong, Linqing; in Jiangsu, Zhenjiang (specifically, the county that included the prefectural seat), Xuzhou (specifically, the county of the prefectural seat, Peizhou, and four other counties), Haizhou, and Huai'an; and in Anhui, Fengyang, Yingzhou, and Sizhou (or particular towns within these jurisdictions). For a list of yeast production centres in Henan, see Yin, *Jianyu Xiansheng fu Yu tiaojiao*, 3:21.

[23] Wang Xianqian, comp., *Donghua xu lu* [Further Records from Within the East Gate of the Palace Compound] (1887 edition), 2:30b.

[24] This edict is quoted at the beginning of Text 5.D.

argument to apply to wheat and the yeast industry. Wheat being perishable, the rational thing for the growers to do is turn their surplus into cash. However, in good years the market for wheat is weak, and the farmers depend on the yeast manufacturers to buy their grain. Otherwise, as they stockpile grain which will already be deteriorating one year later, they face a "deadweight of accumulation." Meanwhile, the concentration of the yeast industry in Henan and Jiangsu offers the advantage that the low wheat prices of these regions are reflected in cheap yeast supplies for other provinces. Once the cheap, commercially produced yeast has disappeared, the people of these other provinces will be forced to make their own, even if the local price of wheat is high. The result will be the worst of both worlds: whether the economy of any given region is bedevilled by low wheat prices or by high ones, the problem will be exacerbated by the commercial yeast suppression policy.

Once again, the emperor took Sun's remonstrance seriously. The memorial was circulated to the governors-general and governors concerned, with instructions to comment. There was a general lack of support for Sun's position. A number of the respondents took issue with his argument that, as wheat cannot be stored for long, the yeast industry is necessary to provide a market for the peasants' surplus. Yin Huiyi, for Henan, implicitly denied this by drawing attention to the lively interregional trade in wheat for use as a food grain. The situations in which wheat was plentiful and cheap were naturally those most attractive to large commercial buyers, and all the indications were that Henan peasants were succeeding in selling their wheat despite the ban on yeast production. In any case, since 50 to 60 per cent of a typical local population was at least partly dependent on the market for its food, the concept of a surplus at, say, the county level was dubious at best. Yin countered Sun's assertion that the yeast suppression policy would provoke domestic yeast production in areas of high wheat prices by arguing that no householder could be stupid enough to divert wheat into yeast making when mere subsistence was uncertain.[25]

---

[25] Ye, comp., "Qianlong nianjian Jiangbei shusheng," Part 1, p. 31. A few months later, Yin claimed that it was thanks to the yeast prohibition that the Henanese

The two respondents for Shaanxi, meanwhile, answered Sun's claim that state intervention buying was not a viable solution to the problem of unwanted wheat by pointing out that in Shaanxi, it was already being carried out. The governor said that the combined effect of official buying and ubiquitous private speculative hoarding had been to keep wheat prices up and avert the possibility of a glutted market. The governor-general wrote at some length about the Shaanxi intervention buying policy, insisting that, deliberately hoarded grain apart, there was no question of a great "deadweight of accumulation" which official funds would not suffice to purchase. The surpluses were very slight, and demand for wheat was high in Shaanxi because of popular enthusiasm for noodles. The question of large stocks of wheat rotting in the official granaries did not arise.[26] Finally, Sun's claim that wheat cannot be stored for long did not go without challenge.[27]

*   *   *

With the provincial consensus in favour of the yeast suppression policy, there was no point in Sun's continuing to voice his dissatisfaction. Meanwhile, neither Fang Bao nor the emperor had relinquished the idea of direct liquor suppression. In the autumn of 1738, the emperor ordered that liquor prohibition be strictly enforced in Zhili because the harvest had again been poor that year. Two or three months later, Fang Bao repeated his more radical proposals, calling for a permanent empire-wide ban on liquor and tobacco. The memorial was his most strident yet. Ebullient in dismissing all the opposition, Fang even improved on a common sense proposal about policy towards a kind of bitter

---

still had enough to eat despite substantial commercial and official redistribution of their grain to dearth-stricken areas largely outside the province. Id., "Qianlong nianjian Jiangbei shusheng," Part 2, p. 16.

[26] The acting Jiangsu governor similarly denied the existence of any problem of surplus wheat production in Jiangsu. In 1740, however, there came an implicit admission from Henan that in the absence of yeast preparation, official intervention buying could be necessary after a good harvest (ibid., Part 2, p. 17).

[27] Ye, comp., "Qianlong nianjian Jiangnan shusheng," pp. 14-16; and "Qianlong nianjian Jiangbei shusheng," Part 1, pp. 31-35.

gaoliang grown in Xuanhua Prefecture, north-west of Beijing. The responsible governor-general had said that distillation using bitter *gaoliang* should normally be tolerated because this cereal was eaten only during famine years. Fang, however, argued that Xuanhua would not be growing so much of the unpalatable variety in the first place were it not for the profitability of liquor manufacture and the long-distance liquor trade. Prohibiting the trade would bring about a spontaneous shift towards the cultivation of more useful varieties.

Fang's main concern, however, was to urge that the court take advantage of the dearth prevailing in several southern provinces to ban liquor for good. His argument was that the best hope of convincing the populace of the desirability of such a measure was to introduce it at a time when hunger threatened. This was, of course, a point already made to E'ertai by Chen Zhaolun. Near the end of the memorial, Fang brought forward a consideration calculated to appeal to those concerned with matters of state finance. Referring to the present dearth, he wrote: "If heretofore the populace had kept more of its grain, for every bushel kept, there would have been a more than twofold saving of State funds, compared with [the cost of] official buying and transport [of relief grain]." The emperor ordered that Fang's proposals be considered, and the Grand Secretaries endorsed them.[28]

It was unfortunate for Sun Jiagan that by now he was serving as Zhili governor-general, and therefore had to implement a policy which he was well known for opposing. He was embarrassed almost straight away by the discovery that those arrested for distilling by the Beijing *gendarmerie* were all from his home province of Shanxi. This would theoretically have laid him open to the charge of being less than disinterested in his opposition to the anti-liquor policy.[29] He carried out liquor suppression for a month or so, until he was provoked to write Text 5.E by reading Fang Bao's new memorial. This was probably during the early

---

[28] *Fang Bao ji*, Vol. 2, pp. 550-53; QSL/QL, 76:15b and 82:2b-3a; and below, Text 5.E.

[29] Indeed, the emperor warned Sun about the talk about him. QSL/QL, 81:29b-30b.

weeks of 1739. Text 5.E is an eloquent expression of distaste for the realities of implementation. Energetic activity in arresting offenders and confiscating their merchandise was not, for Sun, an expression of praiseworthy diligence in furthering the public good. Rather, it was an altogether wretched business, fraught with temptations to corruption and unprincipled fiscality.

To understand how Text 5.E is likely to have struck the emperor, it is useful to consider the kind of message he was receiving from other provincial chief administrators during the anti-yeast campaign. The memorials of two successive Henan governors, Yin Huiyi and Ya'ertu, may serve as an example. These governors believed that they had a major problem on their hands. Yin complained to the emperor about rich Shanxi merchants who, having bought up Henan wheat and opened yeast production workshops, transported the yeast to other provinces in quantities of "some hundred thousand to over a million lumps" per merchant. Henan wheat, in other words, had been fuelling the distillation plants of other provinces on a very considerable scale. The magnitude of the Henan yeast industry was confirmed by Ya'ertu, who mentioned, on the basis of registers submitted by the lower-level jurisdictions, that by the end of lunar 1738 only one tenth, that is over 6 million lumps, of Henan's existing merchant stocks of yeast had still been unsold (see below). The total merchant stocks recorded in Henan since the imposition of the ban in late 1737 must therefore have been over 60 million lumps.[30]

In 1737–38, Yin had exchanges with the emperor about the implementational details of the yeast suppression policy. First, Yin addressed the problem of the merchants' existing stocks of yeast, which would unfortunately keep indefinitely and continue to improve the longer they were kept. The policy eventually agreed was that holders would be required to declare their stocks and sell them off in small amounts within half a year, a deadline which would be extended if need be. Later, Yin proposed an elaboration of the recently enacted supplementary article against large-scale yeast production. Specifically, he wanted a greater range of sanctions (positive as well as negative) to be laid down,

---

[30] Ye, comp., "Qianlong nianjian Jiangbei shusheng," Part 2, pp. 16-17.

to encourage cooperation with the policy, and punish participation in the interregional yeast trade (even by carters and boat operators), as well as negligence, collusion, and corruption.[31]

A report of January 1739 shows that it indeed proved necessary to extend the deadline for selling off existing yeast stocks. Denying an imperial accusation that he had been having his subordinates impound the yeast, so that the merchants' capital was wasted, Yin claimed that he was actually showing the merchants great consideration. Although, he said, the policy of monitored disposal of existing stocks necessitated requiring the merchants to sell within Henan (which they resented), the provincial bureaucracy was helping them by issuing them with permits so that they could travel unmolested in the province. Since scarcity of yeast would soon be pushing up the price, the danger of the merchants making losses was remote.[32]

In fact, it was not until the summer of 1740 that the last of the yeast stocks were cleared, following some firm action by the new governor, Ya'ertu. This, of course, did not end the need for vigilance against clandestine yeast making. In the spring of 1741, Ya'ertu informed the emperor about what he had been doing to ensure that merchants did not take wheat outside Henan to turn it into yeast. He had been requiring that whenever any person from outside the province proposed to export from it a load of wheat exceeding fifty bushels, the responsible broker should report the matter to the local authorities. The latter should then notify their opposite numbers at the merchant's destination, so that they could check that the grain would not be used for yeast production. In 1741, Ya'ertu not only reimposed this measure but also asked the chief administrators of other provinces to have strict surveillance exercised over *any* wheat arriving from Henan during the yeast preparation season. This request was motivated by the consideration that the merchants were quite capable of exporting wheat in loads of under fifty bushels and aggregating the stocks later. By 1743, Ya'ertu was ready to claim that,

---

[31] Ibid., Part 1, pp. 29-30.

[32] Ibid., Part 2, pp. 16-17. Yin suggests that the merchants had deliberately put about the allegation that their yeast was being impounded, in order to embarrass the authorities, and thus obstruct the yeast suppression policy.

although continued vigilance was necessary, illegal yeast making had disappeared over the past few years, and the populace did seem to have more grain than previously.[33]

* * *

In the few years after 1737, the emperor received many memorials such as those cited immediately above. All seemed to reflect provincial chief administrators devoting considerable mental effort to the problem of preventing grain which could have saved the poor from hunger being "wasted" through the irresponsibility of wealthy, mobile capitalists. Given this context, it is hardly surprising that the emperor had little time for Text 5.E.[34] Subsequently, in the autumn of 1739, after an abundant harvest, he ordered Sun by name to enforce liquor prohibition strictly in Zhili, so that local grain stocks might recover from the years of dearth. At this stage, Sun offered no overt resistance. He reported that he was having the local officials buy large quantities of *gaoliang* for the granaries, because the more they bought, the less would be available for making spirits. "What you propose is extremely laudable," came the imperial endorsement. "All that is needful is that you put solid effort into implementing it."[35]

* * *

At least as far as Zhili was concerned, and somewhat further, the court persisted in the policy of strictly interdicting distillation and yeast preparation for about half a decade after 1739. Similar bans were introduced from time to time in areas beyond the original "five northern provinces" plus Jiangsu and Anhui, and there was further prohibitionist activity as late as 1759–60.[36] The

---

[33] Ibid., pp. 18 and 20.

[34] QSL/QL, 83:34b-37a.

[35] Sun Jiagan, *Sun Wending Gong zoushu*, 8:8a-10b.

[36] QCWXTK, 30:5125-26; QSL/QL, 199:13a-b and 217:16a-b; 1818 DQHDSL, 160:27a-b; Kawakubō, "Shindai ni okeru," p. 28; and Ye, comp., "Qianlong nianjian Jiangbei shusheng," Part 2, pp. 19-20, and "Qianlong nianjian Jiangnan shusheng," pp. 17-20.

emperor, however, seems gradually to have shed his original enthusiasm. A general ban remained in place, but all the indications are that, except in periods of particular attention (e.g., following bad harvests), it was honoured more in the neglect than the enforcement.[37] Thus, in terms of eighteenth-century economic history, the anti-liquor policy was probably of limited long-term significance.

The political significance of early Qianlong prohibitionism is perhaps greater. The liquor suppression campaign took place during the early years of the transition period from Yongzheng-style activism to the more relaxed mode of governance character-istic of much of Qianlong's reign. Looking back towards the Yongzheng period, we may see the anti-liquor policy as being like the move to double the reserves of grain held in the ever-normal granaries.[38] Both were early Qianlong policies which imitated Yongzheng interventionism but took it to a new extreme. Looking forwards to the gradual erosion of popular welfare provision in the "mature" Qianlong reign, the liquor suppression policy was one which, at least by implication, called attention to perceived improvidence, intemperance, and irresponsibility among the poor.[39] We have already seen that, in the 1740s, professed concern about such defects featured in Qianlong's early rethinking of aspects of famine relief administration, including the decision to terminate assistance to able-bodied famine refugees.[40]

To return to the documents translated in this chapter, Sun Jiagan's arguments against the liquor suppression policy, no matter whether disingenuous or sincere, richly illustrate how consideration of specific issues could call forth quite sophisticated

---

[37] See the texts of the reasserting edicts; and Kawakubō, "Shindai ni okeru," pp. 30-33.

[38] See above, ch. 2, introduction.

[39] The issue of popular improvidence is mentioned explicitly by both Yin Huiyi and Ya'ertu in the documentation on yeast suppression in Henan. See Ye, comp., "Qianlong nianjian Jiangbei shusheng," Part 1, p. 31, and Part 2, p. 20. Perhaps because of the specific context, the problem which both governors identify is not insobriety, but the perceived proclivity of peasants to sell their wheat and spend the proceeds thoughtlessly. The problem of insobriety was, however, mentioned by the emperor in his initial anti-liquor edict (see above).

[40] See Texts 2.D and 2.E above.

economic discourse from certain Qing officials. While the economic literalists were denouncing a substantial industry as wasteful, Sun perceived it as a constructive and valuable response to structural problems in the north Chinese agrarian economy. While others spoke in simple terms of food and hunger, Sun's thought revolved around considerations of demand, price, market, and the cash income of peasants. Voices like Sun's were to become more influential in the 1740s.

* * * * *

Text 5.A

Letter to the President of the Board of Works, Xu Dieyuan
Date: c. 1720
Author: Fang Bao, as a scholar in residence to the Kangxi emperor.
Source: Fang Bao, *Fang Bao ji*, Vol. 1, pp. 143-45, or *Fang Wangxi Xiansheng quanji* [The Complete Works of Fang Bao] (1851 edition, reprinted in *Sibu congkan*), 6:8b-10a; HCJSWB, 51:7b-8a.

In the drought and famine that afflict the circuits north of the Yellow River, our Sage lord has reduced his victuals, silenced his music, and commanded his court ministers to offer apposite advice. Yet I have yet to learn that any of the company has advanced some admirable plan to aid the common populace in its extremity. Now measures to counter natural disaster should be taken in advance; they cannot be put in hand in time of panic. At present, while the countryside is desolate and the population scattered, and the new grain fails to germinate, the only thing that can be done is not to let the old grain suffer wanton squandering.

The way in which the world was ordered in Antiquity was the acme of minuteness and precision, in consequence of which the grain reserves were fit to be depended on. Under *The Officers of Zhou*, all liquor was produced by the authorities. The common people's opportunities to imbibe it were confined to drinking by the commune head and lineage commander at the changes of the seasons and the year's-end wine-feast. Under the institutions of the Han, if three persons drank together without sufficient reason, they were fined one *yuan* of precious metal.[1] In the time of the Three Kingdoms, anyone with wine utensils in his house was punished without mercy.[2] This showed true appreciation of the fact that there is nothing worse than wine for making good grain vanish, in such a way that the common throng is careless of it and does not investigate.

Nowadays, throughout the Empire, there are wine-sellers everywhere, from the great metropolitan centres and major cities down to poverty-stricken rural areas and minor settlements. In rich and fertile districts where men congregate to dwell, the wine-drinkers are always five persons in ten. As for regions with poor soil and penurious populations, here about one person out of six will drink. The drinking of an average individual invariably wastes the grain that he would eat over two days. If one could put a clear, firm ban on liquor, this would mean that what was saved over three years would give the Empire at large a whole year's food supply. As storage of wealth among the population, this would be equivalent to the ratio, laid down in Antiquity, of "three years' surplus for each nine years' cultivation." Where Master Meng said that "The Sage, in his governance of the Empire, will bring it about that pulse and grain are as freely available as fire and water," can he have been merely polishing his words in order to deceive the age?[3]

Among the uses to which wine is put among the population, there is nothing more seemly than its use in sacrifices, rites, and weddings. And yet the law as instituted by the Duke of Zhou was that "those who did not plough made no grain offerings, and those who did not spin did not wear mourning."[4] If even sacrifices without grain offerings may yet be tolerable, how much the more, the year being bad, to do without the wine? As for the public ceremonies, these come to nothing more than the annual sacrifices at the Temple of Confucius, together with the reception for examination candidates and the neighbourhood drinking ceremony.[5] The authorities can naturally ferment for these as need arises. What in *The Officers of Zhou* is called the ceremony wine is this precisely.[6]

The orders now in force enjoin a comprehensive ban on wine distilled from glutinous setaria, but as for other wines and wine-shops, no ban has been imposed. The consequence is that the common throng look on the ban as nothing but a piece of paper, while official personnel are actually able to exploit it to their evil-hearted profit. It would be appropriate to enact that all wine is entirely forbidden. On the day that they receive the order, the local authorities should tour and inspect their district towns; all wine that is already made should be brought to the official premises, where its owner should be made to sell it under the eyes of the authorities, until it is all gone. If after this there should be any who defy the ban, their shop and equipment should be forfeit. If they brew privily in their own homes, members of the mandarinate should be stripped of their robes, while commoners should be sentenced to a beating with the heavy bamboo, the amercements following the law of Han. If there are wine-shops in a given jurisdiction, and the authorities show themselves incapable of carrying out effective prohibition and surveillance, they should be relieved of their position. He who informs on them should be awarded fifty strings of cash.

Now, if in times of redoubled splendour and of harmony heaped high, when the annual grain crops ripened smoothly, the Duke of Zhou yet caused the Empire to know sacrifices that were without grain offerings, and lamentations where no mourning dress was worn, it was not that he deliberately wished to violate men's proper feelings. Rather, there was no means short of this to equalize the masses and build up their wealth, so that abidingly they might be joyful in his joy, and find their profit in his bounties.[7] After a few years have passed, and grain is flowing in unbroken stream, the authorities should, in adaptation of the law of Han, bestow three pecks of wine upon each household every other year, that they may store it to provide for sacrifices, weddings, and the cherishing of the aged and infirm. Only after there has been some extraordinary sign of grace should the wine-feast be bestowed. If this is done, there will be constant norms to the administration, and it will furthermore be possible to rectify the population's customary practices regarding ritual.

The people of this age find contentment in keeping to their old ways and trying to get off with the least possible expenditure of effort; one who tells of ancient practices and expounds ancient morality they will invariably regard as high-flown and impractical. And yet the fact that dukes, high ministers, grandees, functionaries, and scholars who make a point of being well attuned to what befits the times, and would be ashamed to indulge in high-flown impracticality, have held to this position for some tens of years, may serve to show that it is valid. I would not venture to apprise a person of your years of something that could not well be carried out. One who advocates a counsel of this kind commits no fault; on the contrary, it truly is a splendid plan. I look to you to entertain my purblind words.

Notes

1. The *yuan* was an ancient weight.
2. The Three Kingdoms period was in the third century A.D.
3. "Master Meng" is Mencius.
4. This is an abridged quotation from *The Rites of Zhou*: see Sun, ed., *Zhouli zhengyi*, 7:25, p. 28. The Duke of Zhou, younger brother of the Zhou king Wu, was the supposed author of *The Rites of Zhou*.
5. On the neighbourhood drinking ceremony, see Hsiao Kung-chuan, *Rural China: Imperial Control in the Nineteenth Century* (Seattle: University of Washington Press, 1960), pp. 208-20.
6. Sun, ed., *Zhouli zhengyi*, 3:9, p. 51.
7. There are successive allusions here to the fourth paragraph of the "Kingly institutions" chapter of *The Book of Rites*, to *Kongzi jiayu* [The Family Sayings of Confucius] (*Sibu congkan* edition), 8:7a, and to the third paragraph of the "Great learning" chapter of *The Book of Rites*. Most interesting is the first allusion. The phrase "equalize the masses" occurs in a passage about things which were not to be sold on the markets, whether because they were reserved for court or ceremonial use, because they were sub-standard, or because they would have been a stimulus to luxury. The opening sentence reads: "Wherever a ban is maintained to equalize the masses, infringements, even accidental, are not to be pardoned."

*   *   *   *   *

Text 5.B

Memorial requesting that the ban on liquor be removed
Date: 1737
Author: Sun Jiagan, as president of the Board of Justice.
Source: Sun Jiagan, *Sun Wending Gong zoushu*, 8:15a-21b;
            HCJSWB, 51:9a-10a.

[The memorial begins with a transcription of Qianlong's original prohibition edict. The reader will remember that this ends with instructions to the "Nine Chief Ministers" to formulate proposals for punishments and sanctions.]

Gazing upwards, I perceive Your Majesty's supreme intent of diligence in searching out the people's hidden griefs and cherishing the folk through thrift. My colleagues and I ought naturally to put solid effort into detailed consideration of ways and means of carrying out the prohibition, in obedience to Your Majesty's command. However, I was born and brought up in the countryside. I ate the food of poverty and dwelt in humbleness for twenty years and more. Having long observed the hardships of farmers and merchants, and the realities of life among the people, I am acquainted with them in some detail. I truly perceive that this is a matter of great consequence; my only fear is that, if the measures taken are not skilful, the policy will do nothing but provoke harassment, and will be devoid of benefit to the people. I beg Your Majesty to think on it again.

Prostrate, I read in the Imperial Edict that liquor distillation is rampant in the five provinces north of the Yellow River: "It is only because on drinking but a small amount one promptly becomes merry, and because the price is attractive, and everyone rejoices in its cheapness, that those who prepare the beverage are many." This shows that the cause of liquor-making is already appreciated by Your Majesty. I further read that previous prohibitions have been "ostensibly observed but covertly disregarded by the authorities. . . . Cunning wealthy commoners deploy their resources to enter into collusion with the clerks and runners, and have the temerity to defy the ban and manufacture as they will."[1] This shows that the abuses that attend prohibition are also already appreciated by Your Majesty. If, while being aware of the great numbers who engage in liquor-making and of the difficulties of prohibiting it, Your Majesty remains insistent on the ban, the rationale is no doubt that the liquor-makers are, without exception, wealthy people: it is not a question of the livelihood of the poor. If one banned liquor and preserved the grain, the rich would undergo but a short-lived disturbance, the poor deriving everlasting joy and bounty. This is why Your Majesty is banning it determinedly and is untroubled by doubt.

In my foolish blindness, I believe that—to say nothing of the fact that such a ban will cause harassment—after all the harassment, it will still be impossible to make the ban effective. Even supposing that the prohibition did not cause harassment and could be enforced perpetually, not only would the livelihood of the poor and their reserves of grain remain unbenefited: there would actually be prejudice to them. I ask leave to expound this fully, in the trust that Your Majesty will pardon and adopt my words.

Now the assertion that the consequence of making liquor is the squandering of grain applies to yellow liquor. The yeast for yellow liquor must be made from wheat. For the grain one needs glutinous rice, or glutinous millet or setaria. These cereals are the best and finest of the five grain crops, and to waste them is in truth regrettable. As for white liquor, this is made from *gaoliang*, eked out with bean pods, glutinous millet husks, chaff, and so forth. The yeast is made from barley. *Gaoliang* and barley are not normal daily fare, while the likes of husks and chaff are basically rubbish.[2] When one mixes them together to make liquor, one can gain a substantial price for it, and the dregs can be used to feed domestic animals. This is to transform the useless into the useful: it is not a case of making something useless and thus prejudicing something beneficial. This apart, such things as dates, persimmons, and grapes can all be used in distillation. Here the natural riches of Heaven and Earth permit success without the use of grain.

If now it is proposed to ban both burnt and yellow liquor, there will be nothing to meet the requirements of sacrifices, hospitality, and care of the aged. There would really be some impropriety in this. If one does not ban yellow liquor, but confines the ban to burnt liquor, the effect will be to cause the hundreds and millions of million drinkers of burnt liquor in the Empire to turn instead to yellow liquor. Those who become merry on four ounces of burnt liquor will drink two to three catties of yellow liquor, and still not feel satisfied. Thus the trade in yellow liquor will certainly be ten times what it was before, and the waste of wheat and glutinous rice and millet will be incalculable. While sparing barley and *gaoliang*, which are coarse and cheap, the measure will multiply the waste of wheat and glutinous rice and millet, which are fine and dear. This is what I mean by saying that there would be no benefit to grain reserves.

As to the livelihood of the petty populace, how could this be a matter merely of food for their mouths? They must have iron pots and earthenware steamers with which to cook, and iron implements with which to plough; and with all these products of the hundred craftsmen, they need to acquire them in exchange for grain.[3] There are also the demands of land tax, the requirements of clothing, salt, and vegetables, and the expenses caused by weddings, funerals, and sickness. There is no means of providing for these needs save by the sale of grain. And so if grain is too dear, it spells grief to those who are in secondary pursuits; if it is too cheap, it injures the farmers. Only when the point of equilibrium is found can both be profited.[4] Thus if farmers know disasters caused by dearth, they also know disasters caused by plenty. If, over a decade, the bad years number three, the good years seven, it is appropriate that there be some means of drainage for the grain. One cannot merely pile it up unused.

Now throughout the territory of the five provinces, if one does not grow *gaoliang*, there is nothing to provide for fuel, matting, walls, and roofs.[5] If one grows it and uses the stalks, there ought to be some outlet for selling the seeds. Once stills are banned, the wealthy will not buy *gaoliang*, and the *gaoliang* of the poor will not sell at any price. If, while they cannot sell their *gaoliang*, they are still in need of wine, they will assuredly sell their good-quality cereals in order to buy yellow liquor. Whereas formerly a family of eight could raise seven or eight taels per year through sale of its *gaoliang*, now it will gain but two or three. Whereas the cost of buying white liquor was but two or three taels, their purchases of yellow liquor will take seven or eight. While their income will have been reduced, their outlay will have risen. Not only this, but husks, chaff, and the like will pile up, being no longer exchangeable for cash; fruits of the orchard trees will rot away, deteriorating into uselessness; and ox, sheep, pig, and goose will find food hard to come by, and will not grow fat. The natural riches all having been let slip, it will be possible to meet daily necessities only by putting wheat and millet out on sale. If indeed they can find buyers, the family will lose its grain reserves; but if they find no buyers, tax payments and requirements for clothing, weddings, and funerals will all be compromised. This is what I mean by saying that there will be prejudice to livelihoods.

Besides, the tendency of the petty populace to pursue profit is like that of water to flow downwards. This is not something that can be prevented by government or penal law. If there is no profit in a thing, they will not do it even if rewarded. If there is profit in a thing, forbid it and they will do it the more. If stills are banned, white liquor will be in short supply. If the liquor is in short supply, its price must necessarily be high. If the price is high, the profits in illicit distillation will be tenfold. If there are tenfold profits in a thing, the people will contend for it as if their lives depended on it. With counterfeiting copper coins or making gambling equipment, the punishment is as severe as decapitation, strangulation, or military exile, yet even so the people will occasionally offend. This is for no other reason than their striving after profit.

What punishment are we now to set for illicit distillation of white liquor? Our August Sovereign, in his great sageliness and absolute humanity, will certainly not be able to bring himself to subject the people to the utmost penalty over a mere matter of food and drink. This means that the punishment will unquestionably not be as severe as that for counterfeiting or making gambling equipment. If the punishment is lighter while the profits to be made are even greater, one can hardly expect the folk not to offend. There will be no option but to set severe sanctions for the responsible officials. When the officials fear the sanctions, they will search and arrest. The middling merchants and petty traders will all, without exception, lose their livelihood, while the prominent and wealthy families with their high walls and deep courts, where search and arrest reach not, will dare defy the prohibition. Thus the rich will reap the gains of profiteering more than ever, while the poor, incapable of overcoming their desires, will think to imitate them, using new implements and following new methods.

On this, it will be found that dishes for fermenting vinegar can all be used for fermentation of crude spirits; steamers for preparing rice can all be used for liquor preparation. Where the authorities lack diligence, bribery will claim a part of the resources of these folk; where they are too diligent, sweeping arrests will ruin individual and family. Nor will this be all. When it comes to vinegar dishes and rice steamers, what family does not possess these? If the dish and steamer of one family should perchance be used to break the law, the dishes and steamers of ten thousand families will all be suspect. All who cook will become liable to searching and arrest from door to door; everyday utensils will become the pretext for a free-for-all of blackmail. The courts will hear no other cases but denunciations for distilling, nor will the prisons hold all the offenders. Master Meng said: "The princely man does not harm the folk with what was meant to nourish them."[6] If a measure originally intended for the welfare of the petty populace leads to harassment such as this, it shows how careful one must be in laying down new laws.

In my foolish blindness, I am of the opinion that a ban on stills may be appropriate in years of dearth, but is certainly not appropriate in years of plenty. In years of dearth, when every grain is hard to come by, even barley, *gaoliang*, and the like may assuage hunger, and to put a ban on them is truly advantageous. But one should do this only in districts of actual disaster; there is no need to make the ban of general application. Again, one should confine oneself to earnest exhortation and temporary impounding: there is no need to destroy equipment and inflict penalties and punishments. In good years, when the better grains are plentiful enough to meet the need for food, then as regards such cereals as barley and *gaoliang*, which basically are not normal daily fare, it will naturally be appropriate to lift the ban on liquor preparation. Official personnel will then have no pretext for extortion; the people will be able to divest themselves of grain for which they have no urgent need, the chaff and husks which are no use at all, transacting sales to help with their occasional expenses. Those above and those below will thus alike be spared harassment, while the common folk rejoice in the felicity of their perfected quietude. I look to Your Majesty, for this populace's sake, to think on it maturely. . . .

Notes

1. Sun is quoting out of context, and has omitted the opening words of the sentence. The sentence should begin "There is a failure to realize that monopolization of the market's profits arises out of cunning wealthy commoners deploying their resources...."
2. To say that *gaoliang* was "not normal daily fare" was perhaps an overstatement. Cf. QSL/QL, 81:36a (memorial of 1738 unrelated to the prohibition controversy) for the statement that in Henan, wheat is the most important dietary staple, "miscellaneous cereals" including *gaoliang* coming second.
3. This wording is adapted from the *Mencius* (*Mengzi* 3A/4). The allusion would have been immediately recognized, and provided scriptural authority for the *non*-self-sufficiency of farmers.
4. These are received ideas. Cf., for example, the more sophisticated exposition by the Tang poet Bo Juyi (772–846) in *Boshi Changqing ji* [Mr. Bo's Collection from the Changqing Period] (*Sibu congkan* edition), 46:3b.
5. Yin Huiyi produced a similar list of the uses of *gaoliang* stalks, but added—and indeed emphasized—their importance for stuffing the fascine bundles used in river control. Ye, comp., "Qianlong nianjian Jiangbei shusheng," Part 1, p. 27.
6. *Mengzi* 1B/15.

*   *   *   *   *

Text 5.C

A letter to the Chief Minister, E'ertai[1]
Date: 1737
Author: Chen Zhaolun, as an examining editor in the Hanlin Academy.
Source: Chen Zhaolun, *Zizhu Shan Fang shiwen ji* [Collection of Poetry and Prose from the Zizhu Mountain Study] (edition of c. 1800), 12:3a-4b; HCJSWB, 51:8b-9a.

Bowing my head down to the ground not once but twice, I respectfully submit a letter to Your Worship. A rescript came down yesterday, referring the memorial by the Board President, His Honour Mr. Sun, requesting that the ban on liquor be removed, for deliberation by the joint councils.[2] His Majesty is nobly stooping to consult the councils with an open mind.

Many of the assembly are amused that Mr. Sun has consciously taken issue with a fully promulgated decree. Now, if issue cannot be taken with a promulgated decree, why is our Sage ruler referring Mr. Sun's memorial for deliberation, and why does Your Worship not make up his own mind, but consult with the assembly? If the ruler does not behave in sage-like fashion, and the high ministers become complacent, this will be precisely when all policies become inane. My position is humble, and my status junior; I would not venture to speak out in the assembly. But if, upon withdrawal, I find myself with doubts, how can I allow myself to keep them concealed? I will make so bold as to set out my unenlightened views as follows.

On a previous occasion, I heard your esteemed teaching that "In the midst of mischief, there will be advantage; in the midst of advantage, there will be mischief. Let not one who serves as regional chief functionary lightly speak of bringing in advantage or removing mischief." Your weathered thoughts and aptest of designs swirl ever round about my heart, nor can I be unmindful of them. I take the liberty of thinking that in what His Honour Mr. Sun says about distilling, his words in fact have some affinity with the truth of the matter; why does Your Worship find them so shocking? However, starting from the premise that *gaoliang* is only fit for making liquor, he infers that there will be negative effects from prohibition, once it has been carried out; he claims that prohibition will in fact be detrimental to the people's livelihood. This argument really goes too far. Now, if the penalties were indeed made heavy, and the effect desired instantly secured, with the result that households had reserves of grain while alleyways were free of compotation, would this not be the ultimate desire of an administrator, unmarred by the slightest suspicion of a flaw? If it comes to my foolish opinion, the thought that exercises me is simply that effectively to ban distilling will prove totally and utterly impossible.

Why so? The world having enjoyed protracted peace, the people are accustomed to the joys of ordinary living; how should they understand the harm of wasting grain? To them, distilling liquor is but where their strong desires lie, a constant feature of their daily lives. Thus, whereas the wickedness of gathering to gamble or of counterfeiting cannot necessarily be carried out by anyone or done at any time, preparing liquor is a familiar practice which takes little work. Anyone can make profit in proportion to his capital through liquor preparation, whether that capital be large or small. Therefore do I say that prohibition will be hard.

In my travels as an examination candidate, I have passed back and forth through Qi, Lu, Yan, and Zhao.[3] At the five- and ten-*li* milestones, in hamlets of three families or four, on bare, deserted plains where there is absolutely nothing to be seen, only the distillation eggs are stored in every family, and found in household after household.[4] In the cold winters, there are those who place their children in their bosom so that the two of them can share a garment, while below they have neither jacket nor trousers. Of such people, there is more than one whose face is flushed with drink even as his limbs are shivering. As for those who bind grasses together to make booths, hailing potential customers to stop their horses, they have only to beckon and the latter will respond immediately, gladly searching in their purses. Why? Because without costing the money, liquor gives the warmth of cotton padding. The others, barefoot crones and naked lads, who loiter calling out upon the roads, find not one single cash forthcoming. It is only some few pints of grain that lie between these paupers and the livelihood of a booth-keeper, and yet they are reduced to this degree of wretchedness.

Now how could all these folk of milestones and hamlets command the resources to be able to run stills? But once stills have been prohibited, will it be possible to make an exception for what these folk have in their crocks and jars? If one lets their liquor go, the law will not be carried out; if one bans it, there will be no means of settling this generation, which indubitably fills the whole of Qi, Lu, Yan, and Zhao. As for those families which do have the resources and make this their occupation, if, having been indulgent with them all along, one suddenly brings down harsh laws, it stands to reason that they will stop at nothing, but defy the ban unto the death. And these folk who will defy the ban unto the death are also everywhere in the five provinces north of the Yellow River.

Now mischiefs may be serious and deeply rooted, but be irreversible; while benefits may represent the acme of desirability, and yet be difficult to realize. . . . The Board President's concern is that once the prohibition has been carried out, the benefit may turn to harm; unfortunately, the more he argues, the more inept his argument becomes. My foolish worry is that at the very time of prohibition, harm may manifest itself before there has been any benefit at all. It would seem proper to consider and consider once again. Just now, Lord and Chief Minister, with united virtue, are issuing treasury funds in quantities surpassing millions: I will not trouble you with an enumeration of all the relief grants and tax exemptions. You have, furthermore, given attention to the circuits in the capital's vicinity, repeatedly enquiring as to the population's griefs. The harmony and contentment of the population's present spirits naturally need no affirmation. It would seem wrong, through over-violent pursuit of governance, to prejudice their joy in life to even a small extent. Perhaps, instead, one should leave the matter till a few more years have passed, letting the signs of ruin appear day by day. The population's spirit will then be stabilized, and there will be no measure that will not command obedience. In what I have set out above, I offer something of the common opinion, in prostrate anticipation of your adjudication, and the benefit of your instruction.

Notes

1. There was no position of prime minister in late imperial China. In 1737, however, E'ertai and Zhang Tingyu (1672–1755) were the two senior grand secretaries, and they dominated the government to a very considerable degree.
2. The words "by the joint councils" have been supplied by the translator for the sake of clarity. The reader will remember that Text 5.B was referred to the special mourning-period privy council and the "Nine Chief Ministers" for joint deliberation.
3. The four names roughly indicate the provinces of Shandong and Zhili.

4. To understand why a liquor still should be referred to as an "egg," see the photograph of the "cooling kettle" on p. 144 of Rudolf P. Hommel, *China at Work: An Illustrated Record of the Primitive Industries of China's Masses, Whose Life Is Toil, and Thus an Account of Chinese Civilization* (New York: John Day, 1937). See also ibid., p. 142, for a photograph of the assembled still.

* * * * *

Text 5.D

Memorial requesting that the ban on yeast be lifted
Date: 1738
Author: Sun Jiagan, as president of the Board of Personnel.
Source: Sun Jiagan, *Sun Wending Gong zoushu*, 8:23a-28b; HCJSWB, 51:10a-11a.

On the eighth day of the sixth moon of [lunar] 1738, the Grand Ministers of State, being in the Presence, received the following Edict:[1]

"We have received from Yang Yongbin, provincial governor of Jiangsu, a memorial reporting on his severe measures in pursuance of the ban on yeast making. He is at present having all the equipment of Jiangsu's yeast production workshops either impounded or destroyed, so as to stop illicit manufacture at its source. He further reports that this year the wheat and barley harvests have been rather good, and there is likely to be some commercial traffic in these cereals. Inasmuch as it is truly to be feared that evil-doers in pursuit of profit will take the opportunity to stockpile wheat and barley, hoping to engage illegally in yeast production, he is now ordering all his subordinates to exercise surveillance. He is also having notices printed and distributed in order to inform the public, and dispatching personnel to help with prohibition and surveillance. Finally, he says that he is ordering that the old yeast already made before the prohibition edict was received should be impounded, and that registers be made and forwarded with the implementation reports.

"We bear in mind that all the making of equipment for yeast preparation in the past will have entailed cost. Now that yeast preparation is forbidden, in all conscience one should let the people sell the implements, or convert them to some other purpose, in the trust that this will be agreeable to them. If there is a general impounding, their earlier expenditure on equipment manufacture will all be thrown away. This would be entirely at variance with Our intent to show compassion on the mercantile folk. Such management of the affair is far from satisfactory.

"Where Yang says that there are still old stocks of yeast remaining from before the prohibition edict was received, We do not understand to what time he refers. Our rescript banning yeast was promulgated long ago. If, notwithstanding, there are still some quantities of yeast unsold, this shows that when the regional high officials and local authorities received Our rescript, they regarded it as a mere piece of paper and made no solid effort to observe it. If this year the wheat and barley harvests are indeed abundant, then apart from what the folk directly use to feed their families, the authorities ought either to exhort the populace to save the grain, or else to issue an official price and purchase it. It is essential that there be some positive arrangements if the region is to benefit. How can one simply try to end the matter with a ban on trade, and make no plans whatever on the folk's behalf?

"It is a general principle that senior officials entrusted with managing state business should, where there is something inconvenient to the people, promptly memorialize according to the facts. We have no objection to revoking fully promulgated edicts in such cases. If a policy in fact is to the people's benefit, then the senior officials should carry it out wholeheartedly. Their prompt performance, even after several years or several decades, should ever be as on the first day of receipt. Yet with respect to a matter upon which We had deliberated and sent down an edict, the governors-general and governors involved at first made some indifferent arrangements; before long they were developing an attitude of slackness; and before long again, they had come gradually to neglect it altogether. Surely it ought not to be necessary for Us to issue two or three decrees each year on every matter before they think to take warning and look into themselves! There is no such principle of government at Court; nor should senior officials in external territories have such an expectation. Now, on account of Yang Yongbin's memorial, We command the governors-general and governors of every province to take good note. Respect this."

Gazing upwards, I perceive Your Majesty's ... supreme intent of dedicated pity for the population's griefs. If there are any views in my misguided, foolish heart, I would not dare to refrain from expounding them according to the facts. Prostrate, I find that the directive banning yeast arose out of the ban on liquor. It was felt that, yeast being the genesis of liquor, if its preparation were severely banned, one could avoid the waste of wheat and so enrich the people's grain stores. Once, moreover, the yeast trade was gone, one could do away with liquor manufacture, and thereby spare the five grain crops. This was the original intention of proposals for the ban. Yet since the ban's enactment, while those who have failed to be energetic have regarded the instruction as nothing but a piece of paper, with the result that there are stocks of old yeast scattered everywhere, those who have been energetic have destroyed equipment, torn down workshops, impounded lumps of yeast, and searched for signs of trade or hoarding. The officials are kept hurrying and scurrying along the roads; the *yamen* runners extort blackmail in the villages. It may be presumed that what has been done by the Jiangsu governor, Yang Yongbin, prevails everywhere. Your Majesty has indeed already appreciated the harassment that is being caused, and, in Your compassion, found it hard to bear its contemplation. Now if the policy entailed harassment for a time but was potentially of benefit for later days, it would be inappropriate to ruin the supreme long-term design for the sake of present peace and quiet. Yet, having thought the matter over several times, I have become persuaded that it is devoid of benefit towards the population.

Now the five kinds of grain vary as to whether wet or dry conditions suit their growth; wheat alone is common to both north and south. Over the whole Empire's territory, the percentage of the arable upon which wheat is grown is seventy or eighty. Each time there is a year of plenty, the volume of this harvest is especially great; yet, by its nature, it cannot be stored over long periods. Come next summer, this summer's wheat will turn: if in proximity to moisture, it will be susceptible to worm; if to the open air, to moth. The summer after that, it will grow mildew; the summer after that again, it will turn into ash. Even though stored meticulously, it cannot be preserved.

Where the volume harvested is great but it is hard to keep it, the growers wish urgently to sell the surplus from their own consumption, so as to help them meet their other daily needs. When, however, every family is offering wheat for sale, there are few to buy it. On this, the wheat produced in years of plenty becomes cheap but unsellable. Rich merchants and great traders avail themselves of the popular extremity to buy it in at the low price. When, having bought large quantities, they have nowhere to resell them, they use them for yeast making, for yeast, being light in mass, can be transported for long distances. Although in this the merchants fish the people in pursuit of profit, the farmers genuinely benefit from the provision of an outlet for their wheat, for thus they find relief in their extremity. Each therefore is contented with the other party; from ancient times down to the present, there has been no change.

If now one takes the ancient occupation of the merchant folk and claps a sudden ban on it, not only—with the breaking of equipment and impounding of the yeast—will all the merchants' capital be lost: how will the people's surplus wheat be sold? When wheat and barley have been gathered in abundance, and every household has enough to meet its needs, the local people will not purchase; and now as well, yeast preparation being banned, the merchants will not come. The farming folk must toil at their husbandry: they have no time to engage in distant trade. Upon this, clothing, weddings, funerals, and the everyday necessities of life are all thrown into jeopardy. Besides, the time for the collection of tax-silver is set for when the wheat is ripe. If the wheat cannot be sold, there is no means of paying the tax. Not only is there prejudice towards the population's livelihood: there are also adverse implications for the budget of the State. As the months pass into years, what with the humid heat and mildew, the wheat will all pass into nothingness, which will be entirely devoid of benefit regarding grain reserves. In this situation, even though Your Majesty, in your magnificent humanity bestowed abundantly afar, may issue an official price for purchasing it, the funds within the treasury have limits: how could they suffice to buy up all the population's deadweight of accumulation? Besides, given that once stored in the granaries, it will certainly not keep for long, although the folk's extremity would have been temporarily relieved, the embarrassment to the authorities would be unending. This too is no flawless solution.

I further find that the yeast-making workshops are concentrated in Henan and Jiangsu. All the other provinces draw their supplies from them. Now if, by prohibiting yeast making in these two provinces, one could actually reduce the amount of liquor making in the rest, what would there be wrong with putting hardship on one region so as to benefit the entire Empire? There is, however, a consideration that renders this out of the question, namely, that yeast is a substance which every family must use and every family can make. It is just that heretofore the price in the two provinces was low. It is inevitable that once this low-priced yeast is unobtainable, each family will make its own. Severe as one may make the ban, it will not be possible to prohibit people from making yeast for themselves. This means that whereas heretofore yeast preparation was all done in the two provinces, now it will be scattered everywhere. Whereas heretofore it happened in localities where wheat is cheap, now it will be done in areas where wheat is dear. The quantity of wasted wheat will be the same; but the effect will be that where wheat is dear, it will go dearer still because of yeast production, while where wheat is cheap, it will go cheaper still because there is no yeast production. Besides the merchants' having lost their livelihood, there will be not the slightest fraction of advantage to the farming people. It will be confusion to no purpose.

As for forbidding trade and inspecting for hoarding, this has something still more improper in it. Now the sale of millet and wheat to meet tax obligations is something the authorities enforce with blows and beatings. The enrichment of the people's grain reserves in order to provide against food shortages is something that the rules enjoin with earnest repetition. However, trade and sale, although different matters, are the same in form. Hoarding and keeping reserves, while different in name, are similar in substance. If one prohibits trade, one will inevitably hinder the selling of grain at the same time. If one inspects for hoarding, one will be led to examine people's grain reserves as well. This being so, where will be the limit to the plunderings of the officials? How will the common people flee the legal netting? For when the Empire's farming folk are blessed with times when Your Majesty's supreme sincerity and illustrious discernment bring them to enjoyment of a happy year, and widely shower on them wheat and barley to rejoice their hearts,[2] they will be unable to sell their surplus grain to meet their other needs. If merchants buy it, they will be suspected of yeast-making and severely apprehended; if rich households buy it, they will be pointed to as hoarders and subjected to blackmail; and if the growers market it themselves, they in turn will be accused of trading, and subjected to extortion. To cut off, forcibly, the path of circulation, bringing it about that, in sore straits at home for everyday necessities, hard-pressed abroad by shouts and persecution, they can only fold their hands and wait until their wheat grows mildew; while wives and children sigh in sorrow, numb to the joys of an abundant harvest, but rather finding it a source of misery: this is something that the person of humanity, the princely man, should set his face against with haste.

Now there are naturally major principles for the exercise of government; there are naturally constant norms for the enriching of the people. If one keeps the service levies light and the land taxes low in order to conserve their wealth; if one is lenient with punishments and cancels *corvée* impositions in order to relieve their strength; if one keeps the laws simple and enacts directives sparingly in order to prevent their suffering harassment; and if one nourishes them in peace and quiet, forbearing with them over months and years: then they will of themselves arise into the splendid state where every family and individual rejoices in an adequate provision. There has definitely never yet been anyone who could enrich the people by imposing sterner laws and prohibitions on them, altering their proper occupations, and adding to the plunderings inflicted on them.

I would have Your Majesty broadly revolve Your Heaven-like sagacity and, unshaken by inconstant theories, profoundly appreciate the lasting qualities of broad and simple governance, and recognize the bootlessness of prohibitions, laws, and clauses. All the directives banning liquor, banning yeast, banning trade, or banning hoarding, I would have Your Majesty clear away at one stroke, revoking them completely. The farming folk will be enabled to trade what they have for what they lack; merchants and traders will be enabled to make wealth circulate abundantly. The common folk will all enjoy the natural riches; official personnel will evermore be saved the nuisance of investigating and arresting. Heaven's blessing will arrive repeatedly; the population's spirits will be harmonious and joyful. Such is the straight and level kingly way, the vital art for prolonged peace and lasting governance....

Notes

1. After the close of the emperor's statutory mourning period in early 1738, the special privy council was replaced by a new body known in English as the Council of State, or Grand Council. See Bartlett, *Monarchs and Ministers*, p. 138.
2. There are consecutive allusions here to *Shijing*, Odes 276 and 275.

*   *   *   *   *

Text 5.E

Memorial reporting on progress in banning liquor
Date: 1739
Author: Sun Jiagan, as Zhili governor-general.
Source: Sun, *Sun Wending Gong zoushu*, 8:11a-14b; HCJSWB, 51:11a-12a.

With respect to the ban on liquor, I find: earlier, I received an Edict of enquiry about the fact that the distillers so far taken into custody by the Office of the Gendarmerie have all been men from Shanxi.[1] I respectfully prepared a palace memorial setting out what I was doing to stop the preparation of liquor, and trade therein. Latterly, while perusing the *Metropolitan Gazette*, I saw that the Vice-President Fang Bao has again been advocating his former proposals, this time with further extended scope.[2] He wishes to see a permanent ban imposed in every province, north and south; and goes on to say that in Zhili there has now been a severe distillation ban in force for half a year, while in Shandong the ban has never been relaxed. He has yet to hear that the folk of these two provinces are finding it a source of hardship; and wishes similarly to see a ban upon tobacco-growing. He would have the young tobacco plants uprooted, and the growers beaten.

The Grand Secretaries, having deliberated on his words, endorsed them to the following effect. They said that I was now in process of impounding all the distillation equipment, and that in Shandong the bans on yeast and liquor had already yielded definite results.[3] It would be appropriate, they said, to have all provinces impose the ban severely. Even when good harvests are restored, it should not be permitted to revive proposals to relax the prohibition. All should be instructed to proceed according to the Shandong model. It should no longer be permitted to use even the bitter *gaoliang* of Xuanhua Prefecture, or the dates, persimmons, grapes, and so forth of Shanxi and Shaanxi for liquor preparation. Beginning in 1739, all land under tobacco should be made over to the cultivation of cereal crops or vegetables. The tobacco growers should be punished by analogy with the supplementary article on illicit distillation.[4]

I have considered several times, and am alarmed within. The reason for which I have been impounding distillation equipment is that Your Majesty, deigning to be troubled at the scanty harvests in the Metropolitan Province, had issued an Edict strictly bringing down the ban on liquor.[5] I had only just taken up my post and had submitted no memorial; how would I have dared take it upon myself to lift the ban? Besides, that forbidding distillation is appropriate for years of dearth but not for years of plenty was indeed my own original opinion. I therefore tried putting it into practice, to see whether the thing was workable or not. I have now duly been suppressing liquor for more than a month. There is no day on which arrests of liquor offenders are not reported, no quarter of an hour in which I am not endorsing judgements on liquor offences.[6] I find that during the term of office of my predecessor, Li Wei, within a year there were 364 arrests for distillation or yeast preparation, involving altogether 1,448 offenders. Since I took up my post, within one month there have been seventy-eight arrests for distillation of, or trade in, liquor, involving altogether 355 offenders. The total amount of liquor confiscated comes to over 400,000 catties, the confiscated yeast to over 300,000 lumps. It would be hard to give full figures for the carts, mules, horses, and items of equipment. Even these are only what has been reported to my headquarters; I do not know how many cases have been concluded independently by individual prefectures, departments, and counties. The figures include only those persons who have been detained and brought to the authorities; I do not know how many have been taken by the runners, clerks, and military servicemen, and then released through payment of a bribe. Nor do I know how many functionaries and servicemen have received gifts from offenders, and therefore not arrested them. The figures refer only to the actual offenders; I do not know how many *bao* chiefs and *jia* neighbours from their home localities, or porters and shopkeepers from along the route, have become implicated and are suffering embarrassment.[7]

If it is like this in one province, the situation in the others may be guessed; if it is like this with the ban on liquor, the situation with a prohibition on tobacco may be imagined. If bans on liquor and tobacco were actually implemented, then over the entire Empire, the individuals who would stand convicted, and the families which would be ruined in one year would perhaps indeed be beyond numbering. Our August Sovereign, with Heaven-like love for life, is merciful with punishments and careful with chastisements; even for those who have brought on themselves the gravest sentences through robbery or murder, he will consider twice or thrice, searching for some single thread of grounds for pardon. Will he now, over a matter of food and drink, of everyday comestibles, take tens of millions of guiltless citizens, and drive them into fetters and beneath heavy rods? If one truly wishes to establish a strategy to last ten thousand generations, and to make of our Prince a Yao or Shun, it would appear that one should not make such proposals.

At present, in all the *yamen*, greater or lesser, of Zhili, there are stocks of impounded liquor, and silver realized from disposal of the same. As for the liquor that has not yet been disposed of, if it were wasted that would be a pity; if it were stored, that would be pointless; and to sell it is not consonant with proper dignity. As to the silver already realized, some wish to use it to reward the servicemen and runners, some wish to use it to repair their *yamen*, and some wish to use it to defray public expenditures. Official personnel and servicemen stare down on it with tiger eyes, regarding the arrests for liquor as a hunting-ground for profit. The common people wail aloud, the weak losing their source of livelihood, the strong defying the directives. They form gangs in their tens and hundreds, carrying contraband on backs and shoulders as they sweep over the mountains and traverse the ranges. Before the smugglers of salt are quelled, the smugglers of liquor raise their heads. This is why, day and night, I am sick at heart. Varying my means of exhortation, I order temporary impounding, but promise that the stocks will be released next year. Popular sentiment will place hope in the future, and that is why I show this temporary sign of leniency in the situation that confronts me now. How things stand in Shandong I do not know in detail; but the position in Zhili is what I see with my own eyes. If it is held that tobacco and liquor should be permanently banned, and that the common people will rejoice therein, I really do not dare to join in this deception.

With the world's affairs, one has to put them into practice before one understands them, to have personal experience before one raises difficulties. With all the previous discussion about banning liquor and yeast, it was not only the Grand Secretaries and Nine Chief Ministers who produced nothing but empty theorizing fit only for paper: even where I held that such bans were appropriate in years of dearth but not in years of plenty, this was still the erroneous discourse of a man of books. Only after having personally carried out the policy, and made decisions case by case, do I appreciate the following. If one seizes the people's resources, and throws them into muddle and confusion; if one breaks the people's skin, and beats and cudgels them; and if one takes away their livelihood, and throws them into durance vile; then—given that, after a famine, the people are without firm will—when the number of those who lose their livelihood is great, what will they not do? This would seem to indicate that the undesirability of banning in a year of dearth is even greater than that of banning in a year of plenty.

Thus can we see the grounds for those famine relief injunctions in *The Rites of Zhou*, "discard prohibitions" and "do away with searches." Where *The Book of Documents* says "do not heed words which rest on no enquiry," the meaning is that when one puts forward a proposition, one must have facts to validate it.[8] What the Grand Secretaries and Fang Bao are advocating now is nothing but empty words, without practical application. I dare not, in my turn, use empty words in refutation, but have respectfully abstracted heads from all the cases from Zhili relating to distillation and yeast preparation, and prepared two palace memorials, which I present for the Imperial perusal. These are true histories supported by factual evidence, not something that I could have plucked from my own head.

This thing that is proposed is very simple in the saying, but to implement it is truly difficult. Out of the Empire's whole territory, over half is feeling the disturbance of it. It really cannot be promoted lightly. Prostrate, I trust to Your Majesty to take great care and ponder the issue in detail. Then will the Empire be fortunate exceedingly.

Notes

1. The Office of the Gendarmerie was the headquarters of the Beijing city police force. On this organization, see the recent article by Alison Dray-Novey, "Spatial Order and Police in Imperial Beijing," *Journal of Asian Studies* 52, no. 4 (1993): 885-922.
2. Fang Bao had served as a vice-president of the Board of Rites during the second half of 1737. It was a matter of courtesy to continue to use his title even after he had resigned from the position.
3. On the implementation of the liquor and yeast prohibitions in Shandong, see QCWXTK, 30:5125; QSL/QL, 69:32b-33a; and Ye, comp., "Qianlong nianjian Jiangbei shusheng," Part 2, pp. 18-19.
4. This probably implied 100 strokes of the heavy bamboo, as this was retained as the punishment for "illicitly distilling in contravention of a ban" after the enactment of the 1737 supplementary article on large-scale yeast production. 1767 DQHDZL, 40:28b-29a.
5. The "Metropolitan Province" is Zhili.
6. The translation "quarter of an hour" is of course anachronistic, but it is also rather precise. The division of time in question is a hundredth of a full day and night; this is almost equivalent to fifteen minutes by modern Western reckoning.
7. In speaking of "*bao* chiefs and *jia* neighbours," Sun is referring to traditional arrangements for imposing mutual surveillance on the Chinese population. Under the Qing system, a *jia* was theoretically

composed of 100 households, and a *bao* of 1,000. Below the *jia* was the *pai* (ten households). For details, see Hsiao, *Rural China*, ch. 3.

8. For the quotations, see Sun, ed., *Zhouli zhengyi*, 5:19, p. 94; and the third chapter of *The Book of Documents*. As Fang Bao was an authority on *The Rites of Zhou*, to cite the book against him must have been an enjoyable impertinence.

6. The Grain Trade

In Chapter 5, we saw one minister arguing against one particular form of state intervention in the handling of grain surpluses. His argument was essentially that in turning a portion of the surplus into yeast and liquor, society was making its own arrangements to deal, partially, with the problems of harvest fluctuations in a monetized agrarian economy. His voice, in the late 1730s, was a minority one. This chapter focusses on arrangements for storing and distributing marketed grain surpluses, viewed as essential food supplies. Its purpose is to illustrate further contexts in which there arose the issue of state intervention *versus* reliance on the commercial arrangements generated from within society. The examples are taken mainly from the 1740s, in which the anti-interventionist view gained ground.

The convention in Confucian political economy was to regard the state as guardian of the welfare of society. Unfortunately, however, society was not an undifferentiated whole. People who engaged in commerce were perceived as suspect, because their pursuit of profit appeared to be at least potentially in conflict with the interests of society at large. It was common to describe merchants as "wicked" when their propensity to maximize their profits was perceived as jeopardizing the survival of the poor. Wealthy landowners also might be tempted into "immoral" economic behaviour when local scarcity promised exceptionally high prices to whoever held his grain back from the market longest. The common sense of paternalist administrators was that callous profiteering in the grain business required action, whether moral suasion, outright prohibition, or the subtleties of "stabilizing sales." With private grain storage and distribution in the hands of socially irresponsible and ethically vulgar people, the state had to be vigilant and resourceful.

It is no longer necessary to emphasize that the hostility of the late imperial Chinese state to merchants was not absolute, and that while an eighteenth-century emperor might approvingly invoke the concept of "exalting agriculture and suppressing commerce," he was unlikely to have any policy of the sort under consideration. As Metzger and others have argued, it was recognized that merchants played a necessary role within society and had a legitimate place among the "four orders of the people."[1] What is newer and more problematic is to demonstrate an emerging, rudimentary view, in mid-Qing China, that the very grain business operations conventionally identified as immoral were in society's best interests. This chapter explores some of the complexities involved in such a project, illustrates the evidence that can be found, and sketches the dimensions of the broader topic of state intervention *versus* reliance on the market in the handling of grain surpluses.[2]

The aspects of this broader topic to be addressed here are: policy towards a tendency which may be called "supply protectionism" (Texts 6.A to 6.C); policy towards hoarding grain for speculative purposes (Texts 6.D to 6.E); and policy towards the ever-normal granaries (Text 6.F). Texts 6.A and 6.B show two successive Shaanxi governors discussing the details of temporary prohibitions on interprovincial exports of grain from their dearth-stricken province. Text 6.C, an imperial edict, warns against the selfishness allegedly inspiring such export bans in general, as well as spontaneous efforts by local populations to protect their grain from exportation. Text 6.D is an investigating censor's plea for prohibition of an ingenious form of commercial speculative

---

[1]See, e.g., Thomas A. Metzger, "The State and Commerce in Imperial China," *Asian and African Studies* 6 (1970), pp. 28, 31-32, and *passim*; Will, *Bureaucratie et famine*, pp. 186-87; and Text 4.A above. The statement "Exalting agriculture while suppressing commerce was the constant norm of the ancient Emperors and Kings in their governance of the Empire, and [the tendency of] merchants to injure the people in their greed for profit is, by the same token, something that the nation's law ought to chastise" was made in a 1746 edict of the Qianlong emperor: see QSL/QL, 269:26b.

[2]For a systematic treatment, see my *State or Merchant?*, *passim*. Also relevant is Kishimoto Mio, "Shinchō chūki keizai seisaku no kichō—1740 nendai no shokuryō mondai o chūshin ni" [The Tone of Mid-Qing Economic Policy as Seen in the 1740s Food Grain Crisis], *Chikaki ni arite—Kin-Gendai Chūgoku o meguru tō-ron no hiroba* [Being Nearby: Discussions on Modern China] 11 (1987): 17-35.

hoarding which he calls "hoard pawning." Text 6.E, a critical response to an earlier ban on this same practice, suggests that such hoarding, although undertaken for the sake of profit, fulfills stock conservation functions that are most valuable for the community. Finally, Text 6.F is a well-known contribution, translated practically in full for the first time, to the 1740s debate on the ever-normal granaries. Its wide-ranging discussion includes a firm statement that, once the state granary reserves have reached a certain level, the public is better served by having grain left in the private sector than by being forced to surrender it to the state's well-meaning management.

*   *   *   *   *

The eighteenth-century Qing state had a general policy of free internal circulation of the marketed grain surplus, except, of course, for that portion of it which was purchased by the state. "Free" here means unimpeded by "protectionist" attempts to reserve grain surpluses for the communities which had produced them, or by the activities of speculative hoarders. In adopting this approach, Qing government was somewhat similar to that of pre-1760s France, where free circulation, in this same, limited sense, was pursued under a highly interventionist control system known as "the police of grain."[3] In fact, in China as indeed in early modern Europe, local communities did sometimes undertake determined collective action to prevent grain merchants from removing local stocks for sale on more profitable markets elsewhere. Local and regional officials sometimes imposed, or asked permission to impose, export embargoes on behalf of their own jurisdictions.[4] However, we saw in Text 1.A above that

---

[3] Kaplan, *Bread, Politics and Political Economy in the Reign of Louis XV*, Vol. 1, pp. 10-13, 27, 64-65, and (for description of the control system as it applied to Paris and its hinterland) 66-72. The similarities between the Qing and the pre-1760s French approach should not be exaggerated. From Kaplan's account, interregional grain circulation was much less developed in France than in China, and also much less emphasized in government policy (p. 65).

[4] See, e.g., R. Bin Wong, "Food Riots in the Qing Dynasty," *Journal of Asian Studies* 41, no. 4 (1982), *passim*; and cf. Kaplan, *Bread, Politics and Political Economy*, Vol. 1,

when, in 1709, a certain prefect tried to protect his scarcity-afflicted people with an export ban, the charge that he was "blocking the purchase of grain supplies" was sufficient grounds for his impeachment and dismissal.[5] In general, export embargoes were supposed to be regarded as a policy of last resort, to be imposed only when the dearth in the exporting jurisdiction was so severe as to create real difficulties for its folk's subsistence.[6]

It goes without saying that such a compromise left the door wide open for emotionally charged disputes at local level as to whether a particular situation merited an export ban or not. Little of this emotion has survived in the historical record, except through the usually hostile accounts of popular collective actions written by officials.[7] In practice, decision-making at both regional and central government levels was probably somewhat inconsistent. A convenient way of justifying a ban the case for which was not completely unassailable was to invoke moral criteria, or the distinction between small-scale economic activity and big, quasi-monopolistic business. It is not, let me repeat, that moralistic hostility to big business *per se* was a substantive policy of mid-Qing administration, but that the broader, inherited political culture provided anti-merchant attitudes to be drawn upon when needed. In 1723, the Yongzheng emperor, ruling against protection for Zhili consumers (who, while suffering from high grain prices, were losing grain through a bilateral trade with the earthenware-producing communities of east-central Shanxi) declared that what did merit prohibition was "rich households in

---

pp. 19-20, and 189-96, and Vol. 2, pp. 497-500; and E. P. Thompson, *The Making of the English Working Class* (Harmondsworth: Pelican Books, 1975), pp. 71-72.

[5]The expression "blocking the purchase of grain supplies [by or for other jurisdictions]" (*edi*) goes back to the pre-Qin period. An injunction against this practice was part of a solemn oath sworn by the feudal lords in 651 B.C. at the assembly of Kuiqiu (*Mengzi* 6B/7).

[6]Cf. Will, *Bureaucratie et famine*, pp. 186 n. 78, and 187-88; Wu and Ge, "Qing qianqi de liangshi tiaoji," pp. 132-33.

[7]See, e.g., the 1726 memorial of He Tianpei quoted in Abe, *Shindai-shi no kenkyū*, p. 495. The motives of participants in such collective actions are impugned, e.g., in QCWXTK, 34:5175; Zhao Hong'en, *Yuhua Tang Liang Jiang xi gao* [Directives of the Liang-Jiang Governor-General, from the Yuhua Hall] (1734), 2:70a; and QSL/QL, 311:41b.

their quest for profit habitually removing grain by the full thousand or full myriad bushels." Earlier, in 1708, collective actions in Ningbo forced the local authorities to accept the popular view that, even if grain prices were unusually *low*, the citizens were still entitled to protection against conspiracy by "wicked" merchants, brokers, and "local bullies" to buy up stocks and export them in bulk from the locality.[8] Finally, Texts 6.A and 6.B, from Shaanxi, both invoke the penalties laid down in a regulation mandating temporary prohibition "if a given province has had a poor harvest, and there is not sufficient grain for the folk's sustenance, yet wicked] fellows in pursuit of profit privily transport grain from its borders to the detriment of popular subsistence."[9]

Although the Wei Valley region of Shaanxi was fertile, it was also densely populated, while the province as a whole was prone to drought. Unfortunately, similar conditions prevailed in the adjacent south-western corner of Shanxi. When market grain prices were higher in south-western Shanxi than in the Wei Valley, they were likely to attract the Shaanxi surplus.[10] When Shaanxi harvests were poor, its governors grew apprehensive. Text 6.A is a second document from the Wei Valley dearth of 1748 (cf. Text 1.D above). A directive by the governor Chen Hongmou, issued in late autumn, it illustrates a position midway between belief in commercial distribution of grain surpluses and an assumption of the need for regulation. In other words, Chen's thinking here had much in common with the mentality of those committed to the French "police of grain."

---

[8] QSL/YZ, 7:15b-16b; and *Gongzhong dang Kangxi chao zouzhe* [Secret Palace Memorials of the Kangxi Period] (Taibei: National Palace Museum, 1976; hereafter GZD/KX), Vol. 1, pp. 888-92.

[9] See quotation in Text 6.B.

[10] A 1737 request from the Shaanxi governor for authorization of a temporary export ban specifies that the south-western Shanxi prefectures of Puzhou and Pingyang are attracting Shaanxi grain with higher prices. "The little people in their hope for tiny profits transport the grain . . . in a continuous procession, the effect of which is to increase grain prices in Shaanxi." 1934 *Xuxiu Shaanxi tongzhi gao* [Draft Updated Gazetteer of Shaanxi Province], 127:3a. Wei Valley grain may also have been sold further afield in Shanxi and Henan.

Text 6.A was occasioned by Chen's concern that his subordinates had not correctly grasped the principle that while exports to other provinces must be temporarily prohibited, commercial circulation within Shaanxi (especially the Wei Valley region) must not be impeded. While the risk that merchants would contravene the export ban made it necessary to impose a control system, this was to serve the purposes of efficient distribution of remaining surpluses from "upstream" to the eastern counties of the region. The control system was based on the principle that any merchant intending to buy grain (husked millet, in this case) for resale in Shaanxi must obtain a permit. Anyone caught transporting grain without a permit, creating the suspicion that he planned to export, should in principle be required to put the grain on sale at a reduced price then and there. We can infer from Text 6.B that this was in accordance with the standing rule. However, if the offender was willing to transport the grain elsewhere within the province, the warranty services of a local broker were to be commandeered. With the broker standing surety, a licence was to be issued specifying the quantity of grain and the intended place of sale. Procedures would then be initiated to monitor the progress of the grain towards its destination, and verify that it was duly sold there.[11]

While Chen's control plans seem meticulous by modern standards, it does not follow that he showed no sensitivity to the principles of commerce, or no concern for the survival in the grain trade of offending merchants. He worried that over-zealous implementation by his subordinates might leave the available surpluses "congested" upstream, to the detriment of both downstream consumers and upstream grain dealers. The details of his instructions about requiring would-be exporters to put their grain on sale on the spot show awareness of the need to respect local market conditions. He was also concerned to protect the

---

[11] For comparable procedures in ancien régime France, involving monitoring and the use of permits, but not recourse to brokers, see Kaplan, Bread, Politics and Political Economy, Vol. 1, p. 69. For another Chinese example of close monitoring of a local grain trade in the context of a temporary export (or, perhaps, re-export) prohibition, see the 1755 official notice from Lihe Subprefecture in Northern Jiangsu transcribed in Ye Zhiru, comp., "Qianlong chao miliang maimai shiliao," Part 2, in Lishi dang'an 40 (1990, no. 4), pp. 31-32.

capital of guilty merchants from the arbitrary price cuts that indignant law-enforcers might be tempted to impose. In short, he saw a need to restrain grain merchants from illicit exportation, but he was less concerned with punishment than with ensuring the smooth operation of the province's internal grain trade.

Concern to keep offending merchants in business was shown also by the Manchu Zhongyin, the next Shaanxi governor but one, and author of Text 6.B. This memorial, written in early autumn 1752, shows Zhongyin reporting that he in turn has had to declare an export ban, because of a developing food shortage in the central and south-eastern regions of the province. The focus of the document is, however, quite different from that of Chen Hongmou's directive. Zhongyin was exercised specifically by reports of wealthy but "wicked" merchants hoarding very substantial quantities of grain for eventual export to Shanxi. He saw no harm in allowing petty operators to continue to take grain outside the province, but considered that the "monopolistic" and "speculative" behaviour of the wealthy merchants was unconscionable, and must be stopped.

Zhongyin's understanding of the existing regulation was that the hoarders should be required to put their grain on sale "at the place where it was hoarded." However, although the hoards seem to have been kept in the vicinity of major urban markets, the quantities involved were so large as to make it problematic whether they could be sold quickly (except, of course, to other speculators).[12] The sensible policy therefore seemed to be to have them bought by the authorities, and stocked until the critically hungry seasons of winter and spring. They could then supplement the existing, but inadequate, granary reserves for making "stabilizing sales" to help the people.

Zhongyin's treatment of the merchants had the same dual character that we noticed in Chen Hongmou's instructions. Overtly, there was coercion and hostility: Zhongyin calls the merchants "wicked" five times in Text 6.B, and it appears from a subsequent memorial that the county officials "impounded" the

---

[12] The text mentions hoards in Lintong, Xianyang, and Weinan. Xianyang and Lintong lie, respectively, a short way north-west and north-east of the provincial capital, Xi'an; Weinan is further downstream on the River Wei.

hoarded grain in anticipation of the Xi'an prefect's coming with the funds to buy it.[13] The purchasing arrangements, however, were not unfavourable to the merchants, who were to be allowed a gross profit of 0.2 to 0.3 tl. on each bushel. Thus the possessor of a 10,000-bushel hoard would be presented with a gross profit of 2,000 to 3,000 taels, without the trouble, risk, and cost of transportation and disposal through commercial channels. Zhongyin was solicitous not only about the merchants' capital but also about their time (or rather, speed of turnover). When pointing out the risk of glutting the market by making the merchants release all their stocks at once, he wrote that in these circumstances, "the merchants' capital would be held up." This is a strange concern to have on behalf of hoarders.[14]

*   *   *

Declaring export bans might seem common sense to governors in situations such as those described above. The case against such actions was, however, simple: it was well known that vast populations depended for subsistence on regular imports of grain across provincial frontiers. An export ban in a supplier province could have severe repercussions for consumers elsewhere.[15] In Text 6.C, an edict of 1742, the emperor puts the argument in moralistic terms, with the focus on the duty of regions enjoying surplus to rescue those afflicted with short-term subsistence crises. This is perhaps because it would have gone against the agriculturalist grain of conventional political economy

---

[13] *Gongzhong dang Qianlong chao zouzhe* [Secret Palace Memorials of the Qianlong Period] (Taibei: National Palace Museum, 1982–89; hereafter GZD/QL), Vol. 3, p. 637.

[14] For these reasons, I am able to endorse only the letter, not the spirit, of Will's comment, referring to this same incident, that Zhongyin "sounded rather hostile toward the merchants." It was a question, precisely, of sound rather than substance. See Will and Wong, *Nourish the People*, p. 146 (to which I owe the reference to Zhongyin's memorial).

[15] See Abe, *Shindai-shi no kenkyū*, pp. 492-516 for vivid illustrations of the fact of this dependence; and esp. pp. 505-8 for the chain effect, felt even in Fujian, of a Sichuan export ban in 1731–33.

to draw attention to the fact that sacrifices were required of producer provinces to feed urban consumers.

Text 6.C is not a very sophisticated document. It gives a slipshod explanation of how commercial distribution operates to bring down prices in dearth-stricken regions, and preaches against the "selfishness" and narrow-mindedness of local populations who care nothing for the plight of people elsewhere. The edict's function will have been to remind governors and governors-general that the central government was not generally in favour of supply protectionism and would screen future reports of export bans carefully for signs of callousness and irresponsibility. This did not mean, however, that export bans for which a good case could be made would not receive approval. The emperor endorsed both Chen Hongmou's export ban and Zhongyin's action against would-be large-scale exporters.[16]

In reading Text 6.C, one cannot help being struck by the emperor's statement, "there is definitely no question, in places where grain is in short supply, of forcing men to sell." *Prima facie*, this would seem inconsistent with the regular procedure implemented in Shaanxi by Chen Hongmou and Zhongyin. While this inconsistency can perhaps be rationalized, it remains difficult to see how the theoretical distinction between justifiable and merely selfish export bans could have been applied consistently. Local communities were presumably expected to understand that the higher prices which were drawing their stocks away represented lower food availability elsewhere, but Will has assembled evidence purporting to show that crises were sometimes caused in regions which had surplus by excessive purchases for areas of deficit.[17] Was it "selfish" of the people of the surplus-holding regions to be worried by this possibility?

---

[16] Text 6.B (and, for the emperor's immediate, non-committal response, GZD/QL, Vol. 3, p. 577); and QSL/QL, 421:19a. A similar distinction between defensible and simply selfish export bans had been implied in a new regulation of 1737. This specified administrative penalties for county magistrates who stopped grain from leaving their borders when "a neighbouring province has had a poor harvest and has asked to buy," and for superiors who failed to impeach such. QSL/QL, 49:2b-3a.

[17] Will, *Bureaucratie et famine*, pp. 183-85.

In fact, by the early 1740s, the opposition to supply protectionism was acquiring an answer to this last objection. Merchants would be deterred by rising grain prices from buying on shortage-threatened markets; there was, therefore, no need to worry. Chen Hongmou, interestingly, had made almost such a claim at about the beginning of 1743, a half-decade before he implemented an export ban in Shaanxi as discussed above. In one of his directives as Jiangxi governor, he observed that, contrary to popular report, the high grain prices prevailing in the province were protecting its consumers from _official_ buying on its markets by the agents of other provinces.[18] Meanwhile, in mid-autumn 1742, the Shandong governor Yan Sisheng had reported "daily rising" prices in a flood-stricken coastal prefecture and asked permission for a temporary ban on sea-borne exports. "This," the emperor is said to have replied, "is nothing but the talk of a subordinate official who takes thought only for the single district or commandery. You high functionaries of major territorial responsibility must not be of the mind that would block purchasing of grain supplies. If there were indeed no grain available for shipping, those common folk would naturally refrain from shipping it. How should they await your prohibitions?"[19]

The precise argument that low prices attract commercial grain buyers, while high prices repel them, was not new to Yan Sisheng. He had been confronted with it, and had dismissed it, in an inter-jurisdictional dispute of the late 1730s.[20] Dismissing a looser formulation by the emperor would naturally have been more problematic. Many decades later, Yang Jingren (author of Text 3.C above) was to propose yet another account of the putative safety mechanism: to stop outsiders buying grain within

---

[18] PYTOCG, 15:20b and 22a. In his recent article on Chen Hongmou, Rowe claims, apparently on the basis of this same directive, that Chen argued that "had not the selling price in Jiangxi still been attractively low despite the dearth, extra-provincial buyers simply would not have come" (Rowe, "State and Market in Mid-Qing Economic Thought," p. 12). There is no wording in the directive corresponding to this claim. The translation at the top of Rowe's p. 13 is also surprising.

[19] GCQXLZ, 169:25a.

[20] See Text 7.D below.

one's jurisdiction is unnecessary, because the local brokers will "put the price up even higher," thereby deterring merchants from outside.[21] The formulators of these doctrines may have been content with them; but there is ample evidence that many officials and ordinary people in eighteenth-century China did not share such confidence.

* * * * *

This is the moment to draw a distinction. Commitment merely to free circulation of grain surpluses (*migu liutong*) implied that where impediments existed to such circulation, it was the state's business to remove them. Such an approach in turn indicated opposition to supply protectionism, except in extreme circumstances, and a policy of positive action to draw hoarded grain onto the market. The approach, in short, was interventionist, as was the French "police of grain." A quite different approach, although one also entailing belief in the free circulation of grain surpluses, would have been to argue that the interests of society would be best served if grain merchants (and others) were left to pursue their private interests in the grain trade without interference. Their judgement of their own best interests would tend to produce the best outcome for society possible in the circumstances. Hoarders, for example, should be left to bring their grain out in their own good time. These are, of course, the postulates of economic liberalism, as applied to the pre-modern grain trade. The paradox is thus that belief in free circulation is not the same thing as economic liberalism.

The Qing dynasty's commitment to free circulation can be traced back to the pre-conquest period.[22] The Qing state had, as we have seen, a general policy of opposing supply protectionism; when it conceded the need for grain embargoes, its treatment of the merchant community could be interventionist in the extreme. Action of some sort against speculative hoarders was also considered normal, at least when officialdom perceived a link

---

[21] HCJSWB, 41:17a.
[22] QCWXTK, 34:5169 (entry for 1636).

The Grain Trade

between their operations and an actual rise in local grain prices.[23] Thus conventional practice in eighteenth-century China was interventionist, although less intensely so than in pre-1760s France. However, we have already seen that, in China, by the early 1740s there were the rudiments of an idea that merchant self-interest would see to it that market stocks were not excessively depleted by commercial purchases. Text 6.E (1745) provides evidence of similar thinking about merchant self-interest and grain hoarding. In this case, merchant profiteering is claimed to result in the provision of positive services for the community. The newer thinking on self-interest and the impact of commercial buying offered the state a further rationale for its existing policy: supply protectionism was simply unnecessary. The implication of Text 6.E's argument about self-interest and grain hoarding was, by contrast, that existing policy should be revised: to prohibit speculative hoarding was to harm the public interest.

Text 6.E, although written earlier, in effect rebuts the argument of Text 6.D, a proposal for firm action against one particular form of merchant hoarding. Text 6.D was written in the spring of 1747, and the immediate background was a stiffening of policy (in early 1745) towards landlords and others who held grain off the market during times of dearth.[24] The author, Tang Pin, was a native of Hangzhou; writing as an investigating censor, he was able to bring concerns about his own part of the world to the central government's attention. For Tang, speculative hoarding by rural landowners was small-scale, and of limited significance; the real worry, especially in Jiangsu and Zhejiang, was a capitalistic operation which he called "hoard pawning" (dundang).

Hoard pawning was a way of using a limited amount of capital to accumulate a substantial hoard of rice. All the merchant had to do was buy a certain amount of rice straight after harvest, while the price was low; pawn it for somewhat less than he had

---

[23] See Dunstan, State or Merchant?, ch. 1 for examples of official action against speculative hoarders. One does have the impression that measures against hoarding by wealthy landlords were often more circumspect, and more likely to be based on suasion, than those aimed at merchants or middlemen.

[24] QSL/QL, 230:25b-26a, and 286:24a-25a.

paid for it; and promptly use the loan to buy a second, somewhat smaller quantity of rice, and then pawn that. The cycle would be repeated, as quickly as possible, several times, until the merchant had as much rice as he could have bought with four or five times his original capital. Then, the following year, in the two *soudure* periods of a double-cropping part of China, the merchant would gradually redeem the rice and sell it, taking advantage of the seasonal high prices. Hoards of cotton or raw silk could be accumulated through the same procedure. As far as rice was concerned, the result was that "what the little folk have harvested . . . begins by falling at a low price into merchant hands, and ends by reverting at a high price to the people." The folk, therefore, do "not escape the worry of high food prices even when the year is one of plenty."

It was obvious to Tang that the merchants were wicked, and the situation intolerable. He made proposals for eliminating hoard pawning; these, interestingly, placed the responsibility on the pawnbrokers, presumably to make enforcement as simple as possible. The emperor, who had already approved bans on hoard pawning in the Lower Yangzi provinces within the previous three years, ordered the governors and governors-general concerned to implement Tang's proposals.[25] In doing so, he ignored the counter-argument that Chen Dashou, as Jiangsu governor, had made in February 1745 when faced with Board of Revenue instructions to similar effect. Chen's memorial is Text 6.E.

Chen concedes that it is common for rice merchants to build stocks through serial purchases, and then retain them until the market price has risen. This, however, means that the rice is kept within the local community, and will still be there when the time of scarcity arrives. That the price of rice is high in the *soudure* period is entirely normal; the function of speculative activity is to prevent it from rising higher still. If, on the contrary, one forced the merchants to resell their rice immediately in the season of low prices after harvest, the price of rice would plummet, and the farmers' interests would be harmed. Chen claims that the grain merchants sell once the price has risen (although he agrees that it

---

[25] QSL/QL, 215:24a-b and 286:25a.

would be detestable if they did not), and that practically all the hoarded stocks are sold before the autumn harvest inaugurates the next annual cycle. The speculators thus perform a stock management and conservation service akin to that provided by officialdom. Both speculators and officials stockpile grain in the post-harvest season. While the goals of official management include the maintenance of reserves in case of harvest failure, the existence of the speculators makes it possible for rice to "come onto the market in an unbroken flow" throughout all stages of the annual cycle.

The policy implications of Chen's analysis were liberal, as he himself perceived. As he put it, "purchasing by the people should thus naturally, in every case, be left up to their own convenience. There is no point in circumscribing it with laws and prohibitions." Prudence, in fact, required Chen to report some concrete measures he was taking to implement the officially communicated ban against hoard pawning, as well, perhaps, as the new policy of increased toughness against hoarding generally. He duly reports such measures at the end of Text 6.E. They suggest that Chen's approach was one of minimal compliance.

In an important edict of May 1748, the emperor wrote that "With the affairs of the market-place, for the most part one should let the people carry out the circulation for themselves. If once the government begins to manage it, what was originally intended to be beneficial to the people will, with unsatisfactory implementation, turn out full of hindrances."[26] This pronouncement was provoked by reports of the adverse consequences of the former Zhejiang governor's over-zealous application of the 1747 anti-speculative-hoarding policy. The remark was somewhat casual: as the upshot showed, even now the court was not renouncing the whole principle of intervention against speculative hoarding.[27] However, the 1748 edict does reflect a certain consciousness of how the existing commercial arrangements operated to supply the urban markets of Jiangnan. The background to the edict includes

---

[26] QSL/QL, 314:6b-7a.

[27] Thirteen days later came a reiteration of the prohibition against "wicked merchants seizing opportunities to buy and store, engaging privily in [speculative] hoarding." Ibid., 314:36b.

a small number of memorials, of which Text 6.E was one, expounding how the grain trade functioned, and arguing against anti-hoarding measures and other forms of state intervention.[28] Precise appreciation of the nature of the arguments presented in these memorials is more important, for the historian of Chinese economic thought, than general assessment of the drift of mid-Qing economic policy.

It goes without saying that, compared with Adam Smith's systematic expositions of the social utility of grain speculators, Chen Dashou's is rudimentary in the extreme.[29] Neither does Chen push his arguments with the same assuredness as Smith. One of Chen's central points is that forbidding speculation will mean a flight of grain to markets where the price is higher. Does this mean that he is in sympathy with the motivation for supply protectionism? Smith might have handled this problem at a theoretical level, arguing that the free play of merchant self-interest would assure the optimal allocation of available supplies between communities, as well as over time within the same community. Chen shows no interest in the problem.[30]

Of course, one cannot expect too much of a bureaucratic document. Chen's discussion is coherent, and contains the germs of an economist's understanding of the stock conservation function of grain speculation. His plea for freedom of operation for commercial purchasers was premised on this understanding.

---

[28] Kishimoto, "Shinchō chūki keizai seisaku no kichō," pp. 28-29; and Dunstan, *State or Merchant?*, chs. 3 and 6.

[29] Compare Text 6.E with Adam Smith, *An Inquiry into the Nature and Causes of the Wealth of Nations* (1776, in the 1904 Cannan edition. Chicago: University of Chicago Press, 1976), Vol. 2, pp. 30-31 and 40-41.

[30] See, however, Text 7.E below for an argument, written in 1738, that price incentives suffice to guarantee the best distribution of imported grain supplies between communities in time of famine. The task that Chen left unfulfilled was therefore partly one of synthesis. His failure to synthesize left his defence of speculation vulnerable: Wu and Ge ("Qing qianqi de liangshi tiaoji," pp. 132-33) quote some late eighteenth-century material suggesting that, in the eyes of its bureaucrat authors, one objection to speculative hoarding was precisely that it deterred outside merchants from coming to buy grain for export to other jurisdictions. Since speculation could thus function as an *ersatz* form of "blocking the purchase of grain," it was equally to be condemned, and for the same reason.

The argument of Text 6.E, among other documents, represented significant potential for the development of pre-modern Chinese economic theory. Specifically, it invited policy deliberators to transcend the moralism that obscured debate within the conventional "free circulation" framework and, therefore, to put economic thought on a more scientific footing. That the potential was never fully realized does not detract from its interest for the intellectual and cultural historian.

*   *   *   *   *

In mid-eighteenth century China, there was one policy question which, above all others, brought to the fore the issue of state intervention *versus* reliance on the market. This was the level of stockpiling in the state's ever-normal granaries. If, arguably, the action of self-interested merchants saw to it that marketed grain surpluses were conserved and redistributed, how compelling was the need for the state's traditional pattern of intervention buying and selling, storage and distribution? Did the state's stockpiling operations actually impede the proper functioning of commerce? As explained in Chapter 2 above, a fifteen-year controversy on this issue was unleashed by the decision, which emerged over the course of 1738 and 1739, to attempt a vast expansion of the granary reserves. In some early contributions to the debate, the issue was conceptualized in quite sharp and abstract terms as one of state involvement harming the benign workings of commerce. Text 2.C (1742), while not particularly abstract, puts the case against the state at its most strident.

The debate was far too complex to allow of even a summary discussion here.[31] Suffice it to say that by 1748, when Text 6.F was written, the arguments for and against a high level of stocking in the ever-normal granaries had all been repeatedly rehearsed, and must have been well known to all participants in the controversy.

---

[31] For a full treatment, using archival materials, see my *State or Merchant?*, chs. 4-6. Meanwhile, see Gao Wangling, "Yige wei wanjie de changshi: Qingdai Qianlong shiqi de liangzheng he liangshi wenti" [An Incomplete Experiment: Provisioning Policy and Grain Supply Problems in the Qianlong Period of the Qing Dynasty], *Jiuzhou xuekan* [The Nine Provinces Journal] 2, no. 3 (1988): 13-40; or Rowe, "State and Market in Mid-Qing Economic Thought," pp. 26-28.

Especially after 1743, the debate had focussed on the concern that a high-level stocking policy might be inflationary, either because of the specific characteristics of state purchasing or because of the sheer quantity in store. It is this concern that Text 6.F addresses.

Text 6.F was one of many memorials written by chief provincial administrators in response to an imperial circular, transcribed in the preamble, asking for opinions as to why the price of grain is rising, and, as it were, subtly directing the jury to bring in a "guilty" verdict on the ever-normal granaries. Broadly speaking, most of the governors and governors-general took the hint, and the episode played a certain role in bringing the debate to a conclusion, with the stocking targets reset at quite modest levels.[32] Yang Xifu, author of Text 6.F, was one of the compliant governors. However, besides recommending (among other adjustments) that each province be ordered to cut any "excessive" stocking targets by "10 to 20 per cent," he also offered a multi-causal analysis of the inflation, which he represented as a secular trend beginning in the Kangxi period. The last part of the memorial advocates an empire-wide campaign to promote water conservancy at neighbourhood level.

The memorial won an appreciative comment from the Qianlong emperor. It is regularly cited by modern historians to illustrate mid-Qing officials' consciousness of the eighteenth-century inflationary trend, and their approach towards explaining it.[33] So well regarded a memorial deserves a virtually full translation. Whether it fully deserves its reputation is for the reader to determine. And yet the last section, conventional (by eighteenth-century Chinese standards) and tedious though it may appear, quite possibly had a covert political purpose. Yang must have been aware of the radical nature of some of the criticisms of the ever-normal system. Was a call for a water conservancy campaign (one of so many in Chinese history) a way of trying to

---

[32] See, for the time being, Will, *Bureaucratie et famine*, pp. 171-72, or Will and Wong, *Nourish the People*, p. 143.

[33] QSL/QL, 311:37b; and, e.g., Quan Hansheng, *Zhongguo jingji shi luncong* [Collected Papers on Chinese Economic History] (Hong Kong: Chinese University of Hong Kong, New Asia Institute, 1972), pp. 496-97; and Zelin, *The Magistrate's Tael*, pp. 294-97.

divert attention from the stocking targets of the ever-normal granaries, which some advisers wished to cut more drastically than by a mere fifth or tenth?

*   *   *   *   *

Text 6.A

Decree concerning the circulation under permit of commercial husked millet[1]
Date: 1748
Author: Chen Hongmou, as Shaanxi governor.
Source: PYTOCG, 27:16a-18a.

In the disaster-stricken areas, millet has become expensive, and it is impossible to do other than to ban exports to other provinces. As for commercial distribution within the home province, merchants are still allowed to obtain permits and go and make purchases, putting the grain into circulation relatively close at hand.[2] Any merchant found with millet not covered by a permit at a crossing-point along the Yellow River should be ordered to put it on sale on the spot at a reduced price.[3] It should thus be possible to keep the millet circulating within the home province, while avoiding delays and losses for the merchants.

I have issued the above instructions more than once, and they were all perfectly clear. Nonetheless, in dealing with this matter, the county-level authorities have all been failing to attain the proper mean between over-severity and laxness. There are those who, having seized shipments downstream, have asked leave to investigate why the upstream authorities let them slip through; those who have suggested that odd horseloads of millet should also be held up and made the objects of severe investigation; and those who have asked permission to require the merchant to put his millet on sale at a reduced price already at the place where it was grown, disregarding the congestion of the grain that would ensue. Such requests show failure to grasp the meaning of "circulation within provincial boundaries," and expose their makers to the taunt that they are "refusing food through fear of choking."

What these local authorities have failed to take into account is that, although there have always been many purchasers from other provinces at such upstream locations as Qijiabu in Fufeng County (a place where grain is grown), or Xianyang County in Xi'an Prefecture (where commercial grain collects), purchasers from the home province have also naturally not been few.[4] If one detains and obstructs all purchasers, without enquiring whether they plan export to another province or sale within this one, the grain will all remain congested upstream. The other merchants, catching wind of what is going on, will not dare to come and buy. If merchants do not circulate, on what shall the downstream population's food supply depend? Those upstream who have amassed grain will also suffer when none comes to buy. It will be disadvantageous for both upstream and downstream. This means that the desire to prohibit exports will only have led to the home territory likewise being deprived of succour.

Immediately on receipt of this decree, the provincial administration commissioner is to pass on the following orders to the authorities of the disaster-stricken jurisdictions and the specially assigned officials. At all general checkpoints on the Shanxi border, such as Tongguan, Huayin, Chaoyi, Dali, and Heyang, it is imperative that officials and servicemen exert themselves to carry out surveillance, not letting the slightest quantity of grain slip through their fingers.[5] If there is any laxity, it will definitely be hard for them to avoid censure. At the remaining checkpoints, merchants should, as before, be allowed to proceed upon inspection of their permits.[6] Those who have no permits should be directed to put their grain on sale at a reduced price on the spot. If the place where they are caught is not a town or market, and there is too much grain for the local households, so that it will not sell, they should be ordered to sell it portion by portion in places in the vicinity: there is no need to insist that it all be sold in the one place. Official personnel should be assigned to supervise such sales; once the sales are complete, reports should be submitted to the county headquarters and retained on file.

As for Qijiabu, Xianyang, and other upstream places in which millet is grown or collected, merchants with permits valid for this province should be allowed to proceed after inspection of their permits. In the case of those who have bought millet to export to other provinces, they should be directed to put their stocks on sale at a reduced price. It is, however, impermissible to impose reductions of whatever size one chooses, thereby harming the merchants' capital. If there are merchants who did not originally acquire permits, but who, after being apprehended, declare themselves willing to transport their grain to a named county in this province and to sell it there, there is no need to require them to waste time going to request a permit, and then returning to collect their grain. One should merely halt the boat awhile, and promptly summon a broker, charging him to provide a written bond specifying the place of sale and the quantity of grain. This bond should be presented to the local authorities, who should immediately issue a small licence stamped with their seal, and setting out the merchant's name, the quantity of millet, and the words "to be sold in X County of the home province." At the same time as they issue the licence and let the merchant leave, they should send a flying notification to the authorities of the county of sale. The authorities of both counties should assign personnel to inspect at the checkpoints.

On the boat's arrival, a broker should be summoned to unload the millet and transport it to his premises, where he should sell it at the current price. He should also be directed to provide a bond, and to report to the county headquarters when all the grain is sold, turning the licence in at the same time. The authorities who issued the licence should be notified, so that they can check off the sale. If, some time after the authorities of the declared place of sale have received the notification, the grain-boat fails to arrive, creating the presumption that the merchant has gone off elsewhere, they should inform the authorities at the place of shipment, who should promptly punish the broker who supplied the bond.[7] It may then be hoped that all who have millet will be able to sell it straight away, and all the buyers will be able to trade promptly, with smooth circulation from one party to the next, and without fraudulent use of the permits or procedures to continue to export to other provinces.

To sum up, while exportation ought indeed to be forbidden, it is imperative that there be circulation within the home province. Internal routes should be kept clearly monitored; the routes to other provinces should be kept strictly blocked. This is a critical juncture, and the method is simple, clear, and easy to put into practice. You should also instruct the circuit intendants to monitor and give directions within their jurisdictions, implementing the policy according to local circumstances.

Notes

1. The characters used, here and throughout the directive, to refer to the cereal in question can mean husked grain of any kind. However, in view of the geographical context of the document, and the fact that it was written in late autumn, we may safely assume that the cereal was millet.
2. As opposed to taking it outside the province.
3. Chen presumably means a price below the current market price at the place of sale.
4. Qijiabu (Qi Family Wharf) lay on a tributary of the River Wei in Fengxiang Prefecture.
5. The places listed were all county-level jurisdictions (except for Tongguan, recently elevated into a subprefecture) near, or to the north of, the junction of the River Wei with the Yellow River.
6. Here, Chen is evidently referring to the province's internal checkpoints (or, to translate more literally, [mountain] passes).
7. The words "creating the presumption that" have been supplied by the translator.

*   *   *   *   *

Text 6.B

Memorial reporting the imposition of a temporary prohibition of large-scale trade in grain, and the official buying up of hoarded stocks, as a means of taking advance thought for the people's food supply
Date: 1752
Author: Zhongyin, as Shaanxi governor.
Source: GZD/QL, Vol. 3, pp. 576-77.

I take the liberty of noting that since the second moon of summer, Shaanxi has had little rainfall. As I reported in an earlier palace memorial, much of the territory subordinate to Xi'an, Tongzhou,

Fengxiang, Qianzhou, Xing'an, and Shangzhou is drought-afflicted, and there are places where the autumn harvest is to be despaired of, or will at best be scanty. This is just the time to worry that the population's food supply will be inadequate. Despite this, there are wicked merchants accumulating hoards in the full thousands and heaped tens of thousands of bushels for export to Shanxi.

Although the important thing with stocks of grain is circulation, and it is only right to help one's neighbour jurisdictions, I have heard that this year Shanxi had a good summer harvest. As for the autumn fields, apart from Puzhou Prefecture, which seems to have had a slight shortage of rainfall, the millet is all growing fine and strong throughout that province. This means that in Shanxi the summer and autumn harvests will both have been abundant, and there will be provision for its people's sustenance. Since in Shaanxi many of the autumn fields are at present drought-afflicted, it is still more appropriate to weigh up relative priorities, and keep the folk of the home province abundantly supplied with food. How much the more when the magistrate of Lintong County (in Xi'an Prefecture) reports that his recent investigations show that wicked merchants have accumulated hoards totalling tens of thousands of bushels, while there are also merchant hoards in Weinan and Xianyang. If we allow these hoards to be exported in a continuous flow, the result will be that Shaanxi's stocks of grain will become daily more exiguous, and the people will experience daily greater difficulty in obtaining food. The present daily rising trend of grain prices in each jurisdiction is caused entirely by the wicked merchants designing only to monopolize, speculate, and hoard supplies for export.

I find that the established regulation is that if a given province has had a poor harvest, and there is not sufficient grain for the folk's sustenance, yet wicked fellows in pursuit of profit privily transport grain from its borders to the detriment of popular subsistence, the governor and governor-general shall impose a temporary prohibition in the light of their assessment of the situation. In the Shaanxi dearths of 1747 and 1748, proposals for temporary export bans by the then governors, Xu Qi and Chen Hongmou, received Imperial assent and were reverently implemented, as is on record. I find: although it is not yet time for harvest in the autumn fields, the signs of drought are already fully formed in the above six jurisdictions, and much of the millet is withered. Since it is already the eighth moon, even should sweet showers be vouchsafed, the farmers will only be able to plant the wheat in preparation for next summer's harvest. It is inevitable, in the nature of the case, that from now on reserves will daily shrink. If, on top of this, one permitted the repeated exportation of thousands and myriads of bushels of grain, it would truly be of great harm to the population's sustenance.

With the above in mind, and after close consideration, I have ordered that, while petty traders should be left free to circulate in order to assist the neighbour jurisdictions, all county-level authorities should be instructed to impose a temporary prohibition, according to the established regulation, on all great merchants who have accumulated hoards of thousands or myriads of bushels for export to other provinces. New instructions will be given once there is more than enough food in Shaanxi to feed its people. As for the grain hoarded in Lintong by wicked merchants, according to the regulation, the said merchants should be required to sell it under supervision at the place where it was hoarded. However, since the quantity is in the tens of thousands of bushels, to sell it all at once would probably prove difficult, and the merchants' capital would be held up. This is, meanwhile, just the time for forward planning with respect to relief distributions, loans, and stabilizing sales in the dearth- and disaster-stricken areas. I am at present ordering the provincial administration commissioner to draw up a master plan. Although each county has the stocks held in its ever-normal and community granaries, it is difficult to guess whether these alone will be enough to soothe the afflicted masses of each jurisdiction. As to the highly populous provincial capital, the stocks remaining in the Xianning and Chang'an county granaries (after successive years of loan defaults, and last spring's loans and sales) will in all likelihood be insufficient.[1] This makes it even more incumbent on us to plan in advance.

The grain being hoarded by the aforesaid merchants was all bought while prices were low. If it were made the object of official purchase, with—to be generous—0.2 to 0.3 tl. per bushel added to the original cost price, so that the merchants would still make a profit, then this would be a measure with which they would all happily comply. If, furthermore, we moved the grain to the provincial capital and the dearth- and disaster-stricken areas to provide the wherewithal for stabilizing sales in the winter and spring, this would be greatly beneficial to the people. I have talked the matter over with the provincial administration commissioner and circuit intendant, as well as consulting the governor-general by letter, and we are all of the same mind.

I find: there are at present 400,000 taels of reserve funds in the provincial treasury. They were originally set aside to cover any necessary expenditures in the various parts of the province. I ask permission to allocate 100,000 taels from these funds and have them issued to Cheng De, the prefect of Xi'an, so that he may take them to Lintong, locate the merchants' hoards, and buy them. He will have instructions to make absolutely sure that each merchant is left with a profit, and to carry out the business satisfactorily, refraining from entrusting the task to clerks, runners, village constables, or wicked brokers, recourse to whom might cause corruption and extortion. As for the tens of thousands of bushels which he will buy, he should set aside appropriate amounts for Lintong and Weinan (both of which are drought-stricken). The rest he should transport to the provincial capital, where he should hand it over to the Xianning and Chang'an magistrates for storage, in preparation for the stabilizing sales.

Further: those parts of Weinan and Xianyang which are close to water routes are all sites of merchant hoarding. If enquiry reveals any hoards of full thousands or heaped tens of thousands of bushels which could not be sold off all at once in the locality, they should all be bought by the authorities in the same way. If the aforesaid sum is insufficient, I ask permission to make further allocations from the reserve funds. The important thing is that, without occasioning losses to the merchants, the measure should be of assistance to the people's food supply. As for the funds appropriated to this project, it will be possible to reimburse the provincial treasury once the stabilizing sales have been carried out. I estimate that there should be a surplus, which can be set against the transport costs. If there is any further surplus, this will be retained for public purposes.

I bear in mind that the wicked merchants' hoards were all originally the grain of Xi'an and Fengxiang, which prefectures are now suffering from drought, and will have a poor harvest. If, as I envisage, we buy up the said region's grain in order to eke out its people's food supply, this would truly be much simpler and more economical than the usual process of official buying and transport for relief operations. Because it would be difficult for the merchants to wait for long, I am ordering the provincial administration commissioner to issue the funds and have the buying done; once the buying is complete, a register will be prepared setting out full details of the quantities bought, the prices paid, and (after the stabilizing sales) the transport costs and selling prices. Apart from the memorial I will submit on forwarding the register to the Board of Revenue for audit, I now, in conjunction with the governor-general Huang Tinggui, respectfully report the considerations that lie behind our temporary ban on exports by great merchants, and our decision to buy up the hoarded stocks of grain, in order to assist the people's food supply. . . .

Note

1. Xianning and Chang'an were the two county-level jurisdictions between which the Xi'an prefectural city was divided.

* * * * *

Text 6.C

Edict prohibiting the practice of denying outside buyers access to the stocks of one's own jurisdiction[1]
Date: 1742
Author: Issued in the name of the Qianlong emperor.
Source: *Shangyu dang*, QL 7/11/9; QSL/QL, 178:15a–16a; QCWXTK, 36:5192.

The weather sent from Heaven includes both rain and shine, while the soil furnished by Earth may be of low quality or high; the abundance or otherwise of the harvests depends on these conditions. Given the vastness of the Empire and the distinctiveness of its component territories, if the harvest is poor in one place, it may be good in another. The whole reliance is on intercourse between want and possession, and aid alike to all in times of crisis.[2] Although in the Court's grain buying and reallocation there is naturally some expedient exercise of flexibility, there is definitely no question, in places where grain is in short supply, of forcing men to sell. If merchants converge like spokes into a wheel on regions where the harvest has been good, once they have much grain assembled, the price will naturally come down, and it will be easy for the needy masses to acquire food.[3] Such is the complementary operation of, on one hand, mutual aid between neighbouring provinces, and, on the other, the institution of relief and caring by the State.

Our August Sire and Ourselves have both repeatedly promulgated prohibitions on blocking the purchase of grain by outside buyers. Unfortunately, the outlook of authorities and people at the local level lacks in breadth, nor are they yet reformed from partiality and selfishness. It is thus inevitable that as soon as there is at all a sizeable amount of grain leaving their borders, and the price starts gradually to rise, although the people do not dare overtly to block purchasing, there are none who do not secretly plan for their own selfish convenience and throng to place restrictions on the outside buyers. The authorities thereon show them a biased sympathy, on which they look upon their neighbour provinces as Qin did upon Yue.[4]

This being so, We hereby issue a further edict. The governors and governors-general of all provinces are ordered to exhort and guide the authorities and people of their jurisdictions to the following effect. They must not cleave to the mentality of boundaries and borders, but must be sure to cultivate the sentiments of succour and compassion; that merchants and traders may circulate, drawing upon excess so as to supplement paucity,[5] in order to relieve the difficulties of a single time. If, in the future, their own region should suffer a poor harvest, would it do other than rely upon the selfsame neighbour provinces? Let this too be proclaimed, so that authorities and people may both understand it. Respect this.

Notes

1. This title has been supplied by the translator.
2. The expression "intercourse between want and possession" (*you wu xiang tong*) refers to trade.
3. This sentence seems to be elliptical. The emperor has left out the crucial stage in which the merchants with their stocks of grain "converge" on regions where the harvest has been poor. If, alternatively, "regions where the harvest has been good" contains a scribal error and should say the opposite, the official compilers of both QCWXTK and the *Veritable Records* did not see fit to correct the slip.
4. From the viewpoint of denizens of the ancient state of Qin (in present-day Shaanxi), the people of Yue (in present-day Zhejiang) were geographically and culturally distant, and therefore of no concern.
5. For explanation of this phrase, see n. 7 to Text 3.C above.

*   *   *   *   *

Text 6.D

Memorial requesting severe prohibition of the hoard-pawning of rice, with a view to making the people's food supply abundant

Date: 1747
Author: Tang Pin, as an investigating censor.
Source: "Renhe Qinchuan Jushi," comp., *Huang Qing zouyi* [Memorials of the August Qing Dynasty] (n.d.; 1967 facsimile edn. published by Wenhai chubanshe, Taibei), 44:10a-12b.

I take the liberty of considering that silk, the coarser kinds of cloth, and pulse and grain are matters of life or death for the populace. If the harvest of one year supplies that year's requirements,[1] the folk will not be reduced to extreme hardship as regards their food supply. If the harvest of one year is stockpiled by a small number of families, the folk will necessarily encounter daily greater difficulty in procuring food.

I find that in Zhili, Henan, Shandong, Shanxi, and Shaanxi, the people tend to grow wheat, barley, the two kinds of millet, and various other cereals.[2] In all of the remaining provinces, paddy rice is grown, and the whole reliance is upon the autumn harvest's being bountiful, so that the price of grain is low, and the poor can easily contrive the acquisition of their pints and pecks of grain. Even should there be a year of dearth, merchants accomplish circulation, and the petty folk can still escape the calamity of finding grains of rice as dear as pearls.

In the rice-producing regions, there have always been rich households which have hoarded the unhusked rice from their own fields from one year to the next, firmly refusing to sell unless the market price is high. With them, however, it is only a question of the stocks of individual families constituted from what they have harvested themselves, and in the context of a single county. The harm done is not very great. Of late, however, I have heard that pawnshops have actually adopted the practice of accepting pledges in the form of rice. The interest rates are very low; the clients are very numerous; and the quantities of rice accumulated are very substantial. From the pawnbroker's point of view, it is only a question of expansion of his opportunities for profit, but wicked merchants and artful traders find a way of turning the existence of these pawnshops to their own account, that is to say, to help them all to buy up stocks while prices are low.

Suppose a man has only 1,000 taels of capital. He buys a certain quantity of rice, pawns it for 700 to 800 taels, and then, with the utmost dispatch, buys more rice and pawns it for 500 to 600 taels. Purchases and pawnings follow each other in quick succession; at a rough estimate, the cycle does not stop until one portion of capital has bought four or five portions' worth of rice. Then in the *soudure* periods of the following spring and from late summer into early autumn, the price of rice is bound to rise. The merchants, putting together principal and interest, gradually redeem and sell their grain. This means that what the little folk have harvested in one year begins by falling at a low price into merchant hands, and ends by reverting at a high price to the people. The pawnbrokers and hoarders enjoy handsome profits without stirring from their seats, while the small folk bear the hardship. The harm done by the hoard-pawning of rice is thus extremely serious.

From the small hours until nightfall, Your Majesty knows not a moment's respite from anxious thought about the people's food and clothing. The Imperial breast has frequently been exercised by the problems of official buying for the granaries, a topic on which the great functionaries of every province have likewise repeatedly been planning and devising. Who would have expected that, amidst the populace, the pawnbrokers would enter into symbiotic evil-doing, recognizing only their own profits and not the harm done to the folk at large? I positively fear that, if the practice is not severely eliminated, the little folk will not escape the worry of high food prices even when the year is one of plenty. Besides, when word spreads to other provinces, it will be hard to prevent imitation of the practice. For while the evil of hoard-pawning is especially prevalent in Jiangsu and Zhejiang, the commodities hoard-pawned are emphatically not confined to rice. Each year when the raw silk is newly spun or, at the end of autumn, the cotton crop is ready for harvest, these merchants brazenly spread their nets, proceeding exactly as they do when buying up and pawning rice. It is actually as if the petty folk's plans for securing food and clothing were only intended to supply the wicked merchants' schemes for snaring profit. How could the implications for the populace's livelihood be trivial?

As I write, it is precisely the time when the wheat is nearing readiness for harvest, and the new raw silk is soon to be brought forth. I beseech Your Majesty to command the governors-general and governors of Zhili and the provinces to give strict orders as follows to the county-level authorities. Any pawnshop, urban or rural, which has hoarded rice or such-like goods on hand which it has not yet sold, must be commanded to declare them to the authorities, who must buy them up according to their value.[3] The pawnbroker will be exempt from punishment. If he dares to conceal them, he is to be severely punished according to the "Statute on Violating Imperial Pronouncements" once the matter has been brought to light.[4] Henceforward, furthermore, a quarterly statement is to be obtained from each pawnbroker duly vouching, of his own accord, that he holds no hoard-pawned rice or other goods. These statements should be placed on file. If anyone offends again, he should be duly punished as the statute prescribes. If this is done, it may be hoped that rice will be gradually enabled to circulate, while it will gradually become possible to make the people's livelihood abundant. . . .

Notes

1. Here and throughout the memorial, Tang is referring not to the calendar year, but to the agricultural/consumption year beginning with the main rice harvest in the autumn.
2. The two kinds of millet are glutinous and non-glutinous.
3. It is likely that by "value" Tang means "current market price," but he fails to specify this.
4. The text has *Weizhi lü*, apparently a common abbreviation for *Zhishu you wei lü* ("Statute on Violating Imperial Pronouncements"). The penalty prescribed by this statute was a hundred strokes (effectively forty) of the heavy bamboo.

*   *   *   *   *

Text 6.E

Memorial in response to Board recommendations for a ban on grain-hoarding
Date: 1745
Author: Chen Dashou, as Jiangsu governor.
Source: First Historical Archives, CC, Chen Dashou, QL 10/1/8.[1]

I have received a memorandum from the Board of Revenue ordering immediate prohibition of such mischievous practices as that by which wicked merchants, having purchased rice, do not promptly sell it, but rather pledge it at a pawnshop and then buy anew. The purpose of this prohibition is to stabilize the market price. . . . Prostrate, I recognize that with grain, the most important thing is circulation, and that, according to the regulations, hoarding for trade purposes should be forbidden. However, in eliminating abuses one must be sure to do away with the most harmful, and in establishing laws one must insist that they accommodate the population. There are certainly cases in which one should adapt one's policy to suit the region, closely investigating how to manage matters satisfactorily.

I find that once the folk have gathered in their grain, their whole year's expenses—for paying their taxes, for serving their parents and bringing up their young, for all their operations and activities—must every one of them be met out of the harvest. Thus when the autumn harvest is completed, there are many sellers in the market, and the price will of necessity be low. By the time of the *soudure*, the farmers have no stocks of grain to sell, and the price invariably rises. That the price should be now low and now high, reciprocally falling or rising,[2] is a normal phenomenon and does not arise entirely from hoarding for the purposes of trade.

As for the grain sold by the population, those shopkeepers whose capital is limited already sell as soon as they have bought, realizing but the tiniest of profits with which to keep themselves alive. There are, however, recurrent cases of those merchants whose capital is somewhat more substantial accumulating stocks through minor purchases and awaiting a good price. Although this is the working of the merchant's profit-seeking heart, once the price is high, the rice is sold, and thus remains available for consumption within the local area. The market does not run short of rice; the market price is kept from rising even higher. Investigation and prohibition should certainly not be sweepingly applied!

Besides, in view of the farmers' needs, one cannot prohibit them from selling. If, at the time when rice is cheap, one insists that those who purchase it resell immediately, the market price, contrariwise, will fall still lower, which cannot help but harm the farmers. How much the more since—given that merchants have regard only for profit—it is inevitable that they will pile their stocks onto boats, and go elsewhere to sell. How will the local officials dare to prevent their departure, thereby incurring blame for blocking the export of grain supplies? If, come the time of the *soudure*, there are no stocks at all among the local population, what will it rely on?

I take the liberty of thinking that, when it comes to hoarding by wicked merchants, what one detests is continued refusals to sell even after the market price has risen. As for when the price is low, officialdom itself is required to issue funds and buy, in order to adjust availability; purchasing by the people should thus naturally, in every case, be left up to their own convenience. There is no point in circumscribing it with laws and prohibitions. How much the more since rice is not like other goods, which can be stored for several years. All the grain stocked up by rich households is generally put on sale before the following year's autumn harvest; there is definitely no holding over into the next year. This means that what is harvested in one year in fact supplies that year's requirements. Only a certain given total is produced. Rather than rushing to have it sold cheaply, taking no account of the deficiency to come, would it not be closer to the mark to keep it stored within the population, and let it come onto the market in an unbroken flow? . . .

[*In the remainder of the memorial, Chen reports on the measures he is taking to address the problem of hoard pawning, and speculative hoarding generally. His emphasis is on obtaining results with minimal disruption of existing patterns of behaviour. He reports:*

a) That, as Jiangsu governor, he has been in the habit of instructing his subordinates to issue annual soudure-period exhortations to the local grain-owners, urging them to sell their stocks off gradually "so as to stabilize the market price." Recalcitrant hoarders who did not respond to exhortation were to be given warnings.

b) That, following Board of Revenue instructions, he has already ordered his subordinates to procure pledges abjuring "hoard-pawning" from the local pawnbrokers (as envisaged also in Tang Pin's memorial). This, he opines, should be sufficient to eliminate hoard pawning; there should be no further interference with popular grain transactions.

c) That he has ordered his subordinates to publicize the fact that the new restrictions on the activities of pawnbrokers do not affect the legality of the customary use of pawnshops by poor tenant farmers in the Suzhou-Taicang region. Here, as elsewhere in China, poor peasants were in the habit of pawning their winter clothes for grain in the soudure period, and then recovering their winter clothes after the autumn harvest by pledging grain. Chen evidently saw this popular survival mechanism as vulnerable to bureaucratic or sub-bureaucratic interference in the wake of the new measures against hoards of grain accumulating in the hands of pawnbrokers.]

Notes

1. There is a brief (five lines) abstract of the part of the memorial translated here in HCJSWB, 26:20b. The title I have used was supplied by the HCJSWB editors.
2. Chen must mean "reciprocally with [i.e., in inverse proportion to] the quantity on offer."

*　*　*　*　*

Text 6.F

Memorial setting forth the reasons why grain has become dear
Date:　　1748
Author:　Yang Xifu, as Hunan governor.
Source:　First Historical Archives, CC, Yang Xifu, QL 13; HCJSWB, 39:7b-9b; and, for the edict quoted in the preamble, QSL/QL, 304:16a-18b.[1]

On the twenty-fourth day of the second moon of [lunar] 1748, I received a letter from the Grand Secretariat transcribing the following edict, which was issued on the twelfth day of the twelfth moon of [lunar] 1747:[2]

"... We bear in mind that, for the population, grain is an everyday necessity of life, and yet of recent years one has beheld its price rise daily. How are the needy multitudes to bear this? Take even Sichuan and Hubei, which have always been known for their output of rice: the governor of Sichuan, Jishan, informs Us that merchants are gathering like clouds, and the price of rice is surging upwards; while the governor-general and governor for Hubei report that the reliance of disaster-stricken Jiangnan on the grain supplies of Hubei is creating high rice prices in that province also. Or again, take Zhili, which has always been dependent on the grain of Bagou.[3] This year the Metropolitan Province has in fact had a harvest, yet Bagou also is experiencing high prices because too much has been transported from it.

"Now with commercial circulation, high prices summon low ones. There may occasionally be temporary upsurges, but how should these amount to a progressive increase, year after year, rising but never dropping? If it is held that speculators are at work hoarding the grain, it is to be acknowledged that this is indeed a lair of mischiefs. But this is naturally something that the efforts of local officials can prohibit. Is it conceivable that they are failing altogether in their duty of implementation, but suffer the speculators to burden the folk with their monopolizing; while the governors-general and governors remain without an inkling of it, so that, in the last analysis, there is not one who has put solid effort into stern prohibition, and reaped results therefrom?

"If it is pointed out that the population is multiplying, We reply that the recovery and growth since Kangxi times should have been accompanied by a gradual increase in prices. Why is it that only at the present time there should have been this sudden increase? If one invokes regional calamities, such as floods and droughts, these too have been always with us. Why is it that prices such as those found now have not been heard of previously? Besides, it is to be expected that places which suffer poor harvests have high prices, while places with good harvests enjoy low ones. Why is it that, irrespective of the state of the harvest, the predicament is everywhere the same?

"Another possible suggestion is that whereas in the Kangxi period the granary reserves were kept in silver, not in grain, while in the Yongzheng period, although there was some overhauling of the system, it still had not been thoroughly perfected, now everywhere has stockpiles, and there are annual restocking purchases such that half the population's output goes into the granaries.[4] This cannot help but entail interference with the population's food supply. This explanation would appear extremely near the mark. However, when the provincial grain reserve quotas were set, this was based in every case on the deliberations of the responsible governor-general and governor, and naturally corresponded to the situation in the given province.[5] Those jurisdictions which have so far met their quota have, furthermore, been very few, and there is urgent need of purchasing. This applies everywhere. Such purchasing is relied on as precaution against famine and for the allocation of relief; it would be difficult to advocate its discontinuation. If excessive buying really is the explanation, this ought to be expounded in a realistic way, and thought should be given to an appropriate response. Matters cannot be left to take their own course, with no effort at adjustment.

"We have turned the problem over in Our mind, but are unable to arrive at a deep understanding of the cause. Nor have We found a means of dealing with it satisfactorily. Now if human affairs are not put in order, the population's life will not be blessed with plenty. Wherein lie the defects of present-day governance? What has brought about the present situation? The customs tariff upon grain and beans has already been remitted comprehensively, and although one ought not to expect immediate results from this, it still should not be without some salutary effect upon grain prices.[6] Why is it that the prices do not daily fall, but on the contrary rise day by day? If now one were to resume collection of the tariff, would the prices not go up still further? Since We have been on the throne, We have been dressing before dawn and delaying Our repast till nightfall in the concentration of Our spirit, diligently searching out the hidden sorrows of the people. Of the populace's pains and griefs, there can be none which has been blocked off from Our hearing. And yet, so far from rejoicing in the blessings of grain costing but three cash per peck, We have caused all Our babes to know the burden of difficulty in obtaining food. How much the more shall We afflict Our spirits!

"The governors-general and governors are all personally entrusted with provincial territories, and are duty bound to give mature and detailed consideration to this matter of supreme importance in the people's life, deeply seeking out the cause. If they have indeed discovered whence comes the affliction, with so much the more effort should they be contriving means of succour and release! And yet, some governors do not give the problem their attention, some place the blame upon the neighbouring jurisdictions, and some lay the responsibility at the merchants' door. As for how one ought to deal with the problem, of this they have not thought at all. You should pass on to each governor-general and governor Our orders to investigate with genuine determination, seeking out in detail the factors making for success or failure and reporting in accordance with the facts. If, apart from the points that We have mentioned, there remains some further source of mischief, they ought in every case to tell of it with accuracy and incisiveness. We insistently desire that there be concrete benefit, so that the people's Heaven[7] may be made abundant. Nor, because in this Edict We chanced to touch upon the matter of the transit tax remission, are they to misunderstand Our purpose, and to suppose that Our intent is to resume collection of the transit tax on grain.[8] Respect this."

Gazing upwards, I perceive our Sage Ruler's supreme intent of dedicated thought about the people's Heaven and mature deliberation on achieving a sufficient food supply. . . . Prostrate, I find that, while regional calamities, such as floods and droughts, or speculation on the part of hoarders do indeed suffice to bring about increases in the price of grain, they still are not the fundamental source of the high prices. I venture to submit that the high price of grain arises from the greatness of the number of those who buy food. The greatness of the number of those who buy food arises from the population's poverty. Now that the polity has enjoyed recovery and growth for over a hundred years, the land gone out of cultivation has all been reopened, and one would expect the population to become daily more prosperous. If, on the contrary, it is impoverished, this is the work of cumulative processes. There are four of what I call cumulative processes. One is the multiplication of the population; one is the daily worsening extravagance of customs; one is that land is falling into the possession of rich households; and one is the granary restocking purchases.

With respect to the mischief of the granary restocking purchases, as Your Majesty has put it, "everywhere has stockpiles, and there are annual restocking purchases such that half the population's output goes into the granaries. . . . This explanation would appear extremely near the mark." Your Majesty has evidently already understood the situation, and there is no point in further verbiage. As for the multiplication of the population, . . . the Sage Command remarks that "the recovery and growth since Kangxi times should have been accompanied by a gradual increase in prices. Why is it that . . . there should have been this sudden increase?" In my view, the increase has, in fact, never been other than gradual. I was born and bred in a country village, and my family has for generations toiled at tilling. I recall that in the Kangxi period, rice at the time of harvest was no more than 0.2 to 0.3 tl. per bushel. During the Yongzheng period, one needed 0.4 to 0.5 tl.: the price of 0.2 to 0.3 tl. was no more. At the present time, one must have 0.5 to 0.6 tl.: the price of 0.3 to 0.4 tl. is no more. It is reasonable to observe that if the population is large, so also will be its demand for grain. Although over several decades there has indeed not been a failure to bring more vacant land under the plough, by now the number of places with no vacant land to open has become considerable. It thus stands to reason that multiplication of the population is sufficient to bring about a gradual increase in grain prices.

Where I say that the price increase arises from the daily worsening extravagance of customs, the point is that at the beginning of the Dynasty, men had passed through the griefs of a disordered age and fully tasted hardship. Customs esteemed frugality and simplicity. After several decades of living peaceably and taking pleasure in their occupations, some of the sons and grandsons began to mock their forefathers' low rustic ways. In such things as food and clothing, they vied in their pursuit of delicacy. In marriage and in mourning, they were bent upon fine show. This tendency began in the great cities, but nowadays the farming folk of lonely wastes and unfrequented hillsides are also gradually becoming accustomed to extravagance. In normal times, they borrow as a matter of course, and most of what they gain by toil in the fields goes on repayment. The rest they spend as takes their fancy. When winter first turns into spring, they need to buy grain for their food.[9] If even the daily food of farming folk is drawn from shops and markets, then how can prices fail to rise?

Where I say that the price increase arises from the movement of land into the possession of rich households, the point is that at the beginning of the Dynasty, there was more land than the population needed, and so the price of land was low. After a certain period of protracted peace, the land became just adequate to feed the population, and so its price reached equilibrium. As the protracted peace wore on, the population began to be too large for the land, and so the price of land went high. Land which formerly cost one or two taels per *mu* now costs as much as seven or eight; land which formerly cost seven or eight taels per *mu* now costs more than twenty. People must be poor before they sell, and having sold, they have not the resources to buy back; they must be rich before they buy, and having bought, they have no need to sell again. Of recent times, the proportion of the land that has passed into the possession of rich households has reached some five or six tenths. People who formerly owned land are now all tenant-farmers. It is difficult for what falls to them each year to be enough to meet a whole year's food requirements. They must buy grain to eke it out. The rich households, meanwhile, after the new crop becomes available, are not willing to part with it except at a good price. They actually hold the balance of the level of grain prices. Now if a single commodity is to be bought by one man, its price cannot increase. If there are ten men buying it, its price will all at once shoot up. If ten men offer it for sale, they cannot ask a high price for it; if one man alone is selling it, he can let the price soar upwards. This being so, how can grain be other than expensive?

If we now make an overall assessment of the four causes, the abundance of the population bears witness to the enlightenment upon enlightenment, harmoniousness following harmoniousness with which our present Dynasty has been raising the people into virtue and long life. As for the movement of land into the possession of rich households, the only possible solution is the equal-holdings system.[10] But even if this system were adopted at a dynasty's foundation, there would still be concern lest it provoke confusion; it would be even more difficult to put in practice now, after succeeding generations during which the Empire has been at peace. There is, however, the extravagance of customs, which is susceptible to exhortations and prohibitions.... I have now respectfully received *The Imperially Approved Book of Propriety*, which has been promulgated for observance.[11] It is incumbent on me to instruct the local officials to put solid effort into giving leadership, duly exhorting and admonishing, so that, from gentry down to commoners, from towns and cities out to isolated rural areas, reform may, step by step, be carried out. The tendency towards extravagance may thus, perhaps, be somewhat quelled. However, the human temperament is such that men pass easily from frugality to extravagance, but it is hard for them to revert from extravagance to frugality. One can only guide and transform gradually; the desired effect cannot be realized all at once.

As to the fact that stockpiling in the ever-normal granaries is "relied on as precaution against famine," so that "it would be difficult to advocate its discontinuation," Your Majesty's far-seeing Sage Enlightenment has truly picked out the fundamental point and grasped the essential. However, I have given it repeated thought, and although it would not be appropriate to advocate discontinuation on the grounds that the restocking purchases push up the price, there are still some points requiring consideration and adjustment.

It is reasonable to observe that the only purpose of stockpiling is to have enough for issuing relief. There is no need to store grain to excess. In 1744, the censor Sun Hao memorialized requesting that the quotas for the ever-normal granary reserves be reset so as to stabilize the price of grain.[12] The Board of Revenue advised approval, and instructions were circulated to all provinces. Although the quotas were all duly reset, the governors-general and governors at the time were basically attaching most importance to the idea of "having precautions and being free of worry"; they did not deeply reckon with the daily increase in the price of grain, or the difficulty of making restocking purchases. To speak with reference to Hunan, some of the county-level granaries have reserves amounting to 50,000 to 60,000 bushels. Some of the prefectural granary reserves amount to 70,000 to 80,000 bushels. This cannot help but be excessive. It would be proper to order every province to give detailed re-examination to the quotas set. Any that are excessive should be reduced, as appropriate, by 10 to 20 per cent. After the stabilizing sales, such granaries as have already been restocked according to the present quotas should restore a portion of the silver realized to the treasury. Those which are not yet fully stocked should have their purchasing requirements docked.

Further, according to advice given previously by the Board, once the stocks in each province's granaries have reached the quota, any grain collected subsequently as payment for Imperial Academy studentships need not be replaced through purchase should there arise occasion to expend it in relief. However, the purpose of relief is provided for already by the quota grain-stocks, and, rather than indefinitely storing this non-quota grain in an unnecessary duplication, it would be better to sell it off year by year. At present Hunan annually realizes the price for its non-quota grain, and delivers it to the provincial administration commission for the maintenance of city walls. It would seem that other provinces could do likewise.

Again, the purpose of the ever-normal 30 per cent sales is only to replace the tired grain with fresh.[13] In fact, while after a good harvest year the population basically has no need for stabilizing sales, where the grain within the granaries is firm and sound, there will be some that can be kept for several years. Because the regulations prescribe an annual 30 per cent sale, the officials at the county level are obliged to sell even when the grain is sound and the harvests have been good. I request that henceforward there be no fixed requirement of a 30 per cent sale every year. Since it is perfectly acceptable to sell extra when the harvests have been poor and prices are high, it is equally acceptable to refrain from selling when the harvests have been good and prices are low. The point is that where one bushel more is sold, the masses do not necessarily enjoy that extra bushel's benefit; but as soon as one bushel less is bought, the populace obtains the boon of selling one bushel the fewer.

Prostrate, I read the Edict's questions, "Wherein lie the defects of present-day governance? What has brought about the present situation?" Gazing upwards, I perceive how Sage Virtue in its humility seeks good government only the more where it is already present. This is truly a blessing for the people of the world. I have turned the matter over in my mind, and there is nothing in the governance of the present day, whether in the broad principles or yet in the fine details, which does not display perfection of provision. It is just that in the area of implementation, those who fail to devote their undivided energies but content themselves with nominal performance outnumber those whose efforts are entirely solid.

Take, for instance, the established regulation which provides that county-level magistrates shall exhaustively traverse the country villages, making close enquiries as to what should be promoted or forbidden; that they shall prepare registers and report on the effectiveness of their initiatives; and that the governors-general and governors shall verify their reports and memorialize triennially. Although this does embody the idea of requiring solid performance, if one examines the policies itemized as proper for promotion, they are all things that lend themselves readily to exaggeration and pretence. For leaving solid traces and being hard to cover up with pleasing appearances, there is nothing like an area's water conservancy. And yet because there is much waywardness abroad, it happens in water control also that efforts are not concentrated, and solid results are not obtained. I take the liberty of thinking that at this present moment, of policies for nourishing the people, there is none more worthy of being wholeheartedly pursued than this one matter of water conservancy. It would seem advisable to determine a system of encouragement and admonition, so that every magistrate makes arrangements conscientiously, and the matter does not languish in the sphere of empty words.

Although these days all vacant land has already been opened up, the potential of water conservancy has not yet been exhausted. Now chance irregularities in rain or shine are constantly occurring, and if indeed one can avail oneself of water conservancy techniques, then how (unless, of course, there is an extraordinary flood or drought) will one be left to sit and watch the harvest fail? Although at present in Hunan river and creek conservancy has been methodically put in order wherever major thoroughfares and cities are affected, in hilly neighbourhoods and isolated areas there may be not a few dikes and reservoirs which time has levelled into disuse. Or, in the odd corner of the odd neighbourhood, the springs may be too far apart, or reservoirs and wells inadequate. Although it may be possible to open channels, or to dig and scour, the fact that the land has owners and there is no one to provide supervision often means that the inhabitants let matters slide and wait to see what happens. If there is one such case, there are a hundred. Generally speaking, for every hundred *mu* of the folk's arable, there are one or two *mu* of reservoir which ought to be protected; and yet the foolish people, blind as to long-term considerations, prefer to snatch the grain that can be harvested each year from these one or two *mu*.[14] They do not realize that should there chance to be too little rain, they will abandon the whole hundred *mu*. If the officials closest to the population point this out to them and guide them, there should be none but will be brought back to his senses.

I request that a command be sent down to the provinces, requiring that the circuit and prefectural authorities direct the county-level magistrates to concentrate their efforts on water conservancy, insisting on sincere pursuit of this objective. The magistrates should examine the local gazetteers and make enquiries of the gentry and elders. Whenever they visit the countryside, they should take the opportunity to make careful surveys, so as to ascertain where there are old remains to be restored, or new works to be undertaken. They should plan maturely and engage in detailed deliberations face to face with the local scholars and commoners. They may decide either to urge the local folk to put their strength together, or else to find a way on their behalf; they may see fit either to contribute an appropriate sum from their own salary so as to give the lead, or else to apply for an appropriate amount of public funds in order to assist the project. Provided only that there be solid intent fit to engage the people's confidence, although they may not leap to go about the work, the people will undoubtedly carry out all desirable water conservancy projects of their own accord wherever word of the magistrate's sincerity takes root, even in places that he has not visited in person. Then, as the soil will all be rich and fertile, the output of grain may be increased to twice its former level; once there is provision made for storing and releasing water, regional calamities will be unable to produce disaster. It may be hoped that this will not be without salutary effect on the high price of grain.

As all these works of renovating or creating dikes and reservoirs will leave solid traces, inspection will be possible. The circuit and prefectural authorities should make thorough inspections, and if indeed the people's fields have been benefited, they should submit a request that the responsible official be considered for an administrative reward. As for any who in normal times entirely neglect the matter, with the result that flood or drought is able to produce disaster, the circuit and prefectural authorities should be ordered to ascertain at the time of the calamity inspection whether or not water conservancy had been promoted in the district.[15] Any county-level authorities who, in full knowledge, had failed to put it in hand, should be reported with complete particulars for impeachment and administrative punishment. In this way, it would seem possible to make county-level magistrates put concentrated effort into water conservancy, and single it out for emphasis among those policies itemized as proper for promotion. It is not beyond the bounds of possibility that this would be one way of relieving the high price of grain.

The present high level of the price of grain represents the outcome of cumulative processes. If one wished to have it revert to cheapness in a single day, this would truly be no easy undertaking. As far as I can see, the only possibilities are reconsideration and adjustment of granary restocking purchases, together with concentrated efforts to promote water conservancy, with a view to plenteous output of grain. As to whether or not my views are apposite, prostrate, I can but leave the Sage Enlightenment to make adjudication. . . .

Notes

1. The version of this document held in the palace memorials collection of the First Historical Archives is a copy. It therefore omits the text of the edict to which Yang Xifu was responding, and which he would have transcribed at the beginning of his reply. The HCJSWB version includes a somewhat abridged version of the edict. In view of the importance of this edict, I present an almost full translation here, omitting only the first paragraph, which is the "peg" on which the rest is hung.
2. That is, during January 1748.
3. The old subprefecture of Bagou (modern Pingquan) lies some way north of the Great Wall, to the east of Chengde. On the role in the provisioning of Zhili of the whole "mountainous Mongolian border region" that was administratively incorporated into Zhili under the Qing dynasty, see Will, *Bureaucratie et famine*, p. 141.
4. It goes without saying that the statement "half the population's output goes into the [state] granaries" was a wild exaggeration, but what of the claim that in the Kangxi period, ever-normal granary reserves had been kept in the form of silver? Huang Liuhong's famous 1694 handbook for local magistrates would suggest otherwise: Huang plainly assumes that the magistrate should have actual grain reserves on hand to issue during famines, although it might *additionally* be desirable to give the victims silver for house or tool

repairs, the purchase of seed grain, or the hiring of draught animals. It is true that Huang also envisages the possibility of relief distributions given entirely in monetary form, while R. Bin Wong has shown that by the Yongzheng period, the granaries of certain provinces did sometimes tend to hold silver rather than grain. The official norm, however, remained storage of grain, and it is rather unlikely that actual practice in the Kangxi period consistently departed from this norm. See Huang Liu-hung, *A Complete Book Concerning Happiness and Benevolence: A Manual for Local Magistrates in Seventeenth-Century China*, trans. Djang Chu (Tucson: University of Arizona Press, 1984), pp. 561-65; Will and Wong, *Nourish the People*, pp. 27-37.

5. The emperor refers to the resetting of the ever-normal stocking targets, a process carried out during 1743–44. As Yang Xifu implies in his response, this had been done at the instance of an investigating censor called Sun Hao, and the purpose was to replace the absurdly high targets of 1738–39 with realistic quotas. The result was an empire-wide target significantly lower than that of 1739, but still very much higher than that inherited from the Yongzheng period. For details, see Dunstan, *State or Merchant?*, ch. 5.

6. Cf. above, ch. 4, introduction.

7. That is, food.

8. The transit tax on grain and beans was in fact reimposed about one year later, in January 1749. See QSL/QL, 329:26a-27a, and QCWXTK, 27:5091.

9. Guided both by the sense and by the HCJSWB version, I emend *tiao*, "sell grain," to *di*, "buy grain."

10. The equal-holdings (*juntian*) system was a system under which the state theoretically allotted equal parcels of land to all able-bodied adult males, with reduced entitlements for widows, old men, the disabled, and so on. Introduced by the non-Chinese Northern Wei dynasty (386–534), the system finally broke down in the seventh and eighth centuries. See Denis Twitchett, *Financial Administration under the T'ang Dynasty*, 2nd edn. (Cambridge: Cambridge University Press, 1970), pp. 1-11.

11. Cf. QSL/QL, 245:20b-21a (1745), which confirms that the emphasis of this work is on frugality.

12. The date 1744 is incorrect: Sun Hao's memorial was considered by the Grand Secretaries and Nine Chief Ministers already in 1742. See, e.g., First Historical Archives, *Huke hongben, Cangchu* [Copies of Routine Memorials Made for the Office of Scrutiny for Revenue, Granary Reserves], Bundle 87, Zhang Yunsui, QL 8/2/28. The year 1744 saw the virtual completion of the resetting of the ever-normal stocking targets in response to Sun's memorial (cf. n. 5 above).

13. On the principle and purpose of the annual sale of a set proportion of the ever-normal grain reserves, see above, ch. 2, introduction.
14. The problem of excessive reclamation of land which should have been left for water storage or containment was one with which Yang had recently been grappling on a larger scale. For his attempt to restrain reclamation on the margins of the Dongting Lake, see Perdue, *Exhausting the Earth*, p. 221.
15. There were regular bureaucratic procedures for inspecting disaster-stricken regions. For details, see Will, *Bureaucratie et famine*, pp. 103-6.

7. Commercial Policy and the Development of Market Consciousness

This final chapter has two main objectives. First, it seeks to illustrate the kinds of infrastructural support that many late imperial administrators were willing to provide for commerce, and thereby to reflect a cooperative approach by government towards legitimate commercial operations. Second, and more interestingly, it presents further soundings into the more advanced forms of market consciousness existing among certain Qing officials. As illustrated in the previous chapter, a genuinely liberal economic policy orientation could have developed only on the basis of belief that market mechanisms, and society's existing economic institutions, spontaneously brought about good outcomes for society. In order to assess the prospects for seriously meant, and genuine, economic liberalism in mid-Qing public policy determination, it is therefore necessary (although not sufficient) to investigate the degree of sophistication achieved by mid-Qing market consciousness at its most developed.

Texts 7.A and 7.B show two central China governors assisting commerce in the first case with improved anchorage facilities, and in the second with protection against restrictive practices by mountain porters. The first document comes from the Yongzheng period, the second from the early 1740s. Text 7.C, a document from the ever-normal granaries debate, argues that a portion of the grain collected by the granaries under current policy could well be replaced by silver. Not only does such an approach presuppose that the market has a role to play in bringing food to famine victims; the details of the discussion also show an effort to predict market response to different policy options. Text 7.D highlights, for the last time, the theme of policy dispute. Written from the point of view of a supply protectionist,

it quotes, and rejects, a singularly clear expression of the view
that a price mechanism functions to ensure that merchant
purchases of grain do not deplete markets excessively. As if
building on such consciousness, Text 7.E argues that a price
mechanism ensures the efficient allocation of commercial grain
stocks to the neediest markets in dearth-stricken areas. Of course,
no words corresponding to our "price mechanism" are used;
however, it is quite clear that the author understands the
principle.

*   *   *   *   *

Text 7.A (1728) contains Wang Guodong's proposals, as
Hunan governor, for creating a safe mooring place for merchant
vessels at the provincial capital, Changsha, on the River Xiang.
This was a recurrent concern of Changsha-based administrators,
and, at least in Wang's case, its motivation was probably partly
political.[1] As he describes in the preamble, Changsha was
economically completely overshadowed by its southern neighbour Xiangtan, a mere county capital but a bustling hub of
commerce. Wang seems to have felt that this situation was
improper, and that all that was required to redress it was action
to provide Changsha with safe mooring facilities. He presumably
wanted to build up Changsha's commerce as a means of giving
the city the centrality, wealth, and visual impressiveness
appropriate to a provincial capital. This motivation may have
been the stronger inasmuch as Changsha had only been provincial capital since 1664.[2]

One can only be struck by Wang's vivid depiction of the
commercial prosperity that, he suggests, will be engendered by

---

[1] One or other of the two alternative approaches to the problem was addressed
at least four times in the Ming dynasty, and in 1673, the early 1690s, 1746, and
1763. The "former river course" discussed in Text 7.A had been dug in the early
1690s, but was liable to silting. It had already had to be reopened once by 1728.
1747 *Changsha fuzhi* [Gazetteer of Changsha Prefecture], 5:7b-8a, 15b; PYTOCG,
48:27a-28b.

[2] It was in 1664 that Hunan was established as a separate province. For the
shallow history of the Hunan provincial administration, see 1747 *Changsha
fuzhi*, 18:8b, 11b, 12a, and 13a.

the reopening of a silted artificial inlet at Changsha. Part of his enthusiasm is for the prospect, dear to paternalist administrators, of livelihoods being provided for the poor, who will be able to support themselves as porters. Yet his words also seem imbued with an appreciation for commerce and material prosperity themselves. How far Wang is from the old-fashioned image of the Confucian scholar-official, with his eyes closed to the world of profit!

* * *

Text 7.B (1742) is a directive by Chen Hongmou, as Jiangxi governor. It is one of a number of directives which show him taking action to protect both waterborne and overland trade from crime, restrictive practices, and overcharging. While in Jiangxi, this interventionist friend of commerce took such measures as instituting waterborne patrols to combat piracy; threatening the punishment of beating to death for runners and servicemen who neglected anti-piracy responsibilities; ordering destruction of all "flying shuttle" and "both-ends-busy" boats (two sorts particularly useful for nefarious activities); having all fishing-boats numbered, and prohibiting them from fishing at night; having every passing boat inspected; instructing the merchants to moor only at "police" posts, not at "lonely islands"; providing government lifeboat and salvaging services; addressing the problem of wrecked vessels being plundered by false rescuers; and taking action against overcharging by the state-authorized shipping brokers.[3]

When it came to overland trade, Chen's main concern was apparently to protect merchants from the alleged malpractices and outright criminality of porters and the agencies through which their services were hired. In one directive, he ordered the magistrates of three widely separated jurisdictions on important interprovincial routes to deliberate on the setting of appropriate rates of pay for porters; on a fair system for exacting brokerage fees; and on means of preventing and, if need be, punishing abduction, swindling, and robbery with violence by the agencies

---

[3] PYTOCG, 12:3a-4a, 41a-42a; 13:3a-4a; 14:24a-25b; and 16:21a-23b.

or porters. Simple regulations were to be drawn up and, once approved, inscribed on wooden boards, which were to be placed at the agencies and along the routes.[4] Text 7.B deals with a particular problem in one of these jurisdictions, Yushan County on the Jiangxi-Zhejiang border. Here the porterage agencies had allegedly established a virtual monopoly of transport along the mountain route into Zhejiang by preventing donkey, mule, horse, and cart traffic from using the main road by daylight. They took advantage of their monopoly to charge arbitrary rates. This seemed to Chen unconscionable, since the road was quite level and broad enough to take cart traffic, and had just been repaired. He therefore ordered the local prefect to conduct an inquiry and submit proposals.

Singularly absent from Text 7.B is the paternalist's concern for the livelihood of "small folk" (although Chen does profess concern about the over-exertion which the porters bring upon themselves). He adopts the point of view of the commercial hirers, not the hired. However, what is striking about Text 7.B is that Chen is exercised not only by the merchants' excess costs, but also by the wastefulness and inefficiency of using human labour to carry heavy burdens long-distance on a one-way basis, despite the availability of other options. The emphasis of Text 7.B is thus simultaneously on eliminating lower class wrongdoing and upholding economic rationality. Economic rationality takes precedence over maximizing the number of people to be supported by the montane transport business.

*   *   *   *   *

Text 7.C (1745) comes from a stage in the ever-normal granaries debate in which the stocking targets were somewhat less ambitious than those introduced in 1738–39.[5] Imperial policy, at that time, was to promote sales of Imperial Academy studentships (that is, *jiansheng* titles), so far as possible, *as a substitute* for the established practice of official buying to restock the grana-

---

[4] Ibid., 13:2a-b.
[5] See n. 5 to Text 6.F above.

ries.[6] Text 7.C, by Qin Huitian (a vice-president of the Board of Rites) argues that it is a mistake to accept only grain from applicants for *jiansheng* titles. Rather, payment should be collected indifferently in either grain or silver, so that granary reserves will comprise a mix of grain and silver, in varying proportions.

Qin advocates this policy adjustment for two kinds of reason, the first having to do with the sales prospects for studentships in different circumstances, and the second with the relative desirability of stocking grain and stocking silver. The whole memorial is interesting (if difficult to read in places); however, its originality lies in the brief but systematic discussion of variables affecting the market for *jiansheng* titles, that is, the first set of reasons. Many of Qin's points about the relative advantages of stocking grain and stocking silver were made by others also.

Qin points out that people's willingness to part with grain in order to buy studentships should not be taken for granted, but depends on certain variables. There are, he indicates, circumstances in which people will prefer to buy the studentships with silver; if the court wishes to see the granaries filled, it must accommodate this preference. Specifically, willingness to pay in grain depends on grain being abundant; abundance of grain will be a function both of the state of the harvest within a given region, and of the extent to which that region grows grain in the first place. If grain is scarce (perhaps because of a bad harvest, perhaps because the local economy is based largely on tea), people will prefer to pay in silver. Meanwhile, any given individual's preference will be influenced by his occupation: farmers will prefer to pay in grain, merchants in silver. Payment in silver has, in any case, a built-in advantage for anyone not in a position to deliver grain from his own fields. The price per studentship for each category of applicant was originally set in

---

[6] QSL/QL, 211:16b-18a (1744); and Dunstan, *State or Merchant?*, ch. 5. Possession of a titular Imperial Academy studentship conferred certain social and legal privileges; a short cut to eligibility to sit the triennial examinations for the *juren* (provincial) degree; the opportunity to take these examinations with reduced competition; a limited tax exemption; and the entitlement to purchase various medium- and low-ranking posts in the bureaucracy. See, e.g., Ch'ü, *Local Government in China under the Ch'ing*, pp. 173-75; Chang, *The Chinese Gentry*, pp. 5-6, 22, 29, and 32-43; and Ho, *The Ladder of Success in Imperial China*, p. 34.

silver, and is commuted into grain at a fixed rate. If one has to buy grain to purchase a studentship, market fluctuations may leave one spending more than the set silver price.[7]

So far, Qin is already displaying an unusually well-developed consciousness that the state cannot simply throw a title on the market and expect people to pay for it in a commodity of the state's choosing, without regard for the economic circumstances that may condition the response of the prospective customers. This in itself is very creditable. However, on the boundary between Qin's first and second sets of reasons, he further draws attention to the theoretical implications for grain prices of a policy of requiring payments for studentships to be made consistently in either one form or the other. If all applicants must pay in silver, the extra sales of grain which will be made by farmers will risk aggravating a collapse of prices when the market is well-stocked; if all must pay in grain, the extra purchases of grain which will be made by non-farmers will risk aggravating the high prices of a period of shortage. Unfortunately, Qin does not spell out the theoretical price consequences of allowing applicants to choose how they will pay. Since, however, he has already said that people will prefer to pay in silver when grain is in short supply, he presumably has some sense that individual self-interest will set in train a regulating mechanism, by which additional short-term inflationary harm may be avoided.

Qin's argument for keeping the reserves in a mixture of grain and silver rests on a number of considerations, beginning with the truism that the more grain put in storage in the ever-normal granaries, the less will be available for the people's food supply. In a bad year, this will matter. Then there is the perishability of grain, and the unwelcome liability that the duty of stockpiling grain therefore imposes on magistrates; Qin suggests that county magistrates are in fact already sabotaging the studentship sales policy, so as to minimize their jeopardy. Keeping reserves partially in silver will create new opportunities for flexibility and

---

[7]Provincial officialdom was already well aware of the difficulty of selling studentships as long as the commutation rate was pegged at too high a level— i.e., a level which ignored the on-going inflation in the price of grain. The court addressed the problem in 1744, by ordering a rate reduction (QSL/QL, 211:17b-18a). This, however, did not solve the problem of perennial price fluctuations.

rationalization, with the provincial government redistributing granary resources within the province as the need arises. There will be new possibilities for taking advantage of favourable market opportunities for buying grain. Finally, issuing famine relief partly in the form of silver is by no means as pointless as it sounds. If people are starving, it may be to their advantage to be given money with which to buy food ready-cooked. Otherwise, what with the cumbersome business of preparing for grain distribution to the public, and the fact that the grain issued from the granaries will still need husking, the famine victims may have to wait too long before they eat. Recipients of silver will also be able to use part of their dole as capital, enabling them to gain the cash with which to buy food on the market.

Qin's justification of the practice of issuing food relief partly in monetary form is brief and not very impressive. However, two of his contemporaries, the investigating censor Sun Hao and the Hanlin Academy expositor-in-waiting Li Qingzhi, had between them offered the ingredients of a fully coherent economic rationale. The practice had in fact gained acceptance gradually over the early years of Qianlong's reign. Sun in particular had advocated its wider use, specifically as a way of obviating the necessity to keep replenishing the granaries with grain whatever the inflationary consequences.[8]

As far as Qin's brief treatment is concerned, we can say the following. He assumes that there will be food on the market in a famine-stricken area, although the poor will not be able to afford it without state assistance. The state will, as Sen would put it, boost the "exchange entitlements" of the poor both directly, through monetary hand-outs, and indirectly, by supplying them with capital with which to generate cash for themselves.[9] One suspects that, once a famine has started, it is a little late to try to

---

[8] Will, *Bureaucratie et famine*, pp. 121-23; First Historical Archives, CC, Li Qingzhi, QL 8/5/3 and Sun Hao, QL 8/5; Will and Wong, *Nourish the People*, pp. 477-78; and Dunstan, *State or Merchant?*, ch. 5. Cf. n. 4 to Text 6.F above for possible precedents for the practice in earlier reigns; it is noticeable, however, that Huang Liuhong (1694) seems to envisage silver doles as normally a supplement to food relief, and not a partial substitute for it.

[9] Cf. Amartya Sen, *Poverty and Famines: An Essay on Entitlement and Deprivation* (Oxford: Oxford University Press, 1982), pp. 3-4 and passim.

help the poor to boost their own exchange entitlements; but at least Qin is thinking, however casually, in market terms. The degree to which he is market-oriented is symbolized by the very short shrift he gives to the advantages of keeping granary reserves in grain. If, he suggests, one accepts payment for studentships in grain, one will be able to feel that one is literally carrying out the mandate of preparedness to feed the people; but there is not much more to it than that.

* * * * *

Text 7.D is a letter from Yan Sisheng, as provincial administration commissioner for Western Jiangsu and Anhui, to the governor-general for Jiangsu, Jiangxi, and Anhui. Yan seeks to enlist the governor-general's support in a dispute with the provincial administration commissioner for Eastern Jiangsu, who is stationed at Suzhou. The dispute concerns a conflict of interests between the consumers of Jiangning (that is, Nanjing, or "Nanking"), the Jiangsu provincial capital, where Yan is stationed; and the merchants and consumers of the island of Chongming, in the Yangzi estuary and, therefore, in the jurisdiction of the "Suzhou Commissioner."

The problem is that the Chongming merchants have recently been authorized to buy a limited but still substantial quantity of grain (30,000 bushels) in Jiangning. Yan believes that this is damaging for Jiangning consumer interests; the Suzhou commissioner has argued that it cannot be. The document is included here partly because of the clarity of the Suzhou commissioner's quoted protestation that if Jiangning's food supply is ever in real jeopardy, the Chongming merchants will be deterred by the high prices from depleting its stocks further. However, the text also illustrates the closeness with which Qing administrators might monitor the grain trade, when they saw a need to do so, and, therefore, the amount and kind of information they were likely to have about it. The story as a whole reminds us starkly that, in certain contexts, impulses towards a liberal approach had to battle with entrenched habits of regulation. It was not a foregone conclusion that the liberal impulses would prevail.

Some background is necessary for understanding Text 7.D. Both Jiangning and Chongming needed to import grain, Jiangning because it was a major city, and Chongming because the staple crop was cotton. Both places drew on the substantial flow of grain downriver from the central Yangzi provinces of Jiangxi, Hunan, and Hubei. However, special vigilance was thought to be required in Chongming's case, because the island's position at the mouth of the long river might create temptation for "wicked merchants" to slip out to sea with grain cargoes. This was basically illegal.[10]

Regulation had been introduced in the second decade of the eighteenth century, when the provincial governor had laid down an annual quota (or ceiling) for Chongming's upriver rice purchases. The quota was originally set at 220,000 bushels, in husked rice, to be brought back by a fleet of sixty boats. Subsequently, as the Chongming population rose, a conflict developed between officials sympathetic to Chongming, who did what they could to secure quota increases, and their more security-conscious superiors, who were apt to see increased quotas as an invitation to the "wicked" to sell grain to pirates. Zhao Hong'en, indeed, as governor in the mid-1730s, doubted whether even a quota as high as 220,000 bushels could be justified, especially after a secret inquiry found that during 1730–33, the annual amount of grain imported into Chongming had been only 160,000 to 170,000 bushels. In 1738, ironically, Chongming gained a supplementary quota for imports of a special kind of rice used for making wine and rice-cakes; and then in 1743 or 1744, the Chongming magistrate finally secured a permanent increase in the basic quota to 280,000 bushels. The number of boats was now set at 100. The basic quota was increased again to 340,000 bushels in c. 1760 (with no change in the number of boats). By this time, the whole policy of governing Chongming's rice imports with quotas had begun to look anachronistic, at least to the extent that the security concerns that had originally lain behind the ban on sea-borne

---

[10] On the prohibition of sea-borne export of grain in eighteenth-century China, and its ambiguous status in practice, see Will, *Bureaucratie et famine*, pp. 188-94.

exportation now belonged to the distant past.[11] However, what eventually eroded the control system was growing instability, beginning in 1790 and culminating with the Taiping Rebellion, in the arrangements laid down for the Chongming rice merchants to fill the annual quota.[12]

For, at least from the late 1720s on, the Chongming merchants were not free to buy grain where they chose. Rather, a permit system operated, and the merchants (who were also trading Chongming cloth) were limited to buying, according to sub-quotas, at three Yangzi Valley ports, all situated in Anhui. The nearest was Wuhu, a county seat not very far upriver from Jiangning; almost equidistant was the town of Yuncao, which lay on a tributary of the Yangzi and must have been a collection point for central Anhui rice. Text 7.D refers to the most distant of the ports as Zongyang. It is almost certainly safe to assume that this means Congyang, which was already in Ming times the most important market town of Tongcheng County, and had become the major outlet for the Tongcheng region's rich grain surpluses.[13] Congyang is considerably upriver from Wuhu, although still a fair distance from the Anhui-Jiangxi border. The control arrange-

---

[11] Thus the 1760 Chongming magistrate, commenting editorially in the local gazetteer, hinted that the policy of setting quotas might and should now be reviewed. See 1760 *Chongming xianzhi* [Gazetteer of Chongming County], 5:35b-36a. While the ban on sea-borne exports was inspired partly by concern for food security within the coastal provinces, it was also heir to the policy of keeping grain out of the hands of the Ming loyalists, Zheng Chenggong and family, who had challenged Qing rule in the first four decades after the Manchu conquest. As Will has shown (*Bureaucratie et famine*, pp. 190-93), many exceptions were made to the ban during the eighteenth century.

[12] 1760 *Chongming xianzhi*, 5:34b-35b; 1881 *Chongming xianzhi*, 6:41b-43a; 1930 *Chongming xianzhi*, 7:29a ff.; Zhao Hong'en, *Yuhua Tang Liang Jiang xi gao*, 1:25a, 42a, and *Yuhua Tang Liang Jiang pi'an* [Replies by the Liang-Jiang Governor-General to His Subordinates, from the Yuhua Hall] (1734), p. 18a.

[13] See Hilary J. Beattie, *Land and Lineage in China: A Study of T'ung-ch'eng County, Anhwei, in the Ming and Ch'ing Dynasties* (Cambridge: Cambridge University Press, 1979), p. 36; and Nakayama Mio, "Gōsan sagen ni tsuite" [On Zhang Ying's "Remarks on Real Estate"], *Tōyō Gakuhō* [Journal of Far Eastern Studies] 57, nos. 1-2 (1976), pp. 185 and 198 n. 43. The 1881 Chongming gazetteer specifically mentions Congyang as a designated buying-place in 1790. See 1881 *Chongming xianzhi*, 6:42b.

ments did not stop at this. Official records were kept of the amounts of rice bought by the Chongming merchants, and it is likely that the permits set out the amount that the holder was authorized to purchase.[14]

Yan Sisheng wrote Text 7.D probably in 1737.[15] From Yan's point of view, it should have been enough for the Chongming merchants that (as he mentions) their three designated buying-places were all ports of call for the rice boats from higher up the Yangzi. It was, he suggested, perverse of them to want to buy rice at Jiangning, when their needs could be amply supplied at these other places, which were not so very much further away from Chongming than Jiangning. One could also see what sort of people they were from the fact that they regularly bought more rice than was allowed them by the quotas. Yan knew for a fact, it seems, that the Chongming merchants were "repeatedly" smuggling grain out to sea. He also professed to fear popular alarm in Jiangning if the Chongming merchants showed their faces there.

When one person charges others with a "stubborn and perverse propensity for opting for the more convenient and the nearer," it is hard for an observer not to feel that the boot is on the other foot. From a twentieth-century perspective, Yan is an easy target for ridicule. Resisting this temptation, let us try to see the

---

[14] This may perhaps be inferred from the fact that, in the mid-1730s, Zhao Hong'en assumed that it was possible to calculate the total amount of rice for which permits had been issued in a given year. Zhao, *Yuhua Tang Liang Jiang pi'an*, p. 18a. On the permit issuing procedure, see id., *Yuhua Tang Liang Jiang xi gao*, 1:25a, and "Renhe Qinchuan Jushi," comp., *Huang Qing zouyi*, 61:2b-3a (memorial of 1775). Registers of the Chongming merchants' purchases are mentioned both in Text 7.D, and in a 1741 memorial reproduced in Ye Zhiru, "Qianlong nianjian Jiangnan shusheng xing jin xiqu shaojiu shiliao," p. 19. This memorial, like Text 7.D, claims that the registers show the Chongming merchants to be exceeding their purchase quotas.

[15] Yan served as "Jiangning commissioner" from 1736/2 till 1740/3 (lunar calendar). There was a change of governor-general after the fourth moon (Par. 3) in both 1737 and 1739. Of these two dates, 1737 seems the more likely, on the basis of the information on natural disasters given in 1907 *Jinling tongji, xu* [History of Jiangning: Supplement], 2:1a (cf. Par. 4). There is a not altogether satisfactory treatment of Text 7.D in Chuan and Kraus, *Mid-Ch'ing Rice Markets and Trade*, pp. 62-63, and 202-3, notes 17-19.

dispute clearly. Yan is concerned about the food supply of a large city in a dearth-stricken area. The city is dependent on a continuous stream of rice imports, and it may well be that popular feelings are as volatile as he suggests. The last thing he wants is for outside merchants to be authorized to come and buy 30,000 bushels on the city's markets. The moralism of the broader political culture permits him to strengthen his argument by emphasizing the "wickedness" of the merchants in question, this "wickedness" being evident in their breaking the existing rules for the nefarious purpose of smuggling grain out to sea. In short, a control system has been set up to prevent the Chongming merchants from selling the people's grain to foreigners and pirates; from Yan's perspective, it is in the interests of the Jiangning population that this system be upheld.

The Suzhou commissioner has argued that the Chongming merchants will not come to Jiangning when rice prices there are high.[16] Yan does not seem fully to grasp his point. Moreover, he is sufficiently blind to any sense that the market equitably allocates limited resources as to protest to the governor-general that it is hard on the Jiangning consumers if the Chongming merchants carry their grain away whenever it is cheap. He writes as if urban consumers are entitled to expect at least occasional cheap rice. We may, I think, take it for granted that, whatever the high principles of "free circulation" policy, Yan voices the real sentiments of many at this point.

*   *   *   *   *

The most sophisticated price mechanism argument I have yet found from mid-Qing China was also greeted with resistance, at least in the short term. The short-term resistance can be documented; the longer-acting influence on policy, although very likely real, must remain a matter of conjecture. The argument in

---

[16] If Text 7.D was indeed written in 1737, the commissioner in question will have been Zhang Qu. Zhang Qu's market sense is well reflected in his role in the roughly contemporaneous revision of arrangements for importing copper from Japan. See Helen Dunstan, "Safely Supping with the Devil: The Qing State and Its Merchant Suppliers of Copper," *Late Imperial China* 13, no. 2 (1992), pp. 69-70.

question is found in a 1738 memorial (Text 7.E) which I believe to have helped to clear the ideological way for the 1742–49 experiment with general suspension of the transit taxes upon staple foodstuffs.[17]

We saw in Chapter 4 above that in 1737–38, a policy was adopted of routinely remitting transit taxes on grain cargoes on the routes into dearth-stricken areas. This, at the time, was the furthest the government was prepared to go towards implementing Gan Rulai's suggestion (in Text 4.F) that it attempt to lower the general level of grain prices by abolishing grain transit taxes altogether. However, given the conventional suspicion of merchant morality, even the more limited policy was seen to raise one problem. How could the state prevent merchants who had benefited from a tax remission from slipping off and selling their grain elsewhere than in the famine-stricken zone?

The initial answer given to this troublesome conundrum was control. According to regulations tried out briefly in Jiangsu in 1738, in order to qualify for tax remission, a merchant would have to specify the disaster-stricken county for which his grain was destined. The customs station authorities would issue him with a certificate, which he was to present or forward to the authorities of that county on arrival. The county authorities were to fill in the date of his arrival, stamp the certificate, and return it to him. After his sales were completed, he would be required to go back the same way, so that the issuing authorities could verify that he had earned his exemption. A merchant who secured exemption under false pretences would be punished.[18]

Text 7.E was written as an early protest against these arrangements. The author had seen the memorial proposing them in *The Metropolitan Gazette* and guessed that they would be unappealing to the merchant community. Part of his objection had to do with the requirement that the merchant have his certificate stamped by the authorities in the county of sale. On

---

[17] See above, ch. 4, introduction. The transit tax suspension in fact applied to beans as well as grain.

[18] 1899 DQHDSL, 239:17a-b, amended by reference to Text 7.E and QSL/QL, 79:9b. Cf. Kōsaka, "Kenryū-dai zenki ni okeru kanzei shukoku-zei menjo-rei ni tsuite," pp. 52-53, to which I owe (directly or indirectly) the references used in this discussion. For further detail, see Dunstan, *State or Merchant?*, ch. 2.

one hand, this would expose the merchant to the depredations of official underlings. On the other, whereas merchants liked to travel secretively, for security reasons, the process of going to the *yamen* and applying for the stamp would be publicly visible and would ruin the merchant's incognito. However, more interesting for our purposes is the part of the memorial where the author argues that the requirement that the merchant specify his destination in advance will block the spontaneous operation of price incentives. Left without interference, price incentives will themselves ensure that merchant grain flows to the worst-stricken markets, and does so in a benign sequence.

The argument is very simple. Travelling grain merchants instinctively make for the highest selling prices available within a region at a given time. These will be found in the areas most severely visited by natural disaster. After the merchants have "converged" upon the most severely stricken areas, the prices in these areas will fall, causing the merchants to turn their attention to whichever areas are now offering the highest selling prices. The process will presumably be repeated (although the author does not spell this out) until prices in the region as a whole no longer compete with those available elsewhere. The mechanism will operate most efficiently without state interference. Compelling a merchant to abide by a commitment to sell at a designated place precludes him from responding to more acute need elsewhere.

Text 7.E recommends that the only limitation placed on the freedom of a merchant who has had the transit tax remitted be that he must sell within the province in which the qualifying natural disaster has occurred. The Board of Revenue, however, altogether failed to see the author's point. The Board response restated the position that some jurisdictions would be disaster-stricken, others not; if one did not have a destination specified and check that the merchant duly reached it, there would be nothing to stop "wicked" merchants from slipping off elsewhere to sell their grain once they had won the tax remission. The emperor, however, ordered that the matter be referred to the Jiangsu governor and governor-general for further discussion.[19]

---

[19] QSL/QL, 77:5a-b.

The short-term outcome was a compromise. That even this much was achieved was partly owing to a report of poor merchant response from the superintendent of the key Hushu customs station, on the Grand Canal approaching Suzhou. The report attributed the merchants' lack of enthusiasm for the offered tax incentive specifically to their dislike of the control procedure, which they feared would waste their time. The superintendent and the Jiangsu governor therefore proposed a policy revision which would transfer the onus of verification onto the authorities. The customs station authorities would be required to tell the authorities of the destination county which merchants to expect, and how much grain they should be bringing; the county authorities would be responsible for notifying the customs station of the merchants' arrival, with the full amount of grain. The merchants would still have to go back the same way, in order to surrender their exemption certificates. The emperor endorsed this, with a nod to Text 7.E in the shape of the concession that if a merchant's destination county had already been sufficiently supplied by other operators, there "would be no harm" in letting him change course, and sell his grain in a neighbouring jurisdiction.[20]

The emperor had failed to accept the central implication of the argument of Text 7.E, which was that regulation is simply unnecessary. However, Text 7.E's ringing expression of the view that merchants can be trusted to bring grain to areas of shortage of their own accord may have helped prepare the way for the emperor's decision, in 1742, to try permanent removal of the transit tax on staple foodstuffs after all. If the state did not (as had previously been assumed) need selective tax remissions to attract grain into areas of shortage, it could perhaps experiment with outright abolition as a way of lowering the general level of food prices.

There is one surprise about Text 7.E. Its author was Fang Bao.[21]

---

[20] QSL/QL, 79:9a-10b.

[21] Celebrated Neo-Confucian scholar, author of Text 5.A, and principal proponent of the anti-liquor policy.

*   *   *   *   *

Text 7.A

Memorial asking permission to dredge the old river at the north gate of Changsha

Date: 1728
Author: Wang Guodong, as Hunan governor.
Source: YZZZHB, Vol. 31, pp. 313-14; *Yongzheng zhupi yuzhi*,
            Wang Guodong, 68b-70b; HCJSWB, 117:14a-b.

... Last year, being in receipt of an Imperial command, I proceeded from Zhejiang to my appointment in Hunan. My route passed through the county of Xiangtan, subordinate to Changsha, and I beheld a thousand boats assembled like the clouds, the merchants of the four directions drawn together like the spokes into a wheel. The market towns for several *li* around have merchandise piled high; trade goes between the having and the wanting, and the folk dwell closely packed together, like teeth on a comb. Changsha, meanwhile, is the provincial and prefectural capital, and, what is more, is built hard by the River Xiang. And yet when one surveys the river's banks, one finds no boats in mooring there.

The explanation for this must be that the water of the Xiang rushes tumultuously east into the Dongting Lake to reach the Yangzi.[1] Whereas at Xiangtan the river curves somewhat, and the force of the north wind is gentle, at Changsha not only is the river broad and the north wind's force severe, but there are also no small inlets in which one may take shelter. If the boats were moored in rows, there would be worry lest they bumped each other; if they lay at anchor singly, there would be fear of thieves. If suddenly the wind arose and waves surged forth, it would be hard to withstand them at the instant. There are frequent cases of boats being sunk and people drowned. Thus is it that the boats of the authorities and folk can find no mooring; and if the merchant vessels likewise for the most part go to Xiangtan, it is because, Xiangtan apart, there is no place where they can anchor. It calls to mind the case of the Hukou internal customs station in Jiangxi. This was formerly at Hukou, but what with the greatness of the

Yangzi waters and the shock of the current from the Boyang Lake, the merchants were constantly in danger from the wind and waves when halting their boats to pay the customs dues. Imperial grace being received, the station was transferred to Jiujiang, and men applauded the convenience of it.[2]

I note respectfully that outside the north gate of Changsha, there lies a former river course, three thousand feet in length. It has long been silted up and blocked. Were this river to be dug out deep and wide as it was formerly, a good number of vessels could be moored upon it. It would truly be a thing of great convenience to the folk. Not only could the shipping of authorities and people going back and forth escape from danger: those plying small boats to contrive their livelihood would likewise be enabled to lie peacefully on quiet waters, without being tossed by wind and wave. Moreover, merchant ships would gather from the four directions. If one attracts the hundred crafts, finance will be sufficient; if one causes the hundred wares to circulate, livings will be abundant. As for the people who live by their strength, carrying burdens upon shoulder-poles, once there is merchandise to come and go and to be lifted up and down, even these will gain the opportunity to take load after load, which means that the waterside will also be a hunting-ground for food and clothing for the poor.

The situation stares me in the face; yet as to funding for the proposed project, there is no item that one might appropriate to it. I have before me now a submission from the Postal Relays, Salt, and Grain Intendant, Yang Bi, which reads, in part, as follows: "The dikes in the prefectural jurisdictions of Changsha, Yuezhou, and Changde have not yet been made firm, with the result that when the water swells in spring and summer, it bursts the dikes and overflows. The growing crops are inundated, and it is hard for the people to dwell peaceably. We have reverently received an Edict ordering the restoration of these dikes. . . . I find that this intendancy has always hitherto had 8,000 taels a year of customary salt fee income.[3] At the end of the year I wish to merge the 8,000 tls. still available from . . . 1727 and the 8,000 tls. which will be surplus under 1728, to yield altogether 16,000 tls., and allocate this sum to the dike restoration work. I further note that Changsha is the provincial capital, and the boats of merchants plying back and forth gather like clouds. The plain fact is, however, that what with its mighty waters, as of the great Yangzi, Changsha lacks a place where shipping may be moored. . . . I find that outside the north gate, there lies a former river course. As soon as the 8,000 tls. that will be surplus under 1729 have been delivered, this river can be dredged and opened up for mooring. It may be hoped that this will not be altogether lacking in assistance as regards the people's livelihood in the locality. As for the 8,000 tls. *per annum* of surplus for subsequent years, this should all be deposited in the intendancy treasury for public purposes."

. . . Yang Bi's proposal to allocate the 1727 and 1728 funds for dike restoration, and the 1729 funds for dredging the river bed, is precisely in conformance with my own view. I have now made an estimate of the amount required, and we may anticipate expenditure of approximately 14,000 tls. or so. Yet since the project is concerned with promoting the public good, it would appear that it allows of no delay. According to my foolish view, work might perhaps be started this autumn or winter. As to whether we should use an advance from the tax funds in the provincial treasury to carry out the dredging, awaiting the arrival of the intendant's regularized funds for 1729 to replace the sum expended, prostrate, I beg Your Majesty's Imperial considera-tion. . . .[4]

Notes

1. In fact, the general direction taken by the Xiang downstream from Changsha is north-westerly until quite near the Dongting Lake.
2. Jiujiang and Hukou are on the west and east sides respectively of the confluence of the Yangzi River and Boyang Lake. The Hukou cus-toms station had originally been at Jiujiang, and was moved to Hukou in 1683. It was moved back in 1724. See 1874 *Jiujiang fuzhi* [Gazetteer of Jiujiang Prefecture], 12:1a. A memorial by one Wang Zehong requesting the relocation to Jiujiang states that the move to Hukou had originally been intended as a temporary measure to catch the traffic between Jiangxi and the Lower Yangzi provinces, which could pass straight into the Yangzi from the Boyang Lake without reporting at the Jiujiang customs station. Confirming our present author's remarks, Wang Zehong explains the danger to

shipping arising from the inadequacy of the sheltered mooring area available at Hukou. He argues that the Jiangxi-Lower Yangzi traffic could be caught by means of a branch station at a more suitable spot on the mouth of the lake. See HCJSWB, 51:6a-b.

3. These were non-statutory fees paid by salt merchants; according to Zelin, they had the character of "fixed periodic payments" which the merchants were supposed to make gladly, out of recognition of their privileged position as dealers in state salt. See Zelin, *The Magistrate's Tael*, pp. 204-5.

4. "Regularized funds" is a translation for *guigong yin*, more literally "funds which have reverted to the public coffers." These were the monies claimed for regular state revenues under the Yongzheng emperor's fiscal reforms (see above, ch. 4, introduction). The "regularized funds" in question here were the annual 8,000 tls. of salt fee income accruing to the Hunan Postal Relays, Salt, and Grain Intendancy. Under the new rules of the Yongzheng period, such unofficial revenue had to be declared and formally allocated to administrative expenditures or other public purposes. See Wang, *Land Taxation in Imperial China*, p. 68, and Zelin, *The Magistrate's Tael*, pp. 206-8. In the climate of the Yongzheng period, an official in Yang Bi's position probably had an interest in assiduously proposing socially beneficial ways in which the "regularized funds" pertaining to his office might be used.

*　　*　　*　　*　　*

Text 7.B

Decree ordering that it be ascertained whether or not beasts of burden can be used on the main road through Yushan
Date:　　1742
Author:　Chen Hongmou, as Jiangxi governor.
Source:　PYTOCG, 13:15a-b.

The county of Yushan lies on the main route into Zhejiang. Although the road is described as mountainous, for half its course it crosses rounded hilltops, and the gradient is mostly gentle. There are absolutely no dangerous places. Earlier, because there were many spots where the soil had given way, making it harder for porters to travel back and forth, I ordered the Yushan magistrate to repair the entire course. I have already received memoranda from the said magistrate and vice-magistrate reporting that they have had the whole road repaired, so that the surface is now even. On a gently sloping, major thoroughfare like this, it should be possible for donkeys, horses, and cart traffic to pass: what is the necessity for using a crowd of porters? Not only does it mean extra costs for the merchants, but the exertion of the porters is also excessive. It is absolutely not the proper way to go about things!

On enquiry, I have now heard that in the said area there used to be donkeys, mules, horses, and carts which could be used to transport goods. Their disappearance results entirely from the monopolistic activities of the porterage agencies, which do not permit donkeys, horses, or cart traffic to use the main road. Such pack-horses or donkeys as there are have either to travel at night, or else to take some other, less frequented and remoter route. The result is that the porters, having taken possession of the road by force of numbers, charge whatever rates they choose. Not only do the merchants pay the heavy charges and suffer the porters' swindling and discourtesy, but the porters carry heavy burdens one-way over long distances, coming back unladen. The journeys to and fro involve both wasteful expenditure and physical over-exertion. These various unsatisfactory aspects of the matter call for deliberation, with a view to eliminating the abuses and vexations. Apart from the question of porterage rates, which I have already ordered the provincial administration commissioner to have investigated . . ., it is my urgent duty to order an enquiry as to the best way of opening the main road through Yushan to carts and beasts of burden, for the convenience of merchants and travellers. On receipt of this decree, the responsible prefect shall, at his early convenience, ascertain whether or not this road is suitable for donkeys, mules, and carts; which of the above forms of transport would be convenient; whether one should alternatively use a combination of horses and human porters; and why, up till now, it has not been permitted for donkeys, mules, and carts to use the road together. . . . He is also to write to the magistrate of Changshan county, and involve him in the process of devising satisfactory proposals.[1] The said prefect is to submit a report for my decision.

Note

1. Changshan lay across the border in Zhejiang. Being adjacent to Yushan, it was the first county traversed by this trunk route on the Zhejiang side.

* * * * *

Text 7.C

Memorial advocating that both silver and grain be accepted as payment for titular studentships in the Imperial Academy
Date: 1745
Author: Qin Huitian, as vice-president of the Board of Rites.
Source: First Historical Archives, CC, Qin Huitian, QL 10/6/25; HCJSWB, 39:12b-13b.

[*A long preamble, omitted here, praises the emperor's diligence and devotion in promoting measures for the people's welfare, including a recent decision to give the entire landowning population a one-year holiday from the agrarian taxes that formed by far the largest category of state revenue.*[1] *The author then indicates that he would like to make his own small contribution to his sovereign's efforts in the cause of "cherishing the folk and making resources sufficient."*]

In my opinion, the folk of today are afflicted not so much by poverty as by the inequality between rich and poor; and not so much by lack of resources as by the fact that the resources do not circulate. Because of this the rich grow daily richer while the poor grow daily poorer. The former process gives rise to the mischiefs of luxurious living and failure to know one's place in life; with the latter process, not only do the solitary and supportless suffer the distress of having no one to whom they may turn, but even scholars, being in very many cases without means for the support of life, experience the hardship of having no time for the cultivation of ceremony and right conduct. With folk such as these, it is hard for famine-relief loans and distributions to reach all who need them, nor do they feel the benefit of tax remissions, yet how, in truth, should there be even one of them who is not held within the Sovereign's Sage concern?[2] However, if one wishes to provide for limitless remission and bestowal out of fixed operating funds, this will certainly, by the very nature of the case, be hard. If, on the other hand, confronted with this absolute impossibility, one wishes to seek out a path of assistance through adjustment, then there is nothing that will confer greater kindness or more universal benefit than to "draw on excess so as to supplement paucity," and let the folk be nourished by society itself.

A gracious Edict was earlier vouchsafed permitting, for the sake of famine relief, the retention of the system of soliciting contributions in exchange for studentships in the Imperial Academy. At first, the Board of Revenue was to accept payment in the form of silver; now the provinces are to accept it in the form of grain. This is truly a good measure that exemplifies adaptability to accommodate the people. In my foolishness, I am of the opinion that inasmuch as the present rules only enjoin acceptance of payment in grain, prospective contributors will not be uniformly eager, and the granaries will not be swiftly filled. It will be insufficient as precaution against famine. If one were slightly to adapt the policy, then contributions would be ample, and not only would there be provision for relief, but it would also be possible to use the surplus to do good unto the indigent. Having thought the matter over several times, and exerted my full mental powers in exhaustive exploration of it, I have become persuaded that exclusively accepting grain is less fully excellent than accepting either grain or silver. Besides, already last year Shandong received authorization to carry out the latter policy on a temporary basis. If the authorization were extended to the remaining provinces, the good results would certainly become perceptible at once. I will respectfully expound this for Your Majesty.

The advantages of accepting grain amount to one point, the disadvantages to four. What I call the one advantage is that if one collects and stores payment in kind, it will be handy for making distributions, while the basic idea of providing a sufficiency of food will be preserved.

I bear in mind that grain and money (coin and precious metals) are alike in being handy, but they function according to different principles. The supply of grain is subject to good and bad harvests, while that of precious metal knows neither plenitude nor shortage. There exists a fixed quantity of silver, but there is no fixed price for grain.[3] The folk produce only a limited amount of grain. If it is indeed a good year and there is surplus grain, then to make a timely garnering as precaution against flood or drought is truly excellent. If *at a time of scarcity* those who are fervent in the public cause buy grain in order to make contributions, not only will the price of grain surge up, to the detriment of the poor, but for each extra bushel in store in the granaries there will be one bushel of food less among the people. Besides, the current price will change as time goes by.[4] Even after the amount required per studentship has been reduced, contributors will still be few. This is the first disadvantage.

Grain cannot be kept long in storage. The provinces differ in the humidity of their climates; if stale grain accumulates, mildewing and rotting give cause for concern. The useful turns into its opposite.[5] This is the second disadvantage. When, at the close of a magistrate's term of office, the granary stocks are audited by his successor, the discovery of any spoiled grain encumbers the outgoing magistrate with the obligation to replace it.[6] Officials therefore look upon acquiring new stocks as a path of peril, and secretly restrain would-be contributors or put difficulties in their way. The contributors arrest their steps and fail to come forward. This is the third disadvantage. The nature of the land is different from one province to another. Jiangnan, Zhejiang, Sichuan, and Guangxi are the regions which produce the most grain, while in Fujian, Guangdong, Yunnan, and Guizhou there are places where grain is in short supply. If one insists upon collecting contributions uniformly, it is to be feared that there will arise many cases of one province's granaries being over-supplied while those of another have too little. This is the fourth disadvantage. It is because there are these disadvantages that I worry that prospective contributors will not be uniformly eager, that the granaries will not be swiftly filled, and that the measure will be insufficient as precaution against famine.

If, however, administrators are all instructed to accept both grain and silver, there will be five advantages. In the first place, it is reasonable to observe that the making of contributions is affected by variations in celestial, terrestrial, and human factors.[7] In years when the harvests are good, paying in grain is convenient; in years when they are poor, paying in silver is convenient. This is a matter of celestial factors. In districts where grain is plentiful, paying in grain will be preferred; in areas where it is scarce, paying in silver will be preferable. This is a matter of terrestrial factors. Those who labour in the fields will prefer to pay in grain; those who pursue commerce will prefer to pay in silver. This has to do with human factors. How much the more inasmuch as when one pays in grain, one still has to contend with variations in the current price, while when one pays in silver, values and quantities expended are all uniform![8] This is the first advantage.

If those who possess grain are not required to exchange it for silver, then, when grain is plentiful, one will not risk the price declining to the farmers' detriment; and if those who possess silver are not required to exchange it for grain, then, when grain is scarce, one will not risk the price increasing to the people's detriment. If the choice between silver and grain is left to the contributor's convenience, the response will be enthusiastic, and the granaries will certainly be filled. This is the second advantage.

In principle, contributions for the relief stocks should be made in grain. However, while the need of starving people to be fed is urgent, opening the granaries and transporting the grain is likely to take time, and even when the beneficiaries have received their ration, they must still pound it, winnow it, and cook it.[9] If contributions have reached a sufficient level and relief is issued partially in silver, bought cakes may bring immediate satisfaction to the stomach, while by deploying part as capital, recipients may also contrive their livelihood. Besides, if the relief is issued half in silver, half of the allocated grain may be retained, and the granary reserves will not be too greatly depleted. This is the third advantage.

When flood or drought creates emergency, and there is next to no time in which to act, the regulations enjoin that the provincial authorities send a memorial to the throne on one hand, and release funds for relief upon the other. However, the regular monies from the land and labour service tax are of weighty importance, and if the senior officials are over-cautious with disbursements, there will be risk of famine victims falling through the net. If grain and silver are indeed both ample, there can be generous dispensing at the local level. The poor, unseen, will feel the bounty, while the superior officials will not devour the fat.[10] This is the fourth advantage.

If both silver and grain are accepted, then if one jurisdiction has a deficiency of grain but an excess of silver, there is no reason why one cannot transfer its surplus silver to buy another place's surplus grain, or use the surplus silver from dearth years to buy the surplus grain of years of plenty. With buying cheap and selling dear, grain in the granaries will necessarily be plentiful, and it will also be possible to overcome one limitation of the ever-normal method.[11] This is the fifth advantage.

As for the provincial treasuries, these are the basis of the system of precautionary reserves. If the arrangements I propose are put into practice, although the grain should still be gathered in at local level, instructions should be given for all the silver contributions of each province to be forwarded to the provincial treasury for unified accounting. All these famine relief funds should be retained within the treasury of the home province.[12] In normal times, one would make purchasing decisions according to the level of grain prices; in times of crisis, one would implement relief on the basis of a careful survey of the relative urgency of each area's predicament. If one used income drawn from the entire province to rescue one corner in its hour of need, this would provide for the effective flow of succour and avoid depletion in the face of crisis. . . .

If this is carried out for a long time, there is bound to be a surplus. If so, appropriate subventions can be made within each province for undertakings in the fields of agricultural improvement and water conservancy; for the works of poor relief and care of orphans; for those widows, widowers, and solitary ones who have no one to turn to; for poor students who cannot support themselves; and for the needs of colleges and academies. Further, if one thus draws upon the surplus of the wealthy of the province to relieve the want of its own needy people, so that fullness and depletion counteract each other and resources circulate; then, from this time forward, of those whom relief loans and distributions fail to reach and tax remissions fail to benefit, there will be none who are not equally endued by Sage munificence. . . . It will be bounty free of cost, an inexhaustible resource. This is what I mean by saying "If one were slightly to adapt the policy, not only would there be provision for relief, but it would also be possible to use the surplus to do good unto the indigent. . . ."

[*In the remainder of the memorial, Qin sets out some implementational details of his proposed policy change; explains how his proposal that the silver be deposited in the provincial treasury overcomes the Board of Revenue's previous concern about letting payments in silver be collected at the county level; and takes the precaution of pointing out the difference between his proposal and a recently rejected one by Emida.*]

Notes

1. For the remission edict, see QSL/QL, 242:9a-10b (1745).
2. Government students (*shengyuan*) were entitled to famine relief, as were at least those "solitary and supportless" people (widows, childless old folk, and so on) who belonged among the peasants. Qin's point was presumably that registration procedures, the discretionary decisions of local or regional administrators, village-level corruption, etc., might leave some eligible individuals excluded. Urban "solitary and supportless" people were especially vulnerable, since city dwellers were in general not entitled to relief. Will mentions that the urban "solitary and supportless" might be permitted to register for relief in nearby villages, but such a provision cannot have been fully satisfactory. See Will, *Bureaucratie et famine*, pp. 123-24.
3. The monetary assumptions reflected here seem a little simplistic for the mid-eighteenth century. Qin writes as if silver could be regarded simply as a standard of value, so that fluctuations in the amount of silver available to society were irrelevant (if indeed such fluctuations took place at all). Although questions of silver supply were probably not particularly acute in the mid-eighteenth century (as they had been in the late seventeenth), many of Qin's contemporaries must have been aware that the truth was more complex.
4. The kind of change Qin has in mind is presumably a continuing short-term upward trend as the scarcity of grain grows more acutely felt. In the following brief sentence, he hints that this price increase will force the state to cut the charge per studentship (which in itself, given the circumstances, will lower total receipts of grain), but that it will be impossible to cut the charge sufficiently to maintain the

attractiveness of the grain-for-studentship transaction in a situation of famine or near-famine prices.

5. The framers of the state granary system were, of course, well aware of this danger. For the various countermeasures prescribed in ever-evolving regulations, see QCWXTK, 34:5172-73 and 36:5187, and Will and Wong, *Nourish the People*, pp. 33-36 and 105-10.

6. On the rigorous audits of granary stocks required when an outgoing magistrate transferred his responsibilities to his successor, and on the liability of the outgoing magistrate, see Will and Wong, *Nourish the People*, pp. 204-18.

7. Literally, "variations in Heaven's seasons, Earth's advantages, and human activities." The allusion is to *Mengzi* 2B/1, which argues that in warfare advantageous geographical location is more important than favourable climatic conditions, and human unity more important than either.

8. Qin is referring to situations in which contributors buy the grain which they deliver to the granaries. How much they will spend depends upon the current price. If, however, they are able to pay silver, the amount that they will spend is fixed.

9. Qin is alluding to the problem, addressed also by Emida and others (see Text 1.E above and n. 4 thereto) that grain stored, for durability, in unhusked form was liable to be issued in that form unless administrators took deliberate steps to have it husked. Common administrative practice did, however, provide one partial answer to his point about the burden placed on starving people by the need to husk, winnow, and cook: the local rich could be encouraged to provide ready-cooked relief at "gruel kitchens" until the authorities were ready to begin the official relief distributions (Will, *Bureaucratie et famine*, pp. 126-27). As long as the people were not already starving when they received their relief rations, husking, winnowing, and cooking would not be an abnormal burden in peasant communities; and official famine relief was in principle intended almost exclusively for peasants.

10. Qin alludes to the possibility of relief funds from the provincial treasury falling victim to corruption at the intermediate and upper levels of the provincial hierarchy. To the extent that reserves of grain and money held by ever-normal granaries were under the control of county magistrates, they were, presumably, normally immune to the avarice of senior officials. However, Qin's point here would have been nullified by adoption of his concluding proposal that all silver receipts from sales of studentships be aggregated at provincial level.

11. Qin's use of the expression "buying cheap and selling dear" here seems surprising. The most likely interpretation is that he means no

more than "buying at a lower price than one will charge when selling." His scheme would enhance the likelihood of grain being bought at sufficiently low cost prices to enable granaries to make a modest profit on their operations. The profits would at least give the granaries a certain margin of security, and perhaps also generate sufficient surplus to finance the other social welfare activities which Qin later enumerates.

12. Qin is signalling that each province's silver receipts from sales of studentships should be immune not only to diversion to central government purposes of other kinds, but also to transfer to other provinces.

*   *   *   *   *

Text 7.D

Letter to the Governor-General discussing the grain purchases of cloth merchants

Date: 1737
Author: Yan Sisheng, as provincial administration commissioner for Western Jiangsu and Anhui.
Source: Yan Sisheng, *Chumeng shanfang ji* [Collected Works of Yan Sisheng] (1745), *Shu* [Letters], 2:36a-39a; HCJSWB, 47:19b-20b.

I take the liberty of reflecting that Jiangning, as provincial capital, is a place of great importance. It has a teeming population; and, while those engaged in secondary pursuits are many, those who till the land are few. The city can only rely on Zongyang, Wuhu, and Yuncao, the points at which the rice-boats from Jiangxi and Huguang congregate: a portion of the merchants' surplus grain is shipped directly to Jiangning in order to supply the need for purchases. This truly is the entire city's self-renewing, never-failing store. It is of even more importance than the granary reserves.

The problem is, however, that the wicked merchants of Chongming invariably buy too much at the said points and slip away, exceeding their set quotas. In all three places, wicked brokers and county clerks have joined in mutual collusion, so that it is in the end impossible to ascertain the actual amounts that have been bought. There are repeated instances of cargoes being smuggled onto the high seas in quest of profit, which is a flagrant violation of the prohibition. Take the case of this year's sales at Yuncao, where, according to the quota, they should have bought 80,000 bushels: upon examination of the registers submitted by the county, I find that they have actually bought over 119,000 bushels. This already gives a rough idea of their stubborn and perverse propensity for opting for the more convenient and the nearer, and failing to observe the quotas laid down for them. . . .

I find that in the fourth moon of the present year, authorization was granted to a proposal from the Suzhou administration commissioner to the effect that the Chongming merchants should every year load up with cloth and proceed to Jiangning, there to exchange it for 30,000 bushels of rice, to be deducted, bushel for bushel, from the 100,000 bushels originally set for them to purchase at Zongyang. I responded to this by submitting representations to the effect that Jiangning, being the provincial capital, is large and densely populated; that the rice grown in the area does not amount to much, and the populace's food supply depends entirely on succour from the Jiangxi and Huguang traders; and that it would not be expedient to let the Chongming merchants repurchase the imported grain, thereby pushing up the prices in the city higher still. Your Honour's predecessor instructed the Suzhou commissioner to investigate and report; the latter responded by requesting that his earlier proposal be upheld, and that the merchants be allowed to buy rice in Jiangning. This received your predecessor's endorsement and is on the files. I wish to submit the following considerations.

The provincial seat of Jiangnan has a dense population and requires a very large amount of grain to feed it. It has long depended on outside supplies of rice to meet its needs. If for three to five days the outside traders fail to arrive, the price of rice goes up. At present, the immediate vicinity is suffering from localized natural disasters, and very large amounts of grain are needed for relief and stabilizing sales. It would in the nature of the case be inadvisable to let the Chongming merchants carry the imported grain away again. The situation is before my very eyes, and I am very well acquainted with it. How would it be tolerable if I failed to speak out?

I see that the submission from the Suzhou commissioner has it that "The merchants, in their holding of capital for operation, have nothing other than profit in view. If rice in Jiangning is in good supply and the price is low, those who trade with wares borne on their backs will naturally leap up, vying with each other as they make towards it. If rice should be in short supply and the price elevated, then even if you tried to drive them, it is to be feared that they would not present themselves. How could there be a situation in which their purchases of rice were detrimental to the city population's food supply?" Now to say that when the price is low they will rush to buy, and that when the price is high they will not come, is admirable representation of the interests of the Chongming merchants. But when the price is high, it is to be the citizens who pay it for their food; when the price is low, the rice will be bought and exported by the Chongming merchants. This means that the ordinary people of the provincial capital Jiangning are never to enjoy consuming low-priced rice. Besides, of recent times rice prices in the provincial capital have consistently been higher than those of Suzhou. If the Chongming merchants also are allowed to buy, will the prices not go higher still?

Coming now to where he says "The rice merchants of Jiangxi and Huguang have a long-standing awareness that if they come to Jiangning, there will be cloth for them to buy. Therefore, year after year, they load up with rice and come as expected. If now they hear that the Chongming merchants are taking their cloth elsewhere, I fear that the Huguang merchants will in turn change their destination, which, I would think, would have its harmful consequences." I find that as the rice-boats of Jiangxi and Huguang move eastwards down the Yangzi, there are three major ports of call, and these are Zongyang, Wuhu, and Suzhou. Those boats which visit Jiangning are not more than one or two in ten. If the Chongming merchants wish to exchange cloth for rice, then at a distance there is Zongyang, to which they were originally assigned to make their purchases; closer at hand are Wuhu and Yuncao. The transaction can be carried out at any of these three; why must they insist upon its being at Jiangning? If, for that matter, the Jiangxi and Huguang rice-dealers wish to purchase cloth, they also can avail themselves of Zongyang and

Yuncao; why would they insist on coming all the way to the provincial capital? This would be patent nonsense! How, then, could they "come as expected" when they hear that there is cloth for them to buy, but go elsewhere as soon as there is none?

I find that the Chongming merchants exchanging cloth for rice at Jiangning was always an occasional affair, and, in any case, belonged to the period before the designation of Zongyang, Yuncao, and Wuhu as the ports where the Chongming merchants are to buy their grain. It cannot be taken as a precedent. Already after 1727 or 1728 they were no longer buying rice at Jiangning. It is simply not the case that because in 1732 they had no cloth to sell, they failed to come that year for the first time. Now the wicked brokers of Jiangning are aiding and abetting the Chongming merchants to claim the precedent deceitfully, in the hope of evading the quotas. Thus already in the fifth moon of last year, before the recent authorization, the Chongming cloth merchant Li Zijia and others came directly to Jiangning hoping to buy grain, without so much as reporting to the Chongming authorities so that they could make representations for them. The Suzhou commissioner sent a directive to Taicang Department ordering that they be investigated and brought to justice, as is on the files.[1] This means that not only will the Chongming merchants' trading cloth for rice at Jiangning be detrimental to the city population's food supply: the relaying between the cloth and grain merchants, with one arriving as the other leaves, will inevitably provoke evasion of the quotas, creating yet more problems.

This year, rice prices in the provincial seat are higher than in previous years, and although the Chongming merchants have not yet arrived, once the population hears the news that they have been permitted to buy rice at Jiangning, it will be said that it is being sold for trading onto the high seas, thereby creating the high prices. For since the people have not seen the Chongming merchants in the provincial capital for a long time, they cannot fail to arouse each other to alarm and apprehension. In summary, the wicked merchants of Chongming have repeatedly defied established regulations, while wicked brokers near at hand have helped them on the quiet. Thus, whereas the distance to Zongyang is not more than a thousand *li*, they hold that it is far away and difficult of access; while exceeding their allotted quota at

Yuncao by half as much again, they go pell-mell submitting their appeals. They will not stop until they have drunk dry the source of this town's self-renewing store. Prostrate, I beg you . . . to reset the quotas, severely to forbid evasion, and to order the cancellation of the Chongming merchants' authorization to bring cloth to Jiangning and exchange it here for rice. They must not be permitted to infringe the rules again. It may then be hoped that the food of the inhabitants of the provincial capital will not be dearer every passing day. . . .

Note

1. Since 1724, Chongming had been administratively subordinate to the newly created independent department of Taicang.

*   *   *   *   *

Text 7.E

Address to the throne requesting that the practice of issuing stamped permits to grain merchants be discontinued
Date: 1738
Author: Fang Bao, as a salaried senior scholar and expert on the three canonical texts on ritual.[1]
Source: Fang Bao, *Fang Bao ji,* Vol. 2, pp. 554-55, or *Wangxi Xiansheng jiwai wen* [Supplement to the Collected Works of Fang Bao] (1851 edition, reprinted in *Sibu congkan*), 1:28b-29b.

I learn from the *Metropolitan Gazette* that the Liangjiang governorgeneral, Nasutu, has submitted a memorial with the following proposal regarding famine relief within his jurisdiction. "Pursuant to the established regulation determined by the Board of Revenue last year: whenever a grain boat goes through an internal customs station, the customs authorities, on ascertaining that the boat is proceeding to a specified disaster-stricken countylevel jurisdiction to sell its cargo, should exempt the merchant from paying tax and supply him with a stamped permit. They should instruct the merchant that, after arriving in the designated jurisdiction, he is to forward the permit to the local magistrate, so that the latter may stamp it with his seal. When the unladen boat goes back through the said customs station, the permit is to be presented for inspection and cancellation. If the merchant has the dishonesty to take his cargo to another province, or sells it along the route before arriving at his designated destination, he should be punished by a fine of twice the sum of the remitted tax." It is on record that Your Majesty has already endorsed this with a "Let him do swiftly as he has requested."

Gazing upwards, I perceive how Your Majesty's love for the folk, profound and true, relaxes for never an instant, while the planning of the said governor-general, as he strives to embody Your Majesty's Sage virtue, is detailed and comprehensive. However, with respect to what he says about inspection of the permit, there is that within the established regulation which ought urgently to be adjusted. Every travelling merchant who deals in grain pursues high prices and turns his back on low ones; this principle is something that he grasps without needing to be taught it. The level of the price of grain depends in every case on the severity of the disaster: where the disaster is a mild one the price will be high, and where it is severe the price will of necessity be higher still. If one insists upon requiring that the merchant sell at the appointed place and will not let him change it, then if along the route the price is even higher than in his declared destination, this means that the grain shortage must be even worse than in that further place. The merchant will not dare take it upon himself to break the law and sell, on which the poor folk crying out for food are bound to want to buy by force. I take the liberty of fearing that troubles in the shape of plundering and snatching would certainly start up in even greater numbers.

In general, as soon as merchants have converged upon a place where the grain price is soaring, that price is bound to fall off somewhat. Once the price has fallen off somewhat in one place, the merchants will vie to betake themselves elsewhere. If one lets them do as suits themselves, the circulation will be that much swifter. If not only do they not dare sell in places where the price is high, but they are also forced to sell where it has fallen off, then inasmuch as merchants and traders deploy capital in quest of profit, they are bound to see this as a path of peril and to hold off from it.

As to the notion of the local magistrate of the appointed place of sale stamping the permit, I would point out that even if the regular officials do not dare put difficulties in the merchant's way, the clerks and petty functionaries will be extorting money from him everywhere. By the time he has made two or three trips back and forth, the cost will be some few times more than the remitted tax. Still more disturbing is the fact that merchants, carrying their capital to and fro by lake and river, tend to keep their tracks concealed, their one fear being that some living soul will recognize them. This is how they ward off seizure and extortion under threat of violence by inland pirates. If they are made to go in and out of the government offices to apply to have their permits stamped, everyone will know that they are merchants, and this is something that they fear most deeply. When, in my youth, I travelled in the four directions as a teacher of the scriptures, I regularly took passage in commercial vessels, and gained a deep awareness of these circumstances. It is for this reason that I venture to set forth my foolish views.

Prostrate, I beg Your Majesty to send down a special edict to the following effect. Whenever a grain boat goes through an internal customs station and the merchant is excused from paying tax, he is to be permitted to take his cargo and sell it anywhere within the given province. He is not to ship it dishonestly to another province. It may then be hoped that great merchants and small traders will all leap up, vying to be first, and it will be possible to realize some slight assistance to the people's food supply.

Note

1. In the first few years of Qianlong's reign, Fang Bao was a court scholar, working on such projects as a book of model examination essays, and new commentaries to the three canonical ritual texts. In 1738, he enjoyed the salary of a vice-president of the Board of Rites, although he had resigned from this position early in the year. See Fang Chao-ying, in Hummel, ed., *Eminent Chinese of the Ch'ing Period*, Vol. 1, p. 236.

Conclusion:
Sprouts of Liberalism?

It is, perhaps, a peculiar manifestation of Western vanity to identify certain concepts as "purely Western," while defining them in such a way that only the Western forms can qualify for recognition. "Individualism" is the clearest example of a concept which is routinely so mistreated. At the lower levels of debate, the construct of "purely Western" concepts brings ideological vested interests into play. We all know that Western values are bad (or good, according to ideological preference); hence the attraction of a non-Western antithesis which is happily free of Western values if they are seen as bad, or sadly devoid of them if they are seen as good. Belief in the non-Western antithesis, no matter of which kind, is fiercely cherished. Liberalism, whether political or economic, is generally perceived as good these days (opinions differ about social liberalism); benighted China, that age-old totalitarian giant, simply did not have liberalism.

There is a purely historical objection to such an opinion about the possibility of liberalism in the pre-modern non-West. This is that it involves the assumption that because economic liberalism arose in tandem with political liberalism in the West, and both were products of the much-maligned Enlightenment, it follows that economic liberalism can *only* emerge in association with political liberalism, and depends inseparably on Enlightenment assumptions. Similarly, because the flourishing of economic liberalism as a practical ideology coincided, in the nineteenth-century West, with the triumph of industrial capitalism, economic liberalism can be fallaciously identified as the ideology of modern Western capitalism, without consideration of the possibility that, elsewhere, it may have been something else. The position of the present author is, by contrast, that a rudimentary form of economic liberalism did exist in eighteenth-century China, and that it was indigenous. Whether Chinese economic liberalism was associated with any of the phenomena with which economic liberalism has been associated in the West (not only the development of representative government, but also individualism, the ideology of private property, and a high degree of indifference towards the welfare of the poor) is a separate question, to be treated in the usual way.

The issue of what sort of company was kept by eighteenth-century Chinese economic liberalism cannot be considered here. Suffice it to say that there is not a shred of evidence that eighteenth-century China was on its way to parliamentary democracy. However, Texts 2.D and 2.E do suggest that it may be worth investigating the idea of a link between the rise to influence of economically liberal ideas in 1740s China and a distinctly unsympathetic attitude towards the needy.[1] To address the problems of cultural background, it is true that in China the absence of a deep-rooted commitment to freedom as a value (except in the Daoist tradition) made unlikely any discourse explicitly and extensively trumpeting the concept of liberty. In this, China was unlike eighteenth-century France.[2] However, the Daoist tradition did offer a subtle rhetoric of non-interventionism, and provided models for such paradoxical formulations as "governing by non-governance."[3]

The limited development of the theory reflected in the texts of eighteenth-century Chinese economic liberalism should be noted, and can be easily explained. On one hand, theoretical elaboration could only go so far in a memorial on a specific matter; at the same time, intellectual endeavour in Qing China was excessively identified either with mere scholarship or else with bureaucratic service. As Adam Smith would have put it, there was in China no class of "philosophers or men of specula-

---

[1] I return both to this issue, and to the question of property rights and economic individualism, in Dunstan, State or Merchant?, chs. 3 and 6.

[2] As Kaplan has shown, the 1760s liberalization of the French "police of grain," while inspired by the rather well-developed economic liberalism of the économistes (or physiocrats), was ushered in by a business and "proprietary class" petition campaign whose dominating theme was liberty. Kaplan, Bread, Politics and Political Economy, Vol. 1, pp. 121-25. It is hard to imagine anything of the sort taking place in eighteenth-century China.

[3] Cf. above, ch. 2/introduction.

tion, whose trade it is not to do any thing, but to observe every thing; and who, upon that account, are often capable of combining together the powers of the most distant and dissimilar objects."[4] Smith, with his chair at the University of Glasgow and subsequent pension, may have been such a man, and was able to expound his thoughts both systematically and at wondrous length. The position of a Chen Dashou (author of Text 6.E) was very different.

I will conclude with some disclaimers and clarifications. In the first place, I do not particularly hail the emergence of a Chinese economic liberalism, in the obnoxious belief that Chinese thought is most admirable when it most closely conforms with models which are conventionally perceived as Western. My personal instinct is to regard the discourse of economic liberalism as at best suspect, and at worst pernicious. My basic sympathies have always been with the paternalist tradition. Second, it should be clear that I do not seek (and, indeed, have never sought) to "equate" mid-Qing economic policy "with *laissez-faire* liberalism."[5] I would not even go so far as to describe those who, in certain contexts, put forth liberal ideas as "liberals." The claim is only that in the early Qianlong period economically liberal thought was articulated and had a certain influence.[6] The liberal thought was fragmentary, and competed with persistent interventionist traditions. The expression "sprouts of liberalism" is very apposite, although it leaves one vulnerable to charges of excessive susceptibility to the Marxian "sprouts of capitalism"

---

[4] Smith, *The Wealth of Nations*, Vol. 1, p. 14. On the patronage of scholars in Qing China, see Benjamin A. Elman, *From Philosophy to Philology: Intellectual and Social Aspects of Change in Late Imperial China* (Cambridge, Mass.: Harvard University Press, 1984), pp. 100-112. Although the scholarly activities which patrons supported could, on occasion, include work in astronomy and mathematics, it remains true in general that the scholars patronized were not being paid primarily to think.

[5] *Pace* Rowe, "State and Market in Mid-Qing Economic Thought," p. 33 and n. 71. I was similarly astonished to learn that an earlier manuscript of mine "implicitly agree(s) with Chen and Myers' negative assessment of state intervention" (ibid., p. 8, n. 2). How explicit does one have to be, in order to avoid misreadings of this kind?

[6] I document this influence in Dunstan, *State or Merchant?*, passim.

doctrine.[7] There is, however, no problem as long as one construes "capitalism" as pre-industrial, chiefly commercial and financial capitalism, rather than the capitalism of the Industrial Revolution. A commercialized economy is a prerequisite for the emergence of economic liberalism; and liberal thought is more likely to be articulated by officials if the economy is sophisticated, if commercial capitalism is reasonably well developed, and if there are personal links between officialdom and the capitalist world. All these conditions obtained in eighteenth-century China.[8]

The more interesting question is that of the significance of early Qianlong period economic liberalism both in Qing history and in the two millennia of the evolution of Chinese political economy. As to the former, my working assumption is that the liberal arguments of the late 1730s and 1740s played a certain role in accomplishing the transition from the Yongzheng style of governance to that characteristic of most of the long Qianlong reign. The Yongzheng and early Qianlong periods were characterized by intense interventionism; as leading statesmen of the Yongzheng period retired or died off, however, and as the policy

---

[7] The expression "sprouts of capitalism" (also translated as "nascent capitalism") normally refers to the putative beginnings of capitalist relations of production in Ming and Qing China. According to a once-influential Chinese Marxist school of thought, these endogenous beginnings would have developed into full industrial capitalism but for such negative forces as Western imperialism and traditional China's own "feudal" bureaucratic political system. A representative work in this tradition is the three-volume symposium *Zhongguo ziben zhuyi mengya wenti taolun ji* [Collected Papers on the Issue of the Sprouts of Capitalism in China], compiled by Zhongguo Renmin Daxue, Zhongguo lishi jiaoyanshi (Vols. 1 and 2), and Nanjing Daxue, Zhongguo gudai shi jiaoyanshi (Vol. 3) (Beijing: Sanlian shudian, 1957–60).

[8] An especially suggestive example of a Qing official personally connected with the world of commerce is Wang Youdun (1692–1758). Wang was a man of Huizhou merchant stock who not only wrote an epitaph for that prince of imperially connected merchants Fan Yubin, but also participated in the composition of imperial edicts while a grand minister of state during 1746–58. See GCQXLZ, 22:10b-13b and 452:49a-52a. On the multifarious commercial and financial investments of Qing officials, see, e.g., Sasaki, "Shindai kanryō no kashoku ni tsuite," pp. 29-30, 33, 35, and 39-41. While William Rowe's fascinating study of Hankou-centred commerce (*Hankow: Commerce and Society*) focusses chiefly on the nineteenth century, it paints a vivid picture of the sophistication that could be attained by indigenous Chinese commercial institutions and arrangements.

debates of the 1740s came to conservative conclusions, a banal compromise was reached.[9] In the second half of the eighteenth century, interventionist policies and institutions remained in operation. However, they were no longer being guided, elaborated, and developed by activist imperial direction. The Qianlong emperor may have been a military activist, but he was not a socioeconomic one.[10] The rejection of fiscal positivism shown in his attempted abolition of the investment funding system was consistent with his lack of creative interest in state interventions to promote the welfare of the poor by trying to improve upon the operations of the market.[11] The doctrine that the market could be trusted served to justify Qianlong's relative indolence (as measured by the highest standards of paternalist responsibility). That the problems of paternalism increased with the size of the Chinese population in the later eighteenth century naturally makes the issue of responsibility more complex. The fact remains, however, that thought tending to justify a lower level of state action did emerge at approximately the same time as the first signs of long-term strain began to manifest themselves.[12]

The fact that in the early Qianlong period intensely interventionist policies provoked liberal arguments in reaction to them does not necessarily imply that these arguments were new in Chinese history. To the contrary, already in the seventeenth century Wang Fuzhi had argued, with passion and some sophistication, against official efforts to resist the trend of market prices.[13] Robert Hymes has recently shown that a Southern Song

---

[9] E'ertai died in 1745, while Zhang Tingyu retired in 1750. Exactly what role these men had played in the prolongation of the Yongzheng style of government remains to be determined. However, E'ertai was one of the grand secretaries behind the interventionist eight measures imposed to regulate the Beijing money market in 1744 (above, ch. 2, introduction). His death preceded the final repudiation of this policy by less than a month.

[10] Cf. Beatrice Bartlett's interesting observation that the Qianlong emperor "unlike his father, detested the details of governing" (*Monarchs and Ministers*, p. 175).

[11] See above, ch. 4, introduction.

[12] Cf. Text 6.F above.

[13] See Dunstan, *State or Merchant?*, ch. 3. As I have shown elsewhere, even within the early Qianlong period, episodes of liberalization in different areas of

332 Conclusion: Sprouts of Liberalism?

official called Dong Wei had argued as early as c. 1200 that "forcing down the price" of grain during subsistence crises was a mistake not only because it would deter prospective importers, but also (and more significantly) because the elevated prices would spontaneously correct themselves through their appeal both to importers, and to local wealthy households which controlled reserves of grain. Dong's famine relief manual in which he set out this comfortable doctrine was circulated throughout the empire by the central government. It is not clear, however, whether it was this particular passage that inspired central government approval.[14]

At the present stage of research, it can be argued that the "nascent" economic liberalism of 1740s China represents an advance in sophistication and political significance over the suggestions of Dong Wei in the early thirteenth century, but it cannot be claimed that this kind of thinking was completely new in mid-Qing China. Only future research may permit us to clarify how frequently such thinking was expressed during the intervening centuries, how much influence it had, what level of sophistication it attained, and why more was apparently not built on it by way of economic theory. There may be a new undercurrent of traditional Chinese political economy to be explored; it seems, however, at least as likely that an understanding of price mechanisms, although occasionally articulated, was generally unable to prevail against the interventionist instincts of a bureaucracy steeped in the dual legacy of Confucian paternalism and "Legalist" technique. If this is so, any episode in which awareness of price mechanisms informed one side of an extended policy debate is worthy of historians' attention.

---

policy did not always perfectly synchronize. Thus the limited liberalization of the state-sponsored Sino-Japanese trade began already in 1736, and was fatally compromised in 1744. Dunstan, "Safely Supping with the Devil," pp. 66-73.

[14] Robert P. Hymes, "Moral Duty and Self-Regulating Process in Southern Sung Views of Famine Relief," in Ordering the World, ed. Hymes and Schirokauer, pp. 281-83 and 295-96. Dong does not seem to have had total confidence in the "self-regulating" mechanism: he accepted the need for some administrative action to ensure initial grain imports to set the "process" in motion. Ibid., pp. 296-97.

* * *

The significance of historical phenomena does not necessarily depend upon their novelty. It is always useful for Westerners and others to be reminded that there may be no necessary connection between economic liberalism on one hand, and liberal democracy and respect for a wide range of individual freedoms on the other. Meanwhile, although the main purpose of this book is to contribute to the study of traditional Chinese political economy, assistance from a sinologist in defining what is, and what is not, "purely Western" may be useful for practitioners of "Occidental Studies" also.

Glossary

Aligun 阿里衮
Bagou 八溝
Baling 巴陵
bangding 幫丁
Baode 保德
Baoji 寶雞
Baoning 保寧
benfu 本富
bi 璧
Bo Gui 白圭
Boji 博濟
Cai Shiyuan 蔡世遠
Cai Zhong 蔡仲
Caigou 蔡溝
Cangtou Zhen 倉頭鎮
Changde 常德
changping cang 常平倉
Changshan 常山
Changzhou 常州
Changzi 長子
Chaoyi 朝邑
Chaozhou 潮州

Chen Dashou 陳大受
Chen Gaoxiang 陳高翔
Chen Hongmou 陳宏謀
Chen Zhaolun 陳兆崙
Chengling 城陵
Chenzhou 陳州
Chongming 崇明
Congyang 樅陽
Da Chuanwo 大船窩
Dali 大荔
Danjin 丹津
Daqing 大青
de 德
Deling 德齡
Dengzhou 登州
Dong Wei 董煟
dundang 囤當
edi 遏糴
E'ertai 鄂爾泰
Ehai 鄂海
Emida 鄂彌達
Fan Yubin 范毓馪

Fang Bao 方苞
Fengxiang 鳳翔
Fengyang 鳳陽
Fenzhou 汾州
Fufeng 扶風
Fugu 府谷
Fuzhou 鄜州
Gan Rulai 甘汝來
Gong Erquan 宮爾勸
Gong Zizhen 龔自珍
gongyi hanggui 公議行規
Gu Yanwu 顧炎武
Guan Zhong 管仲
Guangyuan 廣元
guigong yin 歸公銀
Guihua Cheng 歸化城
guoshui 過稅
Guzong 顧琮
Haiyang 海陽
Haizhou 海州
Han Xizuo 韓錫胙
Hancheng 韓城
Hanzhong 漢中
haocai 蒿萊
haolai 蒿萊
Hebao Ying 河保營
He Changling 賀長齡
Hejin 河津
Heyang 郃陽
Hongdong 洪洞
Huai'an 淮安
Huang Liuhong 黃六鴻
Huang Tinggui 黃廷桂
Huangchao jingshi wenbian
    皇朝經世文編
Huayin 華陰
Huazhou 華州
Huguang 湖廣
Huizhou 徽州

Hukou 湖口
huo ji, jia luo 貨集價落
Hushu 滸墅
jiabang 加幫
Jiangning 江寧
Jiangzhou 絳州
Jianli 監利
Jiaxing 嘉興
Jiazhou 葭州
Jin Fu 靳輔
Ji'nan 濟南
Jining 濟寧
Jinshan 金山
Jishan 紀山
Jiujiang 九江
Jizhou 吉州
Kuizhou 夔州
Kunshan 崑山
Lanzhou 蘭州
Lei Cuiting 雷翠亭
Lei Hong 雷鋐
li 禮
Li Fu 李紱
Li Gou 李覯
Li Jin 李璡
Li Kui 李悝
Li Qingzhi 李清植
Li Shenxiu 李慎修
Li Shide 李世德
Li Wei 李衛
Li Yesi 李鄴嗣
Li Zijia 李子嘉
lianfen qihang 斂分齊行
liang ru wei chu 量入為出
Linqing 臨清
Lintao 臨洮
Lintong 臨潼
Liu Yuyi 劉於義
Longmen 龍門

Lu'an 潞安
Lü Kun 呂坤
luodi shuiyin 落地稅銀
Mayang 麻陽
mayangzi 麻秧子
Meixian 郿縣
migu liutong 米穀流通
miju 米局
mingliu 明流
mofu 末富
Mu Tianyan 慕天顏
Muna 穆那
Nasutu 那蘇圖
Niaoshutongxue 鳥鼠同穴
Peizhou 邳州
pingtiao 平糶
Pingyang 平陽
Puzhou 蒲州
Qian Feng 錢灃
Qian Liu 錢鏐
Qian Shisheng 錢士升
Qianzhou 乾州
Qiao Guanglie 喬光烈
Qidiao Kai 漆雕開
qihang 齊行
qihang zhangjia 齊行長價
Qijiabu 齊家埠
Qikou 磧口
Qilang Wo 七狼窩
Qin Cheng'en 秦承恩
Qin Huitian 秦蕙田
Qin Shan 欽善
qiongmin yijing an kui fuhu
　zhi ben 窮民已經暗虧
　富戶之本
Quzhou 衢州
Ronghe 榮河
Ruyang 汝陽
Sanmen 三門

Saokou 潘口
Saoshang 埽上
Shangcai 上蔡
Shangshui 商水
Shangzhou 商州
Shanzhou 陝州
shazhuang 殺莊
shecang 社倉
shengcai 生財
Shengjing 盛京
Shuhede 舒赫德
simin 四民
Sizhou 泗州
Songjiang 松江
Suide 綏德
Suiping 遂平
Sun Hao 孫灝
Sun Jiagan 孫嘉淦
Taian 泰安
Taicang 太倉
Taiyang 太陽
Tang Pin 湯聘
Tang Zhen 唐甄
Tian Wenjing 田文鏡
Tianqiao 天橋
Tongcheng 桐城
Tongguan 潼關
Tongzhou (Shaanxi) 同州
Tongzhou (Zhili) 通州
Tuhai 徒駭
Tunliu 屯留
Tuoketuo 托克托
Wang Fuzhi 王夫之
Wang Guodong 王國棟
Wang Mo 王謨
Wang Pingfan 王屏藩
Wang Youdun 汪由敦
Wang Zehong 王澤宏
Wei Yuan 魏源

Weinan 渭南
Weiyuan 渭源
Weizhi lü 違制律
Wenxiang 閿鄉
Wenyan 文言
Wuding 武定
Wuhu 蕪湖
Xi'an 西安
Xiangcheng 項城
Xiangtan 湘潭
xianmin 閒民
Xianyang 咸陽
Xici 繫辭
Xie Liangzuo 謝良佐
Xiezhou 解州
Xihua 西華
xing 刑
Xing'an 興安
Xiping 西平
Xizhou 隰州
Xu Qi 徐杞
Xuanhua 宣化
Xuzhou 徐州
Xu'yuanmeng 徐元夢
Ya'ertu 雅爾圖
Yan Sisheng 晏斯盛
Yan'an 延安
Yancheng 堰城
Yang Bi 楊祕
Yang Chun 楊椿
Yang Eryou 楊二酉
Yang Jingren 楊景仁
Yang Kaiding 楊開鼎
Yang Xifu 楊錫紱
Yang Tingjian 楊廷鑑
Yang Tingwang 楊廷望
Yang Yongbin 楊永斌
yangmin 養民
Yi Xueshi 易學實

Yichuan 宜川
Yin Huiyi 尹會一
yingyun shengxi yinliang
    營運生息銀兩
Yingzhou 潁州
yin yang yin tian 引養引恬
Yongji 永濟
Yongning 永寧
you wu xiang tong 有無相通
Yucheng 禹城
Yuezhou 岳州
Yulin 榆林
Yumen Zhen 禹門鎮
Yushan 玉山
Yu Tingcan 余廷燦
Yuncao 運漕
Zhang Kunzai 張坤載
Zhang Qu 張渠
Zhang Tingyu 張廷玉
Zhao Dengmo 趙登模
Zhao Hong'en 趙宏恩
Zhao Dianzui 趙殿最
zheng 政
Zhenjiang 鎮江
Zhichuan 芝川
Zhishu you wei lü 制書有違律
Zhongyin 鐘音
Zhouguan 周官
Zhouguan yishu 周官義疏
Zhouli 周禮
Zhu Xiaoyuan 朱曉園
Zhuntai 準泰
Zongyang 棕陽
zuoshui 坐稅

Bibliography

Abbreviations of Works Cited

DQHDSL	*Qinding Da Qing huidian shili.*
DQHDZL	*Qinding Da Qing huidian zeli.*
GCQXLZ	*Guochao qixian leizheng.*
GZD/KX	*Gongzhong dang Kangxi chao zouzhe.*
GZD/QL	*Gongzhong dang Qianlong chao zouzhe.*
GZD/YZ	*Gongzhong dang Yongzheng chao zouzhe.*
HCJSWB	*Huangchao jingshi wenbian.*
PYTOCG	*Peiyuan Tang oucun gao: wenxi.*
QCWXTK	*Qingchao wenxian tongkao.*
QSL/KX	*Da Qing Shengzu Ren Huangdi shilu.*
QSL/QL	*Da Qing Gaozong Chun Huangdi shilu.*
QSL/YZ	*Da Qing Shizong Xian Huangdi shilu.*
YZZZHB	*Yongzheng chao Hanwen zhupi zouzhe huibian.*

Abe Takeo. *Shindai-shi no kenkyū* [Studies in Qing History]. Tokyo: Sōbunsha, 1971.

Balazs, Étienne. *Political Theory and Administrative Reality in Traditional China.* London: School of Oriental and African Studies, 1965.

Ban Gu et al. *Hanshu* [A History of the Han Dynasty]. 12 vols. Beijing: Zhonghua shuju, 1975.

Bartlett, Beatrice S. *Monarchs and Ministers: The Grand Council in Mid-Ch'ing China, 1723–1820.* Berkeley: University of California Press, 1991.

Bauer, Wolfgang. *China and the Search for Happiness: Recurring Themes in Four Thousand Years of Chinese Cultural History.* Trans. Michael Shaw. New York: Seabury Press, 1976.

Beattie, Hilary J. *Land and Lineage in China: A Study of T'ung-ch'eng County, Anhwei, in the Ming and Ch'ing Dynasties.* Cambridge: Cambridge University Press, 1979.

Bol, Peter K. *"This Culture of Ours": Intellectual Transitions in T'ang and Sung China*. Stanford: Stanford University Press, 1992.

Chang Chung-li. *The Chinese Gentry: Studies on Their Role in Nineteenth-Century Chinese Society*. Seattle: University of Washington Press, 1955.

Changsha fuzhi [Gazetteer of Changsha Prefecture]. 1747 edition.

Chen Hongmou. *Peiyuan Tang shouzha jiecun* [Surviving Copies of Correspondence from the Peiyuan Hall]. (1823). 1872 edition.

Chen Zhaolun. *Zizhu Shan Fang shiwen ji* [Collection of Poetry and Prose from the Zizhu Mountain Study]. Edition of c. 1800.

Chongming xianzhi [Gazetteer of Chongming County]. 1760, 1881, and 1930 editions.

Ch'ü T'ung-tsu. *Local Government in China under the Ch'ing*. Cambridge, Mass.: Harvard University Press, 1962.

Chuan, Han-sheng. *See under* Quan Hansheng.

de Bary, Wm. Theodore. "Individualism and Humanitarianism in Late Ming Thought." In *Self and Society in Ming Thought*, ed. de Bary and the Conference on Ming Thought (New York: Columbia University Press, 1970), pp. 145-247.

—————. *Waiting for the Dawn: A Plan for the Prince. Huang Tsung-hsi's Ming-i-tai-fang lu*. New York: Columbia University Press, 1993.

Deane, Phyllis. *The Evolution of Economic Ideas*. Cambridge: Cambridge University Press, 1978.

Dou Zhen. *Guochao shuhua jia bilu* [Jottings on the Calligraphers and Painters of the Present Dynasty]. 1911.

DQHDSL. *Qinding Da Qing huidian shili* [Imperially Authorized Collected Statutes of the Great Qing Dynasty: Precedents and Regulations]. 1818 and 1899.

DQHDZL. *Qinding Da Qing huidian zeli* [Imperially Authorized Collected Statutes of the Great Qing Dynasty: Precedents and Regulations]. 1767.

Dray-Novey, Alison. "Spatial Order and Police in Imperial Beijing." *Journal of Asian Studies* 52, no. 4 (1993): 885-922.

Dunstan, Helen. "Safely Supping with the Devil: The Qing State and Its Merchant Suppliers of Copper." *Late Imperial China* 13, no. 2 (1992): 42-81.

—————. *State or Merchant? Political Economy and Political Process in 1740s China*. In preparation.

————. "'Orders Go Forth in the Morning and Are Changed by Nightfall': A Monetary Policy Cycle in Qing China, November 1744–June 1745." *T'oung Pao*, forthcoming.

E'ertai et al., comps. *Baqi tongzhi chuji* [Gazetteer of the Eight Banners: First Edition]. 1739.

Elman, Benjamin A. *From Philosophy to Philology: Intellectual and Social Aspects of Change in Late Imperial China.* Cambridge, Mass.: Harvard University Press, 1984.

Elvin, Mark. *The Pattern of the Chinese Past.* London: Eyre Methuen, 1973.

Fang Bao. *Fang Wangxi Xiansheng quanji* [The Complete Works of Fang Bao]. 1851 edition, reprinted in *Sibu congkan*.

————. *Wangxi Xiansheng jiwai wen* [Supplement to the Collected Works of Fang Bao]. 1851 edition, reprinted in *Sibu congkan*.

————. *Fang Bao ji* [Collected Works of Fang Bao]. 2 vols. Shanghai: Shanghai guji chubanshe, 1983.

First Historical Archives (Beijing). CC. *Zhupi zouzhe, Caizheng, Cangchu* [Rescripted Palace Memorials, Fiscal Matters, Granary Reserves].

————. HBJR. *Zhupi zouzhe, Caizheng, Huobi jinrong* [Rescripted Palace Memorials, Fiscal Matters, Currency and Finance].

————. *Huke hongben, Cangchu* [Copies of Routine Memorials Made for the Office of Scrutiny for Revenue, Granary Reserves].

————. *Zhupi zouzhe, Caizheng, Guanshui* [Rescripted Palace Memorials, Fiscal Matters, Customs tariffs].

Gao Wangling. "Yige wei wanjie de changshi: Qingdai Qianlong shiqi de liangzheng he liangshi wenti" [An Incomplete Experiment: Provisioning Policy and Grain Supply Problems in the Qianlong Period of the Qing Dynasty]. *Jiuzhou xuekan* [The Nine Provinces Journal] 2, no. 3 (1988): 13-40.

GCQXLZ. Li Huan, comp. *Guochao qixian leizheng* [Classified Biographies of Venerable and Distinguished Personages under the Present Dynasty]. 1890.

Gernet, Jacques. "L'homme ou la paperasse: aperçu sur les conceptions politiques de T'ang Chen (1630–1704)" [Human Beings or Red Tape? An Outline of the Political Ideas of Tang Zhen]. In *State and Law in East Asia (Festschrift Karl Bünger)*, ed. D. Eikemeier and H. Franke (Wiesbaden: Harrassowitz, 1981), pp. 112-25.

Gong Zizhen. *Gong Ding'an quanji leibian* [The Complete Works of Gong Zizhen, Classified by Category]. Shanghai: Shijie shuju, 1937.

―――. *Gong Zizhen quanji* [The Complete Works of Gong Zizhen]. Shanghai: Shanghai Renmin chubanshe, 1975.

Goodrich, L. Carrington, and Fang Chao-ying, eds. *Dictionary of Ming Biography, 1368–1644.* 2 vols. New York: Columbia University Press, 1976.

Graham, A. C. *Disputers of the Tao: Philosophical Argument in Ancient China.* La Salle, Ill.: Open Court, 1989.

Gu Yanwu. *Gu Tinglin shi wen ji* [Collected Poetry and Prose of Gu Yanwu]. Beijing: Zhonghua shuju, 1976.

GZD/KX. *Gongzhong dang Kangxi chao zouzhe* [Secret Palace Memorials of the Kangxi Period]. Taibei: National Palace Museum, 1976.

GZD/QL. *Gongzhong dang Qianlong chao zouzhe* [Secret Palace Memorials of the Qianlong Period]. Taibei: National Palace Museum, 1982–89.

GZD/YZ. *Gongzhong dang Yongzheng chao zouzhe* [Secret Palace Memorials of the Yongzheng Period]. Taibei: National Palace Museum, 1977–80.

Hamashima Atsutoshi. "The Organization of Water Control in the Kiangnan Delta in the Ming Period." *Acta Asiatica* (Tokyo) 38 (1980): 69-92.

Han Xizuo. *Huayi ji* [The Huayi Collection]. 1874.

Hartman, Charles. *Han Yü and the T'ang Search for Unity.* Princeton: Princeton University Press, 1986.

Hartwell, Robert M. "Classical Chinese Monetary Analysis and Economic Policy in T'ang—Northern Sung China." *Transactions of the International Conference of Orientalists in Japan* 13 (1968): 70-81.

―――. "Historical Analogism, Public Policy, and Social Science in Eleventh- and Twelfth-Century China." *American Historical Review* 76, no. 3 (1971): 690-727.

HCJSWB. He Changling and Wei Yuan, comps. *Huangchao jingshi wenbian* [A Statecraft Anthology of Our August Dynasty]. (1827). Reprint of the 1873 edition. Taibei: Shijie shuju, 1964.

He Benfang. "Qianlong nianjian queguan de mianshui cuoshi" [Exemptions from Internal Customs Duties in the Qianlong

Period]. *Lishi dang'an* [Historical Archives] 28 (1987, no. 4): 87–93.

Ho Ping-ti. *The Ladder of Success in Imperial China: Aspects of Social Mobility, 1368–1911.* New York: Columbia University Press, 1962.

Hommel, Rudolf P. *China at Work: An Illustrated Record of the Primitive Industries of China's Masses, Whose Life Is Toil, and Thus an Account of Chinese Civilization.* New York: John Day, 1937.

Hsiao Kung-chuan. *Rural China: Imperial Control in the Nineteenth Century.* Seattle: University of Washington Press, 1960.

Hu Jizhuang. *Zhongguo jingji sixiang shi* [A History of Chinese Economic Thought]. 3 vols. Shanghai: Shanghai Renmin chubanshe, 1983.

Huan Kuan, comp. *Yan tie lun* [The Debate on Salt and Iron]. (1st cent. B.C.). Taibei: Shijie shuju, 1967.

Huang Liu-hung. *A Complete Book Concerning Happiness and Benevolence: A Manual for Local Magistrates in Seventeenth-Century China.* Trans. Djang Chu. Tucson: University of Arizona Press, 1984.

Huang, Ray. *Taxation and Governmental Finance in Sixteenth-Century Ming China.* Cambridge: Cambridge University Press, 1974.

Hucker, Charles O. *A Dictionary of Official Titles in Imperial China.* Stanford: Stanford University Press, 1985.

Hummel, Arthur W., ed. *Eminent Chinese of the Ch'ing Period (1644–1912).* 2 vols. Washington: United States Government Printing Office, 1943–44.

Hymes, Robert P. "Moral Duty and Self-Regulating Process in Southern Sung Views of Famine Relief." In *Ordering the World: Approaches to State and Society in Sung Dynasty China,* ed. Robert P. Hymes and Conrad Schirokauer (Berkeley: University of California Press, 1993), pp. 280-309.

Jin Fu. *Jin Wenxiang Gong zoushu* [The Memorials of Jin Fu]. N.d. Reprinted in *Jindai Zhongguo shiliao congkan* (Taibei: Wenhai chubanshe, 1966–73), no. 143.

Ji'nan fuzhi [Gazetteer of Ji'nan Prefecture]. 1839 edition.

Jinling tongji, xu [History of Jiangning: Supplement]. 1907 edition.

Jiujiang fuzhi [Gazetteer of Jiujiang Prefecture]. 1874 edition.

Kahn, Harold L. *Monarchy in the Emperor's Eyes: Image and Reality in the Ch'ien-lung Reign.* Cambridge, Mass.: Harvard University Press, 1971.

Kaplan, Steven L. *Bread, Politics and Political Economy in the Reign of Louis XV.* 2 vols. The Hague: Martinus Nijhoff, 1976.

Karlgren, Bernhard. *The Book of Documents.* Stockholm: Museum of Far Eastern Antiquities, 1950.

————. *The Book of Odes.* Stockholm: Museum of Far Eastern Antiquities, 1974.

Kawakatsu Mamoru. "Sekkō Kakō-fu no kanden mondai—Minmatsu kyōshin shihai no seiritsu ni kansuru ichi kōsatsu" [The Problem of Cross-Boundary Landholdings in Jiaxing Prefecture, Zhejiang: An Inquiry Concerning the Establishment of Gentry Dominance in the Late Ming Period]. *Shigaku zasshi* [Journal of History] 82, no. 4 (1973): 1-46.

Kawakubō Teirō. "Shindai ni okeru shōshu no seikō ni tsuite" [On the Popularity of Alcoholic Spirits in the Qing Dynasty]. *Shūkan Tōyō-gaku* [Papers in Oriental Studies] 4 (1960): 22-35.

Kessler, Lawrence D. *K'ang-hsi and the Consolidation of Ch'ing Rule, 1661–1684.* Chicago: University of Chicago Press, 1976.

King, Frank H. H. *Money and Monetary Policy in China, 1845–1895.* Cambridge, Mass.: Harvard University Press, 1965.

Kishimoto Mio. "Gōsan sagen ni tsuite" [On Zhang Ying's "Remarks on Real Estate"]. *Tōyō Gakuhō* [Journal of Far Eastern Studies] 57, nos. 1-2 (1976): 171-200.

————. "Shindai zenki Kōnan no beika dōkō" [The Secular Trend of Rice Prices in Jiangnan in the First Half of the Qing Period]. *Shigaku zasshi* 87, no. 9 (1978): 1-33.

————. "Kōki nenkan no kokusen ni tsuite—Shinsho keizai shisō no ichi sokumen" [On the Kangxi Depression: Some Aspects of Early Qing Economic Thought]. *Tōyō Bunka Kenkyūjo kiyō* [Annals of the Research Institute for Oriental Culture] 89 (1982): 251-306.

————. "The Kangxi Depression and Early Qing Local Markets." *Modern China* 10, no. 2 (1984): 227-56.

————. "Shinchō chūki keizai seisaku no kichō—1740 nendai no shokuryō mondai o chūshin ni" [The Tone of Mid-Qing Economic Policy as Seen in the 1740s Food Grain Crisis]. *Chikaki ni arite—Kin-Gendai Chūgoku o meguru tōron no hiroba* [Being Nearby: Discussions on Modern China] 11 (1987): 17-35.

Kōsaka Masanori. "Kenryū-dai zenki ni okeru kanzei shukoku-zei menjo-rei ni tsuite" [On the Suspension of Internal Customs Duties on Staple Foodstuffs in the Early Qianlong Period]. *Bunka* [Culture] 32, no. 4 (1969): 42-78.

Lee, Robert H. *The Manchurian Frontier in Ch'ing History.* Cambridge, Mass.: Harvard University Press, 1970.

Leonard, Jane Kate, and John R. Watt, eds. *To Achieve Security and Wealth: The Qing Imperial State and the Economy, 1644–1911.* Ithaca: Cornell University Press, 1992.

Li Fu. *Mutang chugao* [The Writings of Li Fu: First Collection]. (1740). Contained in *Li Mutang shi wen quanji* [Complete Poems and Prose Works of Li Fu]. 1831.

Li Gou. *Li Gou ji* [Collected Works of Li Gou]. Beijing: Zhonghua shuju, 1981.

Lin, Man-houng. "'A Time in Which Grandsons Beat their Grandfathers': The Rise of Liberal Political-Economic Ideas During the Monetary Crisis of Early Nineteenth-Century China." *American Asian Review* 9, no. 4 (1991): 1-28.

———. "Two Social Theories Revealed: Statecraft Controversies Over China's Monetary Crisis, 1808–1854." *Late Imperial China* 12, no. 2 (1991): 1-35.

Lo, Winston Wan. *The Life and Thought of Yeh Shih.* Hong Kong: University Presses of Florida and the Chinese University of Hong Kong, 1974.

Lü Kun. *Lü Gong Shizheng lu* [Mr. Lü's Notes on Practical Administration]. (1593). 1797 edition.

Ma Feibai. *Guanzi Qingzhong Pian xinquan* [New Exegeses of the "Light and Heavy" Chapter of the *Guanzi*]. 2 vols. Beijing: Zhonghua shuju, 1979.

Marks, Robert B. "Rice Prices, Food Supply, and Market Structure in Eighteenth-Century South China." *Late Imperial China* 12, no. 2 (1991): 64-116.

Metzger, Thomas A. "The State and Commerce in Imperial China." *Asian and African Studies* 6 (1970): 23-46.

———. *The Internal Organization of Ch'ing Bureaucracy: Legal, Normative, and Communication Aspects.* Cambridge, Mass.: Harvard University Press, 1973.

Mu Tianzi zhuan [The Legend of the Emperor Mu]. (c. A.D. 300). *Sibu congkan* edition.

Nakayama Mio. *See under* Kishimoto Mio.

Naquin, Susan, and Evelyn S. Rawski. *Chinese Society in the Eighteenth Century*. New Haven: Yale University Press, 1987.

Needham, Joseph. *Science and Civilisation in China*. Vols. 1-. Cambridge: Cambridge University Press, 1954–.

Nishijima Sadao. *Chūgoku keizai-shi kenkyū* [Studies in Chinese Economic History]. Tokyo: Tokyo University Press, 1966.

Okuzaki Hiroshi. *Chūgoku kyōshin jinushi no kenkyū* [Studies on the Gentry Landlords of China]. Tokyo: Kyūko shoin, 1978.

Ono Kazuko. "Shinsho no kōkeikai ni tsuite" [On the Scripture Study Circle of the Early Qing Period]. *Tōhō gakuhō* [Journal of Oriental Studies] (Kyōto) 36 (1964): 633-61.

Pei Huang. *Autocracy at Work: A Study of the Yung-cheng Period, 1723–1735*. Bloomington: Indiana University Press, 1974.

Perdue, Peter C. *Exhausting the Earth: State and Peasant in Hunan, 1500–1850*. Cambridge, Mass.: Harvard University, Council on East Asian Studies, 1987.

Perry, Elizabeth J. *Rebels and Revolutionaries in North China, 1845–1945*. Stanford: Stanford University Press, 1980.

PYTOCG. Chen Hongmou, *Peiyuan Tang oucun gao: wenxi* [Chance Survivals from the Peiyuan Hall: Directives]. N.d.

QCWXTK. *Qingchao wenxian tongkao* [Comprehensive Scrutiny of Documents: Qing Dynasty] (1786). Reprint of the 1936 *Shitong* edition. Taibei: Xinxing shuju, 1965.

Qian Feng. *Qian Nanyuan Xiansheng yiji* [The Collected Works Bequeathed by Master Qian Feng]. 1872.

————. *Nanyuan wencun* [Surviving Writings of Qian Feng]. 1881.

Qian Shifu, comp. *Qingdai zhiguan nianbiao* [Chronological Tables of High Office-holders in the Qing Dynasty]. 4 vols. Beijing: Zhonghua shuju, 1980.

Qiao Guanglie. *Zuile Tang wenji* [Collected Writings from the Zuile Hall]. 1756.

Qin Shan. *Jitang wengao* [The Prose Compositions of Qin Shan]. 1820.

QSL/KX. *Da Qing Shengzu Ren Huangdi shilu* [Veritable Records of the Kangxi Period].

QSL/QL. *Da Qing Gaozong Chun Huangdi shilu* [Veritable Records of the Qianlong Period].

QSL/YZ. *Da Qing Shizong Xian Huangdi shilu* [Veritable Records of the Yongzheng Period].

Quan Hansheng. *Zhongguo jingji shi luncong* [Collected Papers on Chinese Economic History]. Hong Kong: Chinese University of Hong Kong, New Asia Institute, 1972.

Quan Hansheng and Richard A. Kraus. *Mid-Ch'ing Rice Markets and Trade: An Essay in Price History*. Cambridge, Mass.: Harvard University, East Asian Research Center, 1975.

Rawski, Thomas G., and Lillian M. Li, eds. *Chinese History in Economic Perspective*. Berkeley: University of California Press, 1992.

"Renhe Qinchuan Jushi," comp. *Huang Qing zouyi* [Memorials of the August Qing Dynasty]. (N.d.). Taibei: Wenhai chubanshe, 1967.

Rowe, William T. *Hankow: Commerce and Society in a Chinese City, 1796–1889*. Stanford: Stanford University Press, 1984.

———. "State and Market in Mid-Qing Economic Thought: The Case of Chen Hongmou (1696–1771)." *Études chinoises* 12, no. 1 (1993): 7-40.

Saeki Tomi. *Chūgoku shi kenkyū II* [Studies in Chinese History, Second Collection]. Kyōto: Kyōto University, Tōyōshi Kenkyū-kai, 1971.

Sasaki Masaya. "Shindai kanryō no kashoku ni tsuite" [On Money-Making by Qing Bureaucrats]. *Shigaku zasshi* 63, no. 2 (1954): 22-57.

Sen, Amartya. *Poverty and Famines: An Essay on Entitlement and Deprivation*. Oxford: Oxford University Press, 1982.

Shaanxi tongzhi [Gazetteer of Shaanxi Province]. 1735 edition.

Shangcai xianzhi [Gazetteer of Shangcai County]. 1690 edition.

Shangyu dang [Archive of Imperial Edicts]. Microfilm.

Shangyu qiwu yifu [Edicts Concerning Endorsed Proposals on Banner Affairs]. N.d.

Shih, James C. *Chinese Rural Society in Transition: A Case Study of the Lake Tai Area, 1368–1800*. Berkeley: University of California at Berkeley, Institute of East Asian Studies, 1992.

Sima Qian et al. *Shiji* [The Records of the Historian]. 10 vols. Beijing: Zhonghua shuju, 1972.

Smith, Adam. *An Inquiry into the Nature and Causes of the Wealth of Nations.* (1776). 1904 Cannan edn. Chicago: University of Chicago Press, 1976.

Smith, Paul J. *Taxing Heaven's Storehouse: Horses, Bureaucrats, and the Destruction of the Sichuan Tea Industry, 1074–1224.* Cambridge, Mass.: Harvard University, Council on East Asian Studies, 1991.

————. "State Power and Economic Activism during the New Policies, 1068–1085: The Tea and Horse Trade and the 'Green Sprouts' Loan Policy." In Hymes and Schirokauer, eds., *Ordering the World: Approaches to State and Society in Sung Dynasty China,* pp. 76-127.

Sun Jiagan. *Sun Wending Gong zoushu* [The Memorials of Sun Jiagan]. N.d. Reprinted in *Jindai Zhongguo shiliao congkan* (Taibei: Wenhai chubanshe, 1966–73), no. 541.

Sun Yirang, ed. *Zhouli zhengyi* [The Rites of Zhou, with Correct Exegesis]. (1905). *Guoxue jiben congshu* edition.

Tan Qixiang, ed. *Zhongguo lishi ditu ji* [Historical Atlas of China]. 8 vols. Shanghai: Ditu chubanshe, 1982–87.

Tang Zhen. *Qianshu fu shi wen lu* ["A Book to Be Hidden," with Poems and Prose Texts Appended]. Beijing: Zhonghua shuju, 1963.

————. *Qianshu zhu* ["A Book to Be Hidden," with Annotations]. Chengdu: Sichuan Renmin chubanshe, 1984.

Thompson, E. P. *The Making of the English Working Class.* Harmondsworth: Pelican Books, 1975.

Twitchett, Denis. "Merchant, Trade and Government in Late T'ang." *Asia Major* 14 (1968): 202-48.

————. *Financial Administration under the T'ang Dynasty.* 2nd edn. Cambridge: Cambridge University Press, 1970.

Vogel, Hans Ulrich. "Chinese Central Monetary Policy, 1644–1800." *Late Imperial China* 8, no. 2 (1987): 1-52.

————. *Chinese Central Monetary Policy and the Yunnan Copper Mining Industry, 1644–1800.* Forthcoming.

von Glahn, Richard. "Community and Welfare: Chu Hsi's Community Granary in Theory and Practice." In Hymes and Schirokauer, eds., *Ordering the World: Approaches to State and Society in Sung Dynasty China,* pp. 221-54.

Wang Xianqian, comp. *Donghua xu lu* [Further Records from Within the East Gate of the Palace Compound]. 1887 edition.

Wang Yeh-chien. *Land Taxation in Imperial China, 1750–1911.* Cambridge, Mass.: Harvard University Press, 1973.

Wei Qingyuan. *Mingdai huangce zhidu* [The Ming Population Registration System]. Beijing: Zhonghua shuju, 1961.

———. *Dangfang lunshi wenbian* [Historical Essays from the Archives]. Fuzhou: Fujian Renmin chubanshe, 1984.

———. "Kangxi shiqi dui 'shengxi yinliang' zhidu de chuchuang he yunyong" [The Introduction and Operation of the "Investment Funds" System in the Kangxi Period]. *Zhongguo shehui jingji shi yanjiu* [Journal of Chinese Social and Economic History] 1986, no. 3: 60-68.

———. "Yongzheng shiqi dui 'shengxi yinliang' zhidu de zhengdun he zhengce yanbian" [The Reorganization of, and Evolution of Policy towards, the "Investment Funds" System in the Yongzheng Period]. *Zhongguo shehui jingji shi yanjiu* 1987, no. 3: 30-44.

———. "Qianlong shiqi 'shengxi yinliang' zhidu de shuaibai he 'shouche'" [The Decline and Abolition of the "Investment Funds" System in the Qianlong Period]. *Zhongguo shehui jingji shi yanjiu* 1988, no. 3: 8-17.

Whelan, T. S. *The Pawnshop in China, Based on Yang Chao-yü, Chung-kuo tien-tang yeh [The Chinese Pawnbroking Industry], with a Historical Introduction and Critical Annotations.* Ann Arbor: University of Michigan, Center for Chinese Studies, 1979.

Whitbeck, Judith. "Kung Tzu-chen and the Redirection of Literati Commitment in Early Nineteenth Century China." *Ch'ing-shih wen-t'i* 4, no. 10 (1983): 1-32.

Will, Pierre-Étienne. *Bureaucratie et famine en Chine au 18ᵉ siècle.* Paris: Mouton Éditeur, 1980. Translated by Elborg Forster as *Bureaucracy and Famine in Eighteenth-Century China* (Stanford: Stanford University Press, 1990).

———. "State Intervention in the Administration of a Hydraulic Infrastructure: The Example of Hubei Province in Late Imperial Times." In *The Scope of State Power in China*, ed. Stuart R. Schram (London: University of London, School of Oriental and African Studies; Hong Kong: Chinese University of Hong Kong, Chinese University Press, 1985), pp. 295-347.

———. "Attempts at Reviving the Zhengbai Irrigation System in the Wei River Valley of Shaanxi in the Late Imperial Period: A

Preliminary Investigation." Paper presented at the Conference on the History of the Environment in China, Hong Kong, 13-18 December, 1993.

————. Développement quantitatif et développement qualitatif en Chine à la fin de l'époque impériale." *Annales: Histoire, Sciences Sociales* 1994, no. 4: 863-902.

Will, Pierre-Étienne, and R. Bin Wong. *Nourish the People: The State Civilian Granary System in China, 1650–1850.* Ann Arbor: University of Michigan, Center for Chinese Studies, 1991.

Wong, R. Bin. "Food Riots in the Qing Dynasty." *Journal of Asian Studies* 41, no. 4 (1982): 767-88.

Wu Hui and Ge Xianhui. "Qing qianqi de liangshi tiaoji" [The Adjustment of Grain Supply in the First Half of the Qing Period]. *Lishi yanjiu* [Historical Studies] 194 (1988): 122-35.

Wu Wei-ping. "The Development and Decline of the Eight Banners." Ph.D. dissertation, University of Pennsylvania, 1969.

Xuxiu Shaanxi tongzhi gao [Draft Updated Gazetteer of Shaanxi Province]. 1934.

Yan Sisheng. *Chumeng shanfang ji* [Collected Works of Yan Sisheng]. 1745.

Yan Zhongping. *Qingdai Yunnan tongzheng kao* [An Investigation of the Yunnan Copper Administration in the Qing Dynasty]. Shanghai: Zhonghua shuju, 1948.

Yang Duanliu. *Qingdai huobi jinrong shi gao* [A History of Currency and Finance in the Qing Dynasty]. Beijing: Sanlian shudian, 1962.

Yang Jingren. *Chouji bian* [A Manual of Famine Relief Planning]. (1826). 1883 edition.

Ye Zhiru, comp. "Qianlong nianjian Jiangnan shusheng xing jin xiqu shaojiu shiliao" [Materials on the Yeast and Liquor Prohibitions in Certain Yangzi Valley Provinces in the Qianlong Period]. *Lishi dang'an* 25 (1987, no. 1): 13-20.

————, comp. "Qianlong nianjian Jiangbei shusheng xing jin xiqu shaojiu shiliao" [Materials on the Yeast and Liquor Prohibitions in Several Northern Provinces in the Qianlong Period]. Part 1, *Lishi dang'an* 27 (1987, no. 3): 27-35; Part 2, *Lishi dang'an* 28 (1987, no. 4): 16-21, 59.

————, comp. "Qianlong chao miliang maimai shiliao" [Materials on the Grain Trade in the Qianlong Period]. Part 1, *Lishi dang'an*

39 (1990, no. 3): 23-30; Part 2, *Lishi dang'an* 40 (1990, no. 4): 29-37, 53.

Yichuan xianzhi [Gazetteer of Yichuan County]. 1753 edition.

Yin Huiyi. *Yin Shaozai zouyi* [The Memorials of Yin Huiyi]. N.d. *Congshu jicheng* edition.

———. *Jianyu Xiansheng fu Yu tiaojiao* [Yin Huiyi's Directives as Henan Governor]. 1750. *Congshu jicheng* edition.

Yongzheng zhupi yuzhi [Edicts of the Yongzheng Emperor Issued in the Form of Rescripts]. 1732, 1738.

Yunnan tongzhi gao [Draft Gazetteer of Yunnan Province]. 1826.

YZZZHB. Zhongguo Diyi Lishi Dang'an Guan, comp. *Yongzheng chao Hanwen zhupi zouzhe huibian* [Collected Chinese-Language Imperially Endorsed Palace Memorials of the Yongzheng Period]. Nanjing: Jiangsu guji chubanshe, 1986.

Zelin, Madeleine. *The Magistrate's Tael: Rationalizing Fiscal Reform in Eighteenth-Century Ch'ing China*. Berkeley: University of California Press, 1984.

Zhang Aisheng. *Hefang shuyan* [Record of a Dialogue on River Control]. Late seventeenth century. *Siku quanshu zhenben sanji*, no. 169.

Zhao Erxun et al. *Qingshi gao* [Draft Standard History of the Qing Dynasty]. 48 vols. Beijing: Zhonghua shuju, 1976–77.

Zhao Hong'en. *Yuhua Tang Liang Jiang xi gao* [Directives of the Liang-Jiang Governor-General, from the Yuhua Hall]. 1734.

———. *Yuhua Tang Liang Jiang pi'an* [Replies by the Liang-Jiang Governor-General to His Subordinates, from the Yuhua Hall]. 1734.

Zhongguo Renmin Daxue, Zhongguo lishi jiaoyanshi, and Nanjing Daxue, Zhongguo gudai shi jiaoyanshi, comps. *Zhongguo ziben zhuyi mengya wenti taolun ji* [Collected Papers on the Issue of the Sprouts of Capitalism in China]. 3 vols. Beijing: Sanlian shudian, 1957–60.

Index

Printed and bound by CPI Group (UK) Ltd, Croydon, CR0 4YY

13/04/2025

14656529-0002